Virtual Sound

Sound Synthesis and Signal Processing

Riccardo Bianchini • Alessandro Cipriani

Virtual Sound

Sound Synthesis and Signal Processing
Theory and Practice with Csound

Cinema per l'Orecchio series
Editorial director: Alessandro Cipriani

BIANCHINI R. - CIPRIANI A.
Virtual Sound / by Bianchini R., Cipriani A.
Includes bibliographical references and indexes
ISBN 88-900261-1-1
1. Computer Music-Instruction and study - 2. Computer composition

This edition is an English translation of "Il Suono Virtuale",
Copyright © 1998 ConTempo s.a.s., Rome, Italy
Chapters 1-9 by A.Cipriani
Chapters 10-17 and appendixes by R.Bianchini
The authors have revised and upgraded the text for this English edition

Translated from the Italian by Agostino Di Scipio

Cover and CD Design: Alba D'Urbano and Nicolas Reichelt

Manufactured in Italy
Contempo s.a.s., Rome
e-mail info@virtual-sound.com
info@contemponet.com
URL: www.virtual-sound.com
www.contemponet.com
fax +39-06.355.020.25

Contents

FOREWORD

Digital sound synthesis has for some time been at a remarkably high level of sophistication, flexibility and subtlety. This happy situation is due in large part to the remarkable efforts of Barry Vercoe, the author of Csound and its predecessors, MUSIC360 and MUSIC11. Now thanks to the universality of the C programming language, which guarantees portability between computers running on different operating systems, Csound has become the standard synthesis language wherever there is computer music. The flexibility of the language is already evident in this book: it can be studied by both PC oriented musicians as well as by those using Macintosh.

Of even greater value, the composer who learns Csound on his home computer is fully prepared to accept invitations to work elsewhere, for example in a studio equipped with multi-track recording facilities and expensive external sound processors, all built around UNIX machines which run their version of Csound.

Here, then, is the importance of this book: to learn Csound, especially if you have to do it on your own, you need someone who can explain the hows and whys of this language which offers so many possibilities for digital sound synthesis. The student finds himself here in the capable hands of two superb teachers, Riccardo Bianchini and Alessandro Cipriani. The book is infused with their considerable teaching experience in helping musicians with little or no knowledge of informatics to overcome the initial problems and confusions in order to get started on the road towards a full understanding and mastery of computer music. All the basic techniques of Csound are explained using specific sound synthesis models - additive synthesis, modulation synthesis, the use of filters and delay line effects (reverberation, echo, chorus effects), dynamic control over timbral evolution, interfaces with external sound sources (sampling), etc. - all of which allow the student to build his own experiments and more refined variants using the examples as starting points. In short, the approach here is completely hands-on.

Furthermore, each chapter offers suggestions for more advanced use; that is to say, the book is not just for beginners, but is designed to accompany the musician during various learning phases, from the beginning all the way up to the state of the art. Bianchini and Cipriani have obviously absorbed and worked with a vast range of digital synthesis techniques developed by many specialists in the field, and they provide clear explanations and suggestions for their use and adaptations, always in terms of concise Csound programming examples. For example, we find here a clear description of the famous Karplus-Strong plucked string algorithm, with precise indications about how to modify it. These modifications suggest yet other possibilities for experimentation with yet other potentially fascinating alterations. After following the authors' lessons, the student will be in a position to work with the newest developments in the field, published regularly in such magazines as "Computer Music Journal", "Interface", etc.

An original and valuable idea in this book is the insertion of a few pages called "Extensions" following many of the chapters. The musician who has arrived at a reasonably good level of understanding of the main ideas will find here the technical information that allows him to develop original synthesis ideas. An especially pertinent such "Extension" deals with the issue of "complex events" - the concept that one can construct a Csound instrument for the synthesis of several sound objects where the form, synchronization and the character of each single object are under the control of just a few score parameters. Once such an instrument has been constructed, the composer can conceive of his music in terms of complex large scale gestures rather than always composing at the "note for note" level.

And finally, the book concludes with a selection of writings by other experienced Csound users whose unique applications, fully described here, are extremely useful both for immediate execution and, more importantly, as suggestions to the composer for his own personal developments.

So if you are a beginner or even if you already have a good bit of experience with digital sound synthesis, Bianchini and Cipriani offer here a complete manual for understanding Csound at many levels. And since Csound is continually evolving thanks to the work of a small international group of musicians/programmers who are dedicated to upgrading the language with new methods and with specific adaptations of the latest technical discoveries, the Csound user will find himself on the leading edge of computer music.

Welcome to the Csound universe.

James Dashow

CSOUND : WHAT IS IT?

Csound is a digital sound synthesis program created at MIT (*Massachusetts Institute of Technology*). People from all over the world contribute to develop it further. Indeed, Csound is public domain software: everybody can use it, modify it and contribute to further enhance it. Taking advantage of the power of currently popular processors (such as those inside your PowerMac or PC), Csound performs extremely fast, so fast as to run in "real-time". The program is written in C language, but you don't have to learn C programming to exploit its musical potential. It is sufficient to read this manual through: you will learn how to write Csound orchestras and scores, and how to create any possible sound you can imagine of, right off your personal computer. The important, at the beginning, is not to get scared by the unusual terminology: the learning process, then, will be more natural and quick.

DIRECT SOUND SYNTHESIS BY COMPUTER

What is direct sound synthesis? At the time when analog technology was the mainstream of electronic music, at some point you would have to use, say, nine oscillators and a low-pass filter, and all you could do about that was to go out and purchase nine oscillators and a low-pass. At another point, however, you would need nine low-passes and one oscillator. So you had to go buy eight more low-pass filters. With digital direct synthesis, instead, you can program the available hardware (i.e. your computer) to simulate either nine oscillators and one filter, or nine filters and one oscillator. The process is economic and flexible: you can make your computer simulate any sound generating unit and implement any sound synthesis technique, both old ones and not yet existing ones.

CSOUND : THE BEST SYNTHESIZER IN THE WORLD

The difference between Csound and commercially available audio and music software, is not only that it is free, but also that it doesn't get obsolete: its functionality is such that any new kind of sound synthesis or processing can be implemented. Also, and importantly, such a flexibility allows the musician to create a virtual sound machine that perfectly fits her/his needs. Using Csound you never have to stick to those 30 preset options offered by this or that keyboard or expander: sure, those 30 options are available in your hands right away, and yet they might not give you enough of what is necessary for the sound you have in your mind. On the contrary, Csound is open: as you learn to make competent use of it, you get closer and closer to the sound you're searching for, based on a deep awareness of the synthesis or processing methods involved. Which, by the way, allows you to master any other available tool as well, including commonly used synthesis programs.

This book, in fact, is not only for people already committed to musical research, but also for musicians eager to go deeper into the technological process of their work. What are the basic prerequisites to start reading? Well, nothing more than a basic knowledge of music and acoustics. And, sure, a good familiarity with your computer.

WHAT COMPUTER PRECISELY?

The basic requirement for any sound synthesis language to be successful, is that it is portable to as many types of computer platform as possible. It should not rely on a specific hardware. For that reason, several Csound versions exist, which make the language available on several computers, including PC, Mac, PowerMac, SGI, and others. The more powerful the processor, and the faster the Csound runtime operations. However, by no means the computer speed and power do affect the audio quality of the results you get. Csound doesn't require additional hardware to install on the computer, although you obviously need digital-to-analog converters in order to listen to the actual musical results. Any soundcard on the market will do the job. The soundcard quality will definitely affect the audio quality, especially as in terms of background noise and harmonic distortion. Still, the Csound output is actually stored to some sound file on the hard disk, and as such it is no less than CD quality, and possibly even better. You may want to install, instead of a soundcard, a digital connection to a DAT recorder, using the latter as a high-quality digital-to-analog converter (the only restriction being, then, that only standard sampling rates can be used, namely 32, 44.1 and 48 kHz).

Csound was born for "deferred-time" synthesis. However, as mentioned above, today it can work in real-time provided the computer processor is fast enough (and provided not too complicated sound-generating algorithms are used). To make this notion clear, suppose you want to create one minute of sound: if the synthesis takes more than one minute, such that you have to wait for a sound file to be created on hard disk and play it later, that is "deferred-time". If the synthesis takes one minute or less, such that you listen to the sound while it is being generated, that is "real-time". The time taken by the synthesis process depends on the complexity of the synthesis algorithms, and the latter usually depends, in turn, on the complexity in the generated sound.

WHY "VIRTUAL SOUND"?

The title of this book refers to that obscure moment, in electroacoustic composing, when sound is made "out of nothing", only based on ideas, formulas, desires, methods: prior to listening, it is *virtual*, it has not yet entered the physical world - an experience peculiar to work with digital sound synthesis.

This book was not conceived just as a help to learn Csound and its connection with the MIDI world, or with other tools. It was specially conceived as an introduction to the theory and practice of sound synthesis and processing. The aim was not to survey all of the possibilities Csound offers to you, but to exploit the language to create a bridge for those who are not familiar with direct sound synthesis, making it not too difficult for them to go across the river of knowledge on these matters.

This book comes from afar, rooted as it is in the Electronic Music classes taught by one of the authors in 1977 at the Conservatory of Pescara (Italy). Clearly, having so much time passed since then, and having the matters at issue so radically changed in these years, today very little remains of the original material. At the end of the 1970ies, people at University computing centers around the world were interfacing analog synthesizers and computers. The best-equipped electronic music centers had MOOG or EMS synths among their most advanced sound facilities. To commit oneself to computer music meant to go visit giant University computing facilities and learn about mysterious operating systems. One would then write some computer code and carefully go through a complicated, and quite slow debugging process: launch the program, wait for the results, listen to the sound, make decisions about what was to debug and/or refine, change the code, launch the program again, an so on. Today technological developments tend to hide from users the enormous research work that has been done in order to provide musicians with more handy and effective approaches, possibly based on personal computers. Such enterprise has been stimulated by the enthusiasm raised by the possibilities invented and investigated by computer music research. Csound welcomes everybody to be part of such an adventure, but relieves her/him of the impediments imposed by older technologies.

The authors acknowledge the contribution of Nyssim Lefford, Jon Christopher Nelson, Russell F. Pinkston, Emanuele Casale, Enzo Coco, Gabriel Maldonado, Luca Pavan, Giuseppe Emanuele Rapisarda, Fausto Sebastiani, for their proofreading and clever advice.

Happy Csounding!

1

CSOUND: HOW IT WORKS

1.1 ORCHESTRAS, SCORES, SOUND FILES

In order to generate sound, Csound requires that the user creates two text files. We call these respectively:

1) the **ORCHESTRA** (file extension: *.orc*)
2) the **SCORE** (file extension: *.sco*).[1]

These text files contain everything that is needed to describe the "virtual machine" we want to build and the operations we want it to perform. After saving our orchestra and score files, we use the Csound compiler to *execute* them. The compiler returns a *sound file*, (a file containing a binary code representation of the sound). Once the sound file has been generated, it can be auditioned by merely "playing" the sound file through the computer sound card. The card reads the sound file data and turns it into an electrical signal. By connecting the card's (analog) output to an amplifier, we can send that signal to loudspeakers. At this stage we say that the card performs a "digital-to-analog conversion." It allows us to listen to the sound that is represented digitally in the file.

---

[1] With the latest Csound versions, starting with release 3.50, we can include these two texts (orchestra and score) within one single file bearing the file extension .csd (see section 1.D.1)

Alternatively, it is possible for Csound to read a previously sampled (digitally recorded) sound and modify it in some way. Imagine we have just sampled a flute tone via a microphone plugged into the sound card input (in this instance the card performs an "analog-to-digital conversion"). With the appropriate orchestra and score files, we can specify how that flute tone is to be modified. Csound will then execute the orchestra and score commands and return a new sound file containing the flute tone duly transformed. Finally, we can listen to the modified flute sound by simply playing it through the computer's sound card.

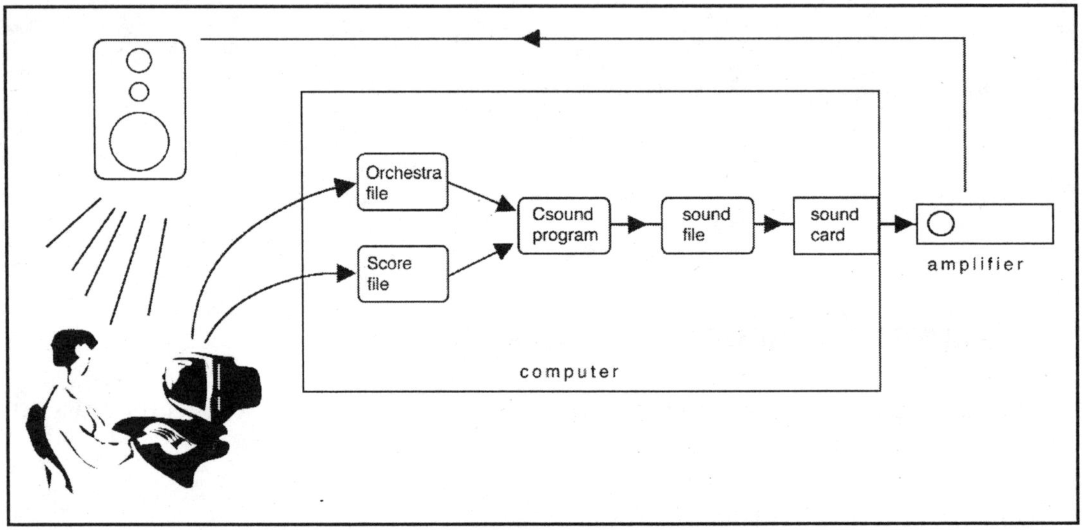

Fig. 1-1

1.2 HOW TO USE WCSHELL FOR WINDOWS [2]

How to run Csound from previously created orchestra and score files, and listen to the result

1. Launch *WCShell* by double-clicking on the *WCShell* icon
2. In the orchestra list, find the file "oscil.orc" and click on it.
3. In the score list, click on "oscil.sco"
4. Click on the *Csound* button to start the synthesis process
5. When the synthesis is complete, close the Csound session by pressing <return>
6. Click on the *PLAY* button to listen

[2] to use Csound without WCShell, see section 1.A.5.

How to create and execute a new orchestra and a new score

1. Launch *WCShell* by double-clicking on the *WCShell* icon
2. Choose *New Orc* from the *Orc* menu. This opens the orchestra editor
3. Type in the orchestra code, and save the file by choosing *Save as...* from the *File* menu
4. Close the orchestra editor by choosing *Exit* from the *File* menu
5. Choose *New Sco* from the *Sco* menu. This opens the score editor
6. Type in the score code, then save the file by choosing *Save as...* from the *File* menu
7. Close the score editor by choosing *Exit* from the *File* menu
8. Click on the two *Update* buttons. Check that the new files are shown in the file browsers
9. Click on the *Csound* button to start the synthesis process
10. When the synthesis is complete, close the Csound session by pressing <return>
11. Click on the *PLAY* button to listen
12. To modify the orchestra, choose *Edit Orc* from the *Orc* menu
13. To modify the score, choose *Edit Sco* from the *Sco* menu

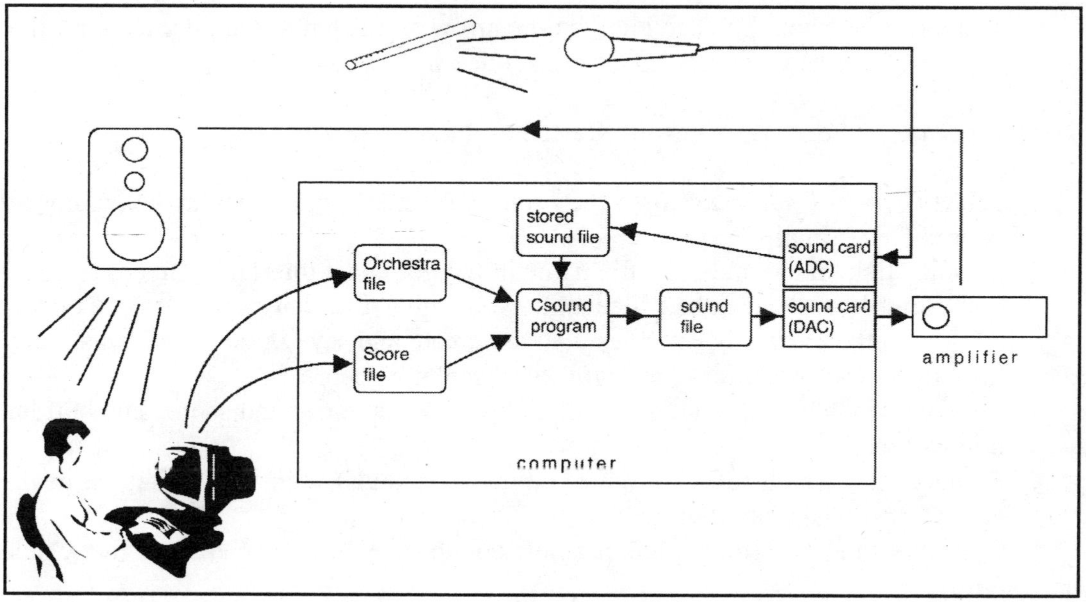

Fig. 1-2

At any time during this process, you may reference either Appendix 1 in this book or the on-line WCShell Help. To start the WCShell Help choose *Help* in the *File* menu or press the F11 key. Please refer to Appendix 1 to learn about WCShell installation and program operation.

1.3 HOW TO USE CSOUND WITH A POWER MAC

How to run Csound from previously created orchestra and score files

1. Find the folder where the Csound program files (*Csound* and *Perf*) are located, double-click on the Csound icon. This starts a graphical interface window.
2. Click the *Select* button next to the orchestra icon. A dialog box will appear where you can browse through folders looking for the desired files. Locate the "oscil.orc" file and double-click on it. The file name will be automatically appear in the orchestra file window, and the "oscil.sco" file name will automatically appear in the score file window.
3. Click on the *Render* button. A message appears to indicate that *perfing* is now running.
4. When *perfing* is complete, a "close" message appears, together with a message box with the text "0 errors in performance". You can listen to the sound by clicking on the *play* arrow (similar to a tape recorder). The play arrow is located on the left side of the message box. You can click on the arrow and listen to the output sound file as many times as you wish. To quit, just click the *Close* button.

How to create and execute a new orchestra and a new score

1. Select *General Preferences* from the *Preferences* menu and select the text editor of your choice (Simple Text is a good start).
2. Double-click on the orchestra file name in the graphical interface. This opens your orchestra file, which can be edited and saved with a different name. You can do the same with the score file. The files that you create and save in the editor must have the extensions ".orc", for "orchestra", or ".sco" for "score".
3. As a test, double-click on "oscil.sco" to open a simple Csound score. The bottom line will read "i1 4 2".
4. Replace "2" (which refers to the duration in seconds) with "10". That creates a tone 10 seconds in duration.
5. Close the window. A dialog box prompts you to save the modified score file. Click *Save*.
6. Now click on *Render*, then listen to the new sound file just created.

How to manage the system folders

As long as you keep all Csound-readable files (*.orc*, *.sco*, *MIDI* files, analysis files, etc.) in the same folder, you don't need to change anything in the window. If you wish to change the default folders, click on the *Default directories* button. Here you can choose any folder as the *Sound File Directory* (SFDIR). The one where Csound will save the sound files. Similarly, *Sound Sample Directory* (SSDIR) will designate the folder in which Csound will look for samples to read, and *Analysis Directory* (SADIR) will designate the folder in which Csound will save analysis files. If you don't type in new folder names, Csound searches for the *perf* program in the default directory.

1.4 HOW TO WRITE AN ORCHESTRA

Warning! This section may appear rather complicated. It introduces new terminology and a unique way of thinking about sound. Nonetheless, it is very important that you go through all sections and subsections that are left in this chapter. This information provides the basic foundation and syntax required in all Csound orchestras and scores. When using Csound in the future, you will simply apply the same set of operations described below..

An orchestra file always consists of two parts: header and instruments. [3]

ORCHESTRA
HEADER
INSTRUMENTS

HEADER
The header assigns some value to four fundamental variables that are shared by *all* instruments.

INSTRUMENTS
Instruments are the "virtual machines" constituting your orchestra. An orchestra can include one or more instruments.

HOW TO WRITE THE HEADER
The header determines the following:
sr sampling rate
kr control rate (see section 1.A.1)
ksmps sr/kr ratio (e.g. if sr = 48000 and kr = 4800, then ksmps = 10); it must be an integer
nchnls number of output channels (1=mono, 2=stereo, etc.)

[3] if the header is dropped, Csound will assume the following default values: *sr=44100, kr=4410, ksmps=10, nchnls=1.*

For all the instruments in your orchestra, the range of technical possibilities depends on the information defined in the header. For example, if you set nchnls = 2, then no instrument will be allowed to generate a quadraphonic output stream, only stereo.

A typical header:

```
sr     = 48000
kr     = 4800
ksmps  = 10
nchnls = 1
```

HOW TO WRITE AN INSTRUMENT

While the header consists of only four assignments, an instrument is usually much more complicated. The level of complication is dependant upon the particular process it is expected to implement.

The first line in the instrument block must contain the instrument “id number”. This is designated by the statement *instr* (instrument) followed by any integer. The statement *endin* marks the end of an instrument. Thus, the general form of a Csound instrument is as follows:

```
        instr 1
...
...     (body of the instrument)
...
        endin
```

For example:

```
        instr   1
aneworc oscil   10000, 220, 1
        out     aneworc
        endin
```

Here, *aneworc* is the name of a *variable*.
What is a variable?

A variable is like a small case, a drawer with a label (such as *aneworc*) where the result of some operation is temporarily stored. In the example, the variable *aneworc* will contain the result of the oscil operation code (opcode). The *oscil* opcode performs the operation of an oscillator to which specific arguments are supplied: amplitude, frequency, and an identification number of a stored waveform function.

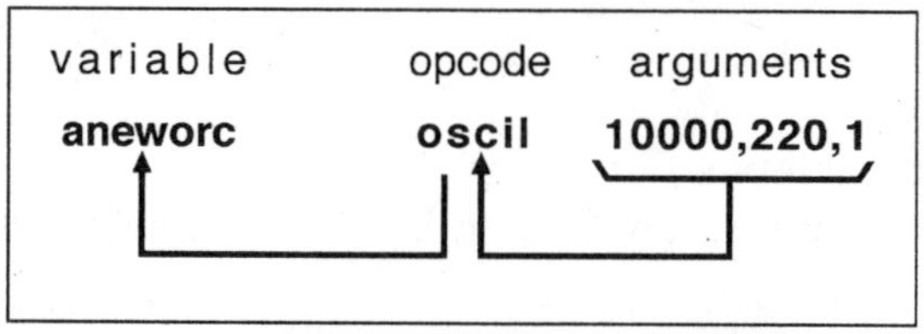

In the example above, the oscillator is given an **amplitude of 10000**, a **frequency of 220 Hz**, and a function that is referenced as **function table number 1** (as we'll see, the actual waveform of function 1 is created by some appropriate opcode in the score file). These values are passed to *oscil* to emulate an audio oscillator with determined characteristics of amplitude, frequency and waveform. The result of *oscil* is deposited in the *aneworc* variable.

In this example, the values of *aneworc* can be used to generate a sound with a frequency of 220 Hz. With this application it is good idea to use a sampling rate that allows for high resolution.

To do so, the variable storing the result of *oscil* must be given a name beginning by an *a* (then it will be an *audio* variable). In Csound, all audio variables are updated at the sampling rate specified in the header (e.g. 48000 times per second). Any variable name that begins with *a* (such as *a1*, *agreen*, *asquare*, *ataraxy*, etc.) can be used to define an audio rate, or a-rate variable. After some result gets stored into an audio variable, the variable name itself can be utilized as an argument to another opcode.

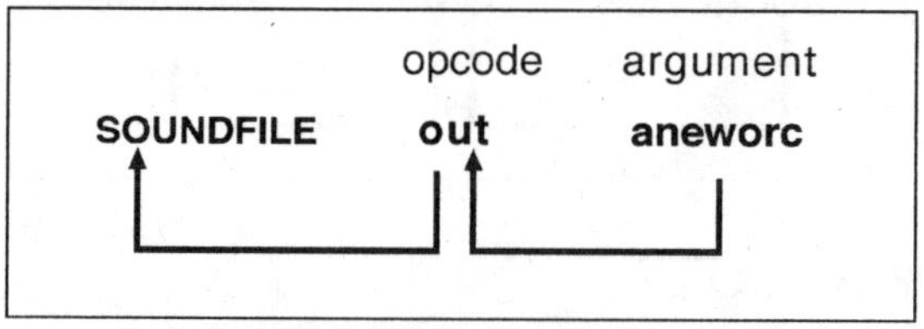

In the example above, *aneworc* is the only argument to the opcode *out*. The *out* opcode stores the value of the argument on the hard disk.[4]

The *endin* (end of instrument) statement marks the end of the instrument body. In the present example, it also marks the end of the orchestra.

In summary:

[4] When we launch Csound to run in real-time, *out* writes the result directly to the sound card buffer

```
        instr   1
aneworc oscil   10000, 220, 1
        out     aneworc
        endin
```

aneworc is an audio **variable**.
oscil is an *opcode* emulating an oscillator. It has 3 arguments: **amplitude, frequency** and **function number**.
out writes its argument (*aneworc*) to the sound file we want to create.

Typically, to ensure predictable performance, an opcode requires that values are given to its arguments (right side of the expression) and that the result of the operation gets stored as a variable (left side of the expression). Once a variable is defined, it can be used as an argument in another opcode, as is the case when *aneworc* is utilized as an input argument for the *out* opcode.
The *out* output is implicitly a hard disk sound file (or the sound card buffer): therefore, the result of *out* does not need to be stored as the value of a variable.

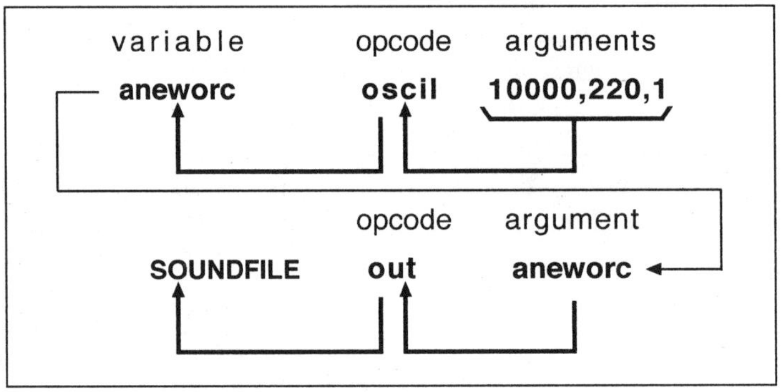

1.5 HOW TO WRITE A SCORE

Like a Csound orchestra file, the score file, usually has two parts: *functions* and *notes*.

SCORE
FUNCTIONS
NOTES

FUNCTIONS

Function statements (f statements) are used to create particular waveforms. When using pre-determined waveforms (sampled sounds), the score file may not require the use of function statements and may be comprised solely of notes.

NOTES

Notes are always necessary (well, at least one note!). It is helpful to not think of notes in terms of the notation of music for an acoustic instrument such as a piano. Rather, notes within the context of Csound scores should be thought of more generally as sound events having any duration ranging from a fraction of a second to days, and as sonic events that may or may not have a precise pitch. The actual pitch depends on the particular instrument we implement in the orchestra and the particular functions we create in the score. Finally, notes can be entered in the score following some linear temporal sequence or any random order. Before the synthesis process starts, the program will sort out all of the score events according to their chronological action time

HOW TO CREATE A FUNCTION

In Csound it is possible to create any kind of function. As you recall, our first orchestra included a reference to some waveform function in the score file labeled as function #1.

```
(aneworc   oscil 10000,220,1)
```

The following f statement generates a sinusoidal waveform for use by this orchestra code:

```
f1   0   4096   10   1
```

where:

f1 determines the **function identification number** (1)

0 is the **action time** for the generation of this function (which determines at what time Csound will create function #1). If this had a value of 3, then the function would be created 3 seconds after the beginning of the score timing.

4096 is the **number of points** in the function. In other words, the waveform will consist in a table of values stored in an array of 4096 memory locations. In most cases, the number of points must be equal to a power of two (256, 512, 1024, 4096, etc.), but there are exceptions where it must be, instead, a power-two-plus-one (257, 513, 1025, 4097, etc.). The largest allowable size is 16777216 points (2^{20}).

10 utilizes one of many different methods for generating functions. We will refer to these methods as **GEN** routines, each has its own id number. With the number 10, we invoke the GEN10 function generating subroutine which is, in fact, a good routine to use if we want to create a sine wave. The different types of GEN routines (GEN01, GEN02, etc.), utilize various methods to create function tables

1 means that we expect GEN10 to create a waveform consisting of one single sinusoidal component. If instead we wrote:

```
f1   0   4096   10   1   1   1
```

we would expect three sinusoids in harmonic ratio (fundamental, second harmonic, third harmonic), all with amplitude level = 1.

At this point some may raise the question: "why do all this just to get a sine wave, when I can press a single key of an electronic keyboard and obtain a complex sound, at any pitch and of any duration?" If you want to modify the sound of your keyboard, you won't be successful unless you have a deep knowledge of the sound-generating process implemented by that keyboard: Csound is an extraordinary tool which allows you to understand and use many existing sound synthesis techniques. Consequently, Csound helps you to better understand your synthesizer and, for that matter, any other electronic music system however complex it may be. Moreover, Csound allows you to do things that no sampler and no synthesizer will ever do. Patience and care are crucial for a composer who is really willing to commit herself/himself to competent exploitation of computer technologies, especially during the early stage of their efforts.

Let's summarize how we create a sine wave in a Csound score:

Function number	action time	number of points in the function (or "table size")	GEN type	amplitude of the fundamental
f1	**0**	**4096**	**10**	**1**

HOW TO WRITE NOTES

. Notes are generated through the use of instrument statements (i statements). An i statement turns on an instrument with the corresponding number in the orchestra file.

Csound i statements consist of *parameters* which are located at particular positions, called *p-fields* (*parameter-fields*). The first three p-fields of any note are the only ones that must always contain values. These three p-fields must contain values for the following pre-defined uses:

p1 (first p-field): determines what instrument in the orchestra is to be played. For example, *i1* selects the instrument #1.

p2 (second p-field): action time. 0 means that the note starts immediately at the beginning of the piece; 3 means three seconds after the beginning, 3.555 means 3 seconds and 555 milliseconds, etc.

p3 (third p-field): duration of the note. The value 2 will generate a note for two seconds, .5 for half a second (you can omit the integer part when it equals zero). Non-american readers should note that a dot (".") must be used as the decimal separator, instead of a comma (","): hence "4.5" is correctly understood by Csound as "four and a half seconds", while "4,5" would not.

One can invent many other parameters (p4, p5, p6, etc.), each for a particular use. How many parameters and for what use, that only depends on the orchestra we ourselves create. In the following example, however, we use only the three pre-defined parameters. Note that it is possible to add comments to orchestra and score codes, e.g. to highlight for ourselves important details, by using semicolons. The Csound compiler ignores anything following a semicolon on any line of code. Lines containing only comments must begin with semicolons.

Example:

```
out a1                      ; this is a comment and
                            ; when running, Csound won't try to execute it
```

Score example:

```
f1   0   4096  10  1        ; function #1, action time, table size, GEN type, amp. of fundamental
i1   0   3                  ; plays instrument 1 starting at the beginning of the piece, lasts 3 seconds
i1   4   2                  ; plays instrument 1 starting at 4 seconds, lasts 2 seconds
i1   6   2                  ; plays instrument 1, starts at 6 seconds, lasts 2 seconds
```

Notice that between the first and the second note there is a silent rest of 1 second. In Csound you don't have to explicitly declare rests and their durations, as they are automatically determined by the time between the end of one note and action time of another.

Careful! In the score file you separate parameters among them by simply inserting a blank (a single space-bar character or a tab character). Do not use commas or any other punctuation mark. In the orchestra file, commas are used to separate opcode input arguments, but in all other cases you must use blank spaces or tabs.

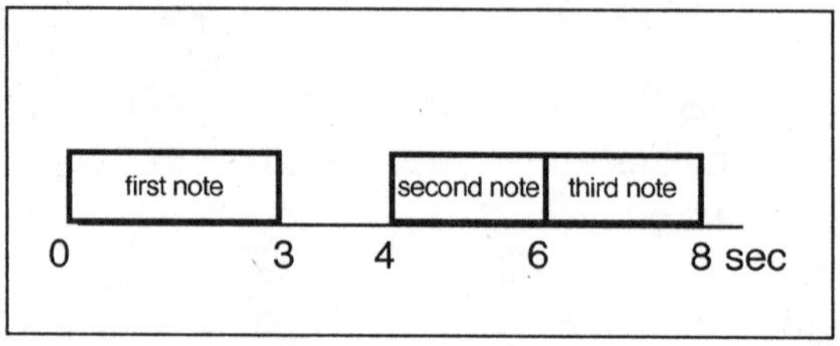

TIPS & TRICKS: it's good idea to usually space out orchestra and score code within a text file (variables, opcodes, arguments, p-fields) using tabs. This helps keep your code easy to read and scrutinize.

Let's summarize:

```
; instrument number   note action time   note duration
i1                    0                  3
i1                    4                  2
```

EXERCISE *Type in the following code and save it as a new orchestra file and a new score file. Insert your own comments explaining the code. Start reading the next section only when you have clearly understood header statements, instrument statements, functions and notes.*

```
; oscil.orc

          sr     =  44100
          kr     =  4410
          ksmps  =  10
          nchnls =  1

          instr     1
aneworc   oscil     10000, 220, 1
          out       aneworc
          endin
```

```
; oscil.sco
f1   0   4096  10   1
i1   0   3
i1   4   2
```

1.6 THE GEN10 ROUTINE

So far we used GEN10 to generate a simple sine wave. However, we can do much more with it. For example, we can create a function with five harmonically related sine waves by including the number "1" five times after the GEN type number:

func.n.	action time	table size	GEN type	amp of fund.	amp. of 2nd hrm	amp. of 3rd hrm	amp. of 4th hrm	amp. of 5th hrm
f1	**0**	**4096**	**10**	**1**	**1**	**1**	**1**	**1**

All partials here have the same amplitude. Notice that we do not have to explicitly specify that the five components be in harmonic ratios since GEN10 creates only harmonically related components. By changing the fundamental frequency in the orchestra, all components will be shifted by the appropriate multiple of the new fundamental. For example, if the fundamental is 220 Hz the second harmonic will be 440, the third 660, the fourth 880, and the fifth 1100 Hz; if we change the fundamental to 100 Hz, the second harmonic will become 200, the third 300, the fourth 400, and the fifth 500 Hz. In this respect,, a table function simply represents a model. GEN10 creates an oscillation of one period (the period of the fundamental), and sums it with four more signals that complete 2,3,4 and 5 oscillations while the fundamental completes one period. The result is a waveform that can be used as a model for whatever note we write in the score. For each note, the model wave is repeated over and over at a rate corresponding to the fundamental frequency. If we want Csound to use this waveform and require a fundamental frequency of 220 Hz, the program simply repeats the waveform 220 times per second (see 2.C.1).

It is important to consider, now, the **amplitude** of each harmonic component. In general, the larger the amplitude value of a given component, the more audible the contribution of that particular component to overall timbre. If we write

```
f1   0  4096   10    1   1   1   1   15
i1   0  5
```

the 5th harmonic will have a 15 times stronger amplitude than all other partials

Synthesize this sound and listen to it, comparing the result with the previous sound example and try to describe how timbre changed.

Next, create a whole set of functions and have notes spaced 3 seconds apart. All of the notes will share a fundamental frequency of 220 Hz, but will have a unique wave function and resultant timbre in the output sound. Modifications in the function can be implemented by simply re-generating function #1 with a differently weighted sum of components. The following score example shows that new values replace older values every three seconds in the generation of the *same* function #1. In other words, a new waveform gets stored in the same memory location, replacing the older one.

```
; oscil1.sco
f1  0   4096   10   10   9   8   7   6   5   4   3   2   1
; with this line, we obtain a waveform made of the fundamental plus harmonics up to the tenth, with
; decreasing amplitude
;
f1  3   4096   10   10   5   3.3   2.5  2   1.6  1.4  1.25  1.1  1
; with this line, components add up to approximate a sawtooth waveform
;
f1  6   4096   10   10   0   3.3   0   2   0   1.4   0   1.1
; with this line, components add up to approximate a squared waveform
;
f1  9   4096   10   1                                    ; a sine wave
f1  12  4096   10   0    1                               ; 2nd harmonic only
f1  15  4096   10   0    0   1                           ; 3nd harmonic only
f1  18  4096   10   0    0   0   1                       ; 4rd harmonic only
f1  21  4096   10   1    1   1   1                       ; fund.+2nd+3rd +4th
f1  24  4096   10   10   0   0   0   0   0   1           ; fund.+7th
f1  27  4096   10   0    0   0   0   0   0   1           ; 7th harmonic only
i1  0   2
i1  3   2
i1  6   2
i1  9   2
i1  12  2
i1  15  2
i1  18  2
i1  21  2
i1  24  2
i1  27  2
```

***EXERCISE** Run Csound using the score above and the previously described orchestra file (oscil.orc). Listen many times to the results. Try to tell the difference between the sounds, especially between those that include only a single component and those containing components that are mixed together to form a more complex tone.*

As seen in this example, different timbres are obtained by adding together different harmonics over one and the same 220 Hz fundamental. The **amplitude** was fixed at 10000, but was physically distributed over the various frequency components according to the various weights. Thus, using a function like

```
f1  0   4096   10  1    1  1    1
```

each of the four components in the output sound have the same level, while in

```
f1  0   4096   10  2    1  1    1
```

the level of the fundamental would be twice as strong as the others.

In the above example, the **fundamental frequency** is 220 Hz, because the constant value was declared directly in the orchestra (frequency argument to *oscil*); but in actuality the sounds contain different frequencies. This is because a function such as

```
f1  0   4096   10  0    0  0    1
```

creates a sound where the 220 Hz fundamental and its second and third harmonics have no energy (amplitude = 0), while the fourth harmonic (880 Hz) is present. The resultant function table contains four complete cycles of a sine.

1.7 HOW TO CHANGE AMPLITUDE AND FREQUENCY FOR EACH NOTE

In addition to creating different functions for each note, it is possible to alter the fundamental frequency and amplitude for each note. What if we wanted to have a different fundamental frequency and a different amplitude for each note? No problem. This is accomplished by replacing the fixed value of 10000 in the orchestra file, the amplitude argument to *oscil*, with "p4". This creates a reference to the fourth p-field in the score which can be given a new value for each note. Clearly, we now have to extend the instrument statements in the score to include one more p-field beyond the three fixed ones. The new field, p4, will determine the amplitude of the note. Similarly, we may want to replace the value 220 Hz, the frequency argument to *oscil*, with "p5". By assigning these values to p-fields, amplitude and frequency will not be fixed to 10000 and 220 Hz, but defined for each note simply by typing in new values in the fourth and fifth p-fields as follows:

```
; oscil2.orc

          sr     =  44100
          kr     =  4410
          ksmps  =  10
          nchnls =  1

          instr     1
asound    oscil     p4, p5, 1
          out       asound
          endin
```

And its score:

```
; oscil2.sco
f1  0   4096  10  1
; p1    p2    p3  p4     p5
i1      0     2   20000  110     ; plays a note starting at 0 sec, with a duration of 2 sec,
                                 ; amp level 20000 and fundamental freq. 110 Hz
i1      3     2   8000   110     ; starts at 3 sec, with a duration of 2 sec, amp level 8000 and
                                 ; fundamental freq. 110 Hz
i1      6     2   9000   440
i1      9     2   15000  440
```

Now run Csound using these files and listen.

Csound can also play several notes simultaneously. Csound instruments are inherently polyphonic and have no restrictions as to the number of overlapping voices. For example:

```
f1  0   4096  10  1
; p1    p2    p3  p4     p5
i1      0     3   7000   261.625    ; C
i1      0     3   7000   329.627    ; E
i1      0     3   7000   391.995    ; G
i1      1     2   7000   466.163    ; B flat
```

1.8 HOW TO CREATE ANOTHER INSTRUMENT

It is possible to create a second instrument. In the following example, instrument 1 plays a sine wave and instrument 2 plays a square wave:

```
; duet.orc

         sr     =  44100
         kr     =  4410
         ksmps  =  10
         nchnls =  1

         instr     1
aone     oscil     p4, p5, 1
         out       aone
         endin

         instr 2
asquare  oscil     p4, p5, 2
         out       asquare
         endin
```

The score for the new orchestra:

```
; duet.sco

f1  0  4096  10  1                                  ; function 1 is a sinusoid, meant for instrument 1
f2  0  4096  10  1  0  .33 0  2  0  .14 0  .11  0 09; function 2 is a square wave, meant for instrument 2
i1     0     3      10000       222                 ; instr 1, lasts 3 sec, freq. 222 Hz
i2     4     3      10000       222                 ; instr 2, lasts 3 sec, freq. 222 Hz
i1     8     3      8000        800                 ; instr 1, lasts 3 sec, freq. 800 Hz
i2     12    3      8000        800                 ; instr 2, lasts 3 sec, freq. 800 Hz
```

Now run Csound using these two new files and listen.

1.9 CONTROL VARIABLES: GLISSANDOS

All the notes we have created so far had a stable frequency—an unvarying, constant pitch. It is possible to create a sound event whose pitch smoothly shifts from one frequency to another over the course of its duration by generating a straight line ramping from an initial frequency value to a final frequency value. This linearly increasing series of values can serve as the second input argument (frequency) to the *oscil* opcode.

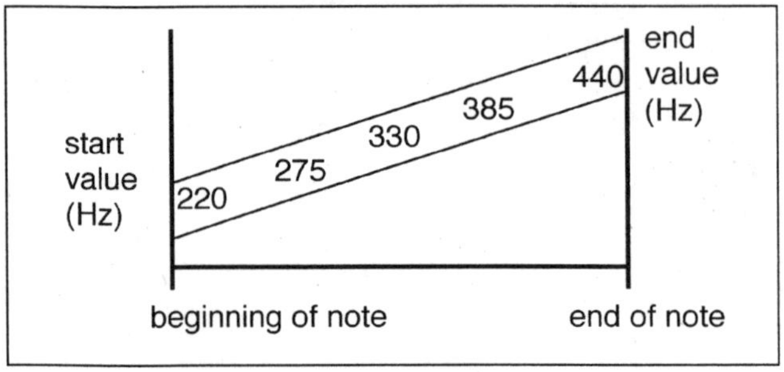

In short, the proper instrument is as follows:

```
        instr 1
kglis   line    220, p3, 440
a1      oscil   p4, kglis, 1
        out     a1
        endin
```

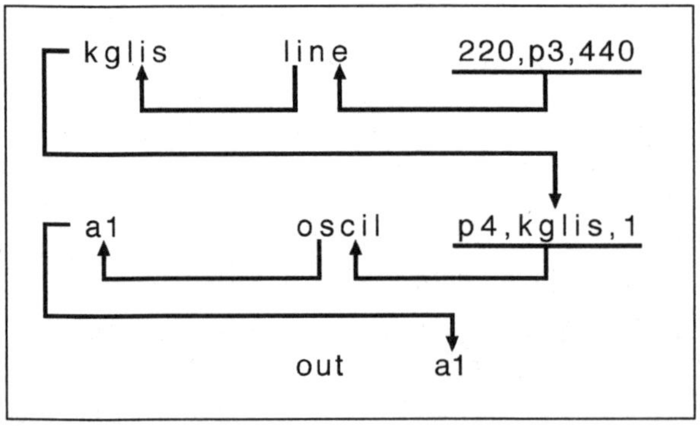

kglis is a *control variabl*e. Unlike audio variables, whose names begin with "a," control variables have names beginning with "k," like *kglis*, *k1*, *karma*, *kernigham*, etc..

To generate a line segment, Csound does not require a very accurate numerical resolution. An audio waveform, which is usually much more intricate and subtle in its development than a straight line, necessitates a much higher resolution. For operations that have less critical aural results, control variables with calculation rates that are lower than the sampling rate should be used. Since control variables are updated at the control rate, the *kr* value in the orchestra header, their use greatly decreases the number of operations performed in the synthesis process and less computation time is needed.

In the above example, *line* generates a series of values linearly increasing from 220 to 440. The result is deposited in *kglis* (we could have used any other name for this variable, the important point being that that name begins with "k"). Afterwards, the contents of *kglis* are passed to the *oscil* frequency argument. Because the values in *kglis* represent a ramp, the oscillator frequency accordingly rises from 220 to 440 Hz, and sounds like a typical gliding tone.

This sine wave tone will take p3 seconds to go from 220 to 440 Hz, , as can be seen from the second argument to *line*. Remember that the third p-field (p3) in any Csound i statement determines the duration of the note: if you set p3 = 0.1 sec., the sound will be a very rapid (1/10th of a second) sweep from 220 to 440 Hz. If you ask for a note lasting 40 seconds, the glissando will accordingly last 40 seconds. It is possible to create more complex glissandos, that are independent of the note duration, but this will be discussed later.

The *line* opcode generates straight lines and requires the following input arguments:

initial value, time (= how long it takes to get from the initial to the final value)**, final value**

For example, if you set the initial value to *ia* and the final value to *ib*, the input arguments for the line opcode will be *ia, idur, ib*. Such variable names begin with an "i" as these are neither audio nor control variables: they are *initialization* variables, meaning that they are given some value right at the beginning of a note and don't change before the next note is started.

In summary, in our new instrument the *oscil* opcode has p4 (= the fourth p-field of i statements in the score) as its amplitude, *kglis* (a straight line raising from 220 to 440 Hz) as its frequency, and the constant value 1 as the function table number. Notes will have only four p-fields (p1=instrument number, p2=start time, p3=duration, p4=amplitude) since we replaced p5 with the *kglis* variable in the oscillator frequency argument.

```
a1      oscil p4, kglis, 1
```

Also, the initial and final frequencies in our glissando are determined as constant arguments to the line opcode:

```
kglis   line 220, p3, 440
```

Here is a complete orchestra for our glissandos that includes useful comments:

```
; gliss.orc
        sr     =  44100          ; sampling rate
        kr     =  4410           ; control rate
        ksmps  =  10             ; sr/kr ratio
        nchnls =  1              ; number of output channels

        instr     1              ; instrument #1
kglis   line      220, p3, 440   ; a straight line going from 220 to 440 in p3 seconds, output in the
                                 ; kglis control rate variable
a1      oscil     p4, kglis, 1   ; oscillator with amplitude p4, frequency following the straight line in
                                 ; kglis, waveform function #1 (as defined in the score), output in the
                                 ; a1 audio rate variable
        out       a1             ; write the contents of a1 to disk
        endin
```

A suitable accompanying score is:

```
; gliss.sco
f1  0   4096   10   1           ; generate function #1, using 4096 memory locations and
                                ; GEN10 routine to obtain a single sine wave component
i1  0   3      10000            ; amp is 10000, the glissando will complete in 3 seconds
i1  4   10     12000            ; amp is 12000, the glissando will complete in 10 seconds
```

EXERCISE *1 Run Csound using these new orchestra and score files.*

EXERCISE *2 Modify the orchestra to create a glissando, falling from 800 to 100 Hz rather than rising from 220 to 440 Hz. Remember that the syntax for the line opcode is:*

kglis line init_value, duration, end_value

EXERCISE *3 Try using p5 as the init_value argument to line, and p6 as the end_value:*

kglisline p5, p3, p6

and write a new score using several notes, all including parameters p5 and p6.

EXERCISE *4 Create a new score with three notes lasting 40 seconds that play simultaneously (same start time and duration). Make the first a rising glissando, the second a falling glissando, the third a constant frequency (init_value = end_value). The initial frequency be 440 Hz for all notes. Choose an end_value for the first and the second note.*

1.10 CONTROL VARIABLES: AMPLITUDE ENVELOPES

Next, we will use a straight line to control the amplitude level rather than the frequency and audition the results.

```
        instr  1
kenv    line   0, p3, 10000     ; a line segment raising from 0 to 10000 in p3 secs; output in the...
                                ; ...control variable kenv
a2      oscil  kenv, 220, 1     ; oscillator with amplitude varying with kenv (increasing from 0 to...
                                ; ...10000), frequency is 220 Hz, waveform function #1 (as defined...
                                ; ...in the score); output in the audio rate variable a2
        out    a2               ; write the contents of a2 to disk
        endin
```

This line control variable changes the level of the sound, creating an *amplitude envelope*. Although this is a very simple and rudimentary envelope, the next chapter introduces more complex glissandos and envelope shapes.

After using the *oscil* opcode you may wonder if the amplitude and frequency inputs should be fixed or dynamic values. For most Csound opcode input arguments there are several modes of operation:

a. **direct** - opcode values are directly specified. The first oscillator example in this chapter included an amplitude of 10000 and a frequency of 220 Hz. Using these direct values, every note played with this instrument will always have the same frequency and the same amplitude.

b. **indirect : using p-fields** - opcode argument values are referenced by p-fields (p4, p5, etc.). Using this model, every new note can have different frequency and amplitude values. However, these frequency and amplitude values will remain static throughout the duration of the note.

c. **indirect : using control variables** - opcode argument values are determined as control variables. These control variables are generated by some other opcode in the orchestra file and subsequently used as an input argument. This model enables frequency and amplitude changes while the note is playing, creating amplitude envelopes and frequency glissandos.

d. **indirect : using audio variables** - opcode argument values are determined as audio rate variables. (This mode of input argument will be discussed in section 7.5).

EXERCISE 1 *Put a header on top of the following instrument and create a new score for the orchestra. Run Csound and listen. Notice that, except for the three basic p-fields, no additional p-field is needed since no argument in this orchestra refers to p4 or p5.*

```
        instr   1
kenv    line    0, p3, 10000
a2      oscil   kenv, 220, 1
        out     a2
        endin
```

EXERCISE 2 *Change the input arguments for* line *to create a line that decreases from 10000 to 0, rather than increasing from 0 to 10000. Remember:* line *arguments are* a, dur, b.

EXERCISE 3 *Replace* a *with p5 and* b *with p6.*

```
;                       a,          dur,        b
kenv        line        p5,         p3,         p6
```

and write a score with several notes, each with its own values in p5 and p6.

EXERCISE 4 *Write a new orchestra which uses control variables as amplitude and frequency arguments for an* oscil.

1.11 CONTROL VARIABLES WITH MULTIPLE LINE SEGMENTS

It is also possible to generate a gliding tone which first rises and then descends. In fact, this and even more complicated glissando shapes are possible with the *linseg* opcode. While *line* generates just one line segment, *linseg* generates many, one segment next to the other. The syntax is as follows:

kx linseg a, dur, b, dur, c ...

For example, the following code results in an oscillator that sweeps from 800 to 1000 Hz and then proceeds down to 400 Hz:

```
        instr   1
ksweep  linseg  800, p3/2, 1000, p3/2, 400
anew    oscil   15000, ksweep, 1
        out     anew
        endin
```

Ksweep above has two segments. Consequently, two partial durations must be specified. In this example, the total duration (p3) is simply divided into two equal durations, so the two ramps of the glissando curve each last precisely half the total duration of the note. For any value in p3, this note will take half the note duration to go from 800 to 1000 Hz, and then half to go down to 400 Hz.

To generate three segments, simply divide the duration by three and add the appropriate arguments to *linseg* as follows:

```
        instr 1
; variable  opcode     from 800 to 1000 in p3/3
;                                        from 1000 to 400 in p3/3
;                                                         from 400 to 900 in p3/3

ksweep  linseg 800,   p3/3,    1000,  p3/3,  400,  p3/3,  900

;              amp    freq     func
anew    oscil  15000, ksweep,  1
        out    anew
        endin
```

The *linseg* syntax is

kx linseg ia, idur1, ib, idur2, ic, idur3, id

but it allows for the addition of as many segments as needed.

Observe that in the example above, all notes are forced to move to and from pre-defined frequency values. These values can change with each successive note, by using appropriate score p-fields:

```
        instr 1
ksweep  linseg  p5,  p3/2,    p6,    p3/2,   p7
anew    oscil   p4,  ksweep,  1
        out     anew
        endin
```

The note statements in the accompanying score include not only the three fixed p-fields (instrument number, action time and duration) and p4 (note amplitude), but also p5 (initial frequency value for the glissando), p6 (frequency value for the glissando at half the note duration) and p7 (final frequency value for the glissando).

Using another linseg opcode, the following instrument adds an amplitude envelope (on envelopes, see 1.C.1), with an attack time, a sustain and a decay:

```
        instr   1
ksweep  linseg  p5,     p3/2,   p6,     p3/2,   p7
kenv1   linseg  0,      p3/3,   10000,  p3/3,   10000,  p3/3,   0
anew    oscil   kenv1,  ksweep, 1
        out     anew
        endin
```

Here the amplitude raises from 0 to 10000 in p3/3 (attack time), holds the value for p3/3 seconds (sustain) and returns to 0 in the remaining p3/3 seconds (decay).

If the three segment durations do not add up to the total note duration (i.e. if their sum does not equal p3), *linseg* will generate values that continue in the same direction as the last defined segment. For example, if we write

```
k1      linseg  0, p3/3, 1, p3/3, 0
```

the duration of *linseg* equals 2/3 of p3, and therefore the values of the second segment will continue decreasing until the end of the note. Strangely enough, in the digital audio realm the resultant negative amplitude values will create a sounding note (negative amplitudes read positive amplitudes with inverse phase).

To avoid this, we can write either

```
k1      linseg  0, p3/3, 1, p3/3, 0, p3/3, 0
```

or

```
k1      linseg  0, p3/3, 1, p3/3, 0, .001, 0
```

In the latter case the continuation of the third segment would result in a horizontal line, generating a series of zeros until the note stops.

1.12 CONTROL VARIABLES WITH MULTIPLE EXPONENTIAL SEGMENTS

In addition to line segments, Csound includes opcodes that create exponential segments. An exponential segment would lend itself better than a straight line to glissandos. Indeed, exponential frequency variations sound more "natural" to the ear, given that pitch raises exponentially, doubling at each higher octave: a frequency glide from 55 to 110 Hz is perceived as the same interval (octave) as 220 to 440 Hz.

The exponential equivalent of *line* is *expon*. The exponential equivalent of *linseg* is *expseg*.

kx expon ia, idur, ib
kx expseg ia, idur1, ib, idur2, ic....

In both cases, the syntax remains essentially the same. The only difference is that exponential opcodes do not accept values of 0 as magnitude levels (even-numbered arguments). Whenever a null value is desired, a small non-zero value like .001 should suffice and result in the desired effect.

```
        instr   1               ; instrument #1
kglis   expon   220, p3, 440    ; exponential segment, raising from 220 to 440 in p3 seconds
                                ; output in kglis
a1      oscil   p4, kglis, 1    ; oscillator, amp is p4, freq. follows kglis, waveform function #1
        out     a1              ; write the contents of a1 to disk
        endin

        instr   2                                       ; instrument #2
ksweep  expseg  p5, p3/2, p6, p3/2, p7                  ; 2 exponential segments (for frequency)
kenv1   expseg  .001, p3/3, 10000, p3/3, 10000, p3/3, .001   ; 3 exponential segments (for amplitude)
anew    oscil   kenv1, ksweep, 1
        out     anew
        endin
```

1.13 ENVELOPES WITH *LINEN*

Csound also contains an opcode that is specifically designed to create trapezoidal envelopes, indicating attack-sustain-release (see 1.C.1):

kenv linen kamp, iatt, idur, idec

where:
kamp is the peak amplitude in the sound;
iatt is the duration of the attack transient (attack time);
idur is the overall duration of the sound (usually equals p3);[5]

[5] Caution: if the third argument to linen (the duration) is smaller than p3, the release segment will continue into negative values, until the end of the note is reached! If this happens undesired results are likely. The same is true for line, expon, linseg and expseg. With these five opcodes, if the actual duration is less than p3 the output will continue in the direction of the last-defined argument.

idec is the duration of the decay

For example:

```
        instr   1
kenv    linen   10000, .1, p3, .5       ; amplitude goes from 0 to 10000 in 1/10th of a second, stays there...
                                        ; ...for a while (= p3 - .1 - .5) and fades away in half a second.
a1      oscil   kenv, 440, 1            ; kenv, generated with linen, is utilized to control the amplitude of...
                                        ; ...the oscillator
        out     a1
        endin
```

When the note duration (p3) changes, this instrument accordingly changes the duration of the amplitude steady state, while attack time and decay time remain the same.

1.14 FREQUENCY ENCODING BY OCTAVES AND SEMITONES. AMPLITUDE ENCODING BY dB

Frequency encoding by "octave point pitch-class"

As noted previously, Csound requires that frequency values be given in Hz and that amplitude levels be specified in raw values (in the range 0-32767). However, one may prefer to express pitch in a more familiar way, such as naming a particular semitone within a register or octave. Csound contains pitch converters that calculate Hz from a given octave and pitch class.

The "octave point pitch-class" representation (hereafter, *pch*) consists of an integer representing an octave and decimal numbers representing semitones. The octave starting on the middle C (261.63 Hz) is named, by convention, octave 8.

Therefore

8.00 = middle C (261.63 Hz)
8.01 = C sharp (277.18 Hz)
8.02 = D (293.67 Hz)
8.03 = D sharp (311.13 Hz)
7.09 = A below middle C (220 Hz)
8.09 = A above middle C (440 Hz)
9.00 = C an octave higher than middle C (523.25 Hz)
5.00 = the lowest C of a piano (32.7 Hz)

Here is the code that instructs Csound to make a conversion from pch to Hz:

```
; pitch.orc
        instr   1
ifreq   =       cpspch(p5)
a1      oscil   p4, ifreq, 1
        out     a1
        endin
```

ifreq is an init-time variable, a variable which is assigned some value before the note starts playing and is then never changed. This contrasts control and audio variables, which are updated many times per second over the note duration. Here *ifreq* is assigned a value in Hz (or *cps*, cycles per second) resulting from the conversion of the *pch* number stored in p5. The conversion itself is accomplished by calling the opcode *cpspch*, which returns the Hz value of pch numbers.

One possible score for the instrument above follows:

```
; pitch.sco
f1  0  4096  10     1
i1  0  1     10000  8.00
i1  1  1     10000  8.02
i1  2  1     10000  8.04
i1  3  1     10000  8.00
```

EXERCISE Provide the instrument above (pitch.orc) with a header. Run Csound using this new orchestra and from the score just above here (pitch.sco). After listening, insert new notes into the score and save. Run Csound again and listen.

Note	**pitch (*pch*)**	**octave (*oct*)**
C	8.00	8.00
C sharp	8.01	8.0833
D	8.02	8.16667
D sharp	8.03	8.25
E	8.04	8.3333
F	8.05	8.41667
F sharp	8.06	8.5
G	8.07	8.5833
G sharp	8.08	8.6667
A	8.09	8.75
A sharp	8.10	8.8333
B	8.11	8.91667

Frequency encoding by "octave point decimal"

Csound also provides an opcode that allows for pitches to be expressed as fractions of an octave. The *cpsoct* opcode evaluates a number as an octave specified by the integer portion of the value (like cpsoct) while the fractional component is interpreted as the true fractional part (decimal) within that octave. The octave space is considered, in this case, a continuum, while in *pch* values are subdivided into semitones. Thus, 8 again stands for middle C, and 9 for the C one octave higher, but 8.5 will stand for F sharp (the interval C - F sharp being half an octave), 8.25 for D sharp (the interval C - D sharp being 1/4th of an octave), etc. (see, above, the table of equivalences between *pch* and *oct*).

Amplitude in decibels

As Csound contains pitch converters, it also contains amplitude converters. In order to express amplitude values in decibels (dB) you only need to create another init-time variable to store the result of a conversion from dB to the absolute value. The conversion is made with the *ampdb* opcode. Be advised, the range of absolute values allowed in Csound is equivalent to a dynamic range of approximately 90 dB.[6]

dB	**absolute value**	**dB**	**absolute value**	**dB**	**absolute value**	**dB**	**absolute value**
90	31622.78	60	1000.00	30	31.62	0	1.000
88	25118.86	58	794.33	28	25.12		
86	19952.62	56	630.96	26	19.95		
84	15848.93	54	501.19	24	15.85		
82	12589.25	52	398.11	22	12.59		
80	10000.00	50	316.23	20	10.00		
78	7943.28	48	251.19	18	7.94		
76	6309.57	46	199.53	16	6.31		
74	5011.87	44	158.49	14	5.01		
72	3981.07	42	125.89	12	3.98		
70	3162.28	40	100.00	10	3.16		
68	2511.89	38	79.43	8	2.51		
66	1995.26	36	63.10	6	2.00		
64	1584.89	34	50.12	4	1.58		
62	1258.93	32	39.81	2	1.26		

```
        instr   1
iamp    =       ampdb(p4)           ; dB to absolute value conversion
```

[6] Csound can save sounds to disk in several sound file formats. The most common formats, however (such as WAVE for Win computers, and AIFF for Macs) allow up to 16-bit digital audio resolution, which is equivalent to a range of 90 dB. See 1.A.2.

```
ifreq   =       cpspch(p5)      ; pch to Hz conversion
a2      oscil   iamp, ifreq, 1
        out     a2
        endin
```

EXERCISE *Answer this question: what happens if the instrument above is edited as follows:*

```
        instr 1
        iamp    =   ampdb(p4)
        ifreq   =   cpspch(p5)
a2      oscil       p4, p5, 1
        out         a2
        endin
```

The right answer is that Csound would convert the dB in p4 to absolute value, and the *pch* in p5 to Hz, and store the results in *iamp* and *ifreq*, but then it would use the original values of p4 and p5 as they are, instead of their equivalents in Hz and absolute amplitude.

1.15 MORE ON THE SCORE

Using the Csound score to compose a musical piece, you may get tired of writing parameter values which don't change from note to note. As a rule of thumb; when a parameter retains the same value over many notes, you can repeat the previous p-field value by simply entering a single dot (.). Imagine you have seven notes all having an amplitude of 10000:

```
i1  0   1   10000   220   ; in this note amplitude is 10000
i1  2   3   .       223   ; in this note too amplitude is 10000
i1  6   2   .       .     ; in this note amplitude is 10000 and frequency is 223
i1  8   3   .       400
i1  8   .   .       420   ; duration is the same as the preceding note
i1  12  .   .       227
i1  15  1   .       220
```

Careful! This works for note statements calling the same single instrument only. If the instrument changes, then you have to enter an explicit value again:

```
i1  0   1   10000   220
i1  2   3           223
```

```
i1   5    2    .       233
i2   7    2    10000   233     ; amplitude value is the same as the previous, but we have
                               ; to re-write it because of the different instrument
i2   9    .    .       .       ; in this case the previous dur., amp., and freq. values can be
                               ; repeated
```

When you write a sequence of adjacent notes with no rests in between them (the second starts when the first stops, the third starts when the second stops, etc.), you can replace each next note's action time with the symbol +, as follows:

```
i1   0    1    10000   220
i1   +    3    .       223
i1   +    2    .       .
i1   +    3    15000   400
i1   +    .    .       .
i1   +    .    .       .
i1   15   1    10000   220
i1   15   1    .       440
i1   +    2    .       427
i1   +    .    .       .
i1   +    .    .       .
```

The last note in this score starts at 20 seconds, lasts 2 seconds, has an amplitude of 10000 and a frequency of 427 Hz. When creating a series of linearly increasing or decreasing p-field values, one can use the score ramping feature, which is implemented by replacing intermediate values with the symbol ">".

For example, this score

```
i1   0    1    60      8.03
i1   +    2    >       8.04
i1   +    1    >       8.06
i1   +    3    >       8.08
i1   +    2    80      8.10
```

is equivalent to the following:

```
i1   0    1    60      8.03
i1   +    2    65      8.04
```

```
i1    +    1    70      8.06
i1    +    3    75      8.08
i1    +    2    80      8.10
```

This creates a linear *crescendo*, from 60 to 80 dB. *Ramping* consists of linear interpolation between any given two end values.

Remember that placing the *e* (end) statement after a group of notes causes all that is written thereafter to be disregarded by the program. If while editing a score file you change a couple of things in the second and third note of a much longer sequence of notes, you can listen to the results of these changes without waiting for the program to generate the entire score by placing an e after the third note. When you run Csound, the synthesis will stop after that line of code.

```
i1    0    1    10000   220
i1    +    3    .       223
i1    +    2    .       .
e                               ; synthesis stops here
i1    +    3    .       400
i1    +    .    .       .
i1    +    .    .       300
```

Csound also provides a mechanism for changing the tempo of your score. It is impractical to re-enter all these action time and duration values. Csound puts at your disposal a statement, specifically devised for this purpose; the *t* (tempo) statement. The syntax for a t statement is as follows:

t   p1   p2   p3   p4   ...

where:

p1	must be zero (beginning of score)
p2	sets the initial tempo (in beats per minutes)
p3, p5, ...	times in beats (in non-decreasing order)
p4, p6, ...	tempi for the referenced beat times (p4 is the tempo value at action time p3, p6 is the tempo value at action time p5, etc.)

With this code, one sets the tempo and specifies accelerandos and decelerandos. If no *t* statement present, Csound assumes a default 60 beats per minute (bpm), which allows for action times and durations to be measured in seconds.

Thus, values of time and values of tempo are pairs of defining points on a "tempo vs time" graph. If we write

```
t0 120
```

then the entire score will be performed at twice the speed. If we write

```
t0 60 5 90 5 120 9 120 15 100
```

the tempo will change as illustrated in the graph on this page. It is 60 bpm at the beginning, gradually speeds up to 90 bpm in five beats; then it suddenly jumps to 120 bpm and stays there until the 9th beat, with no changes; finally it slows down to 100 bpm until the 15th beat of the score.

All accelerandos and decelerandos are computed as linear interpolations between break points (musically, this is not ideal, as in fact our perception of tempo variations follows an exponential curve).

A tempo, once assigned, remains in effect from that time unless another tempo value is indicated. The last specified tempo remains in effect until the end of a section.

What is a *section*? It is a part of an entire score that Csound considers as separate from all others. This means that Csound will compile first all the notes from within the first section, then all those from within the second section, etc. The sorting of notes, too, is done section by section (however, functions remain in effect across the *entire* score).

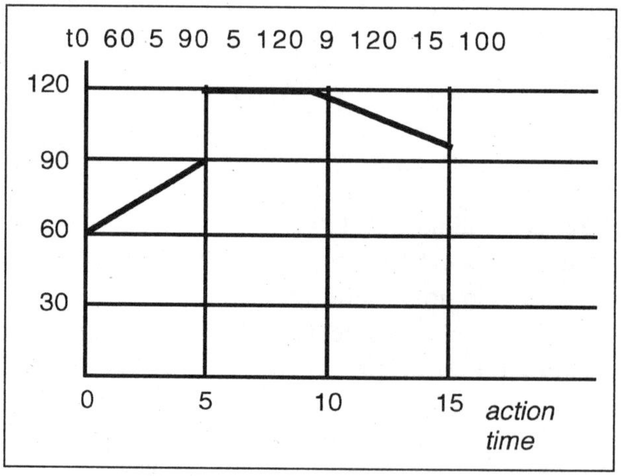

Consider the following score:

```
i1   0   2     80   8       ; first computes this section...
i1   5   1     78   9       ; ... of the score...
i1   3   1.5   80   8.07    ; ... and then, after the last note...
s                           ; ... terminates this section
i1   0   4     60   6       ; starts again here...
i1   3   2.7   65   6.01    ; ... and continues ...
```

Csound will perform the first three notes, according to their actual timing. After the third note (i.e. after the *second* note statement, beginning at 5 seconds and terminating at 5+1 = 6 seconds), Csound resets its clock and re-starts from the first line next to the *s* statement marking the end of the section.

t statements, too, are relative to the section to which they belong. A tempo value of, say, 120 bpm remains in effect until the next section begins. In the new section, the tempo will automatically default to 60 bpm unless a new *t* statement is entered.

1.16 READING THE OPCODE SYNTAX

Since the number of available opcodes is quite large and keeps increasing, it is difficult to precisely remember their details, even for experts. At the end of this book, you can find a description of the syntax for currently available opcodes. The description adopts a symbolic format identical to that in the *csound.hlp* file (this file contains the Csound reference manual and includes briefings on most opcodes). It is important, then, to learn the basic criteria of the syntax description. Consider the following:

```
k1    oscil   kamp, kcps, ifn[,iphs]
a1    oscil   xamp, xcps, ifn[,iphs]
```

These lines provide the syntax of the two versions of *oscil*. The first *oscil* is utilized as a control oscillator whose output is stored in a control variable, *k1*. The second *oscil* is utilized to generate some sound. Consequently, the output is stored in an audio variable, *a1*. In addition to generating outputs at different rates, these exhibit other differences.

Both formats require 3 arguments:

amplitude (amp); frequency (cps = Hz); function (fn)

But they also have an optional argument, the initial phase (*phs*) in the oscillator. Optional arguments are enclosed within square brackets in their manual listings.

Now, observe that the short names *amp*, *cps*, *fn* and *phs* are preceded by "x", "k" or "i". These prefixes indicate the possible input argument rate. The «i» prefix indicates that an argument can be given either a constant or a p-field value, or any expression which does not include control or audio variables. For example, *ifn* means that for the particular argument (function number) only init-time variables are acceptable. Initialization variables are assigned some value right at the beginning of the synthesis process and never change until the next note is played. Csound will not accept control or audio rate variables as an input argument with an i prefix. Therefore

```
a1      oscil   2000, 440, k1           ; will not function, the third argument to oscil only accepts init variables
a1      oscil   2000, 440, ijoe         ; will function
```

The prefix **k** indicates that an argument can accept either an init-time or a control variable. Thus, in the following

```
k1      oscil   kamp, kcps, ifn[,iphs]
```

we are advised that it is possible to express amplitude and frequency by control variables (as we have done in the examples discussed in sections 1.9 through 1.12). However, this opcode will not accept audio variables for these arguments.

The prefix **a** indicates that an argument accepts only audio variables. Thus, if we write

```
a1      reson   asig, kcf, kbw
```

the output from this filter (*reson* is a bandpass filter) gets stored in the audio variable *a1*. The input to the filter, too, must be an audio variable (*asig*, notice that "sig" is short for "signal"). In contrast, the center frequency *cf* and the bandwidth *bw* must be given control or init variables, or some score p-field value like p5.

The prefix **x** indicates that the input argument can be expressed as an init, control, or audio variable.

EXTENSIONS

1.A.1 HOW CSOUND REALLY FUNCTIONS

Csound retains the traditional separation between *instruments* and *notes.* A group of instruments is called an *orchestra*, and actually works as an *executable program* to which data stored in a *score* file are submitted. The score file data represents a sequence of notes.

Csound utilizes two distinct sampling rates, one for audio signals (sample rate, *sr*), the other for control signals (control rate, *kr*). A typical value for the control rate would be 1/10th of the sampling rate. According to the Nyquist law for audio signals, it is necessary to use a sampling frequency at least twice as high as the highest frequency we wish to generate. Thus, to create a sound with a bandwidth as high as 20000 Hz, we have to set a sampling rate of at least 40000 Hz. The choice of the sampling rate directly effects the quality of the audio conversion process. Control signals (e.g. amplitude envelopes, dynamic stereo panning, etc.) have limited bandwidth and can be computed at a lower rate. For such signals we usually don't need high resolution. Their waveform shape is much less varied and detailed than those of audio signals. Using a smaller rate for control signals decreases the number of calculations required and speeds up the overall synthesis process.

When compiling, Csound performs a number of preliminary operations and then begins reading the data from the score. First it computes the required table functions, then the notes. When it generates a note, it goes through an *initialization step* to complete operations that have to be done only once at the onset of the note (pch to Hz conversions, dB to abs value conversions, etc.). Once the init values are set, Csound generates audio signals. This process includes calculating a series of sample values (say 48000 values per second, assuming *sr* = 48000) and another series of control values (say, 16000, assuming *kr* = 16000). If sr=48000 and kr=16000, three audio samples will be generated for each control value (48000/16000 = 3). The process continues until the note terminates.

Fig. 1-A-1 illustrates the procedure followed by Csound as it generates a note.

First, the program reads the complete note statement from the score and initializes the *i*-type variables (including the note's action time, duration, etc.). Subsequently, it begins calculating the values which, when stored in control variables, constitute the control signals. With an amplitude envelope, for example, it would not be necessary to calculate 48000 values per second. Instead, a few thousands calculations per second will be adequate so *kr* can be much smaller than *sr*.

The example shown in fig.1-A-1 sets *kr* to 1/3 the rate of *sr*. This is referenced by *ksmps* in the orchestra header.

At this point, the program moves on to calculating the values which, when stored in audio variables, constitute the audio signals. These signals require a very high sampling rate. After every three audio samples, Csound will calculate a new value for the control signals, repeating this over and over until the end of the note.

To summarize: Csound updates *i*-variables at the beginning of each new note. The *k*-variables are updated at each period of *kr* (i.e. every 1/*kr* seconds). The *a*-variables are updated at each period of *sr* (every 1/*sr* seconds).

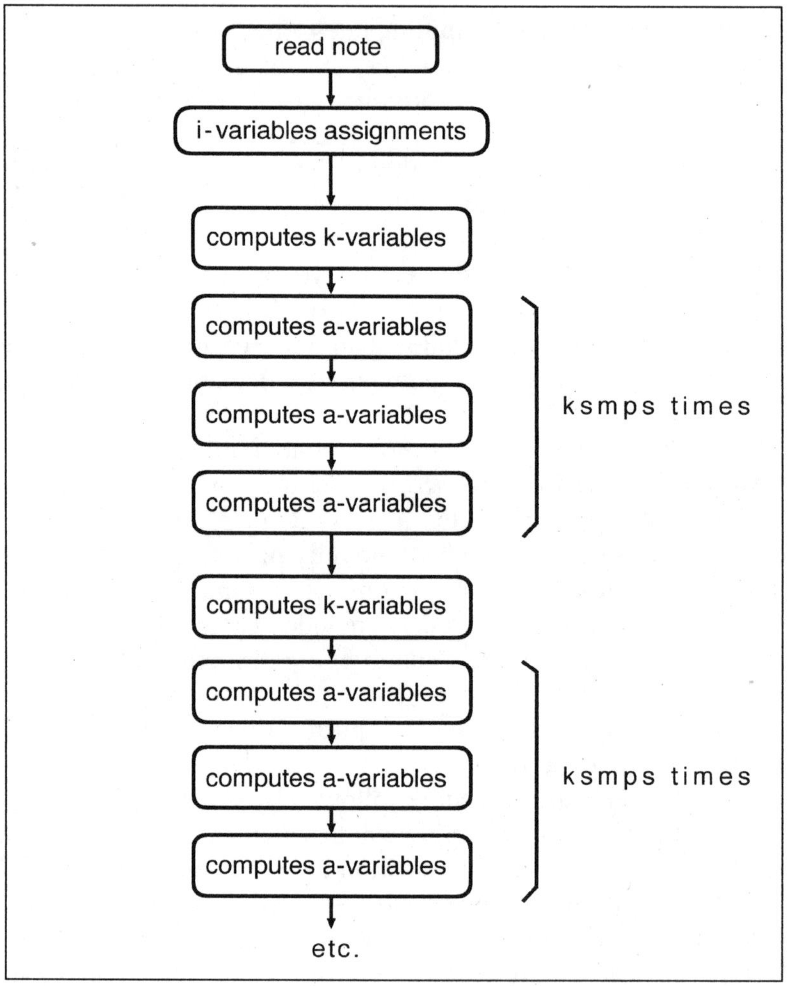

Fig. 1-A-1

1.A.2 CONSTANTS AND VARIABLES

In Csound, there are a number of constants or numerical values that remain unchanged throughout the synthesis process. There are also a number of variables, or memory locations identified by their names (names are given following naming conventions). The internal variable value can change during the synthesis process.

Predefined constants are *the sampling rate for audio signals* (sr), *the sampling rate for control signals* (kr), *the sr/kr ratio* (must be an integer), *and the number of output channels*, which can be 1 (mono), 2 (stereo) or 4 (quad).

There are three types of variables:

initialization variables - their name must begin with an "i". They are computed just once for each note, at the beginning of the note itself. Valid names include: *i1*, *ifreq*, *istart*, *iend*, *i121*, etc.

control variables - their name must begin with a "k". They are computed at k-rate. Valid names include: *k1*, *kfreq*, *kstart*, *kend*, *k444*, etc.

audio variables - their name must begin with an "a". They are computed at sampling rate. Valid names include: *a1*, *aout*, *astart*, *aend*, *a99*, etc.

All such variables are referenced only within the particular instrument where they are defined. There is only one way to pass values among different instruments using variables referenced by all instruments in the orchestra. It requires that you use the *global* variables, whose names begin with "g". Having the attribute of being global, these variables are referenced across the various instruments of an orchestra. Valid names would be: *ga1* (a global variable of audio type), *gkloop* (a global variable of control type), *gi1* (a global variable of init type).

To review, we have:

initialization variables	*i...*
control variables	*k...*
audio variables	*a...*
global initialization variables	*gi...*
global control variables	*gk...*
global audio variables	*ga...*

All variables are mathematically represented as *floating point* numbers. They are 32-bit real integers, with values ranging approximately $2*2^{-127}$ to $2*2^{+127}$. While a 16-bit representation (used in Csound to write a sound file onto disk) allows numbers between -32768 and +32767, floating point variables are comprised of a *mantissa* (base) and an *exponent*. The exponent is a signed 7-bit number, and can assume, according to the rules of binary arithmetic, values between -127 and +127, while the mantissa, or base, can assume values between -2 and +2. Therefore, it is possible in any part of the orchestra to use either very large or very small numbers. However, the values for the audio samples written to a sound file range between -32768 and +32767.

If required, Csound writes sound files in *long integer* format (32-bit integers, in the range -2147483648 to +2147483647), and even in *floating point* format. The *long integer* files cannot be converted to real sounds, they are of use only for further processing, either with Csound or other programs. The *floating point* versions of WAVE and AIFF files can be converted to sound, provided the appropriate drivers are available in the computer operating system.

1.A.3 THE CSOUND SYNTAX

a) Orchestra

Csound is a very powerful sound synthesis language. However, users must follow strict syntactical conventions to exploit its full potential.

A Csound orchestra consists of a text file. The first part of this text file is the header, where *sr*, *kr*, the *sr/kr* ratio, and *nchnls* are declared.

An example of header is:

```
sr     =  20000        ; audio sampling rate
kr     =  1000         ; control rate
ksmps  =  20           ; = sr / kr
nchnls =  2            ; number of output channels
```

Everything that follows a semicolon is a comment, and does not affect the program while it runs.

Following the header is the orchestra itself, which can be composed of one or more instruments. The body of an instrument must be framed between *instr* and *endin*.

```
instr 1
...
...
...
endin
instr 2
...
...
...
endin
```

The general format of an orchestra statement is

[label:] [result] ***opcode*** **[arg1, arg2, arg3...]**

The square brackets imply that the particular syntax element may or may not be present, depending upon the opcode requirements. Thus, the *label* may be absent, just as the *result* and the *arguments* are not required for some opcodes.
Csound instructions read logically from right to left. In order to express

2 + 3 = 5

we would write

5 + 2, 3 if «+» were an opcode with «2» and «3» as input arguments.

The *opcode* is the symbol standing for a particular generating unit. Some examples will clarify this notion.

```
a1      oscil   iamp, ifreq, itab
```

invokes the *oscil* generator (an oscillator). The oscillator will deposits its result in an audio variable called *a1*, using *iamp* (amplitude), *ifreq* (frequency) and *itab* (id number of a function table) as its arguments.

```
        out     a1
```

invokes the *out* opcode (output) and requires only one input argument. This opcode has no resultant output variable but instead writes audio to the specified storage location.

```
ifreq   =   cpspch(8.09)
```

invokes a conversion from pitch (in octave-point-pitch representation) to cycles per second. The pitch being converted here is A3. The result of the conversion (440) is stored in the variable *ifreq*.

Any syntax errors will be detected by Csound when you compile it, and a message will appear referencing lines in the orchestra file where errors occurred. A typical error message looks like this

0 errors in performance

followed by

overall samples out of range: 0

This usually means that your files included no relevant syntax errors.

b) Score

The score is also a text file, but it exhibits a different syntax. The opcode is the first character in each line. Score opcodes are: *i, f, a, t, s* and *e.* The most important are *i* (note) and *f* (function, also called wavetable). Input parameters spaced by blanks or tabs follow the opcodes. Parameters vary in number and the maximum allowed is dependent on the particular version of Csound you are running. Usually up to 50 parameters are allowed.

Here are two typical lines of a Csound score:

```
f1 0 4096 10 1 .5
i1 9 1.5 80 6.078 1 3 6 .66
```

1.A.4 THE CSOUND BUILDING BLOCKS

Writing a Csound orchestra essentially creates connections amongst the available unit generators. In this respect, Csound emulates a classic analog electronic music studio with various modules. However, Csound also has other types of modules.

These opcodes can be classed by their function:

signal generators (oscillators, noise generators, sound file readers, etc.);

signal modifiers (envelopes, filters, etc.);

sensing and control units (envelope followers, amplitude detectors, spectrum analyzers, etc.);

input and output units.

Csound also provides arithmetic operators (addition, subtraction, multiplication, abs value, logarithm, exponential, etc.) and logical operators (equal, greater then, smaller then, not equal, etc.). In the age of analog electronic music a signal was multiplied by another (as in "ring modulation") using a special device called a "ring modulator". In Csound, the simple line of code

```
a3      =  a1 * a2
```

is used to perform this operation. Similarly, mixing signals *a1*, *a2*, and *a3* each scaled by a different factor is accomplished by simply adding the audio signals together as follows:

```
a4      =   a1 * i1 + a2 * i2 + a3 * i3
```

Multiplying an audio signal by a constant *changes the amplitude* of that signal, while *adding* two or more signals together simply *mixes* them.

1.A.5 USING THE CSOUND COMMAND

If you don't use either WCShell or the Power Mac version of Csound, you can launch Csound by typing a command line. The Csound command has its own syntax, including various flags (optional commands) and two file names:

csound [flags] orchestra_filename score_filename

The flags can be either numerical or alphabetical preceded by a "minus" sign (-), for example, *-t60*, or *-Fbach.mid*. If no flag is used, Csound assumes a default value for each of the available flags. If you don't specify any name for the output sound file, omitting the flag *-o filename*, Csound creates a file called "test" as the output file.

Using the Csound command, you simply type the command line following the DOS prompt. In ***Win***, instead, you click on the *Start* button of the *Applications* bar, choose *Run* and type the command line into the text box that appears. You will have also to specify the path name for the orc and sco files so Csound can find them.

Typical command lines are:

csound -o mickey.sf mouse.orc minnie.sco

this generates the sound file "mickey.sf", running from the "mouse.orc" orchestra and the "minnie.sco" score.

csound -W -o goofy.wav walt.orc disney.sco

this generates the sound file "goofy.wav", in WAVE format, running from "walt.orc" and "disney.sco".

c:\audio\csound -W -o d:\soundfiles\goofy.wav c:\audio\orcsco\walt.orc c:\audio\orcsco\disney.sco

here the operating system looks into the "c:\audio" folder for the Csound program to start. The program generates and saves the output WAVE file "goofy.wav" into the "soundfiles" folder of the drive called "d:", running from the "walt.orc" and the "disney.sco" files, both reside in the "audio\orcsco" folder of the drive unit called "c:".

Most important flags are:

-o fnam	where *fnam* stands for the file name you prefer for the new sound file.
-A	the output sound file will be generated in AIFF format
-W	the output sound file will be generated in WAVE format
-m N	specify the level for messages prompted on screen during the synthesis. It is the sum of 1=note amplitude; 2=out of range samples; 4=warnings
-d	prevents the program from plotting the various wavetables required in the score
-t MM	set a metronome mark for the score
-H	allows a "heartbeat" character to appear on screen during the compilation
-z	allows for a list of available opcodes to appear on screen

The most important flag default values are:

-o test
-m 7

1.B.1 A SINGLE FILE INCLUDING ORCHESTRA, SCORE AND FLAGS: THE *CSD* FORMAT

As you have seen, in order to synthesize a sound or an entire musical composition, Csound compiles two distinct files, the orchestra and the score. You have seen, too, that a number of flags must be specified when launching Csound. Sometimes these are too complicated to remember. Some flags change from one Csound release to the next, and it is often the case that a flag takes a different meaning in different releases. Consider, for example, the latest releases running on Windows computers. The flags specific to the particular operating system (enabling you to use the DirectX operating system features, see section 10.3) are collected together under the symbol "+". In order to use DirectX together with your computer's i/o device #2, the following flag is required:

-+X2

To better deal with the ever-growing complexity of such flags, a new format has been introduced, using a single file instead of two. The file extension is *.csd* (*Csound structured data*). A *.csd* file includes orchestra, score and flags, delimited by special instructions, also called *tags*, akin to HTML tags. The HTML language is commonly used to create web pages. Indeed, one of the motivations behind the creation of the CSD format was to include Csound real-time synthesis tasks in web pages.

Tags are always used in pair. The first tag precedes the code body, the second follows it.

```
<CsoundScore>
...
...
...
</CsoundScore>
```

CSD files have the following structure:

```
<CsoundSynthesizer>                 ; CSD code starts here
        <CsoundOptions>             ; flags start here
        ... ;(flags)
        </CsoundOptions>            ; end of flags
        <CsoundInstruments>         ; orchestra code starts here
        ...
        ... ; (orchestra)
        ...
        </CsoundInstruments>        ; end of orchestra
        <CsoundScore>               ; score code starts here
        ...
        ...;(score)
        ...
        </CsoundScore>              ; end of score
</CsoundSynthesizer>                ; end of CSD code
```

When launching Csound, the command line appears as follows:

Csound myfile.csd

You don't have to specify anything, not even the output file name, which is included in the flags specified within the file. Let's see a practical example. (Observe that indentations are used to indicate the different code sections, but they are not strictly necessary):

```
<CsoundSynthesizer>
; a Csound structured data file
<CsOptions>
; flags, including the output sound file, Wave format
-oc:/wave/myfile.wav -W
</CsOptions>
<CsInstruments>
; Orchestra
        sr     =  44100
        kr     =  441
        ksmps  =  100
        nchnls =  1
        instr     1
a1      oscil     10000, 440, 1
        out       a1
        endin
</CsInstruments>
<CsScore>
; Score
f1 0 4096 10 1
i1 0 5
</CsScore>
</CsoundSynthesizer>
```

1.C.1 ATTACK AND RELEASE TRANSIENTS

No phenomenon that includes some amount of energy can ever change its energetic state instantly. Thus, no sound source can change from silence to maximum amplitude value in zero time. It always takes some finite time for this to happen, however short that time might be. That is called the *attack transient* of a sound.
Similarly, there is a *release transient* when the sounds decays to silence.

Figure 1-C-1 illustrates the typical amplitude evolution of a musical tone. You see that the phenomenon consists of four parts:

- *attack*: amplitude gradually raises, moving from zero to the maximum value;

- *decay*: shifts down to a certain level;
- *steady state* (or *sustain*): remains nearly constant;
- *release*: gradually gets back to zero.

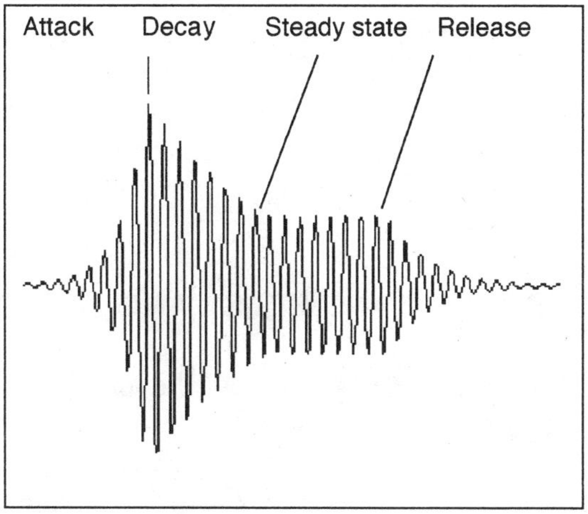

Fig. 1-C-1

The amplitude evolution can be seen as the ideal line connecting the amplitude peaks. We call this line the *envelope*.

Together with the frequency spectrum, the transients play an essential role in determining the timbre of a sound. Sounds having different spectra may be perceived as identical (or at least similar) if they have similar transients in the envelope. And sounds having identical spectra may be perceived as quite different if they have very different transients.

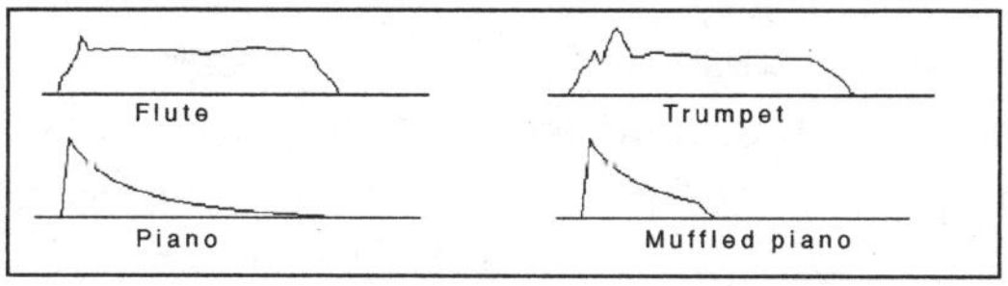

Fig. 1-C-2

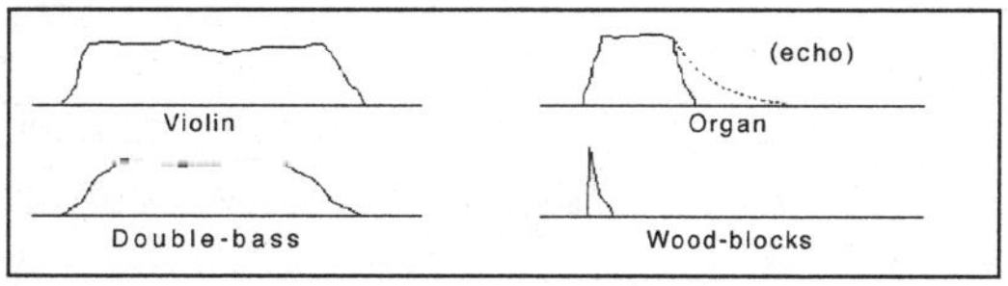

Fig. 1-C-3

Figures 1-C-2 and 1-C-3 illustrate the attack and release transients in typical music instruments. Consider figure 1-C-2. Notice that the sound of the flute is characterized by a rather quick onset followed by short decay (this is the effect of exciting the resonance with the tongue) and by a quick release. The envelope of the trumpet sound (as well as other brass instruments) features a rather peculiar "double attack". The piano has a quick attack followed by an exponential release (which can be dampened by the pedal).

Consider now figure 1-C-3. The violin has a rapid attack and release, while the double bass, due to the greater mass of its strings, is slower in both attack and release. The organ has very quick attack and release transients. Its sound can be characterized by a reverberating coda, too, as an integral element of the organ timbre.

During the transients, a sound can change in amplitude, as well as in frequency, albeit to lesser extent. During the onset time, musical sounds fluctuate in frequency before reaching a stable pitch. This is particularly evident in the "portamento" of certain instruments and the voice. This is also true for any instrument playing the first note in an extended phrase, or for a series of *staccato* notes. During the attack time, the pitch usually is lower than the desired pitch.

1.D.1 BRIEF HISTORY OF SOUND SYNTHESIS LANGUAGES

Direct sound synthesis by computer was born at the end of the 1950's, when computers with sufficient processing power were first introduced. The earliest systems included *MAESTRO* (University of Urbana, Illinois) and the series of *MUSIC* languages developed by Max V. Mathews at Bell Laboratories, *MUSIC III*, from 1960, *MUSIC IV*, from 1963, down to the most renowned (which is still in use today) *MUSIC V*, from 1966. In 1965 Hubert Howe, then at Princeton, developed the *MUSIC4BF* language written in FORTRAN. In 1966 John Chowning developed *MUSIC10*. A few years later, Barry Vercoe from M.I.T. created *MUSIC360* (1969) and its direct descendants, *MUSIC11* (1973) and *Csound* (1986). Other software based sound synthesis languages include *Cmusic* (Moore and Loy, 1982), *Cmix* (Lansky, 1984), *Music4Ci* (Gerrard, 1988), *Common LISP Music* (Schoetthstaedt, 1991), *MUSIC30* (Dashow, 1991), etc.

Nearly all such languages share the two basic concepts of orchestra and score, and hence the concept of the note itself as the minimal event unit. All basically consist of a program (orchestra) to which data is supplied in a specified format (score): the latter represents "what" should be done, the orchestra represents "how" it can be achieved.

One of the major problems with the early sound synthesis languages was that they ran only on the particular kind of computer for which they were created. So, for example, *MUSIC360* ran only on the IBM360 computer (and its descendants, IBM370 and 83xx machines), while *MUSIC11* ran only on the DEC PDP-11 series. The enormous success and quick standardization of the C programming language explains why Csound - written in C - had such a vast distribution. Today Csound can be installed on any personal computer (IBM and compatibles, Apple Macintosh, PowerMac, SUN, SGI, HP).

Of course, in the 1960's there were no *personal* computers (most computer manufacturers believed that powerful machines would never reach desktop size). Work was pursued in the computing centers of the University campus in which many users were sharing a mainframe computer that was less powerful than today's desktop machines. It is easy to imagine the daunting job for computer music composers in these early studios. On top of that processing time was limited, and typically musicians did not rank high on the priority list. In most cases, you would compile the program in the evening and come to listen to the results in the morning. Eventually correcting mistakes by reiterating this process for days, if not weeks or months.

In those years "hybrid" systems were also built. In such systems, all controls were implemented on a computer (usually a *minicomputer*), while the sound synthesis task itself was left to an analog synthesizer, like a MOOG, ARP, Buchla or EMS. In 1967, James Gabura and Gustav Ciamaga linked MOOG modules to an IBM1710. In 1969, at the London EMS studios Peter Zinoviev designed a very sophisticated system based on a DEC PDP-8 computer controlling a big Synthi EMS. Many British musicians worked with that system.

In 1982 a group of music instrument manufacturers set out to produce the standard protocol known as MIDI (Musical Instrument Digital Interface), in order to allow electronic music instruments to communicate with and be controlled by other MIDI devices and personal computers. The MIDI protocol has enabled many people to create music with computers, thanks to the development of personal computers with increased processing power and decreasing price. However, designed for commercial music production, MIDI has its limitations and, hence, can impede the compositional process. At the time when MIDI was introduced, very powerful digital synthesizers were also released (the first was the Yamaha DX-7). But these, too, exhibited severe limitations. Today, synthesizers feature a vast palette of technical possibilities, but their potential remains limited by the constraints of what designers considered marketable.

For these reasons, the speed and accessibility of powerful personal computers opens a new era for direct sound synthesis languages such as Csound. Although more difficult to use, languages such as Csound offer the musician complete freedom in designing sounds, a freedom which was non-existant when the analog synthesizer began to decline in the 1970's. In addition, these languages provide us with a standard and powerful methodology allowing for a vast range of compositional possibilities in the creation, correction and modification of scores.

LIST OF OPCODES INTRODUCED IN THIS CHAPTER

k1	**oscil**	**amplitude, frequency, function**
a1	**oscil**	**amplitude, frequency, function**
	out	**output_signal**
k1	**line**	**init_level, duration, end_level**
a1	**line**	**init_level, duration, end_level**
k1	**linseg**	**init_level, duration, next_level, duration, next_level, ...**
a1	**linseg**	**init_level, duration, next_level, duration, next_level, ...**
k1	**expon**	**init_level, duration, end_level**
a1	**expon**	**init_level, duration, end_level**
k1	**expseg**	**init_level, duration, next_level, duration, next_level, ...**
a1	**expseg**	**init_level, duration, next_level, duration, next_level, ...**
a1	**linen**	**amplitude, attack_time, duration, release_time**

2

ADDITIVE SYNTHESIS

2.1 CONSTANT SPECTRUM ADDITIVE SYNTHESIS

With additive synthesis we can create complex waveforms of any kind, by adding together simple wave components - usually sine waves (see 2.A.1 and 2.B.1).

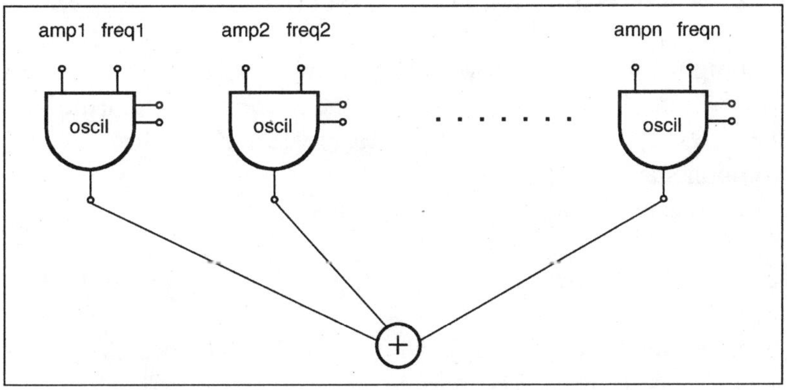

Fig. 2-1

The simplest method dictates a **harmonic relationship between sine waves**. As we have seen, in Csound this can be accomplished using GEN10. Indeed, in order for a complex waveform to be calculated with GEN10, we choose a series of components harmonically related to the fundamental frequency. We also determine the relative amplitude for each component. It is possible to create a sawtooth-like wave, or a square wave, by modifying the amplitude for each component, accordingly (1 / the order number of the particular component within the harmonic series). The sonic difference between a sawtooth and a square wave results from the former being sum of a full series of harmonic frequencies, while the latter is the sum of the odd-numbered harmonics only:

Example of sawtooth wave (10 harmonics only)

```
f1   0   4096   10  10   5   3.3  2.5  2   1.6   1.4   1.25  1.1   1
```

Example of square wave (9 harmonics only)

```
f1   0   4096   10  10   0   3.3  0    2   0     1.4   0     1.1
```

By changing the relative weight of the harmonic components, it is possible to obtain a vast palette of timbres.

In Section 2.3 we focus on how to get rid of the inherent limitations of perfectly harmonic spectra. As spectrum cannot vary over the course of the note, a harmonic spectrum may not produce an interesting output. Still, starting with this simple model, we can achieve better results with little effort.

2.2 VARIABLE SPECTRUM ADDITIVE SYNTHESIS

Frequency components do not have to be harmonically related. A very significant element in the creation of interesting timbres is the presence of inharmonic components, even in pitched sounds. It is also possible to create new timbres exclusively out of inharmonic components.

Harmonics are integers in proportion to the fundamental:

f (fundamental), 2*f (second harmonic), 3*f, 4*f, 5*f, 6*f, 7*f, 8*f, etc.

(here the asterisk denotes a multiply). Thus, if the fundamental is 200 Hz, the second harmonic is 400 Hz, the third 600 Hz, etc.

Wave components which are not integer multiples of the fundamental are called inharmonic. In the remainder of this section, we will play with harmonic frequencies, and make them inharmonic (and viceversa), through the use of glissando. In this way we obtain *variable spectra*, i.e. sounds whose timbre changes over time.

For this, we need *control variables*. Any single harmonic component, has an independent envelope for both its frequency and its amplitude will. The changing of a harmonic's amplitude or frequency - in a way that is independent of the other wave components - is an essential feature of natural sounds. Therefore, it is important for us to control these spectral modifications in order to provide our sounds with a "lively" and natural feel. In Chap.8, you'll learn how to model amplitude and frequency changes based on the analysis of sampled sounds. For now, you should learn how to implement these slight modifications without the help of any signal analysis tools.

In the orchestra example below, we use *oscili*, identical to *oscil* except that it utilizes an interpolated digital oscillator. The syntax is the same, but the audio output is of much better quality (for details, see 2.C.1).

Orchestra example

```
;additive1.orc
        sr     =  44100
        kr     =  4410
        ksmps  =  10
        nchnls =  1

        instr     1

k2hrm   expseg    200, p3/2, 234, p3/2, 200
k3hrm   expseg    300, p3/2, 333, p3/2, 300
k4hrm   expseg    400, p3/2, 376, p3/2, 400
k5hrm   expseg    500, p3/2, 527, p3/2, 500
k6hrm   expseg    600, p3/2, 609, p3/2, 600
k7hrm   expseg    700, p3/2, 715, p3/2, 700
k8hrm   expseg    800, p3/2, 853, p3/2, 800

afund   oscili    3900, 100, 1
ahrm2   oscili    3900, k2hrm, 1
ahrm3   oscili    3900, k3hrm, 1
ahrm4   oscili    3900, k4hrm, 1
ahrm5   oscili    3900, k5hrm, 1
ahrm6   oscili    3900, k6hrm, 1
ahrm7   oscili    3900, k7hrm, 1
ahrm8   oscili    3900, k8hrm, 1

        out       afund+ahrm2+ahrm3+ahrm4+ahrm5+ahrm6+ahrm7+ahrm8
        endin
```

Score

```
;additive1.sco
f1   0   4097   10  1
i1   0   30
```

Observe that the various components are controlled as to create multiple glissandos. At the beginning, the spectrum is harmonic, but then, due to the gradual shifting of all components, it becomes progressively more inharmonic until finally it turns to harmonic again.

Example (instrument #2)

```
        instr  2
k2hrm   expseg  200, p3/2, 220, p3/2, 200
k3hrm   expseg  300, p3/2, 320, p3/2, 300
k4hrm   expseg  400, p3/2, 420, p3/2, 400
k5hrm   expseg  500, p3/2, 520, p3/2, 500
k6hrm   expseg  600, p3/2, 620, p3/2, 600
k7hrm   expseg  700, p3/2, 720, p3/2, 700
k8hrm   expseg  800, p3/2, 820, p3/2, 800

afund   oscili  3800, 100, 1
ahrm2   oscili  1900, k2hrm, 1
ahrm3   oscili  1900, k3hrm, 1
ahrm4   oscili  1900, k4hrm, 1
ahrm5   oscili  1900, k5hrm, 1
ahrm6   oscili  1900, k6hrm, 1
ahrm7   oscili  1900, k7hrm, 1
ahrm8   oscili  1900, k8hrm, 1
ahrm2b  oscili  1900, 200, 1
ahrm3b  oscili  1900, 300, 1
ahrm4b  oscili  1900, 400, 1
ahrm5b  oscili  1900, 500, 1
ahrm6b  oscili  1900, 600, 1
ahrm7b  oscili  1900, 700, 1
ahrm8b  oscili  1900, 800, 1

out  afund+ahrm2+ahrm3+ahrm4+ahrm5+ahrm6+ahrm7+ahrm8+ahrm2b+ahrm3b+ahrm4b+ahrm5b+ahrm6b+ahrm7b+ahrm8b
        endin
```

Score

```
;additive2.sco
f1   0   4097   10  1
i2   0   30
```

Here we use a pair of oscillators for each component. In each pair one oscillator shifts by 20 Hz from its initial frequency, while the other remains fixed. As a result, there is an increasing amount of beatings (up to 20 beatings per second). Then beatings decrease, and the sound reverts to its initial spectrum.

Example (instrument #3):

```
        instr   3
k2hrm   expseg  200, p3/4, 234, p3/4, 244, p3/4, 234, p3/4, 200
k3hrm   expseg  300, p3/4, 333, p3/4, 323, p3/4, 333, p3/4, 300
k4hrm   expseg  400, p3/4, 376, p3/4, 386, p3/4, 376, p3/4, 400
k5hrm   expseg  500, p3/4, 527, p3/4, 517, p3/4, 527, p3/4, 500
k6hrm   expseg  600, p3/4, 609, p3/4, 619, p3/4, 609, p3/4, 600
k7hrm   expseg  700, p3/4, 715, p3/4, 705, p3/4, 715, p3/4, 700
k8hrm   expseg  800, p3/4, 853, p3/4, 863, p3/4, 853, p3/4, 800
k2hrmb  expseg  200, p3/4, 234, p3/2, 234, p3/4, 200
k3hrmb  expseg  300, p3/4, 333, p3/2, 333, p3/4, 300
k4hrmb  expseg  400, p3/4, 376, p3/2, 376, p3/4, 400
k5hrmb  expseg  500, p3/4, 527, p3/2, 527, p3/4, 500
k6hrmb  expseg  600, p3/4, 609, p3/2, 609, p3/4, 600
k7hrmb  expseg  700, p3/4, 715, p3/2, 715, p3/4, 700
k8hrmb  expseg  800, p3/4, 853, p3/2, 853, p3/4, 800

afund   oscili  3800, 100, 1
ahrm2   oscili  1900, k2hrm, 1
ahrm3   oscili  1900, k3hrm, 1
ahrm4   oscili  1900, k4hrm, 1
ahrm5   oscili  1900, k5hrm, 1
ahrm6   oscili  1900, k6hrm, 1
ahrm7   oscili  1900, k7hrm, 1
ahrm8   oscili  1900, k8hrm, 1
ahrm2b  oscili  1900, k2hrmb, 1
ahrm3b  oscili  1900, k3hrmb, 1
```

```
ahrm4b  oscili   1900, k4hrmb, 1
ahrm5b  oscili   1900, k5hrmb, 1
ahrm6b  oscili   1900, k6hrmb, 1
ahrm7b  oscili   1900, k7hrmb, 1
ahrm8b  oscili   1900, k8hrmb, 1

out  afund+ahrm2+ahrm3+ahrm4+ahrm5+ahrm6+ahrm7+ahrm8+ahrm2b+ahrm3b+ahrm4b+ahrm5b+ahrm6b+ahrm7b+ahrm8b
     endin
```

Score:

```
;additive3.sco
f1  0  4097  10 1
i3  0  30
```

This combines the previous two examples. The note duration is subdivided into 4 segments. At first the spectrum turns from harmonic to inharmonic. Subsequently, beatings are introduced, up to 10 per second. Then only inharmonic frequencies are heard, without beatings. Finally, the spectrum reverts to its initial harmonic state.

These modifications in the spectrum follow frequency changes. Let's see now how we add amplitude envelopes and integrate these modifications.

Example

```
          instr   4
k2hrm     expseg  234, 1, 200, p3-1, 200
k3hrm     expseg  333, 1, 300, p3-1, 300
k4hrm     expseg  376, 1, 400, p3-1, 400
k5hrm     expseg  527, 1, 500, p3-1, 500
k6hrm     expseg  609, 1, 600, p3-1, 600
k7hrm     expseg  715, 1, 700, p3-1, 700
k8hrm     expseg  853, 1, 800, p3-1, 800

kampodd   linseg  0, .1, 4000, .1, 2000, 2, 2000, 2, 7000, p3-6.2, 1000, 2, 0
kampeven  linseg  0, .1, 4000, .1, 2000, 2, 2000, 2, 0, p3-6.2, 6000, 2, 0

afund     oscili  kampeven, 100, 1
af        oscili  kampodd, 100, 1
ahrm2     oscili  kampeven, k2hrm, 1
```

```
ahrm3    oscili   kampodd, k3hrm, 1
ahrm4    oscili   kampeven, k4hrm, 1
ahrm5    oscili   kampodd, k5hrm, 1
ahrm6    oscili   kampeven, k6hrm, 1
ahrm7    oscili   kampodd, k7hrm, 1
ahrm8    oscili   kampeven, k8hrm, 1

         out      afund+af+ahrm2+ahrm3+ahrm4+ahrm5+ahrm6+ahrm7+ahrm8
         endin
```

Score

```
;additive4.sco
f1  0  4097  10 1
i4  0  8
```

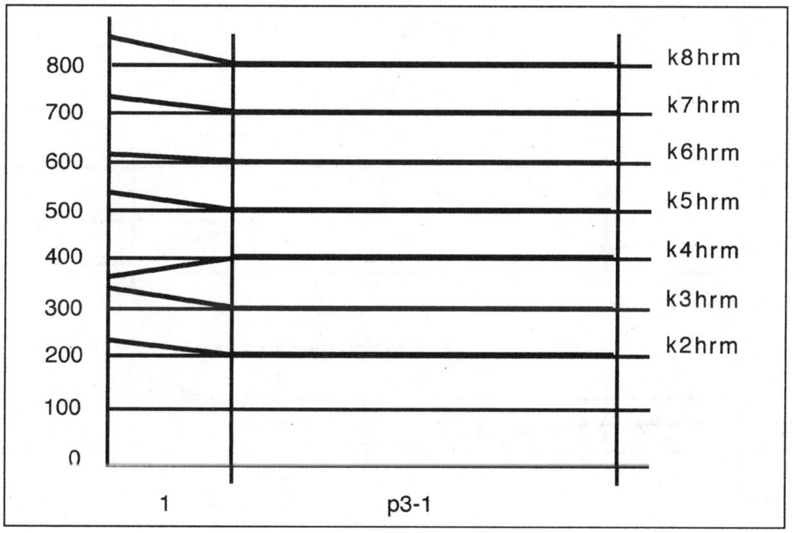

Fig. 2-2

The above example creates a sound with a sharp attack and a long decay. At onset, the timbre is first inharmonic, then it becomes harmonic. As soon as the harmonic relationship is reached, the odd-numbered wave components change in amplitude, as do the even-numbered components, but each has different envelopes. Let's take a closer look:

```
k2hrm    expseg    234, 1, 200, p3-1, 200
```

This opcode determines the glissando for the second component, from 234 to 200 Hz. The frequency remains at 200 Hz until the end of the note. All components behave like this, but scaled to their own frequency. It is clear that if the overall duration of the note were shorter than 1 second, this control would make no sense.

There are two amplitude envelopes, one for to the odd-numbered and one for the even-numbered components:

```
kampodd   linseg  0, .1,4000, .1,2000, 2, 2000, 2, 7000, p3-6.2, 1000, 2, 0
kampeven  linseg  0, .1,4000, .1,2000, 2, 2000, 2, 0, p3-6.2, 6000, 2, 0
```

Both have a rather sharp attack (1/10th of a second) and a decay as short as the attack itself. The steady state phase is 2 seconds. Then, the even-numbered harmonics slowly disappear, while the odd-numbered raise to an amplitude of 7000. Subsequently, the even-numbered return and raise up to 6000 while the odd fade to 1000.

Observe that the last modification takes place in a time equal to the duration-minus-the-time-it-takes-for-the-other-changes-to-happen, i.e. .1+.1+2+2+2 = 6.2 seconds.

Finally, in the last two seconds both the odd- and even-numbered components fade down to zero.

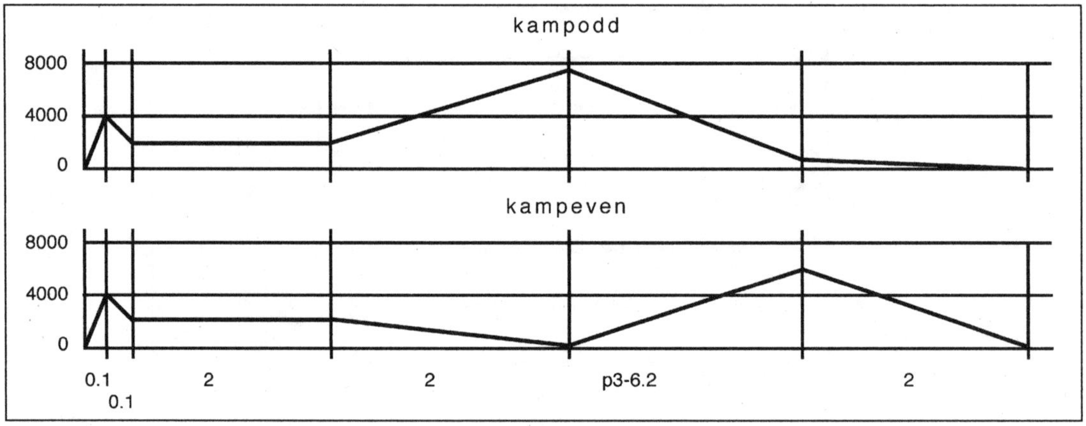

Fig. 2-3

```
ahrm2     oscili  kampeven, k2hrm, 1
ahrm3     oscili  kampodd, k3hrm, 1
```

Observe that the oscillators for the even-numbered components get their amplitude from the *kampeven* control variable, while the odd-numbered get theirs from kampodd. Each component has its own specific control variable which determines the glissando (*k2hrm*, *k3hrm*, etc.). All oscillators use the same wave function, namely #1. It is defined in the score as a sine wave.

EXERCISE 1 *: Create an orchestra with 4 components, each with independent amplitude and frequency envelopes. Declare arguments to the control signal opcodes as p-fields in the score (p4, p5, etc.).*

EXERCISE 2 *: Create an orchestra with 10 components. The highest five to be present during the attack transient, then fade to zero and finally return during the note release.*

EXERCISE 3 *: Create an orchestra with a slow attack time (at least 8 seconds), with at least 3 harmonic components and 3 inharmonic components, each at a fixed frequency. At the beginning feature only the harmonic. Then a "timbre glissando", from a harmonic to inharmonic spectrum. Avoid frequency sweeps, use only amplitude modifications.*

EXERCISE 4 *: Compose a small musical study using the additive synthesis methods explained so far.*

2.3 PHASE AND *DC OFFSET*: GEN09 AND GEN19

With GEN10 you create a sine wave by simply declaring the relative amplitude of the fundamental period in the waveform

```
f1   0   4096   10  1
```

With GEN09 you have to declare three parameters: the component number ("1" for the fundamental, "2" for the second harmonic, etc.), the relative amplitude and the initial phase (in degrees). That allows you to

1) determine a sequence of components in any order
2) determine the phase relationships among components (with GEN10 all have initial phase = 0).

For example, the f statement

```
f1   0   4096   09   1   1   180
```

creates a sine waveform 180 degrees out of phase (the negative half of the period in the wave is followed by the positive half).

What's the use of phase? Acousticians explain that the human ear is insensitive to the absolute phase of a sound signal, and, in general, that it is insensitive to phase differences between different sound signals. However, phase differences may have a relevant role in attack transients. The ability to precisely determine a particular phase value is very useful when it comes to the creation of control signals, such as stereo panning (see section 5.2), vibrato (see 5.3), tremolo (see 5.4) and filter.(5.5).

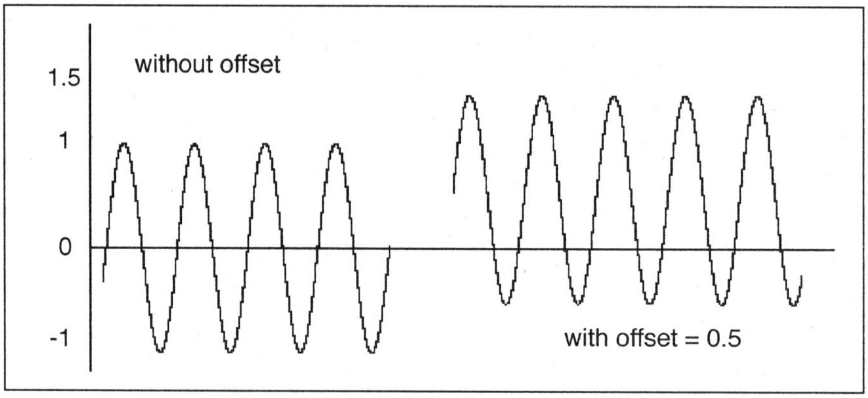

Fig. 2-4

GEN19 allows you to also determine a DC offset (direct current offset) in the waveform (a constant number added to all points in the function). As an example, consider the two sinusoids in fig. 2-4. The left one has no offset and it is symmetric with respect to the horizontal axis. The right one, on the contrary, has a DC offset of 0.5, and therefore to each one of its points an absolute amplitude value of 0.5 was added, which causes a shifting of the signals in the positive fields.

The DC offset is applied after the waveform is scaled.

What is scaling? Imagine we use GEN10 and determine the following summation of five sine waves:

```
f1  0  4096  10  1  5  2  7  10
```

In that case, we created a waveform whose fifth harmonic has an amplitude 10 times louder than the fundamental. In general, Csound rescales these amplitude values so that the peak amplitude is 1. But there is a way to avoid rescaling function values. This requires that you invoke the particular GEN routine not by its actual id number (a positive number), but its negation. So, if you wanted to use GEN10 and avoid rescaling, you would not write 10 but -10 as the fourth p-field in the f statement. That leaves the values in the table function unrescaled.

```
f1   0   4096   -10 1  5   2   7    10
```

The above gives a waveform with an absolute peak value of 22.108 (if we hadn't required the rescaling, it would have peaked at 1). Observe that if we use that waveform function as in the following line

```
a1 oscil 10000, 500, 1
```

the output signal amplitude will not be 10000, but 10000*22.108 = 221080!

In short:

GEN09, GEN10 and GEN19 all create a wave table by the weighted sum of sinusoids. For each sinusoid, GEN09 utilizes 3 p-fields, while GEN10 utilizes 1 and GEN19 four.

```
fn   t   d    9    h1   a1   phs1   h2       a2       phs2 ...
fn   t   d    10   a1   a2   a3     a4 ...
fn   t   d    19   h1   a1   phs1   dco1     h2  a2   phs2  dco2...
```

n	function id number
t	action time for the calculation
d	size (must be a power of 2 or a power-of-2 plus 1. Examples are 1024, 2048, 1025, 2049, etc.)
9, 10, 19	GEN id number. When positive, the wavetable is scaled to a maximum absolute value of 1 after generation. A negative value causes the scaling to be skipped.
h1, h2...	component number (relative to a fundamental which, if present, would cover the full table size with a single period). It must be positive, but does not need to be integer. Components can be specified in any order.
a1, a2...	relative amplitude. Negative values are permitted (implies phase shift).
phs1...	initial phase of components, expressed in degrees.
dco1...	direct current offset, applied after scaling. A value of 2 will cause the oscillation range [1,3] instead of [-1,1].

Examples:

```
f1   0   1024   9    1    3    0  3    1  0    9   .3333    180
f2   0   1024   10   1      .5     .33  .25       .2
f3   0   1024   19   .5     1      270   1
```

f1 is made of 3 harmonics, namely the 1st, the 3rd and the 9th; each has an amplitude equal to the reciprocal of its order number (the 3rd harmonic has an amplitude of 1/3rd). The 9th is in reverse phase (180 degrees phase shift).

f2 is made of 5 harmonics, approximating a sawtooth wave.

f3 is a sigmoid, i.e half a sine wave period beginning at its negative peak (phase = 270 degrees).

Let's take a closer look at f3. If we required a component number equal to 1, we would end up with a full wave period covering the full wavetable size. Similar, if we required a component number equal to 2, we would obtain two periods over the full size. But we actually asked for .5 period, that is, half a sine wave period. Shifting the initial phase of this half period by 270 degrees, we obtain a function which corresponds to the midsection of a sine wave, going from -1 to 1. However, we also specified that a DC offset of 1 be added to the function. That causes the oscillation range [0,2] instead of [-1,1].

Using GEN09 or GEN19, we may want to determine a waveform including non-integer component numbers. But that would be appropriate in principle only. The various sine fragments of inharmonically related components do not perfectly fit in the table, they remain "broken" at some random amplitude value. Using such a waveform, an audio function will make the shift from one cycle to the next to create higher harmonic frequencies (harmonic distortion), which is quite incontrollable as in this example

```
;                  fund           integer ratios              non integer ratios
f1  0  2048  09  1 2 0      2 1 0    3 1 0    4 1 0    3.4  2  0  9.23  1  0
```

2.4 COMPLEX OSCILLATORS: *BUZZ* AND *GBUZZ*

Csound opcodes include two special oscillators, *buzz* and *gbuzz*. The former generates a series of equal-amplitude, harmonically related sine waves. The latter generates a series of cosine waves of varying amplitude. Both are useful especially in subtractive synthesis (see Chap.3).

a1 buzz xamp, xfrq, knh, ifn[, iphs]
a1 gbuzz xamp, xfrq, knh, klh, km, ifn[, iphs]

a1	output signal
xamp	amplitude
xfrq	frequency in Hz

knh number of required harmonics (must be positive)

klh (only for *gbuzz*) component number for the lowest harmonic in the series. Can be positive, zero or negative. If negative, all components below zero will reflect as positive components without phase change (the cosine is an even function. It is symmetrical with respect to the vertical axis).

km (only for *gbuzz*) multiplier in the series of amplitude coefficients. This is a power series If the *klhth* component has an amplitude coefficient of A, the (*klh* + n)th will have a coefficient A*(*km***n). That means that the amplitude values fall on an exponential curve. Can be positive (increasing amplitude values), zero or negative (decreasing amplitude values). Changing this value during a note yields interesting effects. Also, both *buzz* and *gbuzz* can be modulated in amplitude or frequency by other audio signals.

ifn table number of a stored function containing, for *buzz*, a sine wave or, for *gbuzz*, a cosine wave. In either case, a large table of at least 8192 points is recommended.

iphs initial phase of the fundamental frequency, expressed in fractions of a cycle [0 to 1]. A negative value causes phase initialization to be skipped, so that there is phase continuation between notes.

The effect of a line such as

```
a1  buzz    iamp, ifrq, 10, 1
```

using the function

```
f1  0  8192   10  1
```

is the same as

```
a1  oscil   iamp, ifrq, 2
```

using the following function

```
f2  0  8192  10  1  1  1  1  1  1  1  1  1  1
```

as, in fact, we required, in either case, 10 harmonically related components with equal amplitude.

Example using *buzz*:

```
;buzz.orc
        sr     =  44100
        kr     =  4410
        ksmps  =  10
        nchnls =  1
        instr     1
kharm   line      1, p3, 20            ;control ramp, from 1 to 20
a1      buzz      10000, 440, kharm, 1 ;number of harmonics in the buzz increases
                                       ;from 1 to 20
        out    a1
        endin

;buzz.sco
f1      0      8192   10     1         ;sine wave
i1      0      3
```

Example using *gbuzz*:

```
;gbuzz.orc
        sr     =  44100
        kr     =  4410
        ksmps  =  10
        nchnls =  1
        instr     1

km      line   .1, p3, .7                  ; ramping from .1 to .7
a1      gbuzz  10000, 440, 20, 2, km,1     ; 20 harmonics, starting with the 2nd
                                           ; amplitude series multiplier varies with km
        out    a1
        endin

;gbuzz.sco
f1      0      8192   9 1 1 90             ;cosine wave
i1      0      3
```

Opcodes such as *buzz* and *gbuzz* are often used in the computer synthesis of speech by linear prediction code (LPC, see section 8.7).

EXTENSIONS

2.A.1 WAVE SUMMATION

No matter the number of sound sources surrounding us, only *one* wave reaches our eardrum. It consists of the sum of the several waves produced by each of those sources. The human hearing system is capable of isolating single components in the sound source, just as it can distinguish among several instruments in an orchestra.

Moment by moment, the amplitude value of one wave is added to the amplitude value of all other. This happens to be an *algebraic* addition. The values added together retaining their sign.

In fig. 2-A-1 two sound waves are shown, called A and B. It is easy to observe that their sum, C, is obtained by adding the instant values of one wave with the instant values of the other. If, at a certain point, either A and B amplitude values are positive, then the result in C will be their addition. If, at a different point, A has a positive amplitude value while B has a negative one, the resulting instant value in C will equal the subtraction of the one from the other.

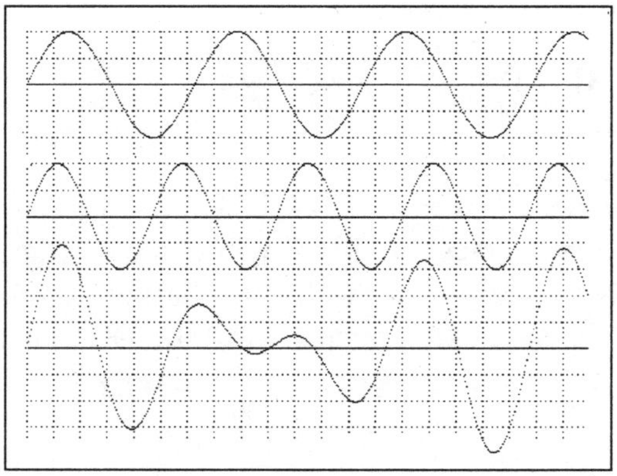

Fig. 2-A-1

2.A.2 TIMBRE

The majority of sounds we hear in the real world, are not *pure* but *complex* sounds. It is possible to decompose them into their pure *wave components*. To better understand this phenomenon, we may consider a famous analogy from the field of optics. It is well known that some colors are primaries, or not further separable into partial elements (red, orange, yellow, etc.). These colors correspond to a certain wavelength of the light beam. By having a beam of white light pass through a prism (which filters white light into the seven colors of the light spectrum) we can isolate a single wave component.

The same happens in sound. A certain wavelength correspond to a certain pitch. If no other frequency is present, that will be perceived as a pure sound.

A pure sound has a sinusoidal waveform, and can be represented as a trigonometric function

sin (x)

(for more details, see section A.2.4). When components are scaled by an integer relationship to the lowest component, we call them *harmonics*. The lowest is called the *fundamental*, or first harmonic. The component having twice the frequency of the fundamental is the *second harmonic*, the one having three times frequency as the fundamental is the *third harmonic*, and so on. In order to determine the spectrum of a harmonic sound, suppose **all** harmonics are present (harmonic frequencies within the limits of hearing, as in fact ultrasonic frequencies do not affect timbre perception). It is sufficient to give each harmonic an amplitude value. Consider, for example, a scale function like this:

HARMONIC	**I**	**II**	**III**	**IV**	**V**	**VI**	**etc.**
AMPLITUDE	**1**	**.8**	**.6**	**.75**	**.4**	**.3**	**etc.**

which can be rendered graphically as in fig. 2-A-2. This is the *spectrum* of a sound. On the horizontal axis are frequencies, in kHz, while the vertical axis represents amplitude values in dB. You can clearly see that this is a harmonic spectrum by the fact that all frequencies are equally spaced. That means, they are harmonically related to the

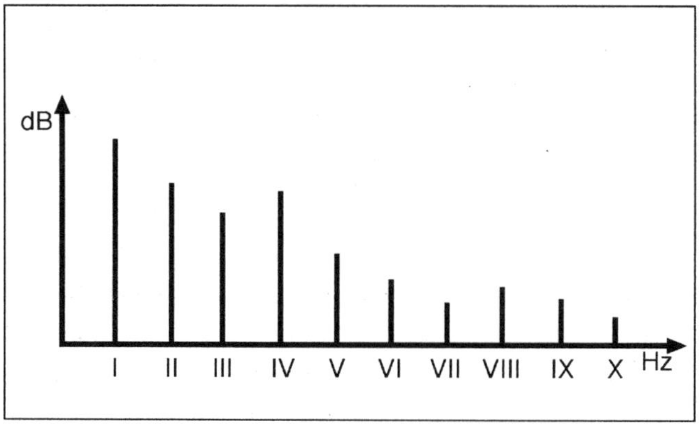

Fig. 2-A-2

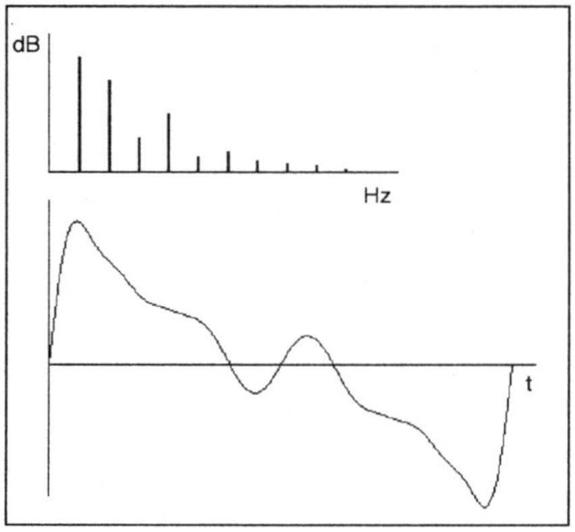

Fig. 2-A-3

fundamental as, in fact, you can see that the frequencies are .1, .2, .3, .4, .5, .6, .7, .8, .9, and 1 kHz. In short, we have here all harmonics up to the tenth. In general, the phase of each component does not affect our perception of the timbre.

In fig.2-A-3 we see a harmonic spectrum and its corresponding wave. Observe that harmonic spectra give rise to *periodic* waves.

Components may be in *inharmonic* relationship to the fundamental, as is the case with the spectrum shown in fig. 2-A-4, where frequencies are not equally spaced and their relation to the fundamental is not an integer ratio (indeed, such relationships may be expressed by irrational numbers).[1] Waves resulting from inharmonic spectra are *aperiodic*.

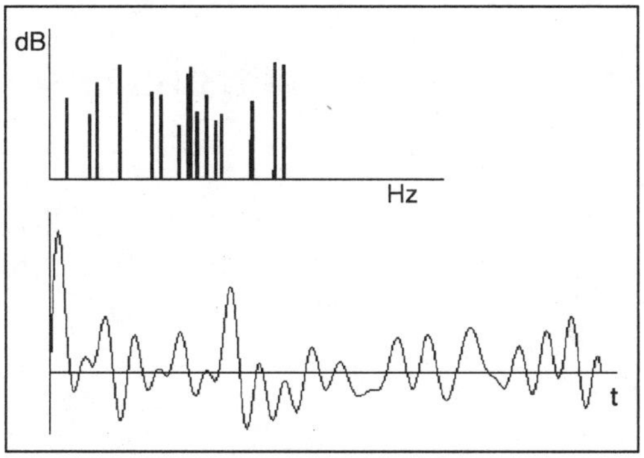

Fig. 2-A-4

Periodic sound waves (or quasi-periodic because in physics perfect periodicity implies infinite duration) are usually heard as having a precise pitch. This is the case with most musical instruments, and with the vowel sounds of the human voice.

Aperiodic sound waves, instead, are not heard as having a precise pitch. At best, we may be able to identify a *range* or a *frequency bandwidth*. That's the case with musical instruments of indetermined pitch (cymbals, gongs, etc.) and with the consonants of the human voice.

So far we discussed the building up of complex sounds by summation of simple components. That implies a *synthesis* process. However, it is also possible to go the other way round, decomposing a complex sounds into its components. This implies an *analysis* process.

The Fourier theorem (from the name of the XIX century French philosopher and scientist Jean-Baptiste Fourier) states that all periodic waveforms can be represented by a series of harmonics, each one having its own amplitude. Therefore, it is possible to

[1] An irrational number is a number not representable with a finite amount of digits: for example, 1/3, π, etc.

determine the *spectrum* of any periodic sound. From all this it should be clear there is a relationship between timbre and the frequency and amplitude parameters. While the latter are both unidimensional magnitudes (a single number is enough to determine the particular value, and a whole set of values is represented as a straight line), timbre (or the spectrum) is a multidimensional parameter. It can only be determined by a series of numbers each being a measure for the amplitude of a particular component. One important consequence is that while values of pitch and amplitude can be arranged in musically understandable "scales", timbres cannot, as in fact a particular spectrum cannot be represented as a single point on a line, but as a point in a multidimensional space - a space with *n* dimensions, where n is the number of components having an amplitude level other than zero.

2.B.1 ADDITIVE SYNTHESIS: HISTORICAL SKETCHES AND THEORY

Historically, additive synthesis was the first sound synthesis method exploited by electroacoustic composers. The search for new timbres led the electronic music pioneers (most notably Herbert Eimert and Karlheinz Stockhausen) to experiment with the construction of sound by wave summation, with either harmonic and inharmonic spectra.

The equipment available then was rather poor compared with today's technology. It was necessary to copy and paste the sounds from several analog tape tracks which resulted in poor audio (a tape recorder from the early 1950's had a frequency response of 60-12000 Hz and a signal-to-noise ratio of less than 50 dB). The very small number of oscillators made it necessary to implement additive synthesis by mixing sine waves from many tapes in order to get a more interesting sound. The most advanced technology available was perhaps that of the Studio di Fonologia of the Milan RAI (Italian State Radio), where as many as 9 oscillators were available to the electronic musician. That allowed for complex sounds to be synthesized in "real time".

Additive synthesis was the basis of one of the most relevant electronic music works of that time, **Komposition 1953 Nr.2 (Studie I)**, by Stockhausen. This was a music of many *mixturen*, as the composer called his groups of sine waves whose frequencies followed very precise serial compositional rules.[2] The basic material was drawn from the harmonic series, with components tuned according to ratios 12/5, 4/5, 8/5, 5/12, 5/4. Based on this set of numerical relationships, Stockhausen built many *mixturen* by successive derivations from that basic set of relationships. The derivation itself was bound by the limits of hearing. Upper and lower frequency

[2] K.Stockhausen., "Komposition 1953 Nr.2 (Studie I)", in Technische Hausmitteilungen des NWDR, VI, n.1-2, Hamburg, 1954.

hearing limits were considered, as well as upper and lower amplitude limits. Sound in its raw form remained the very goal of Stockhausen, however abstract his operations may seem to us.

From the second half of the XIX century (and especially following the work of H.Helmholtz), timbre was said to be dependent on the amplitude weights of the various harmonics in a complex sound. The early electronic music composers started there. But soon, they had to admit that real sounds are far more complex and subtle than those that followed the classical theory. The point was that Helmholtz took a static view of sound, and was concerned with the steady state of tones, or *sustain*. In contrast, natural sound phenomena are dynamic. Indeed, attack and release transients are to be considered at least as important as the spectrum of the sound in its steady state. Also, the spectrum itself may change significantly over the duration of a sound.

Perhaps these problems explain why Stockhausen, Berio, Maderna and others, started to integrate sounds created by additive synthesis with sounds obtained using other techniques. First, they used substractive synthesis and the montage and manipulation of recorded "concrete" sounds.

Additive synthesis has its origins in the *Fourier theorem* which states that any periodic function can be expressed as a weighted sum of sinusoids and cosinusoids. By *periodic function* we mean a function whose shape repeats, always in an identical pattern, over an infinite number of cycles. In the real world, however, no sound would behave like that.

All phenomena have a beginning, an internal evolution, and an end. Still, if we limit ourselves to the observation of very short chunks of a sound waveform, then the Fourier theorem can anyway prove useful.

According to the Fourier theorem, we can write:

sound wave = 1st harmonic + 2nd harmonic + 3rd harmonic + 4th harmonic ...

How many harmonics do we need to get a precise representation of a sound wave? Mathematics answers: *infinitely many*!

However, take into consideration that our ear is not able to hear frequencies beyond some upper (ultrasonics) and some lower limit (infrasonics). The number of audible harmonics is bound within the range of audible frequencies. Furthermore, some harmonics contribute to the overall sound to such a small extent that they are imperceptible and can be dropped.

From trigonometry, we know that a sinusoid is characterized by its three different parameters: **amplitude**, **frequency** and **phase**. A sinusoid can be expressed in the following terms

$$\mathbf{A = A_0 * \sin (2\pi\omega t+\phi)}$$

where A is the *instantaneous amplitude* of the resultant waveform, A_0 is the *peak amplitude*, $2\pi\omega t$ is the term representing *frequency*, and ϕ is the *phase*. For clarity, we replace$2\pi\omega t$ with the symbol **f**.

Then we can write

$$\mathbf{A = A_1 * \sin (f + \phi_1) + A_2 * \sin (2*f + \phi_2) + A_3 * \sin (3*f + \phi_3) + A_4 * \sin (4*f + \phi_4) + ...}$$

where $\mathbf{A_1}$, $\mathbf{A_2}$, $\mathbf{A_3}$, etc. are the peak amplitudes for each harmonic component, **f** is the fundamental frequency (hence **2*f**, **3*f**, **4*f**, etc. are the harmonic frequencies, i.e. the integer multiples of the fundamental), and finally ϕ_1, ϕ_2, ϕ_3, etc. are the initial phase for each harmonic component.

With a more compact mathematical notation, we can re-write the above formula as

$\mathbf{A = \Sigma_i^n\ A_i * \sin(i * f + \phi_i)}$ (the symbol Σ_1^n denotes the summation of 1, 2, 3... n terms)

Because the phase is, within a single sound, almost irrelevant to the ear, we can omit the phase terms and further simplify our notation

$$\mathbf{A = \Sigma_i^n\ A_i * \sin(i * f)}$$

Thus understood, additive synthesis lends itself quite well to the creation of sounds with either harmonic and inharmonic spectrum. In fig.2-B-1, we see a number of sine wave oscillators whose output signals are added together in a mixer. When the oscillator frequencies are integer multiples of some fundamental frequency, the resultant sound wave has a harmonic spectrum. Otherwise, it has a inharmonic spectrum.

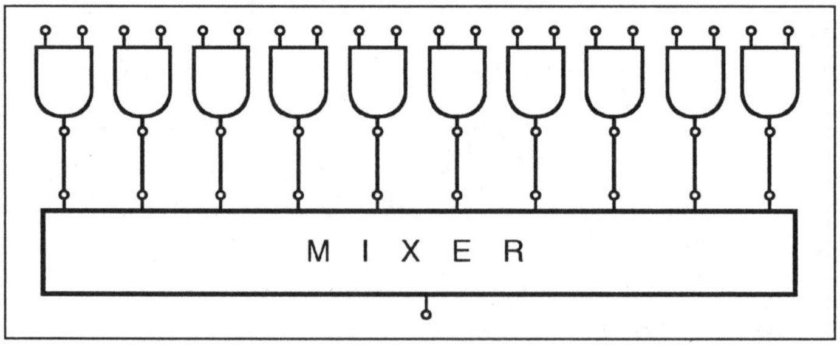

Fig. 2-B-1

Fig. 2-B-2 shows four different examples of additive synthesis, all including sounds of harmonic spectra.

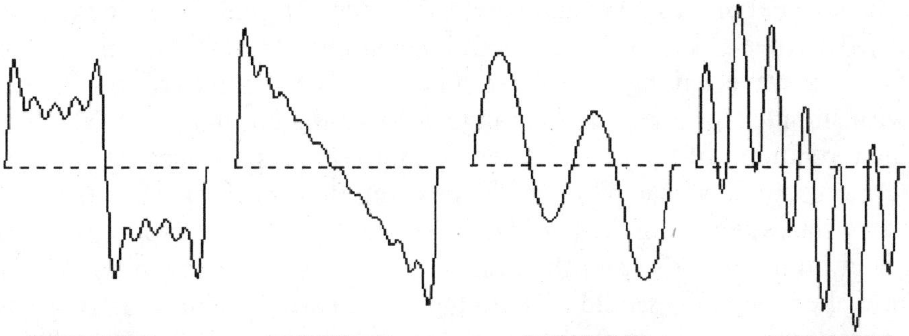

arm	amp
1	1
2	0
3	.5
4	0
5	.33
6	0
7	.25
8	0
9	.2
10	0

arm	amp
1	1
2	.5
3	.33
4	.25
5	.2
6	.16
7	.13
8	.12
9	.11
10	.1

arm	amp
1	.5
2	1
3	0
4	0
5	0
6	0
7	0
8	0
9	0
10	0

arm	amp
1	1
2	0
3	0
4	0
5	0
6	0
7	0
8	0
9	0
10	0

Fig. 2-B-2

2.C.1 THE DIGITAL OSCILLATOR: HOW IT WORKS

In this and the preceding chapter, we have been using the *oscil* but we have not examined its internal process. We ask now; how does a digital oscillator work?

In fig.2-C-1 we see a table, or array[3] with 20 positions. We fill these positions with the values of a sine wave having a peak amplitude of 10. Each position in the array is denoted with an index, or phase, in the range 1-20. In the bottom part of the figure, there is a graphical rendition of the array values. It approximates a sinusoid.

To generate a sound, we can pick the values from each successive position in the array. At the end we start again from the beginning (leftmost position). In order for this to work as a computer program, let's call *i* the index to the array and *T* the array, or table, itself. For example, the index *T(2)* would point to the second array position. In this way, we can "read" the array through, picking the value off each array position. The process can be represented as a computer program using the following pseudo-code (here the symbol ← stands for a value assignment, some value, on the right of the symbol, is assigned to a variable, on the left).

```
i     ← 1                        ;assign some initial value to index
start loop
          output ← T(i)          ;send i-th value from array to the output
          i ← i+1                ;increment index, so it points to next position
          if i > 20 then i ← 1   ;when table end is reached, let's start the loop again
end loop
```

indexes	1	2	3	4	5	6	7	8	9	10	11	12	13	14	15	16	17	18	19	20
values	0	3.1	5.9	8.1	9.5	10	9.5	8.1	5.9	3.1	0	-3.1	-5.9	-8.1	-9.5	-10	-9.5	-8.1	-5.9	-3.1

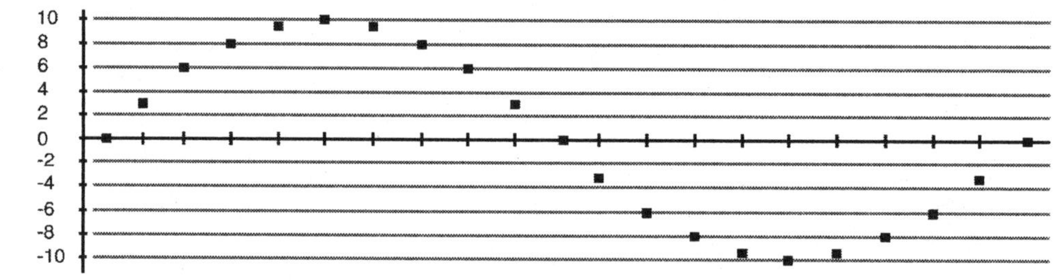

Fig. 2-C-1

[3] An array is an ordered set of values, each value being represented by a particular index. For example, index 4 in the array [2, 3.5, 6, 1, -12] points to the value 1, while index 5 points to the value -12, etc.

This pseudo-code (this code is “pseudo” insofar it is written in an intuitively clear, but inexistent programming language) implements a digital oscillator, reading a sine wave contained in the table T.

But what frequency does this sine tone have? Let’s call the sampling rate *sr*, as usual. We can calculate how many cycles of this sine tone we hear in the resulting sound. Given that one cycle corresponds to 20 reads, we have

cycles/sec = sr / 20

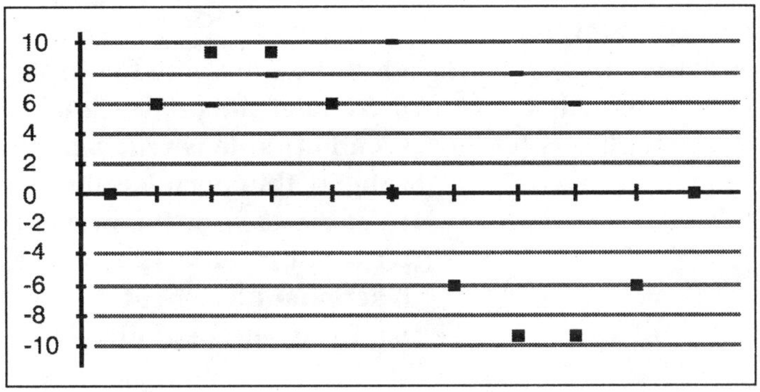

Fig. 2-C-2

So, for example, with sr = 44100 we have

cycles/sec = 44100 / 20 = 2205

The frequency we hear is 2205 Hz. How can we change this? A method would consist of changing the wavetable size, but this is not very practical. Instead, what happens if we read the values from each second position? We end up covering a full cycle with only 10 values (see fig. 2-C-2). The resulting frequency is

cycles / sec = 44100 / 10 = 4410

Similarly, we could read the value from each position twice, in which case we get a lower frequency

cycles / sec = 44100 / 40 = 1102.5

This method has a limit in that it does not allow us to obtain all frequencies we may possibly require. What can we do? So far, we incremented our index to the table by an integer step. We now introduce a new variable, called *phase*. It expresses decimal numbers, and is denoted as *ph*. The index to the table will be taken from this variable, except that the actual index value will result by truncating the phase to an integer. The index must be an integer, as it would make no sense to point, say, to the array position 2.6.

```
ph ← 1.0                              ;assign initial value to phase
increment ← 1.3
start loop
        i ← integer_part_of_ph
        output ← T(i)                 ;send the i-th value to output
        ph ← ph + increment           ;increment the phase value
        if ph > 20 then ph ← ph - 20  ;if end of table is reached, wrap the phase
                                      ;value within permissible value range (1-20).
                                      ;In contrast with the previous pseudo-code
                                      ;ph is not reset to 1, as we have to save the
                                      ;fractional increment.
                                      ;So, for example, if ph = 21.3, then ph = 1.3.
end loop
```

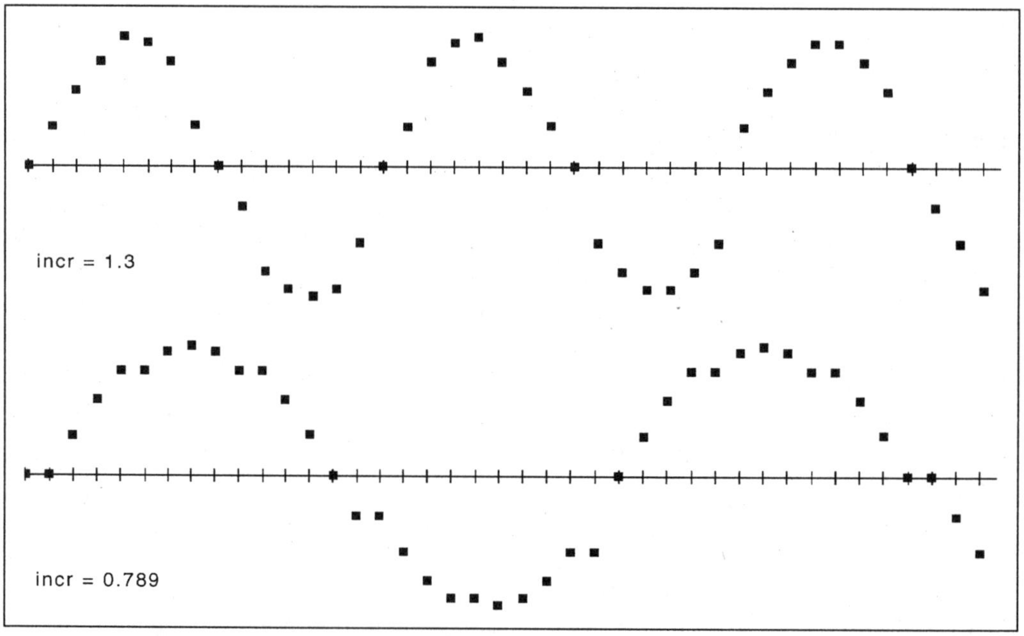

Fig. 2-C-3

Using this new pseudo-code, the process will take place as shown in fig. 2-C-3. On the top graph, the increment is 1.3, the resulting frequency is 44100 / 20 * 1.3 = 2866.5. On the bottom graph, the increment is 0.789, the resulting frequency is 44100 / 20 * 0.789 = 1739.745. By simply specifying a different increment step, we obtain a different frequency. If we call **freq** the resultant frequency, **size** the table size and **incr** the incremental step, we create a more general formula:

freq = sr / size * incr

Therefore, to determine what increment value corresponds to some required frequency, the formula is:

incr = freq / (sr * size)

Observe now the bottom graph in fig.2-C-3. Some values are repeated twice in a row (with the first, the second, the fifth, the sixth, etc.). Observe, too, that some values in the array were simply ignored. Admittedly, our "sine" tone has a rather angled profile. This accounts for the harmonic distortion in the sound, (the appearance of unwanted harmonics).

We used a rather crude approach in order to get an integer value for our table index. We simply truncated the phase, dropping off the decimal part. For example, if *ph* were 2.9, then *i* would be 2, and the program would read the value of the second position in the array, just as it would if *ph* were 2.1. A more refined approach would consist in rounding the phase to the nearest integer.

But that is still not enough. We can do better using *linear interpolation* between one value and the next. Take a look at figure 2-C-4. We have, there, some table position *k* and

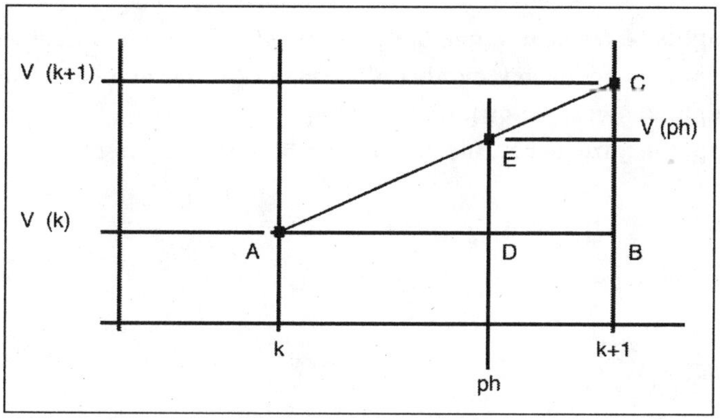

Fig. 2-C-4

the next, *k+1*. Suppose the precise phase value falls in some point in between. Points A, B, and C constitute a right-angled triangle, as do A, D, and E. It is easy to verify that the two triangles are similar. The three sides of one are proportional to the corresponding sides of the other. Accordingly, we can send the value of E, which falls between *V(k)* and *V(k+1)* - to the output. We call this value V(ph), the interpolated value for the table in that particular point. The formula is simple.

Given the proportion

DE / BC = AD / AB

we can write

DE = AD / AB * BC

But **AB = 1**, therefore we get

V(ph) = (ph - k) * (V(k+1) - V(k)) + V(k)

This is the formula for linear interpolation. It greatly improves the audio quality, by radically abating harmonic distortion. However, it requires a slightly longer computation time for the digital oscillator. In Csound, many opcodes have their relative "interpolated" variant. For example, we can use either *oscil* and *oscili*, *table* and *tablei*, *foscil* and *foscili*, etc.

LIST OF OPCODES INTRODUCED IN THIS CHAPTER

a1	**buzz**	**amplitude, frequency, number of harmonics, function id number[, initial phase]**
a1	**gbuzz**	**amplitude, frequency, number of harmonics, order number of the lowest harmonic, amplitude scale factor [, initial phase]**
a1	**oscili**	**amplitude, frequency, function id number[, initial phase]**

3

SUBTRACTIVE SYNTHESIS

3.1 WHITE NOISE AND FILTERS

Subtractive synthesis utilizes the notion that a new sound can be generated by decreasing the amplitude of the components in a spectrally rich sound source. This requires the use of filters. A filter is a device which allows some frequencies to be emphasized over others.

First, let's consider how we create white noise[1] using Csound. For this we use the *rand* opcode, whose only argument is amplitude. Why does *oscili* have three arguments (amplitude, frequency and waveform) while a noise generator such as *rand* has one? White noise is the sum of all audible frequencies, at equal energy at all frequencies. That means that *rand* generates random waveforms (void of periodic patterns), and that it does not need to be assigned any specific waveform function. The only parameter that makes sense for this opcode, then, is the peak amplitude in the random waveforms it generates.

```
;noise.orc
        sr     =  44100
        kr     =  4410
        ksmps  =  10
        nchnls =  1
```

[1] We call "white noise" a sound made of all audible frequencies, in analogy with the optical phenomenon of the color white, made of all the colors of the visible spectrum.

```
        instr   1
a1      rand    p4
        out     a1
        endin
```

Score example:

```
;noise.sco
i1   0   3   20000
```

Thus we create a white noise lasting three seconds, with a peak level of 20000.

Now, let's see how we submit such a sound to the filters beginning with high- and low-pass filters.

The sound we want to filter is the input signal to the filter. We can determine some of the filter's characteristics such as the frequency bandwidth that will be attenuated, or eliminated, after passing through the filter. Finally, the output from the filter is stored in an audio variable. The following opcodes implement a low-pass and a high-pass, respectively

a. Low-pass filter
a1 tone input_signal, cutoff_frequency [2]

b. High-pass filter
a1 atone input_signal, cutoff_frequency

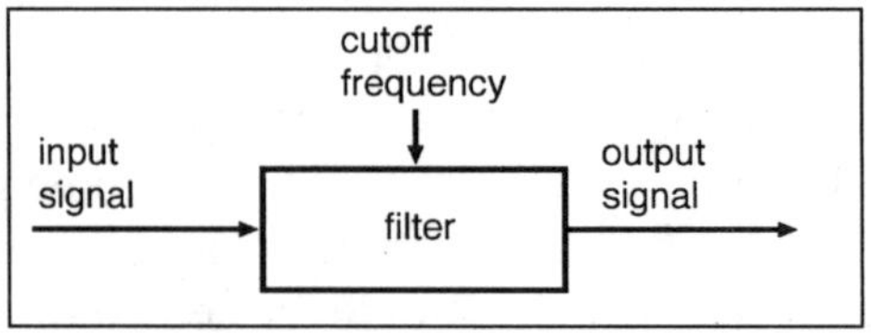

3.2 1st-ORDER LOW-PASS FILTERS

A low-pass filter attenuates all frequencies above the cutoff frequency. A "low-pass" filter allows the only frequencies lower than the "cutoff" frequency to pass through the filter, without substantial energy loss. It attenuates frequencies higher than that.

[2] The opcodes *tone* and *atone*, just like *reson* and *areson* (discussed later) have one more, optional, argument, *istor*. If set to 0, *istor* clears the internal memory storage for the filter at the beginning of the note. If set to 1, it skips the clearing stage during initialization. This stage has minimal effect on the sound.

```
        instr   1
a1      rand    20000
afilt   tone    a1, 1000
        out     afilt
        endin
```

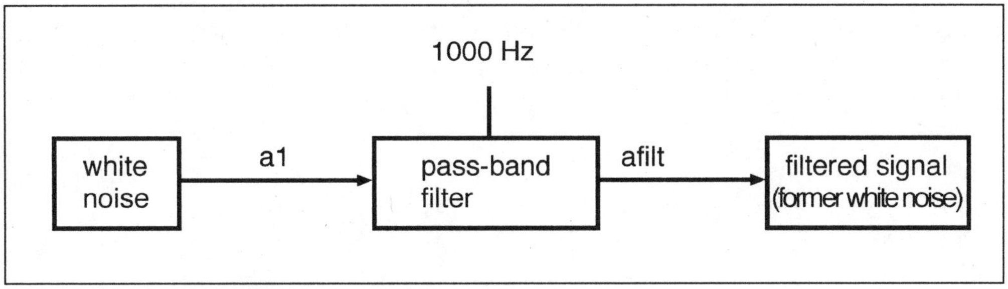

Fig. 3-1

This instrument replicates the process shown in fig.3-1. The output consists of a noise in which frequencies higher than 1000 Hz have been attenuated, following a certain decay curve, while frequencies lower than 1000 Hz remained untouched (see section 3.B.1). We hear a darker sound, the higher frequencies now have a lower amplitude than in the original noise.

What is the decay curve regulating the attenuation of higher frequencies? It depends on the *order* of the filter. If we use a 1st-order filter, as is our example, and set the cutoff frequency to 1000 Hz, then the 2000 Hz component will be attenuated to approximately half of its original amplitude, while the 4000 Hz component will be attenuated to 1/4th of its original amplitude, etc.

If we set the cutoff to 300 Hz, then 600 Hz will have half the amplitude (-6 dB), 1200 Hz will have 1/4th (-12 dB), 2400 will have 1/8th (-18 dB), etc. (See the amplitude/dB equivalence table in section 1.14). Notice that this explanation describes *ideal* filters. In *real* filters (such as those implemented either in hardware circuit or in Csound codes) the cutoff frequency of some filters (be it low- or high-pass) is defined as the frequency at which attenuation reaches -3 dB (accordingly, the frequencies spaced by an octave from the cutoff, will be attenuated by -6 dB).

Amplitude	Frequency	Frequency	Frequency	Frequency
0 dB	300			
-6 dB		600		
-12 dB			1200	
-18 dB				2400

Later we will explain how to utilize higher-order filters, with a steeper attenuation curve.

3.3 1st-ORDER HIGH-PASS FILTERS

A high-pass filter attenuates all frequencies below the cutoff frequency. A "high-pass" passes only frequencies higher than the cutoff frequency. Frequencies lower than the cutoff, are attenuated, according to a decay curve.

```
        instr   1
a1      rand    20000
afilt   atone   a1, 1000
        out     afilt
        endin
```

The ouput is a noise in which all frequencies below 1000 Hz have been attenuated, following the decay curve, while frequencies higher than 1000 Hz remain untouched. We hear a brighter sound, the lower frequencies now have a lower amplitude than in the original source sound.

Like *tone*, *atone*, also, is a 1st-order filter. If we set the cutoff frequency to 1000 Hz, the frequency at the next octave lower, 500 Hz, will be attenuated by half its original amplitude (-6 dB), while 250 Hz will have 1/4th (-12 dB) and 125 Hz 1/8th (-18 dB), etc. Here, too, in a *real* filter energy is attenuated at the cutoff frequency by -3 dB.

Amplitude	Frequency	Frequency	Frequency	Frequency
0 dB				1000
-6 dB			500	
-12 dB		250		
-18 dB	125			

3.4 HIGHER ORDER FILTERS

Let's now consider a 2nd-order low-pass filter. If the cutoff frequency is 300 Hz, then the amplitude at 600 Hz will be attenuated by 12 dB, while at 1200 Hz it will be attenuated by 24 dB, etc. In short, the attenuation is doubled with respect to a typical 1st-order filter. A 3rd-order filter would have a three times as much attenuation, a 4th-order will have a four times as much attenuation, etc.

Let's try, now, to create a 2nd-order high-pass filter:

```
        instr   1
a1      rand    20000
afilt   atone   a1, 1000
afilt2  atone   afilt, 1000
        out     afilt2
        endin
```

a1 is white noise, the input to the first *atone* filter. The output from the first filter becomes the input to the second, and this simple operation will further attenuate all frequencies below 1000 Hz. We say that these two filters are "cascaded". Notice that we maintained the same cutoff frequency for both. The output from the second *atone* represents the output of a 2nd-order high-pass filter. Given that a single filter attenuates the cutoff frequency, 1000 Hz, by -3 dB, two such cascaded filters will attenuate the 1000 Hz by -6 dB. For results closer to the theoretically ideal filter response, we'd better resort to the special filters known as "Butterworth filters" (see section 3.7).

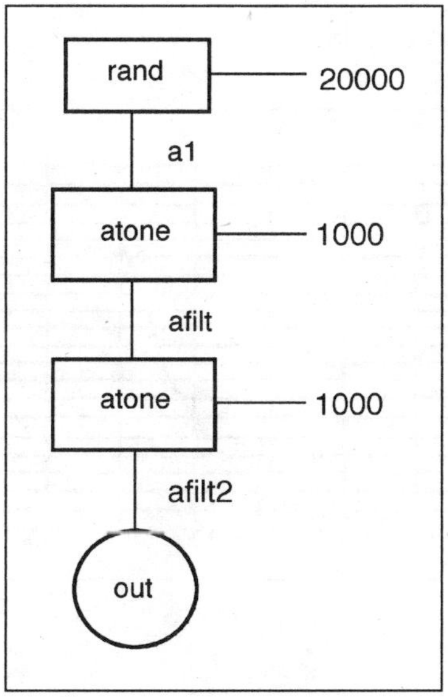

Fig. 3-2

Here is an example of 3rd-order filter:

```
        instr     1
a1      rand      20000
```

```
afilt   tone    a1, 1000
afilt2  tone    afilt, 1000
afilt3  tone    afilt2, 1000
        out     afilt3
        endin
```

***EXERCISE**: Comment each line in the following instrument.*

```
        instr   1
a1      rand    20000
afilt   atone   a1, 1000
afilt2  tone    afilt, 2000
afilt3  tone    afilt2, 2000
        out     afilt3
        endin
```

In fig.3-3 the response curves of three typical filters are shown: a 3rd-order low-pass, a 3rd-order high-pass and a band-pass.

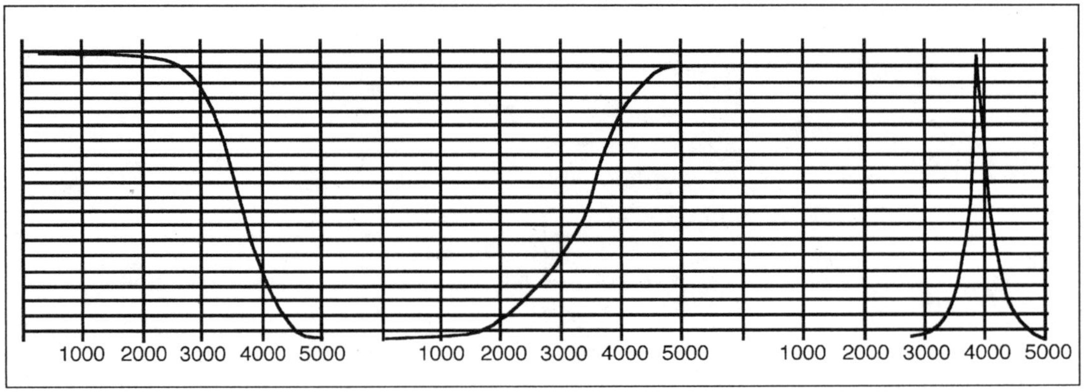

Fig. 3-3

3.5 BAND-PASS FILTERS

Band-pass filtering allows us to attenuate components below and above specified frequencies. For example, if the lower frequency in the filter bandwidth is 1600 Hz and the higher is 2000 Hz, the filter will attenuate frequencies lower than 1600 Hz and higher than 2000. Each time we use such a filter we have to determine how wide we want the pass band and what is the value of the center frequency. In the example, the *bandwidth* is 400 Hz (2000 - 1600), and the *center frequency* is 1800 Hz.

In Csound, we can perform band-pass filtering with the use of the opcode *reson* (2nd-order).

a1 resoninput_signal, center_frequency, bandwidth

Let's now filter some white noise with *reson*.

```
        instr   1
awn     rand    20000
afilt   reson   awn, 1800, 400
        out     afilt
        endin
```

In practice, the frequencies which lay between 1600 Hz and 2000 Hz are not completely untouched by the filtering process. The only frequency that remains untouched (0 dB, no attenuation) is the center frequency itself.[3] In an ideal band-pass, the two ends of the pass band must be 3 dB softer than the amplitude of the center frequency. Symmetric attenuation curves exists across the higher range 1800-2000 Hz, and the lower range 1800-1600 Hz. Both curves decay by -3 dB.

Amplitude	Freq	Freq	Freq	Freq	Freq	Freq	Freq
0 dB				1800			
-3 dB			1600		2000		
-12 dB		800				4000	
-24 dB	400						8000

In an ideal 2nd-order filter, the lower octave (800 Hz) of the bandwidth's lower end (1600 Hz) is attenuated by 12 dB, and so is the higher octave (4000 Hz) of the bandwidth higher end (2000 Hz). The respective double octaves (400 and 8000 Hz) are attenuated by 24 dB, etc. As the filter implemented with *reson* is far from ideal, the center frequency is slightly amplified. The greater the ratio of center frequency to bandwidth, the stronger the center frequency amplification. Again, for results closer to an ideal band-pass filter, we should use a Butterworth filter (see section 3.7).

[3] *reson* implements a 2nd-order resonant filter, and that causes the center frequency to be slighlty amplified, an effect indirectly proportional to the ratio of the center frequency to the bandwidth.

We can create a 4th-order band-pass cascading two *reson* filters:

```
            instr   1
awn         rand    20000
afilt       reson   awn, 1800, 400
afilt2      reson   afilt, 1800, 400
            out     afilt2
            endin
```

What happens if we radically reduced the bandwidth? We would be left with smaller and smaller portions of the source noise spectrum, until eventually we would hear the central frequency ringing similarly to a sine tone. In the following orchestra, we use a fixed central frequency and set a time-varying bandwidth:

```
            instr   1
awhitenoise rand    20000
kbandwidth  expseg  1000, p3-2, 1 , 2, 1        ;ramp from 1000 to 1 in p3-2 secs, then 1 until end
afilt       reson   awhitenoise, 800, kbandwidth
afilt2      reson   afilt, 800, kbandwidth
            out     afilt2
            endin
```

The output of *expseg* narrows the bandwidth of the two filters. The bandwidth changes from 1000 to 1 Hz in p3-2 seconds. Then for the last two seconds, it remains 1 Hz wide. The output from *expseg*, called *kbandwidth*, becomes the bandwidth argument to the two *reson* filters.

In principle, this process causes the central frequency to progressively increase in amplitude, but this is not the actual result with the *reson* band-pass filters. Furthermore; depending on the particular input signal, we may want to check the amplitude of the output and scale it. This is made possible by the 4th optional argument to *reson*:

a1 reson input_signal, center_frequency, bandwidth[, scale code]

Only three values are accepted as the scale code:

0 = no scaling, in case the signal amplitude is unpredictable and heavily dependent on both the spectrum of the input and the filter parameters.

1 = peak response value is 1, all frequencies are attenuated except for the center frequency, according to the normalized response curve.

2 = the output RMS value is made the same as that of the input signal.

TIPS & TRICKS : Scale codes 1 and 2 are used when one assumes all frequencies are physically present in the input signal. If that is not the case, scaling is not recommended. If one needs to adjust the output level anyway, the only practical solution is to multiply the output signal by a quantity determined at each instance, dependant upon whether one wants to amplify or attenuate the output.

Let's now see how we can use the band-pass filter to create glissandos, fix the bandwidth and change the filter's center frequency with a control variable. Oddly enough, this will sound very reminiscent of the gliding tone we created in the first chapter. It's no surprise that if we set a very narrow bandwidth, then only the central frequency will be heard, no matter how noisy the original sound submitted for filtering. Therefore, if we gradually change the central frequency over time, that will create in a glissando effect.

Observe this example

```
            instr   1
awnoise     rand    5000
kcentralfrq expseg  50, p3, 10000
afilt       reson   awnoise, kcentralfrq, 1, 2
afilt2      reson   afilt, kcentralfrq, 1, 2
            out     afilt2
            endin
```

Clearly, the input to a filter may be something other than white noise. We used white noise, simply because we know it contains all possible frequencies. So, we don't have to analyze the input sound before we filter its spectrum to allowing particular frequencies to pass through the filter unaltered. Sampled sounds, too, could be band-pass filtered. In such a case we are not in the position to emphasize, nor attenuate, just *any* frequency. For example, it would be meaningless to filter a soprano sound with a narrow band-pass centered around 50 Hz as a typical soprano spectrum lacks such low components.

3.6 GAIN UNITS: *RMS, GAIN, BALANCE*

Because it is not always easy to foresee the effects of filtering, especially when using sampled material as the source sound, Csound made available a number of opcodes for regulating the RMS amplitude value:

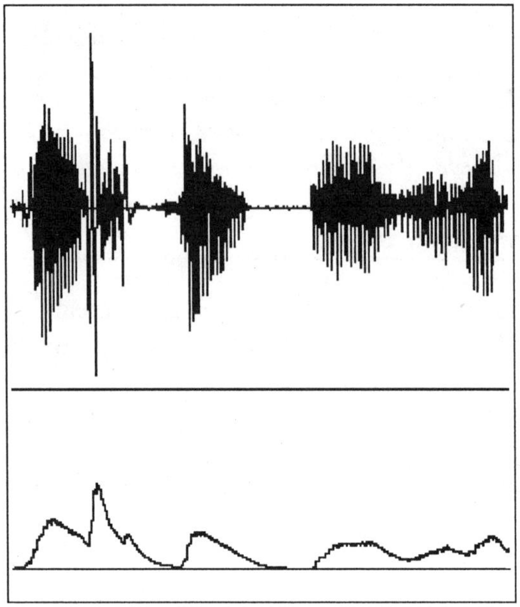

Fig. 3-4

k1	**rms**	**asig[, ihp, istor]**
a1	**gain**	**asig, k1[, ihp, istor]**
a1	**balance**	**asig, acomp[, ihp, istor]**

rms deposits in *k1* an estimate of the RMS value for the input signal *asig*. The RMS value represents the energy present in a signal. Observe in fig. 3-4, it is easy to see that the RMS value is not always the same as the amplitude peak value. There is no direct relationship between RMS and peak level. The two are interrelated by the sound waveform. For example, a sine wave that peaks at 1, has a RMS value of 0.707.

The *gain* opcode allows modification of the amplitude of a signal in such a way that the RMS in the output, *a1*, equals the level *k1*. Hence, if used in conjunction with *rms*, this opcode allows flexible control over the RMS of any given signal (see instrument #1 in next orchestra example).

The *balance* opcode implements the operations of *rms* and *gain* together. The amplitude of the input signal *asig* is modified as to match the amplitude of a compared signal *acomp*. Be careful! *rms* works by analyzing small successive small chunks of the input signal. So, its output is always shortly delayed.

ihp (optional) is the cutoff frequency of an internal low-pass filter. The default is 10 Hz.

istor (optional) (see footnote 2 in this Chapter).

```
;gain.orc
        sr     =  44100
        kr     =  4410
        ksmps  =  10
        nchnls =  1
        instr     1
a1      soundin   "voice.wav"
k1      rms       a1
afilt   reson     a1, 500, 200
aout    gain      afilt,k1
        out       aout
        endin

        instr     2
a1      soundin   "voice.wav"
afilt   reson     a1, 500, 200
aout    balance   afilt,a1
        out       aout
        endin
```

Instrument #1 reads a sound from the "voice.wav" file, copying it into the variable *a1*. It then extracts the RMS value of *a1* and stores that number in *k1*. The signal *a1* passes through a band-pass filter, *reson*, and the resulting signal is stored in *afilt*. The amplitude of *afilt* is modified, using *gain*, to match the RMS value of *a1*, previously stored in *k1*.

Instrument #2 does exactly the same thing, using *balance* instead of the couple *rms-gain.*

3.7 MULTI-POLES FILTERS AND RESONANT FILTERS

It is possible to apply more complex filtering methods than the ones described so far. To do so, we must now introduce four new filters, the so-called *Butterworth* filters (from the name of the physicist who first devised them).

a1	**butterhp**	**asig, kfreq [, iskip]**	**(high-pass)**
a1	**butterlp**	**sig, kfreq [, iskip]**	**(low-pass)**
a1	**butterbp**	**asig, kfreq, kband [, iskip]**	**(band-pass)**
a1	**butterbr**	**asig, kfreq, kband [, iskip]**	**(band-reject)**

These opcodes can also be written as **buthp**, **butlp**, **butbp** and **butbr**.

These are 2nd-order filters with a particular internal structure (named "Butterworth filter structure"), and are called IIR filters (infinite impulse response filters). They feature a certain stability in the passing band, a great precision and an exceptional attenuation of frequencies outside the passing band. As expected, in Csound such filters demand slightly more computation time than *tone*, *atone* and *reson*.

asig	input signal
kfreq	cutoff frequency (*butterhp* and *butterlp*) or central frequency (*butterbp* and *butterbr*)
kband	bandwidth (*butterbp* and *butterbr*)
iskip	is = 1, causes the initialization to be skipped (see *reson's istor*)

Here, we want to use these filters to build a multi-poles filter, (a filter with multiple peaks in the frequency response curve). This is useful in *formant synthesis* (see section 15.4), which is a kind of subtractive synthesis that is particularly powerful for modeling the voice by filtering out sound sources with many harmonic components.

When building a filter, it is useful to test its functionality by feeding it with a sine wave sweeping across a large frequency range, (10-10000 Hz), in order to check the frequency response of the full curve. In the orchestra example below we didn't use p5. So in the score, the value for p5 is always 0 (but it could have been given any other value, and that would not affect the synthesis process).

```
;4poles.orc
        sr     =  44100
        kr     =  4410
        ksmps  =  10
        nchnls =  1

        instr     1
        iamp   =  p4                ;sine wave amplitude
;- - - - - - - - - - - - - - - - - - - - - parameters of filter 1
        ifilt1 =  p6                ;center frequency in Hz
        ibw1   =  p7                ;bandwidth in Hz
        iamp1  =  p8                ;formant amplitude
;- - - - - - - - - - - - - - - - - - - - - parameters of filter 2
        ifilt2 =  p9                ;center frequency in Hz
        ibw2   =  p10               ;bandwidth in Hz
        iamp2  =  p11               ;formant amplitude
;- - - - - - - - - - - - - - - - - - - - - parameters of filter 3
```

```
        ifilt3  =  p12                 ;center frequency in Hz
        ibw3    =  p13                 ;bandwidth in Hz
        iamp3   =  p14                 ;formant amplitude
;---------------------- parameters of filter 4
        ifilt4  =  p15                 ;center frequency in Hz
        ibw4    =  p16                 ;bandwidth in Hz
        iamp4   =  p17                 ;formant amplitude
;---------------------- control signal for the frequency sweep
kfrq    line       10, p3, 10000
;---------------------- sine wave generation
a1      oscili     iamp, kfrq, 1
;---------------------- filtering :
af1     butterbp   a1, ifilt1, ibw1    ;filter 1
af2     butterbp   a1, ifilt2, ibw2    ;filter 2
af3     butterbp   a1, ifilt3, ibw3    ;filter 3
af4     butterbp   a1, ifilt4, ibw4    ;filter 4
;---------------------- sum of the 4 filtered signals
        aout    =  af1*iamp1+af2*iamp2+af3*iamp3+af4*iamp4
        out        aout
        endin
```

Let's try this score:

```
;4poles.sco
f1  0  4096   10  1
;                          fc1  lb1 amp1 fc2 lb2 amp2  fc3 lb3 amp3 fc4  lb4 amp4
i1  0  10   5000  0  400  200   1   900  300  .5  1500  200  1.5  3000  400  1
```

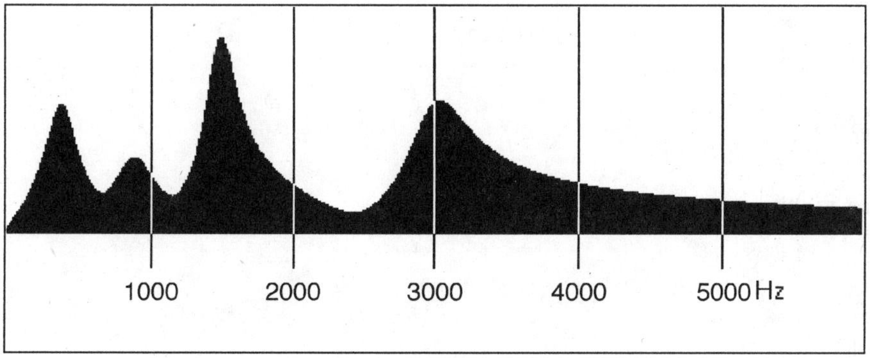

Fig. 3-5

Once the synthesis is completed, open the newly created sound file from a sound file editor. You will see something like the graph in fig.3-5, which is a frequency/amplitude graph (frequency on the horizontal axis, amplitude on the vertical axis). Notice the four peaks at 400, 900, 1500 and 3000 Hz. Their amplitude exactly matches what we indicated in the score (1 at 400 Hz, .5 at 900 Hz, 1.5 at 1500 Hz, and again 1 at 3000 Hz). What we have built is a *parametric equalizer*. The difference between programming Csound to implement a parametric equalizer and using an existing hardware eq, lies in Csound's flexibility allowing you to include any number of peaks.

Another kind of low-pass is the *variable resonance low-pass filter,* well-known to those who worked with analog synthesizers such as the modular Moog. To build this filter, we shall use a *butterlp* low-pass and a *butterbp* band-pass in parallel (as opposite to "cascaded"). To test the frequency response, this time, we use a sine slowly gliding from 0 to 10000 Hz.

```
;resfilt.orc
        sr      =  44100
        kr      =  4410
        ksmps   =  10
        nchnls  =  1

        instr      1
        ifrq    =  p5               ;cutoff freq
        ibw     =  ifrq/p6          ;calculates the bandwidth
                                    ;as a fraction of the cutoff frequency
kfrq    line       0, p3, 10000         ;control signal for the sweep
a1      oscili     p4, kfrq, 1      ;gliding sine wave
;- - - - - - - - - - - - - - - - - - - - filters
af1     butterlp   a1, ifrq*2       ;low-pass
af2     butterbp   a1, ifrq,ibw     ;band-pass
;- - - - - - - - - - - - - - - - - - - - - sum of filtered signals
        aout       =  (af1+af2)/2
        out        aout
        endin
```

A score for this orchestra would be:

```
;resfilt.sco
f1 0 4096 10 1
;in     act dur amp   ifrq Q
i1      0   5   15000 2000  1
```

```
i1    +  .   15000  2000   2
i1    +  .   15000  2000   4
i1    +  .   15000  2000   8
```

The so-called "filter Q", or *resonance factor*, corresponds to p6, and is defined as

Q = cutoff_frequency / bandwidth

In our orchestra, it is necessary to calculate the bandwidth *ibw* (for *butterbp*) as a function of the cutoff frequency. If we require constant bandwidth relative to musical intervals (e.g.: 1/2 octave), its absolute value changes depending on the particular center frequency. If we set *ifrq* to 100 Hz and ask for a 1/2 octave bandwidth, the actual bandwidth size is 50 Hz. If we set *ifrq* to 1000, a 1/2 octave bandwidth is, this time, 500 Hz.

The frequency response graphs illustrated in fig.3-6 correspond to the four different Qs in the above score, assuming a fixed center frequency of 2000 Hz.

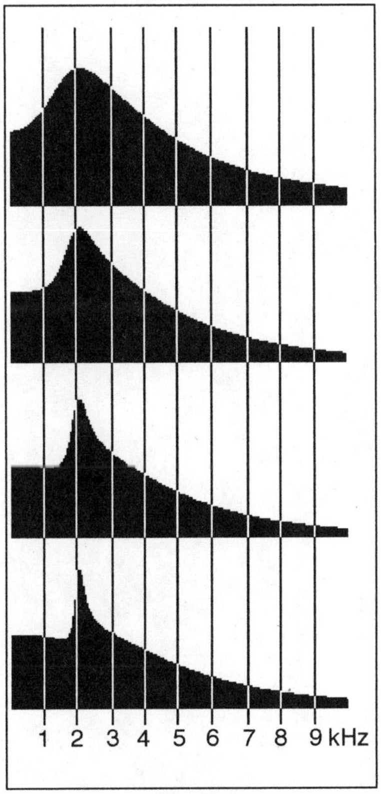

Fig. 3-6

It is not too difficult to modify the above orchestra in such a way as to vary both the Q and the cutoff frequency during the note.

Starting with the 3.47 release, Csound allows us to use a special opcode, *lowres*, which is a built-in implementation of the variable resonance low-pass. The syntax is:

ar lowres asig, kcutoff, kresonance [,istor]

ar	output signal
asig	input signal
kcutoff	cutoff frequency
kresonance	resonance value: a greater value causes a greater amplification of the cutoff frequency

EXTENSIONS

3.A.1 SUBTRACTIVE SYNTHESIS: HISTORICAL SKETCHES

As observed in section 2.B.1, subtractive synthesis was utilized in the 1950's as an alternative to additive synthesis. It became an important compositional device, although for many it remained basically in the shadow of after additive synthesis.

Just as in additive synthesis, subtractive synthesis, too, is theoretically rooted in the Fourier theorem. If we have a complex waveform (with either harmonic or inharmonic spectrum, or even a completely flat white noise spectrum), we can use filters to cut away, or to simply attenuate, some of its components, thereby modifying the spectrum and, hence, the timbre.

In the electroacoustic music studios from the 1950's, three types of filters were available:

full-octave band-pass filters, usually with preset frequencies (which were often built in-house by the studio technicians);

1/3rd-octave band-pass filters, usually with preset frequencies and general purpose, high and low-pass filters, with controllable cutoff frequency.

Of course, these filters were manually operated making quick filter changes unfeasible, and prevented precisely repeatable operations. As a matter of fact, composers preferred to keep the filter parameters fixed, thus using unvarying spectra.

Some filtering systems supplied an alternative way to create amplitude envelopes and to determine the duration of a sound. A typical band-pass filter would always make the attack and release transients last a bit longer than necessary. This was caused by the relationship between the center frequency and the pass bandwidth (which was proportional to the so-called "filter Q"). If we filter a pulse signal (with shortest attack and release times) using band-pass filtering, with narrow bandwidth, the output would sound very different from the initial pulse. In fig. 3-A-1 you see the waveform of a short pulse (top), and the effect of its filtering by a narrow band-pass (bottom). Not only does the resultant signal have a prominent frequency (a sine wave) which was not at all evident in the initial pulse, but it also has a longer duration and an envelope curve (an exponential decay).

Here is a Csound orchestra, with its score, that you can experiment with using this synthesis method. They were written to create the effect illustrated in fig. 3-A-1. The output pulse will be heard in the left stereo channel and the filtered signal in the right channel.

```
;xsubtr.orc
        sr      =   44100
```

```
        kr      =   44100  ; notice kr = sr!
        ksmps   =   1
        nchnls  =   2

        instr       1
a1      linseg      10000, 1/kr ,0, p3-1/kr, 0
a2      reson       a1, 2000, 100
        outs        a1, a2*.3
        endin

;xsubtr.sco
i1 0 1
```

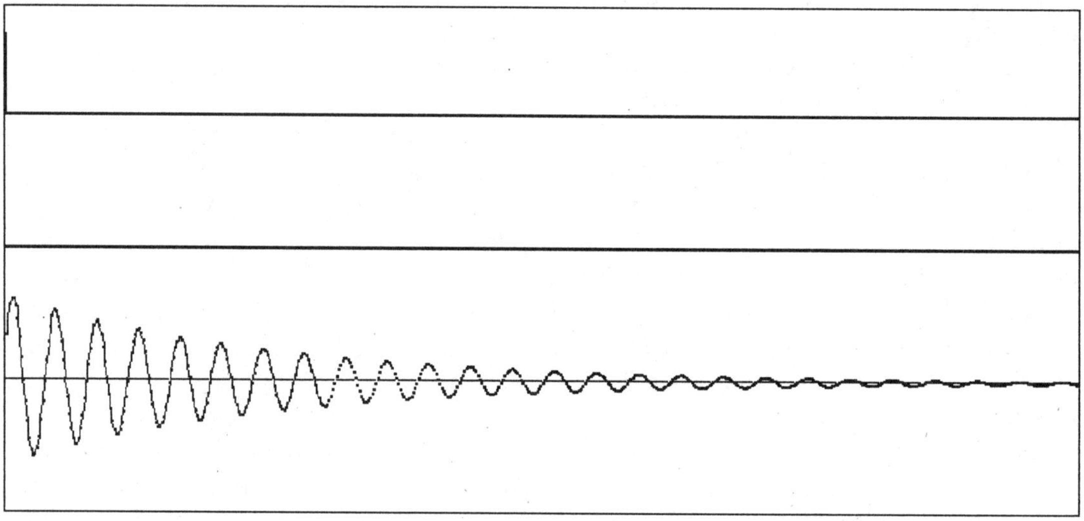

Fig. 3-A-1

The pulse is generated with the *linseg* opcode and is stored in the audio variable *a1*. It has the shortest possible duration, and is equal to a single control cycle (*1/kr*). *a1* becomes the input signal for *reson* whose arguments include a 2000 Hz center frequency and a 100 Hz bandwidth. The filter output, *a2*, is finally scaled so that its amplitude level is similar to *a1*. In the stereo output, *a1* is sent to the left stereo channel (first argument to *outs*), *a2* is sent to the right stereo channel (second argument to *outs*).

The timbre of the output is reminiscent of a marimba hit with rubber-head mallets. It is interesting to make a comparison between this sound and the percussive sounds created by Stockhausen for his *Gesang der Jünglinge* and *Kontakte*, two works largely based on subtractive synthesis methods, and other sophisticated studio techniques.

Clearly, if we change the filter center frequency and the bandwidth, we obtain sounds of different pitches and with different timbre qualities. In general, the wider the bandwidth, the more "noisy" the result and vice-versa. The narrower the bandwidth, the more clearly definite pitch is audible. In truth, the determining factor in the sound's quality is the ratio of the bandwidth size to the center frequency, the so-called filter Q.

In works of electroacoustic music from the 1950's, a widely used effect was involved filtering *white noise* to achieve *colored noise*.[4] The filters available then, were not particularly sophisticated, compared with the Csound filters. There were basically two kinds: band-pass (usually with a full or a 1/3rd-octave pass band), and low-pass or high-pass with manually controlled cutoff frequency. Among those former types, a celebrated (and expensive) model was the Danish Bruel & Kjäer, which offered a series of linear faders, for each independent output control from each filter. Equally expensive was the Krohn-Hite, which offered two knobs to adjust the cutoff frequencies of the high and low-pass filters. When used effectively variable band-pass filtering (high-pass cutoff point lower than low-pass cutoff point), or variable notch (band-rejection) filtering (high-pass cutoff point higher than low-pass cutoff point) was possible.

Another filter worth mentioning here, was the peculiar filter built up by Dr. Alfredo Lietti at the Studio di Fonologia of the Milan RAI radio station. Basically, it appeared to be a band-pass with a variable bandwidth (as narrow as 2 Hz!), but it used two ring-modulators, one main filter and a number of auxiliary filtering circuits. With this filter, Bruno Maderna created the sounds that open his *Notturno*, characterized by their peculiar evocative power.

3.B.1 SUBTRACTIVE SYNTHESIS: THEORY

As in additive synthesis, subtractive synthesis can be described with reference to the Fourier theorem we briefly discussed in section 2.B.1. Given any sound source with a complex spectrum, we can modify the spectrum to obtain new spectral configurations. In principle, if the source is as rich in harmonics as the pulse we discussed in the preceding section, then we can synthesize *any* sound by appropriately filtering out some frequencies in that pulse. However, this approach is not very practical. Subtractive methods are more commonly used in order to render musically interesting modifications

[4] by *colored noise* we mean here a kind of noise which, different from white noise, does not include all audible frequencies, but only larger or smaller regions of frequencies.

Let's consider a signal with harmonic spectrum

$$A = A_1 * \sin(f) + A_2 * \sin(2f) + A_3 * \sin(3f) + A_4 * \sin(4f) + ...$$

where A_1, A_2, etc. represent the amplitudes of the various harmonics, and *f, 2f, 3f*, etc. represent their harmonic frequencies. If we filter this with a low-pass filter having a response of -6 dB per octave, and a cutoff frequency equal to the fundamental, *f*, we obtain

$$A = A_1 * \sin(f) + (A_2\text{-6dB}) * \sin(2f) + (A_3\text{-9dB}) * \sin(3f) + (A_4\text{-12dB}) * \sin(4f) + ...$$

Here the component with the frequency *2f*, one octave higher than *f*, is attenuated by 6 dB; *3f*, a twelfth (= approx. 1.5 octave) higher than *f*, is attenuated by approximately 9 dB; *4f*, two octaves higher than *f*, is attenuated by 12 dB, etc. In short, if we call Π(t) the time-varying spectrum of some original signal, and Ω(t) the filter *transfer function* (or response curve, eventually it, too, time-varying), we can write

$$Z(t) = \Pi(t) \otimes \Omega(t)$$

where the symbol ⊗ denotes the *convolution* (multiplication of two spectra, see section 13.6) of Π(t) and Ω(t).

Fig.3-B-1 illustrate this effect. It shows the spectrum of some signal (top), the filter response curve (middle) and the spectrum in the signal after filtering (bottom).

Clearly, all this applies to inharmonic sounds and sounds with time-varying spectrum, as well. Furthermore, it is also possible to use filters whose response curve is itself time-varying (*dynamic filtering*), or filters whose operations are dynamically dependent on spectrum of the input signal (*adaptive filtering*).

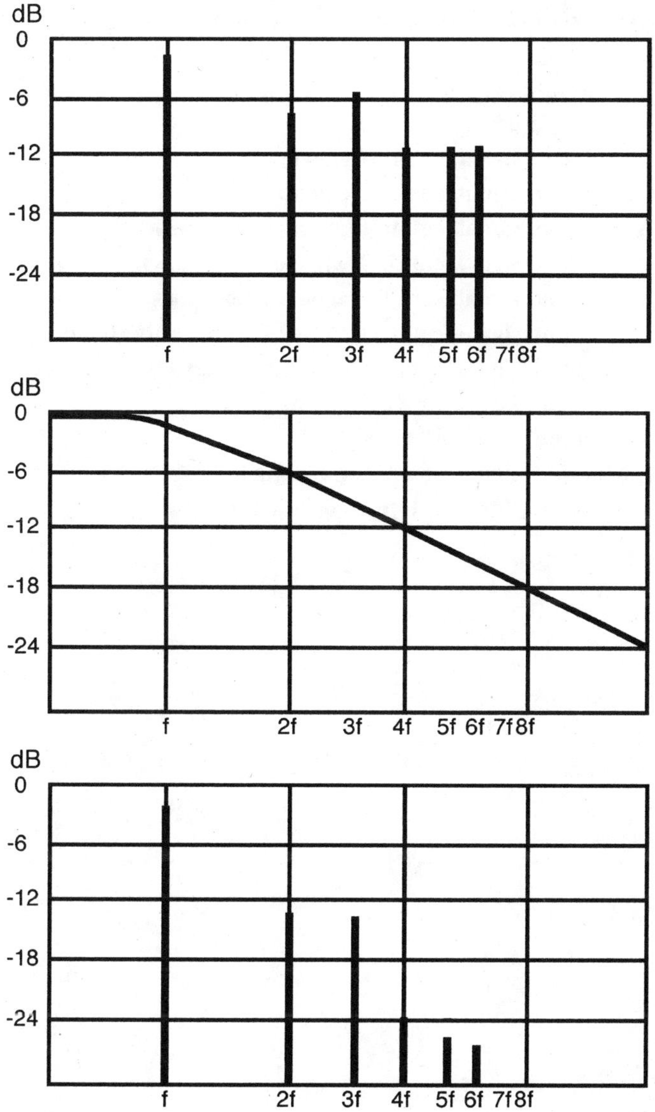
dB
0
-6
-12
-18
-24
f
2f
3f
4f
5f
6f
7f
8f
dB
0
-6
-12
-18
-24
f
2f
3f
4f
5f
6f
7f
8f
dB
0
-6
-12
-18
-24
f
2f
3f
4f
5f
6f
7f
8f

Fig. 3-B-1

LIST OF OPCODES INTRODUCED IN THIS CHAPTER

k1	**rand**	**amplitude**
a1	**rand**	**amplitude**
a1	**tone**	**input_signal, cutoff_frequency**
a1	**atone**	**input_signal, cutoff_frequency**
a1	**reson**	**input_signal, cutoff_frequency, bandwidth**
a1	**butterhp**	**input_signal, cutoff_frequency (high-pass)**
a1	**butterlp**	**input_signal, cutoff_frequency (low-pass)**
a1	**butterbp**	**input_signal, cutoff_frequency, bandwidth (band-pass)**
a1	**butterbr**	**input_signal, cutoff_frequency, bandwidth (banda-rejection)**
k1	**rms**	**input_signal**
a1	**gain**	**input_signal, RMS_value**
a1	**balance**	**input_signal, comparator_signal**
ar	**lowres**	**input_signal, cutoff_freq, resonance**

4

FLOW-CHARTS

4.1 GRAPHICAL REPRESENTATION OF PROCEDURES

Any sequence of linked events, or *procedure*, can be represented in several ways: by text, by graphics, or even by acoustical representations. A Csound orchestra is a written description of a set of particular procedures whose result is a generated sound. It is not a very "readable" representation. We can hardly grasp its complete functionality at first glance. Especially, if the orchestra was created by someone else, or if it is complex, you may find it difficult to understand all of its details. What can we do then?

A good solution is to adopt a representation other than text, like a graphical representation, for example. The kind of graphical representation we are going to use here is based on *flow-charts*. Flow-charts are useful in many fields, because they make it easy to grasp the structure of a set of linked events in an intuitive manner. Consider the analogy of a city map. Draw yourself a little map, that's usually more handy than remembering directions like "take the third right turn, when you get to the pay-phone turn left, go straight to the gasoline station...".

4.2 LET'S GO TO THE SEASIDE

Imagine a situation like this: a friend suggests that you go with him/her to the seaside, in your car early Sunday morning provided it doesn't rain. What are the operations and choices to make in such a situation? Here's a list of some choices including those which are banal and self-evident:

1. Set the alarm clock - then wake up.
2. Look outside. Is it raining? If it is, go back to bed.
3. Pack a seaside bag, go outside and get in the car.
4. Start the engine. Does it start? If it doesn't, go back to bed.
5. Drive to your friend's place.
6. Is she/he ready? If he/she's not, wait.
7. Drive to the seaside.

Let's see how this simple procedure, called "Go to the seaside", can be represented in a flow-chart. The diagram is in figure 4-1. In the graph, time moves from top to bottom, and also from left to right sometimes. Each rectangular box is labeled (e.g. "Set alarm clock and wake up). Diamond boxes have question marks (e.g. "Watch outside, is it raining?"). Rectangular boxes denote *actions*, and have a single output. Diamonds denote *tests*, and have two outputs, one for tests evaluated as true, one for those evaluated as false. Thus, if we answer the question "is it raining?" with a "yes" (true), the diagram flows to "go back to bed" and the procedure ends with the action "STOP". If, instead, the answer is "no" (false), we can continue the process.

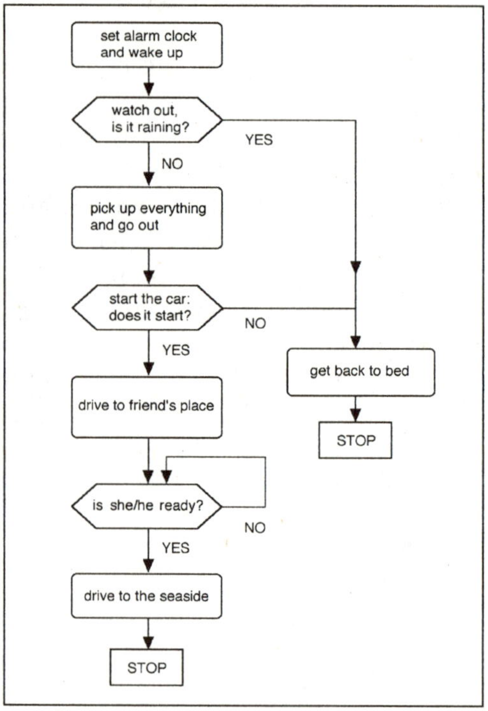

Fig. 4-1

Today, the graphical representation of musical procedures is rather common. In fact, much computer music *software* includes a graphical user interface. As in MAX, KYMA, Patchwork, etc. Therefore, it is useful to learn how this kind of graphical representation works.

4.3 SYMBOLS

Our representation should use graphical symbols or icons that can be easily recognized and associated to a single object. Every Csound *unit generator* (UG, usually described as an opcode) can be denoted by a particular symbol. However, Csound includes many unit generators, such that it is confusing to have a different symbol for each one. It is better to limit the number of symbols and use text labels to distinguish them.

The signal flow proceeds from top to bottom, and from left to right. Whenever possible, audio signals are represented by vertical connections, while control signals are represented by horizontal connections. If a unit generator accepts both audio and control signals, the audio input is placed on the upper side of the symbol, and the control input is placed on the right side. The output is always a line issuing from the bottom side of the symbol.

Fig.4-2a and 4-2b illustrates some of the Csound signal generators. Observe the *oscil* symbol. It has two inputs on top (amplitude and frequency), and two inputs on its right (function number and phase). The output is a line from the bottom.

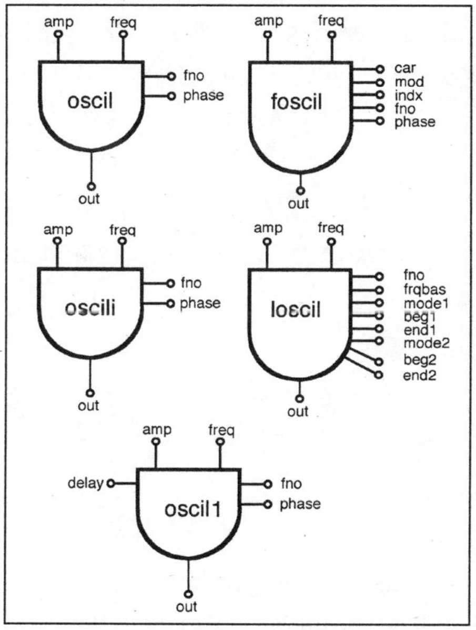

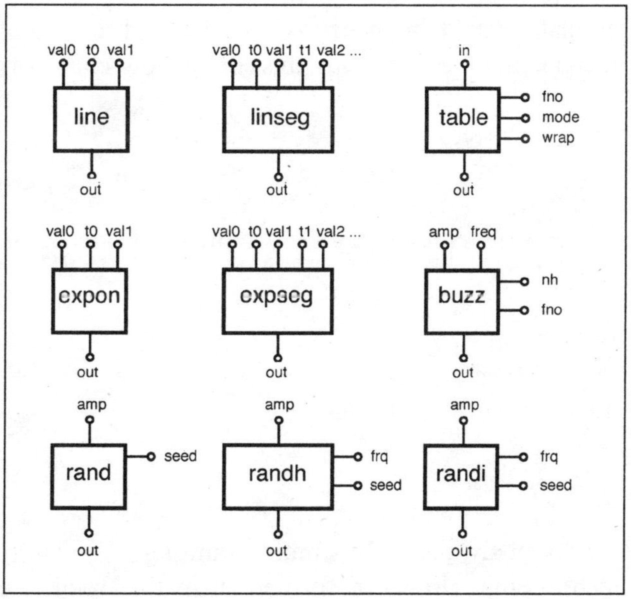

Fig. 4-2a unit generators (1) Fig. 4-2b

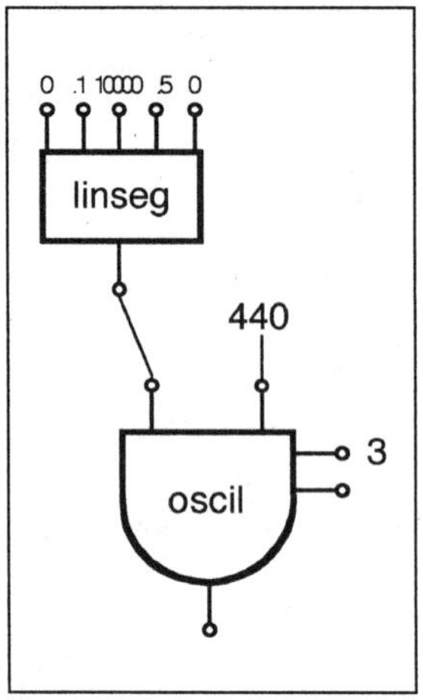

Fig. 4-3a

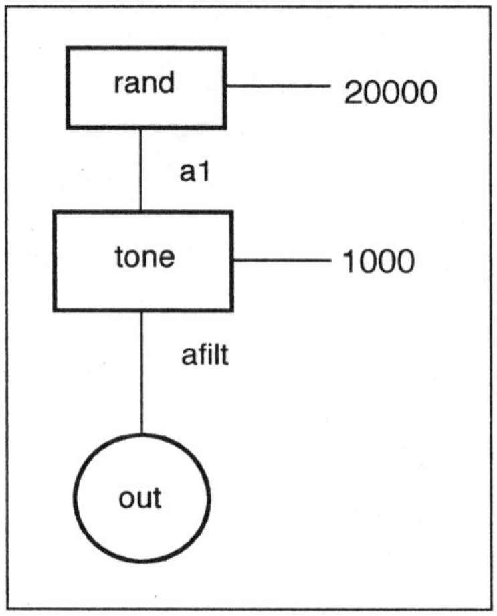

Fig. 4-3b

UGs with a variable number of inputs (arguments) are more complicated. Think of *linseg*, for example. In the figure, *linseg* has 5 arguments (*val0, t0, val1, t1, val2*). It is important not to omit any data.

A simple flow-chart, in fig. 4-3a, illustrates an (incomplete) instrument with two UGs, *linseg* and *oscil*. The first generates two line segments, as indicated by the arguments listed on top of the relevant symbol (0, .1, 10000, .5, 0). The output could be called *kenv*. The oscillator has a frequency of 440 Hz and an amplitude that varies with *kenv*. The audio function number is 3. Thus, this simple flow-chart corresponds to the following Csound code:

```
kenv    linseg    0, .1, 10000, .5, 0
a1      oscil     kenv, 440, 3
```

The flow-chart in fig.4-3b represents one of the Csound instruments we created in Chap.2

```
        instr     1
a1      rand      20000
afilt   tone      a1, 1000
        out       afilt
        endin
```

Obviously, these are simple examples. We would not need flow-charts for such simple instruments. However, further on in this book we will encounter orchestras that will appear more difficult, if not impossible, to understand without the help of flow-charts.

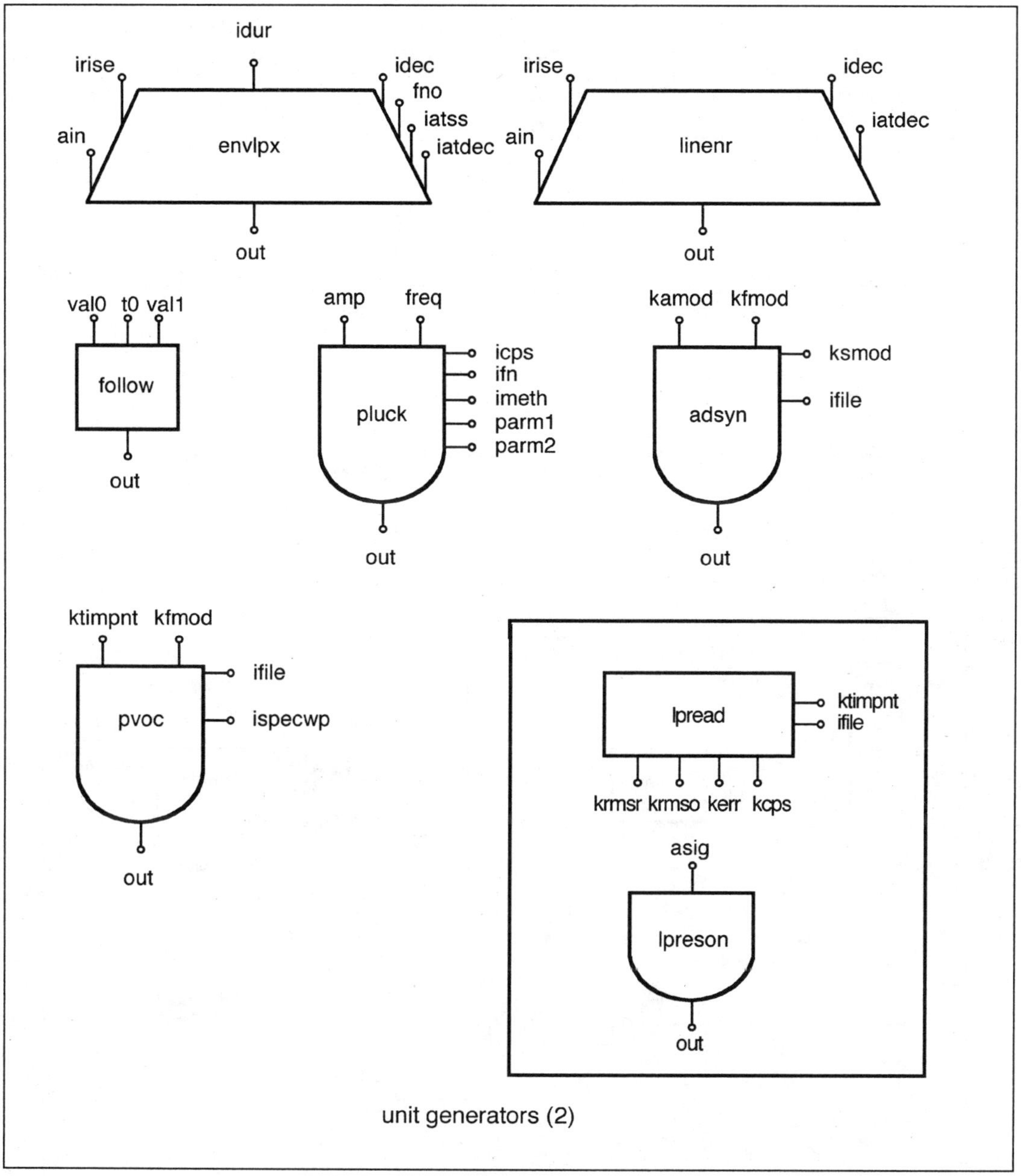
idur
irise
idec
fno
iatss
ain
envlpx
iatdec
out
irise
idec
iatdec
ain
linenr
out
val0 t0 val1
follow
out
amp freq
icps
ifn
imeth
parm1
parm2
pluck
out
kamod kfmod
ksmod
ifile
adsyn
out
ktimpnt kfmod
ifile
pvoc
ispecwp
out
lpread
ktimpnt
ifile
krmsr krmso kerr kcps
asig
lpreson
out
unit generators (2)

Fig. 4-4

More *signal generators* symbols are illustrated in fig.4-4. Symbols for the most common *signal modifiers* are listed in fig. 4-5, and finally symbols for *sound input* and *output* are listed in fig.4-6.

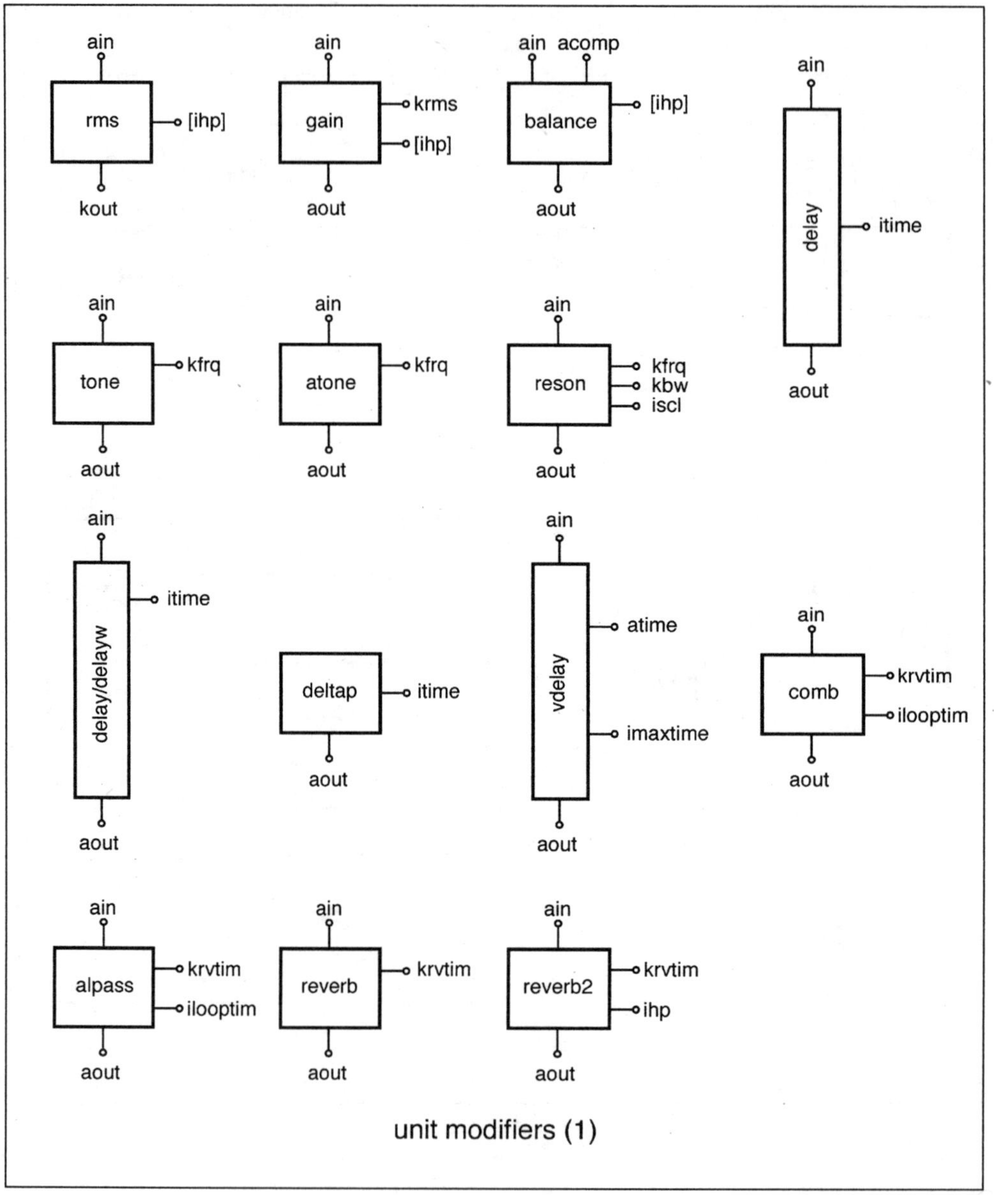

Fig. 4-5

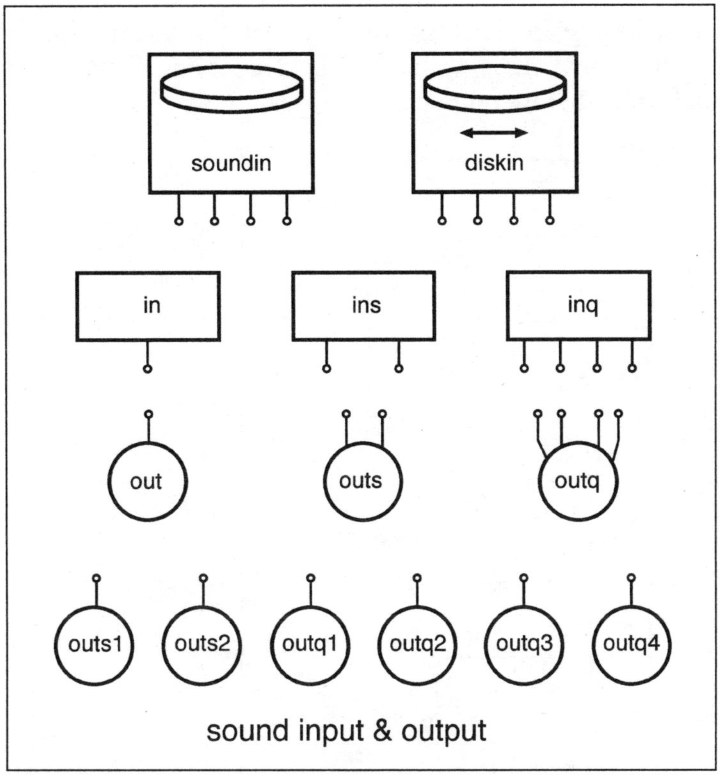

Fig. 4-6

4.4 COMPLEX DIAGRAMS

Fig.4-7 illustrates a flow-chart of greater complexity. This is the physical model of a flute, introduced by Perry Cook and coded in Csound by Hans Mikelson. Physical modeling is discussed in detail in Chap.16.

An envelope generator produces a signal, *kenv1*, by determining the variable amplitude of a noise generator (*rand*). The noise signal is called *aflow1*. But *kenv1* is added to *aflow1*, creating the audio signal *asum1*. The latter is added to a feedback signal called *aflute1* (the output of a delay and filter, see below), and the new signal, *asum2*, is sent to a delay line (*delay*) whose delay time is *1/ifreq*.25* seconds. The delayed signal, *ax*, is passed through a transformation, the polynomial function $x - x^3$. The modified signal, called *apoly*, in turn is added to *aflute1* and multiplied by 0.4. This creates *asum3*, an audio signal which is sent to a low-pass filter (*tone*) with a cutoff frequency 8 times higher than the desired output frequency. The output from *tone* is called *avalue* and becomes the input to a second delay line, this time with a delay of *1/ifreq*.75* seconds.

The delayed signal is the feedback signal *aflute1* that we mentioned before. *avalue* is the final output audio signal. It is scaled by the proper level, p4, and multiplied by the envelope signal *kenv1* before output.

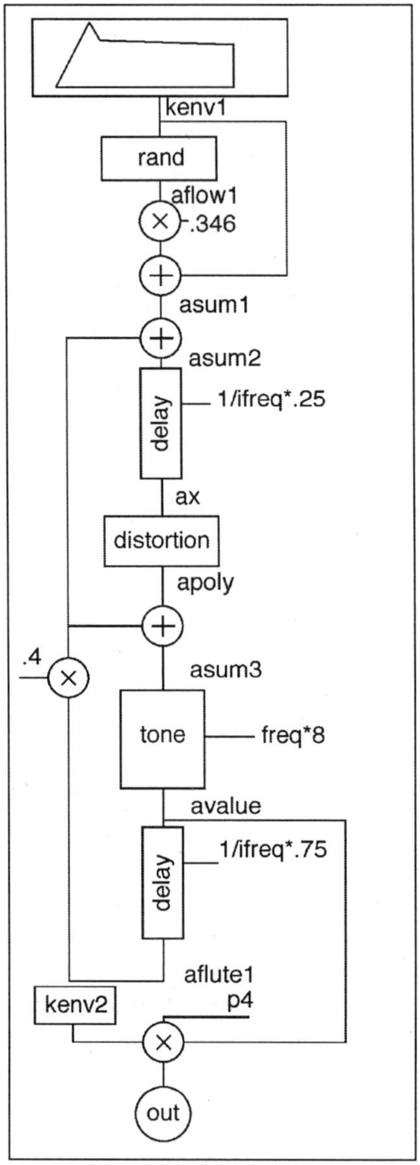

Fig. 4-7

```
            sr      =  44100
            kr      =  4410
            ksmps   =  10
            nchnls  =  1

            instr      1

aflute1 init 0
; ------------ air flow
;
kenv1       linseg     0, .05, 1.1, .1, .98, p3-.15, .95
kenv2       linseg     1, p3-.01, 1, .01, 0
aflow1      rand       kenv1
asum1              =   aflow1*.0356 + kenv1
asum2              =   asum1 + aflute1*.4
;
; ------------ embouchure
;
ax          delayr     1/p5/4
            delayw     asum2
apoly              =   ax - ax*ax*ax
asum3              =   apoly + aflute1*.4
avalue      tone       asum3, 8*p5
;
; ------------ tube
;
aflute1     delayr     1/p5*.75
            delayw     avalue
            out        avalue*p4*kenv2
            endin
```

Fig.4-8 consists of two more diagrams, which illustrate two frequency modulation (FM) instruments. FM is discussed in chap.12. For the moment, let's simply take a look at these diagrams and compare them with the Csound code below (*fm_2.orc*). After studying FM and physical modeling in chap.12 and chap.16, do not forget to turn back to the flow-charts in this section.

```
;fm_2.orc
        sr     =  44100
        kr     =  4410
        ksmps  =  10
        nchnls =  1

        instr     1                          ;FM, 1 carrier and 1 modulator
iamp              =  p4
icar              =  p5
imod              =  p6
indx              =  p7
amod    oscili       imod*indx, imod, 1
acar    oscili       iamp, icar+amod, 1
        out          acar
        endin

        instr     2                          ;FM, 1 carrier e 1 modulated modulator
iamp              =  p4
icar              =  p5
imod1             =  p6
indx1             =  p7
imod2             =  p8
indx2             =  p9
amod1   oscili       imod1*indx1, imod1, 1
amod2   oscili       imod2*indx2, imod2+amod1, 1
acar    oscili       iamp, icar+amod2
        out          acar
        endin
```

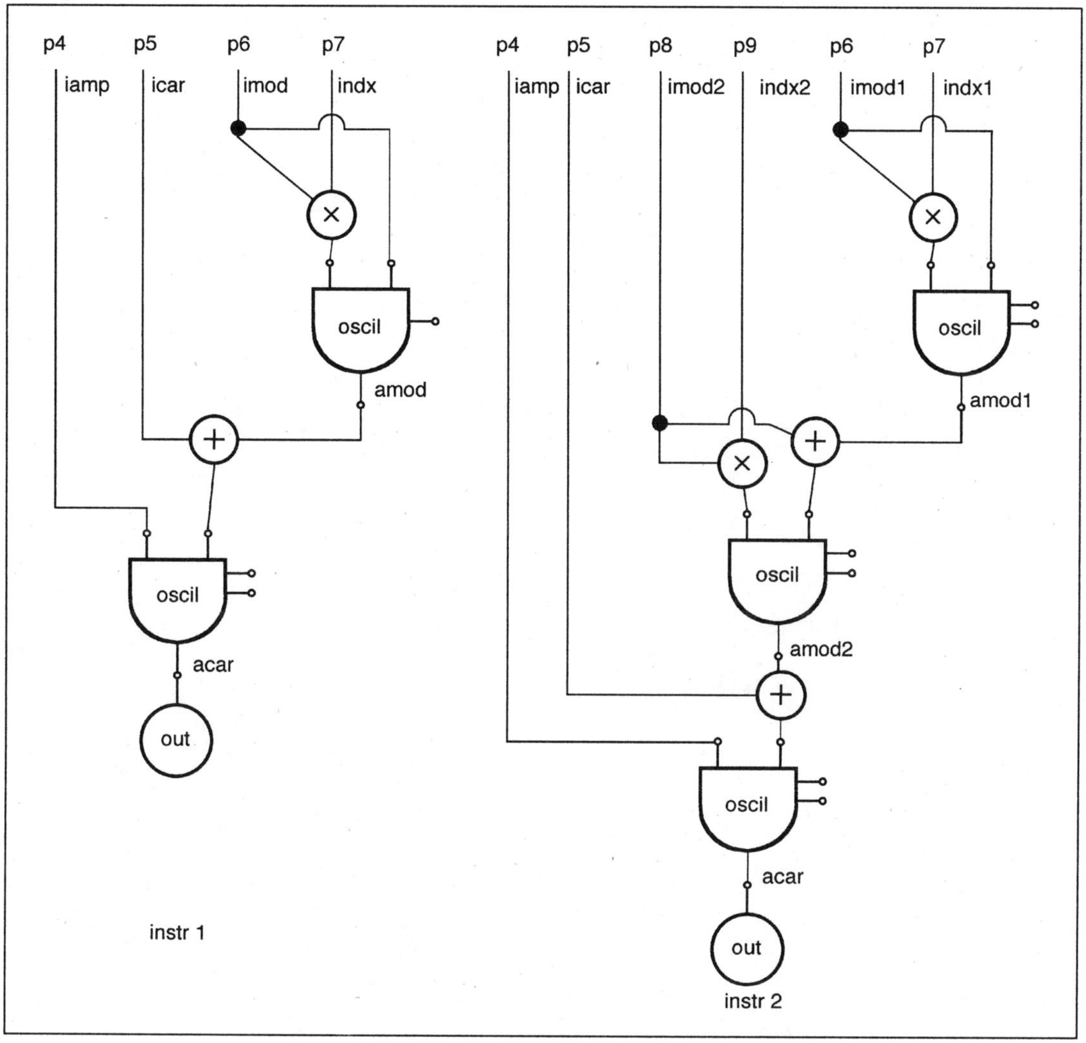
p4
p5
p6
p7
iamp
icar
imod
indx
oscil
amod
oscil
acar
out
instr 1
p4
p5
p8
p9
p6
p7
iamp
icar
imod2
indx2
imod1
indx1
oscil
amod1
oscil
amod2
oscil
acar
out
instr 2

Fig. 4-8

5

STEREO, CONTROL SIGNALS, VIBRATO, TREMOLO, 3-D SOUND

5.1 STEREOPHONIC ORCHESTRAS

So far, your orchestra headers always included the assignment *nchnls = 1*, and thus all instruments were generating mono signals. Let's now introduce the possibility of choosing among mono and stereo instruments.

For stereo output, use *outs* rather than *out*. The syntax is as follows

outs left_out_signal, right_out_signal

Observe the following example:

```
;stereo.orc
        sr      =  44100
        kr      =  4410
        ksmps   =  10
        nchnls  =  2            ;notice nchnls=2
        instr      1
asine   oscil      10000, 1000, 1
```

```
asquare   oscil   10000, 220, 2
          outs    asine, asquare  ;asine on left channel, asquare on right
          endin
;
          instr   2
awn       rand    10000
          outs    awn, awn        ;awn on both left and right channels
          endin
```

A score for this orchestra would be:

```
;stereo.sco
f1   0   4096  10  1
f2   0   4096  7   1   2048  1   0  -1   2048  -1
i1   0   5
i2   6   5
```

Here we have a stereo orchestra (*nchnls=2*) which includes two distinct instruments

instr1: generates two signals, *asine*, heard in the left channel, and *asquare*, heard in the right channel
instr2: generates only one signal heard in both output channels, for monophonic effect.

Let's now create a new orchestra which positions notes in three distinct locations in the stereo field, left, center and right.

```
;stereo1.orc
        sr     =  44100
        kr     =  4410
        ksmps  =  10
        nchnls =  2
        instr     1
ast     oscili    p4, p5, 1
        outs      ast*(1-p6), ast*p6
        endin
```

In this example, the first argument to *outs* (left output) is assigned the *ast* signal multiplied by 1 minus the p6 value from the score (notice that multiplication is denoted by an asterisk, *); the second argument (right output) is assigned again *ast*, but this time multiplied by p6.

Here's a score for this new instrument

```
;stereo1.sco
f1   0    4096   10   9    8    7    6    5    4    3    2    1
i1   0    1           10000          200            1         ;right stereo output
i1   1.1  1           10000          200            .5        ;center stereo output
i1   2.2  1           10000          200            0         ;left stereo output
```

How come the first note is audible in the right channel? Notice that for that particular note we set p6 = 1, and according to the orchestra code, the left output is *ast* multiplied by 1-p6, in this particular case, *ast**(1-1), equals *ast**0. All audio samples in the *ast* signal are set to zero. The right output, on the other hand, is *ast* multiplied by p6, i.e. *ast* * 1. Thus, all audio samples remain untouched (any number multiplied by 1 gives the number itself). Therefore, the sound will come to our ears via the right channel only.

Let's take a look at other stereo panning possibilities. As a general procedure, consider the following

```
outs [audio variable]*(1-p6), [audio variable]*p6
```

Now consider some specific cases. For p6=1

outs [audio variable]*(1-1) = 0, [audio variable]*1 = audio variable

which means: no signal on the left, the whole signal on the right.

For p6=0

outs [audio variable]*(1-0) = audio variable, [audio variable]*0 = 0

hence we get no signal on the right, and the whole signal on the left.

For p6=.5

outs [audio variable]*(1-.5) = audio variable / 2, [audio variable]*.5 = audio variable / 2

which means: The signal appears at equal amplitude in both speakers (monophonic effect).

For p6=.75

outs [audio variable]*(1-.75) = audio variable * 1/4, [audio variable]*.75 = audio variable * 3/4

we get the signal at 1/4 amplitude on the left, and three quarters amplitude on the right.

This way, we are able to allocate a specific position for each note across the stereo front.

If we want a sound to move from, left to right and back, over the course of the note duration, we have to set some control variable with linear values going from 0 to 1 and then back to 0. Let's see an example of this dynamic stereo panning

```
;dynamic stereo panning programmed from the orchestra

        instr   1
kstereo linseg  0, p3/2, 1, p3/2, 0
ast     oscili  p4, p5, 1
        outs    ast*(1-kstereo), ast*kstereo
        endin
```

```
;dynamic stereo panning programmed from the score

        instr   2
kstereo linseg  p6, p3/2, p7, p3/2, p8
ast     oscili  p4, p5, 1
        outs    ast*(1-kstereo), ast*kstereo
        endin
```

Observe that the second instrument exploits three stereo positions: p6 = initial position, p7 = middle position, p8 = final position (values in the range [0,1]).

Here's a score for this orchestra

```
f1  0   4096  10     1
i2  0   5     20000  500  .5  1   0    ;from center to right, then to left
i2  6   5     20000  500  0   .5  .5   ;from left to center, then remains there
i2  12  4     20000  500  0   .5  1    ;from left to right
```

This method is quite simple, but it is not completely rewarding. If you listen carefully to the third note (shifting from left to right), you may notice that the sound is weaker at the center of the stereo field, and louder when it moves across the left (beginning) or the right (end) channel. That happens because the perceived sound level is proportional to the signal power which is itself proportional to the square of the amplitude.

There are several ways to solve this problem. Perhaps the most effective one was suggested by Charles Dodge, and consists in defining the gain factors for the two channels (i.e. *kstereo* and *1-kstereo*, in our orchestra) as the square roots of the stereo panning control signal.

Here's that solution:

```
; stereo panning with control signal square root

        instr   1
kstereo linseg  0, p3/2, 1, p3/2, 0
ast     oscili  p4, p5, 1
kleft   =       sqrt(1-kstereo)         ; square root of 1-kstereo
kright  =       sqrt(kstereo)           ; square root of kstereo
        outs    ast*kleft, ast*kright
        endin
```

Besides *outs*, two more opcodes exist for modifying stereo output, *outs1* and *outs2*. The former sends the signal to the left channel only, the latter to the right channel only.

For quadraphonic sound, the opcode is *outq*, but we can also use *outq1*, *outq2*, *outq3*, and *outq4* to determine the four outputs separately. (Clearly, a quadraphonic sound card is needed to listen to quad sound output).

Let's summarize the syntax of the Csound output signal opcodes

```
out     asig                        ; one output channel (mono output)
outs    asig1, asig2                ; left channel, right channel (stereo output)
outs1   asig                        ; left channel only
outs2   asig                        ; right channel only
outq    asig1, asig2, asig3, asig4  ; 1st chan., 2nd chan., 3rd chan., 4th chan.,
                                    ; (quad output)
outq1   asig                        ; 1st channel only
outq2   asig                        ; 2nd channel only
outq3   asig                        ; 3rd channel only
outq4   asig                        ; 4th channel only
```

5.2 STEREO CONTROL SIGNALS

Observe in the orchestra example above that the speed of stereo motion depends on the note duration. The two line segments determine the control variable *kstereo* and both have a duration of p3/2, so that a shorter duration would result in a higher panning speed. There is a way to control the speed independently of duration. To do so, we use an oscillator to generate the control variable. This oscillator doesnít produce audio signals, but simply a series of values from 0 to 1 and back to 0, at a specified speed. These values are multiplied by an audio variable. We do not use *linseg* (as we did in the last orchestra example), but *oscili* to generate either a sine wave or some other waveform, (e.g. a triangle waveform), with instant amplitude bound by the range [0, 1].

Further explanation is needed, however. Suppose that function #1 is a sine wave, and that the required amplitude is 10000:

```
k1      oscili      10000, 440, 1
```

This creates a sine wave with a period that repeats 440 times per second, and an instantaneous amplitude that oscillates between -10000 and 10000. If we write

```
k1      oscili      .5, 2, 1
```

the wave completes 2 periods per second, and has an instantaneous amplitude that oscillates between -.5 and .5. However, if this signal *k1* is to guide sound movement in the stereo field, it must oscillate between 0 to 1. For this reason, we add a DC offset (see section 2.7) of .5 to it. So it oscillates within the proper range [-.5+.5=0, .5+.5=1].

```
;stereo movement with oscil

          instr     1
k1        oscili    .5, 2, 1
kstereo   =         k1+.5
asound    oscili    10000, 220, 2
          outs      asound*kstereo, asound*(1-kstereo)
          endin
```

An oscillator with such low a frequency (2 Hz) will produce no audible sounds! But this is correctly used here, as its purpose is not to generate any sound, but to control some other signal. The rate at which the control values are generated is now dependent on the oscillator frequency. Had we used a 1 Hz oscillator, the sound would have moved from left to right and back at a rate of once per second. Had we required a 220 Hz, the stereo movement would be too fast to perceive, as well as, create unwanted side-effects, because the frequency (220 Hz) is in the audible range.

5.3 VIBRATO CONTROL SIGNALS

When looking at a violinist's left hand while playing a vibrato note, we notice the finger's swinging on the fingerboard. The wider the swing, the deeper the pitch deviation. The action may be slow or fast. The vibrato speed depends on the frequency of the swinging motion of the finger, moving from some higher-pitch position to some lower one. The vibrato depth depends on how wide the finger swing is. Now, imagine that our violinist acts as a control oscillator

```
;vibrato.orc
        sr     =  44100
        kr     =  4410
        ksmps  =  10
        nchnls =  1
        instr     1
k1      oscili    2, 3, 1              ;control oscillator, amplitude peak=deviation peak,
                                       ;frequency=vibrato speed
asound  oscili    10000, 220+k1, 1     ;audio variable
        out       asound
        endin
```

```
;vibrato.sco
f1    0   4096    10  1
i1    0   3
```

In this example, the violinist plays a 3 seconds note having a pitch of 220 Hz. The pitch oscillates with the movement of the finger. As we said, the wider the finger swings on the fingerboard, the more the pitch deviates. Observe the arguments to the control oscillator (henceforth called the "modulator"). Notice that its amplitude is 2 which means that it generates values between -2 and 2. Note the arguments to the audio oscillator (henceforth called the "carrier" oscillator). The output from the modulator, *k1*, is added to the carrier's frequency value. The frequency will oscillate between 218 and 222 Hz. At what rate? At a rate proportional to the number of cycles per second in the modulator (the speed of the violinist's finger). In this particular case, we set the modulator to 3 Hz, such that the pitch deviation pattern (220 / 222 / 220 / 218 / 220 Hz) is repeated 3 times per second.

In fig.5-1 a flow-chart is shown with two oscillators connected in such a way as to create the vibrato effect just described. *amp* is the overall amplitude (e.g. 10000), *freq* is the carrier frequency (e.g. 220 Hz), *vib depth* is the amplitude of the modulator (e.g. 2), and *vib freq* is the modulator frequency (e.g. 3 Hz).

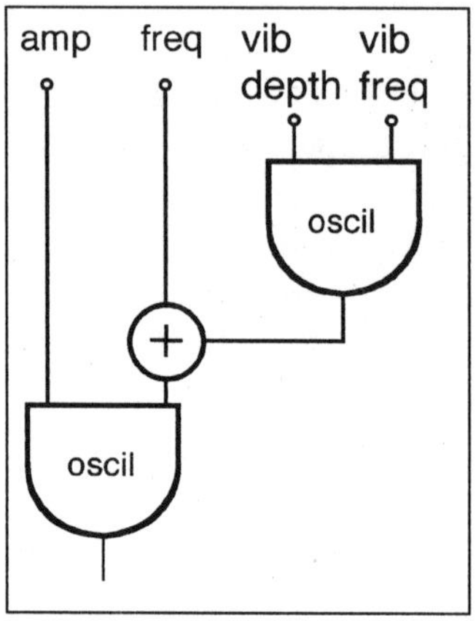

Fig. 5-1

We may think this is a good method for adding a vibrato effect to any note. Alas, this is not so! In music, vibrato is not an *absolute* frequency fluctuation, but is a shift *relative* to the base frequency. We can measure it in terms of *percentages* of the base frequency value. A 2 Hz vibrato applied to a 880 Hz note causes a more subtle result as compared to the vibrato effect in the preceding example. A 2 Hz vibrato applied to a base frequency of 220 Hz corresponds to approximately a 0.9 % deviation. When applied to a base frequency of 880 Hz, it corresponds to a 0.23 % deviation. The following orchestra is more consistent with our actual perception of vibrato sounds:

```
;vibrato1.orc
       sr     =  44100
       kr     =  4410
       ksmps  =  10
       nchnls =  1
       instr     1
k1     oscili    .009, 3, 1            ;control oscillator, amplitude peak=deviation peak in %,
                                       ;frequency=vibrato speed
asound oscili    10000, p4*(1+k1), 1   ;audio variable
       out       asound
       endin
```

```
;vibrato1.sco
f1   0     4096   10    1
i1   0     3      220
i1   3.1   3      440
i1   6.2   3      880
```

Here the vibrato depth is expressed as a multiplier of the base frequency (0.009 determines a 0.9 % deviation). The base frequency is multiplied by 1+*k1* so that the control signal causes a deviation of 0.9 % for all possible base frequencies. This consistent effect is achieved independently of the particular base frequency.

5.4 TREMOLO CONTROL SIGNALS

To create a tremolo effect, we modulate the amplitude (not the frequency) of the carrier oscillator.

Observe the example illustrated below: the control variable *k2* (values ranging from 0.8 to 1.2) multiplies the amplitude value *iamp*, which results in small amplitude deviations in fact perceived as a tremolo. This tremolo completes a full cycle in half a second, when the modulator frequency is set to 2 Hz.

```
;tremolo.orc
        instr   1
ifrq    =       220
iamp    =       10000
k1      oscil   .2, 2, 1                ; control oscillator (modulator)
k2      =       k1+1                    ; oscillates between 1+.2=1.2 and 1-.2 = .8
a1      oscili  iamp*k2, ifrq, 1        ;carrier with tremolo
        out     a1
        endin
```

EXERCISE *: create an instrument similar to the one above (tremolo.orc), but with an amplitude envelope for the tremolo (this is illustrated in fig. 5-2). The notes begin with no tremolo, then the tremolo width gradually reaches its maximum width at half the note duration, and finally the note ends with no tremolo.*

Here's the solution:

```
        instr   1
ifrq    =       cpspch(p5)
```

```
iamp        =        10000
k1          oscil    .2, 2, 1                  ; control oscillator (modulator)
kenvtrem    linseg   0, p3/2, 1, p3/2, 0
k2          =        k1*kenvtrem+1
a1          oscili   iamp*k2, ifrq, 2
            out      a1
            endin
```

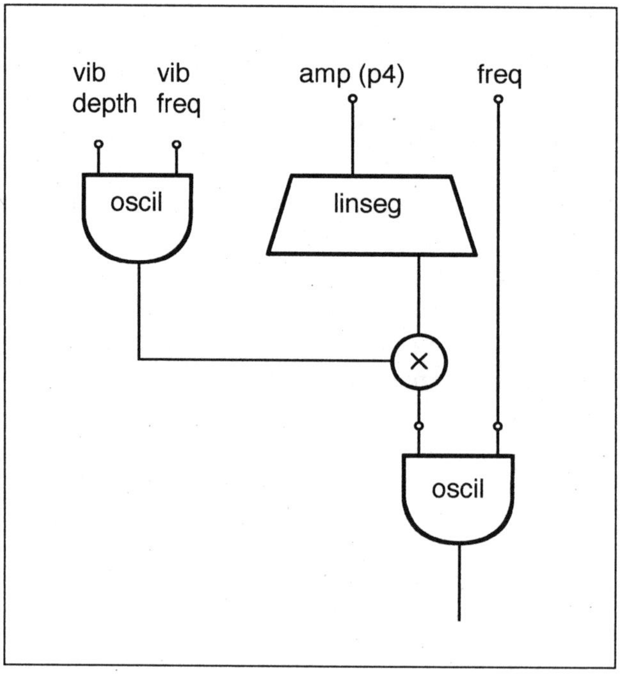

Fig. 5-2

5.5 FILTER CONTROL SIGNALS

It is also possible to use control signals to drive some filter parameters, thus affecting the timbre of a sound. To achieve a kind of dynamic filtering (e.g. the well-known wah-wah effect), we can use a control oscillator to drive the filter frequency and/or its amplitude (i.e. the amount of variation in the filter parameters).

As an example, let's create some instrument (#1) which is to include a control signal *kfilt1*, oscillating between -1000 and +1000, and to this we add a constant value, 1100. The result is stored in *kfilt2*, and varies between 100 and 2100. Finally, this signal is used as the center frequency of a band-pass filter, *reson*.

```
;band-pass filter with center frequency controlled with an oscillator,
;input signal is generated with rand

        instr   1
a1      rand    10000
                                        ;control signal determining the filter center frequency
                                        ;has a frequency of .1 Hz, period = 10 secs
kfilt1  oscil   1000, .1, 1             ;kfilt1 oscillates between -1000 and 1000; add the constant 1100
                                        ; so that...
kfilt2  =       kfilt1 + 1100           ;...the result, kfilt2, oscillates between 100 e 2100
                                        ;(unipolar signal)
;               input sig.  center freq.  bandwidth
afilt   reson   a1,         kfilt2,       p4
out     afilt
        endin
```

Let's create another instrument (#2), which will include a control signal *kbw1* that varies between -200 and +200. We add to that a constant offset of 210 and get *kbw2*, a quantity that oscillates between 10 and 410. This quantity drives the bandwidth of *reson*.

```
;band-pass filter with bandwidth controlled with an oscillator,
;input signal is generated with rand

        instr   2
a1      rand    10000
                                        ;control signal determining the filter bandwidth
                                        ;has a frequency of .1 Hz, period = 10 secs
kbw1    oscil   200, .1, 1              ;kbw1 moves between -200 e 200; add to that the constant 210...
kbw2    =       kbw1 + 210              ; so that the result, kbw2, moves between 10 and 410

;               input sig.  center freq.  bandwidth
afilt   reson   a1,         500,          kbw2
        out afilt
        endin
```

It is possible to combine center frequency and bandwidth controls. Write such an instrument yourself, using two oscillators with separate controls over the two parameters.

5.6 ENVELOPE CONTROL SIGNALS

Using the *envlpx* opcode it is possible to create envelopes with onset curves of any complexity. The *envlpx* syntax is:

k1 envlpx kamp, irise, idur, idec, ifn, iatss, iatdec [, ixmod]

kamp amplitude
irise rise time in seconds. 0 or negative values signify no rise modification
idur envelope duration (usually = p3)
idec decay time in seconds. 0 means no decay modification. A value greater than *idur-irise* will cause the decay to be truncated.
ifn function table number of stored rise shape. This points to a table having an extended guard point, or a table whose size equals a-power-of 2-plus-1 (e.g. 1025, 4097, 8193, etc.). It is important that the last value in the table be 1, to avoid discontinuities after the attack transient.
iatss attenuation factor after *irise* seconds. A value of 1 will maintain a true steady state after at the last rise value. A value > 1 will cause an exponential growth, while a value < 1 will cause an exponential decay. The length of this envelope portion is directly proportional to *idur*, and, in fact, equal to *idur-idec-irise*. 0 is illegal.
iatdec attenuation factor for the decay. It must be positive, and normally must be in the order of .01. A larger value, or a too small one, generally causes an audible cutoff. 0 or negative values are illegal.
ixmod (optional) influences the "steepness" of the exponential curve determined by *iatss* (when the latter is other than 1). It is normally set to a value in the range [-.9, +.9]. Negative values will cause an accelerated growth or decay. Positive values will cause a slower growth or decay.

Orchestra example using *envlpx*. Rise shape stored in function #2.

```
;envlpx.orc
        sr      = 44100
        kr      = 44100
        ksmps   = 1
        nchnls  = 1
        instr     1
ifrq    =         cpspch(p5)
iamp    =         ampdb(p4)
```

```
;ar     envlpx  kamp, irise, idur, idec, ifn, iatss, iatdec

k1      envlpx  iamp, .2,   p3,   .2,  2,   .5,   .01
a1      oscil   k1, ifrq, 1
        out     a1
        endin
```

A score for this new orchestra:

```
;envlpx.sco
;a table function with 5 harmonics (for use with oscil)
f1   0    4096   10   1   5    .3   .2  .1
;
;attack function table (for use with envlpx), brass-like,
;notice table size is 4097, and the last value is 1
f2   0    4097    7    0    2102   .873    856    .426    1139   1
i1   0   4    80     8
```

In order to create envelope curves, we can also use the *oscil1* opcode. It works just like any other oscillator, except that it generates one only cycle of the waveform. It exists both as a regular and an interpolated oscillator. The syntax is:

k1 oscil1 idel, kamp, idur, ifn
k1 oscil1i idel, kamp, idur, ifn

idel delay in seconds before the oscillation starts. During this time, the output value equals the first amplitude value in the function table *ifn*.
kamp amplitude
idur duration in seconds, relative to one cycle of the waveform. 0 or negative values cause all initialitation to be skipped.
ifn function table number.

Let's now create a function table (#2) containing a signal properly utilizable as an envelope, such as a trapezoidal shape with the classic *attack-sustain-release* pattern. We will use that function table in the following orchestra:

```
;envosc.orc
        sr  =  44100
        kr  =  4410
```

```
        ksmps =   10
        nchnls =  1
        instr     1
iamp    =         p4
ifrq    =         p5
kenv    oscil1    0, iamp, p3, 2
a1      oscil     kenv, ifrq, 1
        out       a1
        endin
```

Let's generate function #2 with the GEN07 routine. This particular routine is discussed in section 14.3. Here, suffice it to say that GEN07 works a bit like *linseg*.

Here's a score for the new orchestra

```
;envosc.sco
f1   0  4096  10     1
f2   0  4096  7      0    512   1  2560  1  1024  0
i1   0  2     10000  500
```

It could be possible to use the rise envelope shape of a sampled sound. That, however, is an extraordinarily complicated task. First we should extract the envelope from some given sound file (using, for example, the *follow* opcode, see section 7.5), and save the attack portion to a new sound file. Of course, the new sound file must have the appropriate duration (a-power-of-two-plus-one) and have the final sample set at the maximum amplitude. Then we should copy the new file to some function table that can be utilized with *envlpx*. Good luck!

5.7 *RANDI, RANDH, PORT*

We may want to utilize random signals as control signals. Indeed, random signals are often of real help when trying to enrich the sound while avoiding the quite artificial quality of many electronically generated sounds. In such cases, we do not use *rand* (which will only add white noise) but one of its variants:

```
ksig  randh    kamp, kcps[, iseed]
ksig  randi    kamp, kcps[, iseed]
asig  randh    xamp, xcps[, iseed]
asig  randi    xamp, xcps[, iseed]
```

ksig and *asig* are pseudo-random sequences, with values in the range [*-xamp, + xamp*]. *iseed* is an optional initialization value for the random generator, and usually determines the very first output number in the pseudo-random sequence. For example, if *iseed* = .8 and *kamp* = 10000, then the first output number is .8*10000=8000. A negative value will cause the initialization to be skipped, so that a different random number will be produced as the first output value for each note. The default value is .5. *xamp* is the maximum output level.

randh generates pseudo-random numbers at a rate of *xcps* times per second. For example, writing

```
k1      randh   1,5
```

we get a new random number in the range [-1, +1] every 1/5 = 0.2 seconds.

randi is similar to *randh* but it introduces straight-line interpolation between successive numbers. The difference between *randi* and *randh* is illustrated graphically in fig.5-3.

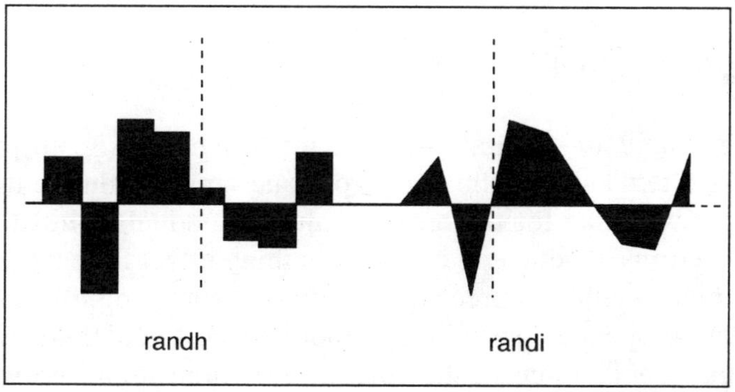

Fig. 5-3

Let's experiment with the following orchestra, where a vibrato control signal is generated with *randi*:

```
;randivbr.orc
        sr     =   44100
        kr     =   4410
        ksmps  =   10
        nchnls =   1
        instr      1
iamp    =          p4
```

```
ifrq      =        p5
kenv      linseg   0, p3/4, iamp, p3/2, iamp, p3/4, 0
kvibr     randi    p7, p6, -1
a1        oscili   kenv, ifrq*(1+kvibr), 1
          out      a1
          endin
```

Try this score:

```
;randivbr.sco
f1   0   4096   10      1
i1   0   3      10000   440   8   .01      ;vibrato depth...
i1   +   3      10000   440   8   .02      ;...gets wider...
i1   +   3      10000   440   8   .03      ;...and...
i1   +   3      10000   440   8   .04      ;...wider
```

Another useful opcode used to create control signals is *port*:

k1 port ksig, ihtim[, isig]

It applies a "portamento" to a step-valued input signal, *ksig*. In practice, the input signal is low-pass filtered so that the jump from one sample value to the next is smooth. *ihtim* is the time it will take for the present value to gradually shift to the new one. In other words, it determines the length of the smoothing effect for each input value. *isig* is some internal, initial value (it precedes the first input sample), similar to the *istor* argument of filtering opcodes (see Chap.3, footnote 1). The default value is 0. Fig.5-4 shows four separate applications of the *port* filter (bottom) to a step-valued signal (top) with increasing values of *ihtim*.

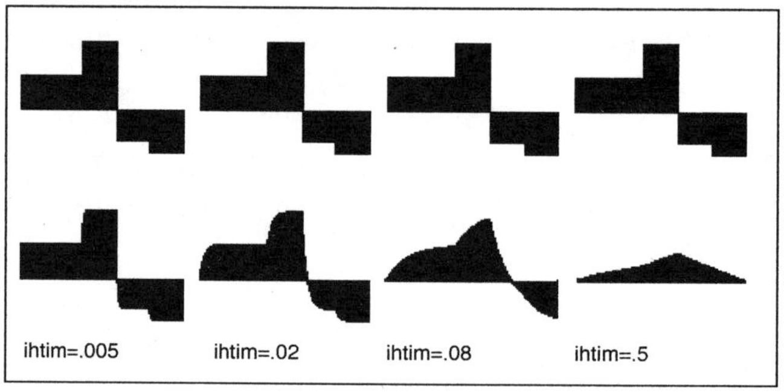

Fig. 5-4

5.8 3-D SOUND

Since the beginning of electronic music, sound spatialization has been of great interest to musicians. Actually it had been of interest earlier, to 16th-century composers like Adrian Willaert and, most notably, Andrea and Giovanni Gabrieli, who orchestrated many of their compositions for 2 choirs and 2 organs facing one another in the Basilica di S.Marco, in Venice.

In the 1950's, Karlheinz Stockhausen used five loudspeakers for the public performances of his tape piece *Gesang der Jünglinge* (four loudspeakers placed at the four angles of the hall, the fifth high above the audience). Such a loudspeaker configuration was not used afterwards, mainly because tape recorders with more than 4 tracks were not readily available. In 1958, Edgar Varèse's *Poeme Electronique* was played through 120 loudspeakers placed all around the shell-like structure of the *Philips Pavillon* (designed by Le Corbusier), at the Brussels Expo. Many analogous cases could be mentioned.

However, here we would like to focus on the simulation of spatial cues starting with two or four output channels.

Eli Breder and David McIntyre implemented a Csound opcode, *hrtfer*, specially devised for the simulation of 3-D sound field, which is effective when listening on headphones. The fundamental principle in this approach is to consider the *azimuth* (horizontal position) and the height or *elevation* (vertical position) of the sound relative to an artificial head (*hrtfer* is an acronym for *head-related transfer function*). The head model serves to precisely measure the frequency attenuations caused by the physical structure of the listener's head and the pinnae of the outer ear.

The model is effective only when listening on headphones because many cues in spatial field are masked by the resonances in the real environment (requiring more filters, reverb, etc.).

The term 3-D *audio* refers to systems capable of simulating the head distortions and the outer ear reflections using digital filters. The method allows us to position a mono sound source within a virtual space surrounding the listener. It takes into account the spectral modifications created by the head structure and the pinnae (depending on the spatial orientation of the source sound), and employs filter parameters based on experimental data representing each particular orientation. The data was originally gathered by measuring the sound response of an artificial head and its pinnae, while exposed to a very broad-band sound signal.

The most recent Csound versions include the *hrtfer* opcode:

aleft, aright hrtfer asig, kazim, kelev, "HRTFcompact"

asig is the input signal to be positioned in the virtual 3-D space

kazim is the azimuth value in degrees. Positive values indicate the spatial field on the right of the listener, negative values indicate the spatial field on the left.

kelev is the height in degrees. Positive values indicate the spatial field above the listener, negative values indicate the spatial field beneath.

"*HRTFcompact*" is a file containing experimental data included in the Csound library. This is the only file name that you should type in here.

aleft and *aright* are two output signals. Normally, it is good idea to scale them either with *balance* or simply multiply them by a constant.

Using this opcode, you have to set the orchestra sampling rate to 44100 Hz, as the "HRTFcompact" file is compiled based on that frequency.

Let's take a look at a concrete example:

```
;hrtf.orc
        sr      =   44100
        kr      =   4410
        ksmps   =   10
        nchnls  =   2
        instr       1
kazim   linseg      0, p3, -360                          ;sound moves around the listener...
kelev   linseg      -40, p3, 45                          ;...and increase in elevation
ain     soundin     "voice.wav"
al,ar   hrtfer      ain, kazim, kelev, "HRTFcompact"
alscl   =           al * 200
arscl   =           ar * 200
        outs        alscl, arscl
        endin

;hrtf.sco
i1      0   10
```

LIST OF OPCODES INTRODUCED IN THIS CHAPTER

```
        out     asig                        ; one output channel (mono output)
        outs    asig1, asig2                ; left channel, right channel (stereo output)
        outs1   asig                        ; left channel only
        outs2   asig                        ; right channel only
        outq    asig1, asig2, asig3, asig4  ; 1st chan., 2nd chan., 3rd chan., 4th chan. (quad output)
        outq1   asig                        ; 1st channel only
        outq2   asig                        ; 2nd channel only
        outq3   asig                        ; 3rd channel only
        outq4   asig                        ; 4th channel only

k1      envlpx  amplitude, rise_time, dur, dec_time, function_number, transition_from_rise_to_decay,
                attenuation_factor_for_decay [, steepness_of_transition_from_rise_to_decay]

k1      oscil1  initial_delay, amplitude, duration, function_number
k1      oscil1i initial_delay, amplitude, duration, function_number

k1      randh   amplitude, frequency [, seed_for_pseudorandom_generation]
k1      randi   amplitude, frequency [, seed_for_pseudorandom_generation]
a1      randh   amplitude, frequency [, seed_for_pseudorandom_generation]
a1      randi   amplitude, frequency [, seed_for_pseudorandom_generation]

k1      port    input_signal, transition_time_to_new_value[, init_value_for_internal_filter]

aleft, aright   hrtfer  input_signal, azimuth_value, height_value, "HRTFcompact" file
```

6

DIGITAL AUDIO

6.1 DIGITAL SOUND

Music played back from vinyl discs (LPs), open-reel tapes, cassette tapes, radio, and television, consists of electrical signals converted to sound by the loudspeakers. Such signals are "analog" signals, meaning that their voltage variations are proportional to the pressure variations in the represented sound signal.

Music played back from CDs, DATs, MiniDiscs, and computers, are comprised of "digital" signals, which represent the sound pressure variations by means of a sequence of binary digits, or information units (bits).

As is well-known, any sound is completely defined by its instant amplitude values. A digital device generates a sequence of numbers, each corresponding to a single instant amplitude.

In digital media (either based on mechanical technology, such as the CD player, or magnetic technology, such as the DAT recorder) signals are written and read as sequences of binary digits, 1 and 0. Correction mechanisms are usually applied during the playback process, to prevent moderate flaws and defects in the physical material (e.g. small scratches or dust on the CD surface) and even minute demagnetization (of the DAT tape) from causing serious problems. Digital copies are always perfectly identical to the original but analog copies, no matter how good, introduce signal degradation.

Finally, the signal-to-noise ratio in digital media is much better than analog media It is approximately 96 dB for CD and DAT (the two having more or less the same audio quality) while it is only 60 or 70 dB for analog tape recorders not using noise-reduction systems.

6.2 ANALOG-TO-DIGITAL AND DIGITAL-TO-ANALOG CONVERSION

Digital audio systems include special circuits capable of converting signals from analog to digital and from digital to analog. These are called A-D converters (ADC) and D-A converters (DAC).

Let's briefly examine the functionality of the A-D process. The process is to translate a series of electrical magnitudes into a sequence of numbers, so that each number in the sequence captures a particular voltage at a specific time. In fig.6-1, the continuous line is an analog signal, i.e. the unfolding in time of an electrical voltage. We divide the time-axis into equally-spaced, shorter segments and register the corresponding amplitude values from the analog signal. Each value, or "sample", remains unchanged until the next is registered. We obtain a step-valued signal which is a rough representation of the original.

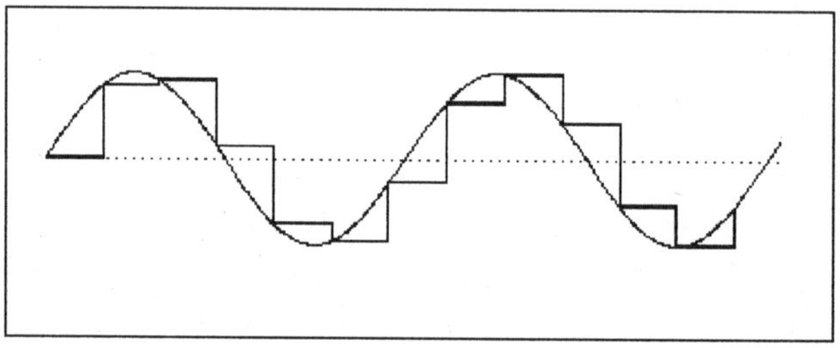

Fig. 6-1

Clearly, the smaller the time between successive samples the more accurate the representation. In theory, if we could divide the time-axis into infinitely small portions, the two signals would be identical.

The time between successive samples is called the *sampling time*. Its inverse, 1/*sampling time*, is the *sampling frequency*, or *sampling rate* (*sr*). To correctly perform an analog to digital conversion, the sampling frequency must be at least twice as high as the frequency of the highest component in the recorded signal. Thus, to convert a sound including components up to 20000 Hz, for example, we need a sampling rate of at least 40000 Hz. A lower sampling rate causes the phenomenon known as *foldover* where components with a frequency higher than half the sampling rate are folded back into the audible range.

With *sr* = 20000 Hz, an analog signal with a frequency of 11000 Hz would result, after the conversion process, in a frequency of 9000 Hz (see section 6.B.1).

Another crucial factor in the digital domain is the number of binary digits available to store the amplitude values after the conversion process itself. Of course, we are bound to a finite number of digits, typically 16 bits, that allows for the coding of integer numbers within the range [-32768, +32767], and corresponds to 65535 different amplitude values. With 7 bits we would be limited to as few as 127 different values, and a very poor audio quality (for details, see section 6.A.1). Indeed, 16-bit numerical resolution is a basic pre-requisite for high quality digital audio. Recently some proposals were put forth, for better audio quality: the DVD (Digital Versatile Disc) allows 5 audio channels with 24-bit resolution, and at sampling rates as high as 48 or even 96 kHz.

To conclude, we should notice that a digital signal converted to analog remains a step-valued signal, and its spectrum includes many replicas, or *alias* images, of the expected spectrum (fig.6-2).

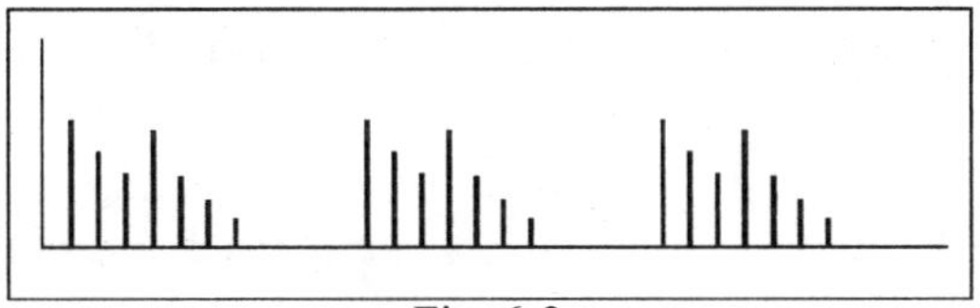

Fig. 6-2

This phenomenon is caused by harmonic distortion introduced by the discrete steps between any two successive samples. To avoid the audible artifacts of this phenomenon, D-A converters have a built-in analog filter to remove the alias spectra (*anti-aliasing* filter). This filter is a low-pass with cutoff frequency (*fc*) set to half the sampling rate

fc = sr / 2

The frequency response of anti-aliasing filters is far from ideal, and no such filter is capable of completely removing the unwanted frequencies. Even a sharp cutoff would be of little use, as it would cause new artifacts in the frequency response curve (such as a rippled response curve) and other side-effects (phase distortion). To get rid of this problem, today D-A converters work at much higher sampling rates (*oversampling*), of at least 4 times the nominal value, such that the aliased components are shifted far above the pass band of the anti-aliasing filter (fig. 6-3).

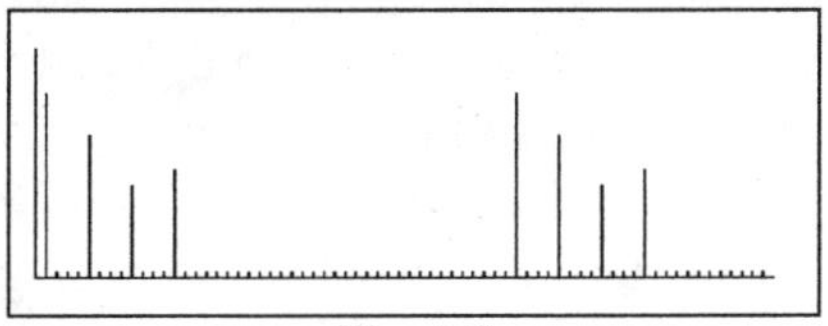

Fig. 6-3

6.3 SOUND CARDS AND AUDIO FILE FORMATS

Some computers have their own built-in sound recording and playback systems. That is the case with the Power Macintosh. Most PCs, instead, require that you install a separate sound card. Many models of sound cards are available on the market, each having its own technical features, performance benchmarks and price. Important for our purposes is the quality of the sound card's A-D and D-A converters and the available on-board connections to external devices. We are not interested in the synthesis methods implemented by the sound card's chip.

The best available sound cards have two basic elements: the interface card itself, which fits into the computer, and the signal conversion unit. Normally, a great deal of electrical noise is present inside the computer case due to the magnetic fields of the hardware circuits (these noise signals propagate at very high frequencies, in the order of hundreds of MHz). That makes it quite impossible to avoid noise when handling analog signals. Therefore, audio converters should be placed externally. Today, however, good sound cards can be found with on-board converters. Using sophisticated engineering approaches, designers are able to isolate the system from the electromagnetic pollution inside the computer.

Low-priced sound card manufacturers are not keen to declare the technical details of their D-A and A-D converters. The predominant use of such cards is in multimedia applications (such as video games) and seldom requires high standards. When comparing these products, the essential features to take into account include *harmonic distortion* (should be lower than 0.5 %) and *signal-to-noise ratio* (should be higher than 85 dB).

Digital i/o connections are widespread (DAT, ADAT, CD players equipped with digital output, MiniDisc, etc.). It makes sense, then, to install a sound card featuring digital i/o for exchanging digital signals between the computer and other devices. This way, we avoid the unnecessary conversions, from digital to analog (e.g. DAT output) and from analog to digital (e.g. sound card input). A pure digital copy guarantees no signal degradation, when the same communication protocol is utilized for coding and decoding the signal. Today two standard protocols are commonly accepted for stereo digital audio: AES/EBU and S/PDIF. The AES/EBU is mainly found in professional equipment, and requires tripolar Cannon-type (XLR) connectors. The S/PDIF (*Sony/Philips Digital Interface Format*) requires either coaxial (RCA plugs) or optical connectors.

Several audio file formats exist, depending on the hardware/software platform. All are based on the PCM (*Pulse Code Modulation*) principle, but differ on a number of details.

On Windows platforms, the standard sound file format is WAVE, which is an instance of the RIFF format (*Resource Interchange File Format*). WAVE files have a file header of at least 44 bits, which includes the file format id, sampling rate, number of channels, number of bits per sample, and length of the audio data chunk.

On Macintosh computers, the standard sound file format is AIFF (*Audio Interchange File Format*). Also, Macintosh computers support the SDII (Sound designer II) format.

Other computer manufacturers offer proprietary formats. As with the SUN Microsystems, and the IRCAM sound format, etc.

When necessary, we can convert sound files from one format to another using computer programs especially designed for the purpose. Many sound file editors, too, allow for loading and saving audio data in several formats.

6.4 SOME ANNOTATIONS ON DIGITAL AUDIO FOR MULTIMEDIA APPLICATIONS

Multimedia applications are becoming more and more important and interesting. There sound is an essential component, and several audio formats and standards have been developed specifically for multimedia applications. However, these formats usually do not meet professional audio requirements, when designed to fit a particular field of application. Consider, for example, the problem of mass memory storage. Storing audio data requires enormous memory banks. Indeed, with a sampling rate of 44100 Hz, a stereo signal of 1 second fills as many as

2 Bytes * 2 channels * 44100 samples per second = 176400 kBytes

10 MBytes are needed to store 1 minute of audio. To reduce such exorbitant memory costs, multimedia applications resort to audio data compression algorithms. Unfortunately, all such algorithms are *destructive*, as they omit some portions of the digital signal. The most promising compression format today is MPEG. With MPEG, one can choose among variable compression ratios, depending on the necessary signal quality.

Consider, however, that the audio components of any multimedia application are often far from professional. 8-bit resolution and 22050 Hz sampling rate are considered accepted standards. Furthermore, audio formats designed for multimedia are different from the professionally accepted formats. For example, the soundtrack of digital movies may be coded either in AVI format (*Audio Video Interleaved*), where chunks of audio data are interleaved with video frames, or in *Real Audio* format, which was introduced mainly for sound playback over the Internet.

Given that professional audio processing on computer music requires a tremendous data storage capacity, many efforts are being made today in order to find optimal data-compression methods. Unfortunately, methods called "non-destructive" (where the original data can precisely be re-constructed from the compressed data) are of little use for musical applications because the compression ratios are largely insufficient. Some "destructive" methods, though they do not allow for a perfect reconstruction of the original data, are more useful, at least in so far as they drop only data that is inaudible. In any case, these methods let the user determine the compression ratio. This led to the success of the MPEG format (Motion Picture Experts Group), which is available in four different versions (MPEG 1, 2, 3 and 4). MPEG offers significant compression ratios, in the order of 1/10 (compressed sound file is 10 time smaller than the original), while allowing for a limited loss of audio quality. For Internet applications, a well-known audio compression format is *Real Audio*.

EXTENSIONS

6.A.1 DIGITAL-TO-ANALOG AND ANALOG-TO-DIGITAL CONVERSION

Let's see what happens when we use different sampling rates to convert an analog signal to digital.

In fig. 6-A-1, we see the effect of sampling a signal at three different rates. From top to bottom, the sampling rate gets higher and, hence, the sampling time gets shorter. A shorter sampling time means smaller discrete steps in the digital signal. It is easy to see that with higher sampling rates the digital signal becomes more and more similar to the analog original.

Now, if we are to make sure that the digital is a correct representation of the analog, how high should the sampling rate be? And how large should the steps in the digital signal be? The Nyquist theorem states that we need a sampling frequency that is twice the highest frequency component in the analog signal.

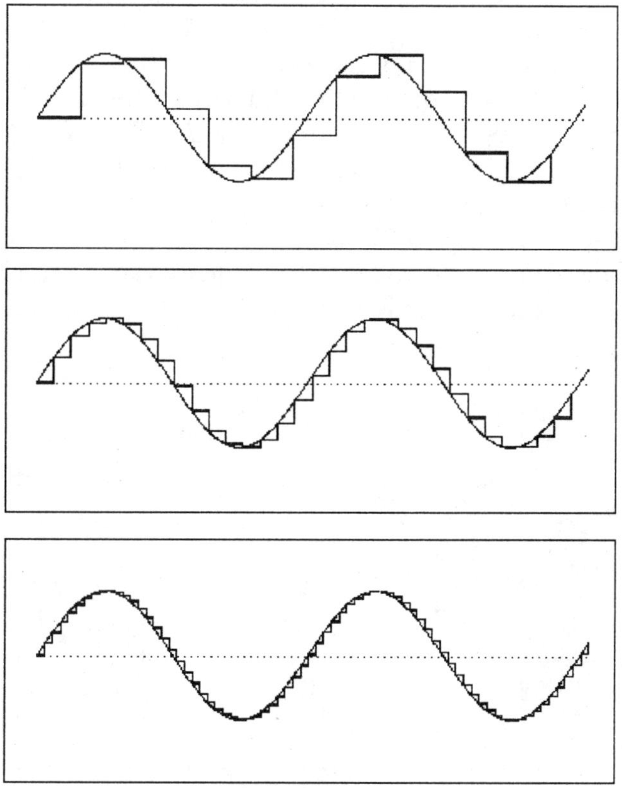

Fig. 6-A-1

Thus, if we call *fmax* the highest frequency to convert, the sampling rate must be:

sr >= 2*fmax

The term *Nyquist frequency* is half the sampling rate (*sr/2*). Given some sr, the Nyquist frequency is the highest reproducible frequency.

As the audible frequency range is less than 20000 Hz, any *sr* higher than 40000 Hz is acceptable. For reasons explained later, the actual sampling rate is a little higher than strictly necessary. The sampling rate of CD players, for example, is 44100 Hz, and that of DAT recorders/players is 48000 Hz.

Analog-to-digital conversion is the process of translating a variable voltage into a numerical signal, such that the latter represents the voltage values at equally spaced time intervals in the signal. The number of floating points utilized for every single voltage value affects the *dynamic range* and the *signal-to-noise ratio*. The dynamic range is defined as the ratio between the maximum and the minimum representable amplitude values. The signal-to-noise ratio is the ratio between the maximum amplitude value and the level of the background noise (either digital or analog noise). The number of digits also affects the precise representation of the analog signal's shape.

As it is not possible to work with an infinite number of binary digits, the numerical *precision* in the conversion process is always *limited.* This causes *quantization*, and results in a loss of information in the digital signal. A digital signal is not a continuous curve, but a curve made of successive discrete steps, or information *quanta* (with 16 bits, there are 32767*2+1=65535 quantized values).

Clearly, a smaller number of bits causes a larger quantization error as in the example in fig.6-A-2. To clarify, these amplitude values are within a rather small range, [-5,+5].

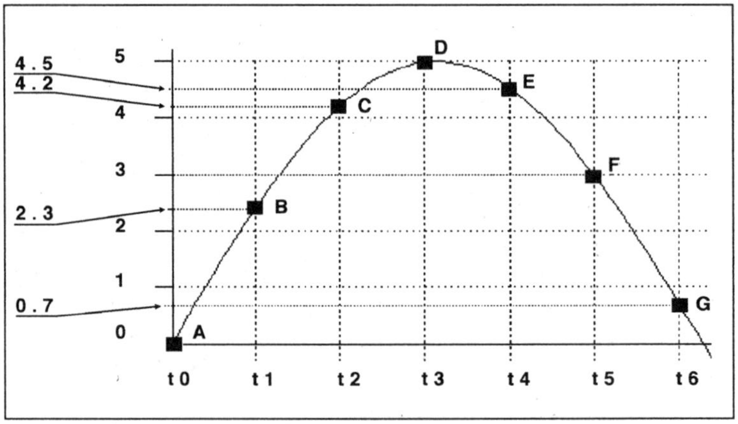

Fig. 6-A-2

The analog signal to convert is half a sine wave period with a peak amplitude of 5, and the sampled values from the signal are represented by capital letters (A through G).

The first voltage value, A, is zero and its digital representation poses no problem. The second value, B, is 2.3. The digital sample is truncated to 2 (the integer number closest to the actual voltage) and the resolution is poor. That introduces a quantization error of 15 %. The following chart lists the true voltage values, the resulting sampled values and the corresponding quantization error (in percentage and absolute terms) for the overall process illustrated in fig. 6-A-2.

Sample	true value	quantized value	error (%)	error (abs)
A	0.0	0	0	0.0
B	2.3	2	15	0.3
C	4.2	4	10	0.2
D	5.0	5	0	0.0
E	4.5	4	11	0.5
F	3.0	3	0	0.0
G	0.7	1	30	0.3

Now, to what extent is the quality of the sound is really affected by quantization errors? To answer this question, consider that by using just one more bit of numerical precision, we actually double the range of representable voltage values. In other words, we get a dynamic range which is 6 dB greater (remember the dynamic range is the actual distance between the minimum to the maximum representable amplitude values).

A 16-bit digital signal, then, has a dynamic range of

16 * 6 dB = 96 dB

which is a greater dynamic range than is available with any analog tape recorder, even a professional machine. The next chart illustrates the dynamic range possible with higher numerical precision:

bits	8	12	16	18	20	24
dB	48	72	96	108	120	144

With 16 bits (today a standard accepted in professional audio, computer music, CD and DAT manufacturing) the maximum quantization error amounts to half-a-bit-against-16-bits, which is equivalent to

$$\mathbf{(1/2) / 2^{16} = 0.5 / 65536 = 0.0008\ \%}$$

That is a negligible quantity by professional standards.

The digital-to-analog process poses no particular theoretical problem. It is sufficient to check that the sampling rate is appropriate, given the highest frequency component present in the analog signal. Notice too, that the available bits per sample have to be converted at simultaneously.

6.B.1 FOLDOVER

What happens if the analog signal includes some frequency higher than the Nyquist frequency? In fig.6-B-1 we see an analog, sine wave signal (dotted line) and the effect of three different sampling rates on the digital conversion (continuous lines).

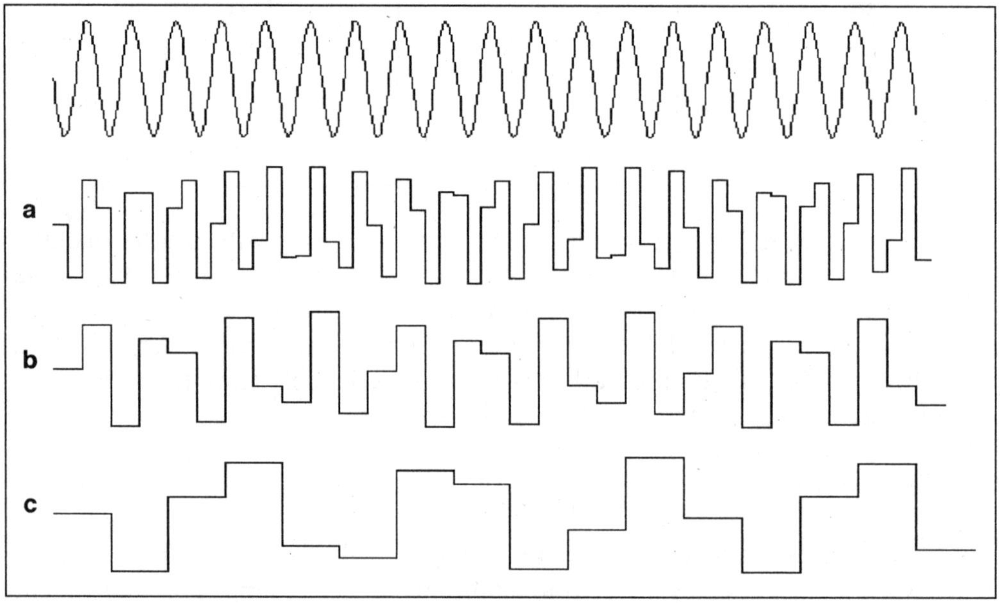

Fig. 6-B-1

In the first example (a) the frequency of the analog signal is lower than the Nyquist frequency ($(sr/2)/fmax = 8$), so the conversion is effective. In the second example (b) the frequency of the analog signal is as high as the Nyquist frequency itself ($sr/2=fmax$), so there, too, the conversion is effective. In the third example (c), however, the frequency is higher than the Nyquist frequency ($(sr/2)/fmax = .75$). Notice that the digital signal has a period three times as long as that of the analog signal. In other words, the digital signal has a frequency three times lower than the analog signal. This phenomenon is known as *foldover*. Intuitively, we observe that the sampling process takes place at a lower rate than twice per period, so that the sequence of samples cannot correctly reproduce the original frequency. Thus it happens that components higher than the Nyquist frequency are folded over the Nyquist frequency itself, and appear as frequencies lower than their true frequency in the analog domain.

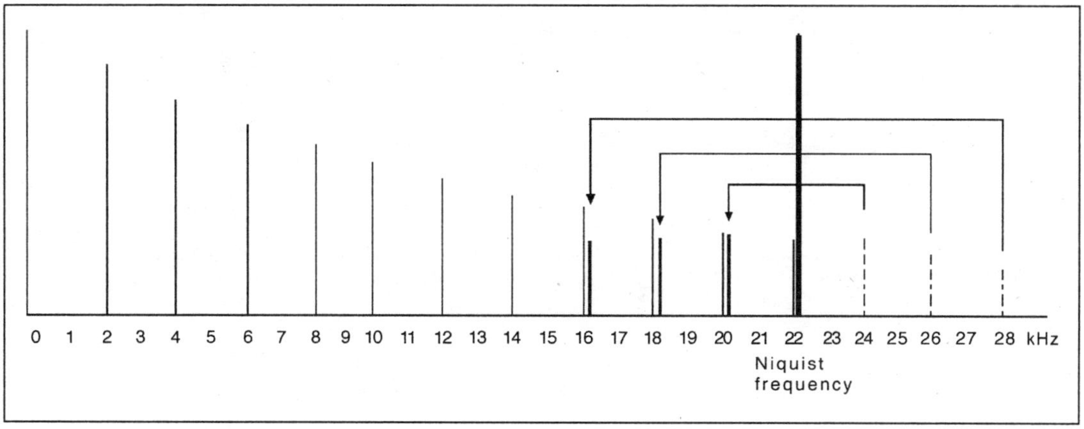

Fig. 6-B-2

Clearly, the above observations apply not only for sine wave analog signals, as they in fact apply for any component of any complex analog signal that we want to convert to digital. Fig.6-B-2 shows the foldover phenomenon in an improper A-D conversion of some periodic sound with a fundamental of 2000 Hz. Straight vertical lines are the frequency components in the digital signal, while dotted lines are the frequency components of the analog signal which are higher than the Nyquist frequency (here *sr/2* = 22050 Hz). These are folded back over the Nyquist frequency (bold lines) and are audible together with the correctly sampled components.

Depending on the sampling rate available on your sound card, you must always make sure that the analog sounds you want to convert to digital do not include frequencies higher than *sr/2*. If they do, you should low-pass filter them to remove the higher components.

7

SAMPLING AND PROCESSING

7.1 THE *SOUNDIN* AND *DISKIN* OPCODES

In Csound we can play back sampled sounds by using the *soundin* opcode. It provides no processing possibilities, but, on the other hand, it is fairly simple to use.

Basically, it is an audio signal generator whose output samples are taken directly off a pre-existing sound file. This requires no function table, as the generated waveform is that of the played back sound file itself. Also, it requires no frequency and amplitude arguments, as Csound uses the sound file default playback.

The syntax is the same for mono, stereo and quad output signals:

audio variable	opcode	filename	initial time to skip	sound file format	comment
a1	**soundin**	**ifilcod**	**[, iskptim]**	**[, iformat]**	**; mono**
a1, a2	**soundin**	**ifilcod**	**[, iskptim]**	**[, iformat]**	**; stereo**
a1,..., a4	**soundin**	**ifilcod**	**[, iskptim]**	**[, iformat]**	**; quad**

As you see, only the first argument is required, and its meaning is self-evident. It is the name of the sound file that we want to play back.

For example, we may write:

```
a1      soundin "cork.wav"           ;the filename must be within double quotes
```

Csound looks for the required sound file in the current directory first, then in the SSDIR and finally in the SFDIR directory (if specified in the Csound system preferences). You can also specify the entire path for the sound file:

```
a1      soundin "c:/corks/cork.wav"    ;path and filename within double quotes
```

Notice that, starting with the Windows 3.50 Csound release, to write pathnames you should use a regular slash ("/"), not the back-slash ("\"). The latter is now used as a line continuation symbol - very useful when you type in very long lines of Csound code. For example, the following line:

```
f1  0  4096  10  1  2  3  4  5  6  7  8  9  10
```

can be written as:

```
f1  0  4096  10  1  2  3  \
4  5  6  7  8  9  10
```

To reference the sound file, we can also call it with the special name "soundin" plus the number of the particular extension. For example: *soundin.1*. That implies that the file to be read had been previously saved to hard disk with that particular name and extension:

```
a1      soundin.1             ; in such case quotes are omitted
```

Let's now consider the *skiptime* argument (optional). Suppose the file we want to play contains the sound of a voice speaking the word "beetle". If we want to play back the entire file, we do not need to specify anything, as the *skiptime* default value is 0 (Csound reads the file through, starting from the beginning). However, if we want to play only the final portion of the word, "tle", omitting the "bee", the file being read will have to start at some point other than the beginning, say at 0.1 seconds.
Then we write:

```
a1      soundin "beetle.wav", .1        ; generates "tle", omitting the "bee"
```

The third argument, *iformat*, can often be dropped. It is necessary only when the sound file was created with some non-standard format lacking a readable header.

A Csound instrument can feature as many *soundin* opcodes as desired, limited only by the operating system setup options and by the particular Csound release being used. Within an instrument, *soundin* opcodes can refer either to a single sound file or to several sound files. When many *soundin* opcodes refer to the same sound file, they can have either the same or a different *skiptime.*

Be aware that the *soundin* opcode cannot be re-initialized (this is explained in section 17.3).

EXERCISE 1 *Create a new instrument with a sound file submitted to some filtering.*

EXERCISE 2*: Create a new instrument playing back a sound file. The soundin skiptime values are assigned from the score (p4), such that the file is read starting from a different point at each note. After that, try notes with durations shorter than the actual sound file duration such that the playback is interrupted at some random point before the end of sound file is reached.*

diskin is similar to *soundin*, but it also allows changes in the playback speed and direction, and for creating simple sound loops. The syntax is as follows:

a1[,a2[,a3,a4]] diskin ifilcod, kpitch[,iskiptim][, iwraparound] [,iformat]

ifilcod	name of the sound file; works just as in *soundin*.
kpitch	ratio between the output frequency and the sound file original frequency.

e.g.:

kpitch = 1	the sound file is read through and played back with no modification;
kpitch = 2	double playback speed, resultant pitch is one octave higher;
kpitch = .5	half the normal speed, resultant pitch is one octave lower;
kpitch = 3	three times the normal speed, an octave-plus-a-fifth (= a 12th) higher

See the ratio-to-interval chart in the appendix to Chap.8. If *kpitch* is negative, the sound file is played in the reverse direction, from end to beginning.
For example:

kpitch = -2	double speed (one octave higher), from the last to the first sample (reverse playback).

iskiptim	(optional) *skiptime*; works just as with *soundin*.

iwraparound	(optional) useful for implementing a sound loop. It must be 1 (= on) or 0 (= off). When on, if note duration is longer than the sound file duration, playback returns to the beginning everytime the end of sound file is reached (the reverse is true when *kpitch* is negative).
iformat	(optional) works as with *soundin*.

Like *soundin*, *diskin* cannot be re-initialized (see 17.3).

7.2 COPYING SOUND FILES TO FUNCTION TABLES (GEN01)

The GEN01 function generating routine transfers a sound file to a function table. The transfer allows you, then, to submit the sound file waveform to operations which would be impossible to perform using *soundin*. The sound file waveform becomes a general model that can be utilized in several different ways. In the simplest instance, we may want to change its frequency.

function no.	action time	table size	GEN type	filename	skiptime	file format	channel
f #	**time**	**(size)**	**(1)**	**(filcod)**	**(skiptime)**	**(format)**	**(channel)**

With AIFF or WAVE files, setting *table size* to 0 automatically causes the *table size* to be the same as the file length, so we do not need to do any calculations. The *filename* has to be put in double quotes. *skiptime* works the same as *soundin* and *diskin*.

The *format* argument may be set to 0, causing the format to be determined by the sound file header.

The *channel* argument may be set to 0 as well, causing all channels to be transferred from the sound file to the table.

The transfer terminates when the end of the sound file is reached, or (if *table size* is smaller than the sound file length) when all table locations are filled in. If *table size* is larger than the sound file length, the remaining locations are filled with zeroes. Notice that when *table size* is 0 (*deferred allocation*), the table can only be accessed by the *loscil* opcode (see next section).

If the GEN type number is negative (-1) the sound file waveform will not be scaled during the transfer. If it is positive (1), the waveform is scaled to the normal amplitude range [-1,+1] (*post-normalization*). In the former case (no scaling), you should use appropriate scaling factors to control the signal amplitude, either to boost it (greater than 1) or to attenuate it (smaller than 1). In the latter case (scaling, post-normalization) you can set any applicable absolute amplitude value, as usual.

Examples:

```
f   1   0   0   -1  "beetle.wav"    0   0   0
```

the above copies the "beetle.wav" sound file to function table #1. Deferred allocation is required. No scaling is applied.

```
f   2   0   16384 1    14 1   0   0
```

Here the "soundin.14" file is copied to function table #2, for which 16384 memory locations are allocated. The first second of sound in the sound file is skipped (*skiptime* = 1). Notice that in order to reference the filename "soundin.14", only the extension number is specified, without quotes (see section 7.1).

Special attention must be paid when we use *oscil* to read a function table generated with GEN01. Normally, a function table utilized with *oscil* represents one cycle of the waveform, while any sound imported with GEN01 is likely to have many cycles. If some table #1 contains 300 cycles of a flute sound, we have to divide the oscil frequency by 300 to get the duration of a single cycle.

*TIPS & TRICKS: to calculate how many cycles are in a sound stored as a mono WAVE file, a typical formula is: cycles = (file length in bytes - 44) / sr * sound frequency / 2.*

7.3 READING A SOUND FILE TABLE WITH *LOSCIL*

The *loscil* opcode (mono or stereo) reads function tables created with GEN01. It offers signal processing possibilities similar to those available with commercial "samplers". We can modify the amplitude, the frequency and the loop points in the sampled sound (the start and end loop points identify a shorter portion of the sound to loop and read). Different from *loscil*, no "sampler" would allow you to dynamically modify those parameters and exert precise and independent controls over each of them. We may use *loscil* to drive the pitch of a sampled sound (glissando) while, at the same time, radically change its amplitude envelope (and maybe sending the result to some band-pass filter, etc.).

The syntax for *loscil* is as follows:

ar1 [,ar2] loscil xamp, kcps, ifn , ibas [, imod1, ibeg1, iend1] [,imod2, ibeg2, iend2]

ar1[, ar2] output variable(s) (1 variable for mono input files, 2 variable for stereo input files)

xamp amplitude

kcps	required frequency
ifn	function table number where the recorded sound file is copied; it is good idea to use amplitude normalized tables
ibase	base frequency in Hz of the recorded sound (see below)
imod1	play mode for the sustain loop; 0 = no looping; 1 = normal looping; 2 = forward-backward looping
ibeg1	start point for the sustain loop, in samples
iend1	end point for the sustain loop, in samples
imod2	play mode for the release loop; 0 = no looping; 1 = normal looping; 2 = forward-backward looping
ibeg2	start point for the release loop, in samples
iend2	end point for the release loop, in samples

With *loscil* you are expected to enter a special argument, beside the one or more output variables and the most common arguments (amplitude level, frequency, function table), that is the "base frequency". More special arguments include the optional loop values.

Let's see what is the use of these arguments, starting with *ibas*.

Usually, the sound we copy into the function table has a particular, recognizable fundamental frequency (there are many computer programs that allow you to analyze any sound and precisely determine the fundamental). If you enter that frequency value into the *ibase* argument of *loscil*, that will "tune" the pitch of the Csound output with the original pitch. For example, suppose you enter a particular *ibase* value. When you require an output sound of 440 Hz, Csound will calculate the ratio between the latter value and the original base frequency, and will then play back the sample at the required pitch (440 Hz, i.e. A above middle-C). When using AIFF files, the *ibas* argument is optional, as their header already includes the base frequency. Therefore, you may omit the *ibase* value, as it will be read from the AIFF header. However, you can still type in a different *ibase* value, in which case Csound will skip the built-in base frequency.

Let's see an example, illustrating a typical mistake when using *loscil*. Suppose we have just copied a trumpet tone, 220 Hz (A below middle-C), into some table function #1. And suppose we want to play back that tone, at pitches C, D, E. Here's the appropriate score:

```
i1  0  1  80  8
i1  +  1  80  8.02
i1  +  1  80  8.04
```

If we provide *loscil* with a value *ibase* equivalent to G (above middle-C, 392 Hz), i.e.

```
a1      loscil   iamp, ifrq, 1, 392
```

then Csound will play B-C-D, which is not what we wanted it to do. Why is that? Csound "tuned" the trumpet sound file to the pitch we had specified, and calculated the ratio between the output pitch and the specified fundamental. Clearly, as the latter was not correct, Csound can only play unexpected notes.

We suggest you check the base frequency of AIFF files, too, as the base frequency in the header is not always equivalent to the pitch we hear, especially if the sound spectrum includes inharmonic components. The best way to determine the base frequency (and, by all means, the best way to work with sounds) is by maintaining a **close interaction between our auditory perception and more objective knowledge data**.

Now, about loops... What's the use of *sustain loops* and *release loops*? Sustain loops make it possible to prolong the steady-state, or sustain, of the sound by looping a short chunk of sound in the steady-state portion. We can set the beginning and end points of the loop by specifying the value in arguments *ibeg1* and *iend1*. The release loop makes it possible to elongate the release transient of the sound, i.e. the portion of the sound that decays to zero after the end of the note (see section 7.4).

Let's go back to our "beetle.wav" file. Suppose it has a duration of 1 second, and suppose it was sampled at 44100 Hz. Which means that the entire file contains 44100 audio samples. Suppose we actually need a longer note duration, say 5 seconds. Normally, Csound would play back the word "beetle" and then return all zeroes until the end of the note. But we may want to create a loop to repeat the word many times over the note duration:

```
abeetleloop     loscil   10000, 150, 1, 150, 1, 0, 44100
```

The above reads out samples stored in function #1, with an amplitude value of 10000 and a frequency of 150 Hz. The base frequency, too, is 150 Hz. The required loop covers the full duration of the sampled sound (0 - 44100). The loop mode (*imode*) is 1 (sustain loop). What we hear is something like

```
1    2    3    4    5    seconds
beetlebeetlebeetlebeetlebeetle
```

as in fact the sampled sound repeats 4 times after the first read.

Now, imagine that we want to loop only the final segment in the sound ("tle"), lasting 0.5 seconds. The loop we have to determine, then, starts at the 22051st audio sample and ends at the 44100th:

```
abeetleloop     loscil  10000, 150,    1,  150,    1,  22051, 44100
```

What we hear is

```
0    1    2    3    4    5    seconds
beetletletletletletletletletleltetletletle
```

as the 2nd syllable portion of the sampled sound repeats over and over until the note stops.

Any point in a sampled sound can be selected as *istart* and *iend*. To determine the precise position within the sound, we can load the sampled sound to a sound file editor and browse through its waveform looking for the appropriate points.

We may want to utilize loop mode (*imode*) 2:

```
abeetleloop loscil      10000, 150, 1, 150, 2, 22051, 44100
```

The result is:

```
0    1    2    3    4    5    seconds
beetleelttleelttleelttleelttleelttleelttle
```

The looped portion is read in forward and reverse direction alternately until the note stops. Loop mode 2 is also useful for delaying the release until *after* the note has stopped. This is explained in next section.

7.4 RELEASE LOOP WITH *LINENR*

The *linenr* opcode detects the nominal end of a note and extends its duration to the final release time.[1] The syntax is:

k1 linenr kamp, irise, idec, iatdec
a1 linenr xamp, irise, idec, iatdec

irise	rise time
idec	decay time
iatdec	bias amplitude values for *idec*, usually in the order of 0.1 (zero or negative values are illegal).

[1] In most Csound versions, *linenr* works for notes activated by some external MIDI event, either coming from a MIDI file or a MIDI controller device.

linenr is unique because it involves "note-off" sensing and a release time extension. If some instrument includes two or more such opcodes, time extension will automatically conform to the largest *idec* value featured.

Let's experiment linenr with the following example:

```
;linenr.orc
        sr     =  44100
        kr     =  4410
        ksmps  =  10
        nchnls =  1
        instr     1
ifrq           =  cpspch(p5)
iamp           =  ampdb(p4)
kenv    linenr    iamp, 0, 2, .01       ; upon sensing of "note-off", duration is extended
                                        ; by 2 seconds
aout    oscil     kenv, ifrq, 1
        out       aout
        endin
```

```
;linenr.sco
f1   0    4096   10    1
i1   0    1      80    8
i1   +    .  .         8.02
i1   +    .  .         8.04
i1   +    .  .         8.05
i1   +    .  .         8.07
```

Compile orchestra and score above in Csound. Listen and notice that some notes overlap even though no overlap is indicated in the score.

Now, let's go back to the example illustrated in the preceding section and introduce both a sustain and a release loop:

```
kenv         linenr  10000, .001, .5, .01
abeetleloop  loscil  kenv,   150, 1, 150, 1, 22050, 30000, 1, 30000, 44100
```

We added the last three arguments which are required for the release loop (1, 3000, 40000), and makes the note fade away in half a second after the "note-off".

7.5 THE *FOLLOW* OPCODE

With *follow*, we extract the amplitude envelope from an external sound file. The extracted envelope then can be applied to another signal.

The syntax is:

asig follow ain, idt

ain input signal
idt duration of each next chunk in the input signal whose amplitude gets measured
asig output signal, containing the envelope values extracted from *ain.*

In the example below, we extract the envelope from a given sound file ("voice.wav") to drive the amplitude of an oscillator:

```
;follow.orc
        sr     =  44100
        kr     =  4410
        ksmps  =  10
        nchnls =  1

        instr     1
ifrq    =         cpspch(p5)
ain     soundin   "voice.wav"         ;input sound file
aenv    follow    ain, .002           ;take the amplitude each 2/1000 seconds
aenv1   tone      aenv, 50            ;low-pass filter (50 Hz cutoff) useful to...
                                      ;..."round off" the signal envelope
kenv    downsamp  aenv1               ;downsampling aenv1 to change it to...
                                      ;...a k-variable, kenv
a1      oscil     kenv, ifrq, 1       ;amplitude driven by kenv
        out       a1
        endin


;follow.sco
f1    0    4096    10    1
i1    0    3       0     8
```

7.6 *LIMIT* AND *ILIMIT*

Another opcode which is useful when modifying sampled sounds (and other signals, as well) is *limit*. The syntax is:

a1 limit asig, klow, khigh

where:

a1	output signal
asig	input signal
klow, khigh	lower and upper thresholds (values at which the input signal will be limited)

If the *asig* amplitude is lower than *klow*, its value will be changed to *klow*. If it is higher than *khigh*, itís value will be raised. In other words, the signal will be clipped, causing distortion artifacts. The transformation can also be applied to i- and k-variables

i1 ilimit isig, ilow, ihigh
k1 limit ksig, klow, khigh

All such opcodes cause some harmonic distortion in the signal by adding odd-numbered harmonics to its spectrum. The result is similar to the electric guitar "overdrive" effect introduced in the 1960's.

Let's experiment

```
;limit.orc
        sr     =  44100
        kr     =  4410
        ksmps  =  10
        nchnls =  1
        instr     1
ifrq           =  cpspch(p5)
iamp           =  ampdb(p4)
kenv    linseg    0, .01, iamp, p3-.01, 0   ;generate a triangle envelope...
a1      oscil     kenv, ifrq, 1             ;...and apply it to some periodic signal
krms    rms       a1                        ;get the rms power of that signal...
a2      limit     a1, -p6, p6               ;...and limit it between -p6 and +p6
a3      gain      a2, krms                  ;scale the result...
```

```
                                                ;...to match the initial amplitude level
        out     a3
        endin

;limit.sco
f1      0       4096    10      1   .5  .4  .3  .2  .1
;instr  act     dur     dB      pch     limit
i1      0       .9      90      8       30000
i1      1       .       .       .       20000
i1      2       .       .       .       10000
i1      3       .       .       .        5000
i1      4       .       .       .        1000
```

Notice as you listen that as the limit level (p6) decreases the output sound gets more and more distorted.

LIST OF OPCODES INTRODUCED IN THIS SECTION

a1[,a2][,a3,a4]	**soundin**	**filename[, initial_skip_time] [, format]**
a1[,a2][,a3,a4]	**diskin**	**filename, freq., [, initial_skip_time] [, loop_flag][, format]**
a1	**loscil**	**amp, freq, func_table_no. [, base_frequency] [sustain_loop_flag, loop_start_time, loop_end_time] [decay_loop_flag, loop_start_time, loop_end_time]**
k1	**linenr**	**amplitude, rise_time, decay_time, decay_bias_value**
a1	**linenr**	**amplitude, rise_time, decay_time, decay_bias_value**
a1	**follow**	**input_sig, time_window**
a1	**limit**	**input_audio_sig, lower_limit, upper_limit**
k1	**limit**	**input_control_sig, lower_limit, upper_limit**
i1	**ilimit**	**input_init_variable, lower_limit, upper_limit**

8

SOUND ANALYSIS AND RESYNTHESIS

8.1 INTRODUCTION

Analysis/resynthesis is one of the most interesting approaches to sound processing. The following is an overview of the approach:

1) A sound file is separated into its spectral components using an some particular computer program. The analysis data are stored in an analysis file.

2) The analysis file can be edited, and its data modified. The new data may differ from the original sound.

3) The modified data is used to synthesize a new sound file.

This way it is possible to stretch the sound duration while leaving the frequency unchanged or change the frequency leaving the duration unchanged. Such transformations may be dynamic (accelerando, glissando, etc.). Depending on the modifications to the analysis data, a vast palette of very interesting sound effects can be created.

Several analysis/resynthesis methods exist. We will focus on the following ones in Csound

kind of analysis technique	analysis program	analysis file type	resynthesis method	Csound resynthesis opcode
phase vocoder	*pvanal*	fft (**Win**) or pv (**Mac**)	inverse FFT phase vocoder	*pvoc*
heterodyne analysis	*hetro*	het	oscillator banks or additive synthesis	*adsyn*
LPC (linear prediction code)	*lpanal*	lpc	filter banks	*lpread/lpreson*

Phase vocoding is widely utilized today even by proprietary, commercial programs. Such programs, however, only allow limited modification of a number of parameters, and provide little or no explanation regarding the effected output. We'll discuss the theory behind the phase vocoder in next section. It will help you to fully exploit not only the potential of Csound phase vocoding, but any other phase vocoder as well.

8.2 PHASE VOCODER ANALYSIS

The program *pvanal* is included in the program library that comes to you with Csound. It implements a kind of FFT (*Fast Fourier Transform*) known as STFT (*Short-Time Fourier Transform*), which breaks the sound signal into many chunks, or *windows*, whose length range from 1 ms to .3 seconds in duration. Each windowed chunk is analyzed separately, creating separate sets of FFT data - usually called "frames". The *pvanal* analysis generates a sequence of these analysis frames, and stores that sequence in a file. Normally, the sound source to is mono. However, it is possible to analyze stereo or even quad files, by selecting the particular channel to be analyzed. A complete analysis requires as many analysis steps as there are channels (see the **How to use pvanal** subsection and the list of command line flags, at the end of this section).

a. Choosing the frame size

A crucial factor is the frame size (*FRMSIZ*), or the number of points (samples) in an analysis frame. It must be expressed as a power-of-two (such as 64, 128, 256, 512, etc.).

Framesize = number of points

Choosing the appropriate frame size can be a difficult task. The optimal frame size is dependant on the particular sound being analyzed. Accurate analysis leads to accurate resynthesis.

But why is the frame size so important? It affects many aspects of the analysis process including:

1) frequency precision (bandwidth of the "analysis channels", or *STFT* bins)
2) time precision (*TIME INTERVAL*)

Unfortunately, high frequency precision typically leads to bad temporal resolution. Therefore it is crucial for us to find a good balance between the two. Let's take a closer look at the factors we should consider when choosing a good solution to this problem.

b. Frequency

The analysis process divides the entire frequency range into adjacent frequency channels. The bandwidth in each channel is calculated by dividing the sampling rate by the frame size:

analysis channel bandwidth = sr / frame size

A larger frame size results in a narrower channel bandwidth and in a more precise frequency representation. Let's consider this: Suppose you have a sound sampled at 44100 Hz, and in order to analyze it, you choose a frame size of 1024. The channel bandwidth is

44100 / 1024 = 43.06 Hz

The analysis frame will include a series of frequency channels each having a bandwidth of 43 Hz. Channels are equally spaced between 0 and 22050 Hz (the Nyquist frequency). If the input sound has a harmonic spectrum with a fundamental frequency of 70 Hz, the fundamental will fit in the first channel (43-86 Hz), the second harmonic (140 Hz) will fit in the fourth channel (129-172 Hz), the third harmonic will fit in the fifth channel, etc.

This is fine as long as each single harmonic component falls in a separate channel. However, suppose you used a frame size of 256:

44100 / 256 = 172.27 Hz

first channel 0-172 Hz
second channel 172-344 Hz
third channel 344-516 Hz
etc.

Now, both the fundamental (70 Hz) and the second harmonic (140 Hz) fall in the first channel (0-172 Hz), both the third (210 Hz) and the fourth harmonics (280 Hz) fall in the second channel, while the fifth, sixth and seventh harmonics fall in the third channel, etc. That illustrates poor frequency precision, because many components fall in a single analysis channel.

Clearly, a 172 Hz bandwidth, which is critical for lower frequency components, is fine for frequencies higher than 3000 Hz (in that frequency range even musical intervals as small as tones and semitones are larger than 172 Hz). Therefore, a bandwidth of 172 Hz separates higher frequencies quite well. And yet, it may span more than a full octave in the lower frequency range.

We can say: **a large frame size is recommended to achieve a good frequency precision in the analysis.**

c. Time

As observed above, the analysis process divides the sound signal not only into frequency bins, but into time windows as well. A larger window size will translate into a smaller total amount of windows. In other words, **a small frame size is recommended to achieve good temporal precision**. The FFT algorithm analyzes a time interval whose length can be calculated by dividing the frame size by the sampling rate.

time interval = frame size / sr

Consequently, a finer frequency resolution implies a coarser time resolution and vice-versa. For example, consider that using the *sr* = 44100 and *frame size* = 8192, the analysis channel bandwidth is a rather fine 5.38 Hz, while the time interval is a gross 0.1858 seconds. Now, if the sound we want to analyze has an attack transient shorter than 0.18 seconds, the analysis will be completely ineffectual as the FFT would return a few average values representing the amplitude evolution within the transient. So, we end up with a precise representation of the frequencies, but with a poor representation of how their amplitude changes over that small time, and, hence, leaves us with a poor resynthesis.

d. Solution: overlapping windows

One way to get rid of this problem is to use overlapping analysis windows. That takes full advantage of large frame sizes yet doesn't cause poor temporal precision. We speak of the *windows overlap factor* (*WINDFACT*) to describe many successive windows overlapping. Fig. 8-1 illustrates this. There are four windowed sound segments (windows) equally spaced in time, overlapping such that the beginning of the fifth window lines up with the ending of the first. Hence, we have here *WINDFACT* = 4. Therefore, we can still have a good temporal resolution with a large frame size.

In short, the two most relevant factors to remember for accurate analysis are *FRMSZ* and *WINDFACT*. In principle, two more parameters are involved: *window type* (Hamming, Hanning, Gauss, Blackmann-Harris, Kaiser, rectangle) and *FFT* size (which must be at least twice as large as *FRMSZ*), but they are preset in Csound and we don't have to worry about them.

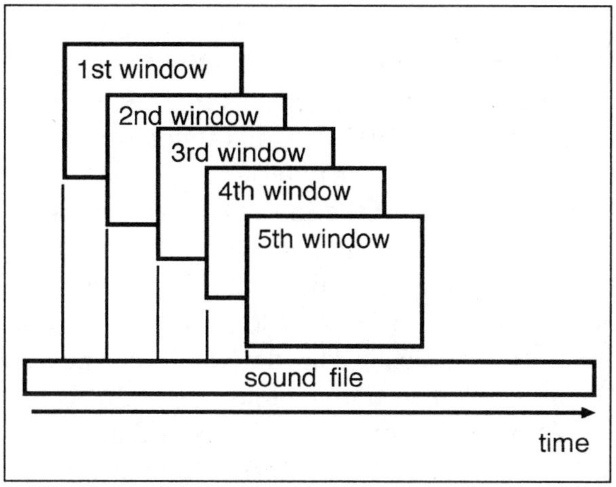

Fig. 8-1

e. How to use *pvanal*

To run *pvanal* we write a command line such as:

Csound -U pvanal [flags] infilename outfilename

Here's an example:

Csound -U pvanal [flags] lana.wav lana.fft (*Win*) or
Csound -U pvanal [flags] lana.aiff lana.pv (*Mac*)

The analysis data is stored in the file called "lana.fft", or "lana.pv". The analysis process will use the parameter default values (*FRMSZ*=256, *WINDFACT*=4, etc.), which is fine for sounds with simple temporal characteristics. Remember that even very simple harmonic sounds may not be easy to analyze. Such was the case with our sound with the fundamental of 70 Hz, discussed above. The optional flags in the command line allow more precise tuning of various parameters.

For example, to include a frame size of 1024 samples and an overlap factor of 8 (8 windows), we write:

Csound -U -n1024 -w8 lana.wav lana.fft (*Win*), or
Csound -U -n1024 -w8 lana.aiff lana.pv (*Mac*)

These two flags, *-n* and *-w*, are the most useful and indeed the most often used. Here's a complete list of the *pvanal* flags:

-s<srate> sampling rate of input sound file. If the sound file has a header (as is the case with WAVE and AIFF files), the flag can be omitted. Notice that the sound file sampling rate can be different from the resynthesis sampling rate.

-c<channel> for stereo or quad sound files, this flag indicates which channel is to be analyzed. The default is 1 (= stereo left channel).

-b<begin> start time (in seconds) of the sound file segment to analyze. The default is 0.0 seconds.

- d<duration> duration (in seconds) of the sound file segment to analyze. The default is 0.0 seconds, meaning that the entire sound file must be analyzed.

-n<frmsiz> frame size (in samples). The default is the power-of-two close to the number of samples for a 20 milliseconds sound (e.g. 256 samples, at sr = 10 kHz, resulting in a frame of 25.6 milliseconds). Be advised that, in some Csound releases, frame sizes larger than 1024 cause problems during the resynthesis process.

-w<windfact> overlap factor between analysis windows (default is 4).

-h<hopsize> used as an alternative to *-w* (can be used only when *-w* is omitted). Determines the distance, in samples, between the beginning of one present window and the beginning of the next.

The output file, "lana.fft" or "lana.pv", can be used with the *pvoc* opcode in order to resynthesize the original sound, or to change the original duration and pitch.

How to launch the *pvanal* analysis (*Win*)

Enter the menu "*Util*" of WCShell and select first "*Analysis*", then "*Pvanal*". A dialog box will appear with the *pvanal* command line. The program default selects the current WAVE file as the input to analysis and will give the analysis file the same name as the WAVE file, but with the file extension *.fft*. You can change the command line flags, and then click the OK button. Csound will then create the required analysis file.

> ***TIPS & TRICKS (Win):*** *You can save the analysis file with another name. It is good idea not to change the file extension (.fft), so the file is easily recognizable as an analysis file.*

How to launch the *pvanal* analysis (*Mac*)

In the "*Utility preprocess*" menu, select "*PVANAL*" and choose the sound file to analyze. The program will give the analysis file the same name. If the sound file is called "bug.aiff", the analysis file will be called "bug.pv". If a file with this name already exist, you can type in a new name for it. It is recommended, however, that the output filename extension remain *.pv*. You can set the *frame size* and the *windfact* values. You can change the duration of the sound file segment to analyze when appropriate. The default is the complete sound file. When you are done with these settings, just click the "*analyze*" button. Csound will generate the analysis file.

f. Some hints

To perform a correct analysis, **the analysis window size must be at least as large as the number of samples required to cover the full cycle relative to the lowest frequency** (the cycle of the fundamental). For example, if the lowest frequency in your sound is 100 Hz, its cycle is 1/100 seconds; with *sr* = 44100 Hz, then, the frame size must be at least 441 samples. The power-of-two closest to that is 512. So the analysis window size should be at least 512 samples, 256 would not be a good choice.

Be aware of the properties of the sound to analyze.

- a larger frame size is suitable for low-pitched sounds with slow attack transients;
- a smaller frame size is suitable for high-pitched sounds with very short attack transients;
- for low-pitched sounds with short transients (e.g. fundamental frequency = 65 Hz and rise time=0.01 secs) you can try 512 samples (assuming the sound was sampled at 44100 Hz), meaning a time interval of 0.00115 secs (1/9th of the rise time) and a bandwidth of 86 Hz. That is fine for harmonic sounds. But for a bass-drum, which is inharmonic, such analysis settings would make it impossible to capture the lower frequencies, all falling in the same analysis channel. In such a case, better frequency resolution is needed. We should enlarge both the frame size (2048) and the overlap factor (8) so that the higher frame size is not detrimental to the time resolution (which would result in a poor analysis of the attack);
- finally for a high-pitched inharmonic sound having short attack transients, use a large frame size and a large overlap factor.

8.3 PHASE VOCODER RE-SYNTHESIS

From the user's viewpoint, resynthesis is not as complicated as analysis. It may however require more time for the calculations (depending on the particular orchestra and score, and on the computer's internal clock).

The opcode that performs resynthesis based on *.fft* and *.pv* files is *pvoc* (phase vocoder). The syntax is

ar pvoc ktimpnt, kfmod, ifilcod [, ispecwp]

ktimpnt (time pointer) determines, moment by moment, which frame is read from the analysis file. For example, suppose we had performed the analysis of a sound lasting 2.5

seconds. To re-generate the entire sound, we may want to determine the *ktimpnt* variable in the following way:

```
ktimpnt	line 0, p3, 2.5
```

kfmod is the pitch transposition factor:

1= no transposition
1.5=a fifth higher
2=an octave higher

ifilcod is the name of the analysis file.
ispecwp (optional) if non-zero, it attempts to preserve the spectral envelope when the frequency content is changed (as in *kfmod*). The default is 0 (spectral envelope is not preserved).

a. ktimpnt
Let's run some examples demonstrating the practical use of the *ktimpnt* argument beginning with an instrument which changes the sound duration, but not the frequency.

```
;pvoc.orc
		sr	=	44100
		kr	=	4410
		ksmps	=	10
		nchnls	=	1
		instr		1
ktimpnt	linseg		0, p3/2, .5, p3/2, 0
aluna	pvoc		ktimpnt, 1, "luna.fft"
		out		aluna
		endin
```

In this instrument we use the "luna.fft" analysis file (generated earlier with pvanal), without a frequency transposition in the original sound (suppose it is the sound of a voice speaking the word "luna", lasting 0.5 seconds). The resynthesis is performed by reading the analysis file through, first from beginning to end (in p3/2 seconds), then from end to beginning (in the remaining p3/2 seconds). It sounds like this:

L U N A A И U ⅃

Observe that the instrument reads through the analysis file at a rate specified by p3. If we do not want to alter original timing (0.5 seconds), the required duration would be 1 second (half a second in each direction).

Example:

```
i1 0 1
```

output:

```
0      .2     .4     .6     .8     1 seconds
L   U    N    A   A    И   U    ⅃
```

If we want to lengthen the sound, it is sufficient to specify a longer duration. For example, p3=2 will generate a sound with a duration twice as long. On the contrary, with p3=0.5, the sound will have half the original duration. Such changes do not affect the frequency, which remains the same as the original.

Examples:

```
i1 0 2
```

```
0     .2    .4    .6    .8    1     1.2   1.4   1.6   1.8   2 seconds
L      U        N        A        A        И        U      ⅃
```

```
i1 0 .5
```

```
0   .1   .2   .3   .4   .5 seconds
L  U  N  A  A  И  U  ⅃
```

Let's see now more orchestra examples:

```
;pvoc1.orc
          sr      =  44100
          kr      =  4410
          ksmps   =  10
          nchnls  =  1
          instr      1
ktimpnt   line       0.5, p3, 0
```

```
aluna   pvoc    ktimpnt, 1, "luna.fft"
        out     aluna
        endin

;pvoc2.sco
i1 0 1
```

results in:

```
0       .2      .4      .6      .8      1 seconds
A               И           U           ⅃
```

```
;pvoc2.orc
                sr     =  44100
                kr     =  4410
                ksmps  =  10
                nchnls =  1
                instr     1
ktimpnt         line      0, p3, 0.25
aluna           pvoc      ktimpnt, 1, "luna.fft"
                out       aluna
                endin

;pvoc2.sco
i1 0 1
```

```
0       .2      .4      .6      .8      1 seconds
L                   U
```

```
;pvoc3.orc
                sr     =  44100
                kr     =  4410
                ksmps  =  10
                nchnls =  1
                instr     1
ktimpnt         line      0, p3, .5
aluna           pvoc      ktimpnt, 1, "luna.fft"
                out       aluna
                endin
```

```
; pvoc3.sco
i1 0 1

0       .2      .4      .6      .8      1 seconds
L        U        N        A
```

b. kfmod

Let's see how we can modify the frequency, now. The second *pvoc* argument is *kfmod*, a multiplier of the original frequency. Values less than 1 will result in pitches lower than the original (e.g. 0.5 = an octave lower, 0.75 = a fourth lower), while values larger than 1 will result in higher pitches.

Here's an example:

```
;pvoc4.orc
          sr      =  44100
          kr      =  4410
          ksmps   =  10
          nchnls  =  1
          instr      1
ktimpnt   line       0, p3, .5
aluna     pvoc       ktimpnt, 2, "luna.fft"          ; an octave higher  (kfmod=2)
          out        aluna
          endin

; pvoc4.sco
i1  0  .5
```

8.4 HETERODYNE ANALYSIS (*HETRO*)

While the phase vocoder analysis lends itself to sounds with either harmonic and inharmonic spectra, heterodyne analysis is effective for harmonic (and quasi-harmonic) sounds only. On the other hand, while the phase vocoder resynthesis is a very slow process, resynthesis based on heterodyne analysis is relatively quick.

Heterodyne analysis focuses on a certain number of harmonic components (specified by the user) and for each harmonic it measures the amplitude and the frequency at every given time interval (which is specified by the user). As it can track individual harmonic frequencies, it can also follow frequencies that deviate from the harmonic spectrum, like the frequency components in the attack transients of a piano sound. Resynthesis is made possible by the *adsyn* opcode.

The Csound heterodyne analysis program is called *hetro*. Its command line is:

csound -U hetro [flags] sound file analysis_file

The flags are as follows:

-s<srate> sampling rate of input sound file. If the sound file has a header (as with WAVE and AIFF files), the flag can be omitted. Notice that this sampling rate can be different from the resynthesis sampling rate.

-c<channel> for stereo or quad sound files, it indicates which particular channel must be analyzed. The default is 1 (= stereo left channel).

-b<begin> start time (in seconds) of the sound file segment to analyze. The default is 0.

- d<duration> duration (in seconds) of the sound file segment to analyze. The default is 0, meaning that the entire sound file must be analyzed.

-f<begfreq> estimated fundamental frequency, necessary in the algorithm to initialize the analysis filters. The default value is 100 (Hz). We suggest that *begfreq* is slightly smaller than the lowest frequency in the sound file.

-h<partials> number of harmonics to track. The default value is 10. The highest possible number depends upon the Csound release being used.

-M<maxamp> largest amplitude value obtained in the sum of all the harmonics at any time in the analyzed sound. The default is 32767.

-m<minamp> amplitude threshold. Components having an amplitude below the threshold are discarded by the analysis. Typical values are 128 (=-48 dB), 64 (=-54 dB), 32 (=-60 dB), 0 (= no threshold). The default is 64.

-n<brkpts> number of separate analyses to perform across the sound file segment. This represents just the highest allowable value, as in fact not all the analyses will be actually performed, depending on how many components are above the amplitude threshold (*-m*) within a given segment. Also, it depends on the way *hetro* internally arranges the analysis data (components with the same amplitude could be temporarily grouped together). The default is 256.

-l<cutfreq> this flag causes the internal default filter (a *comb* filter) to be replaced with a 3rd-order Butterworth lowpass (18 dB per octave) with cutoff frequency of *cutfreq* Hz. That makes the analysis slower, but provides you with better results. The default is 0 (= use the default *comb* filter).

Here's a heterodyne analysis example:

csound -U hetro -f250 -h16 -n100 pianoC3.wav pianoC3.het

This command line launches the analysis of the lowest 16 harmonics (-h16) in the "pianoC3.wav" sound file with an estimated fundamental frequency of 250 Hz (-f250). 100 analysis breakpoints (-n100) are required and equally spaced across the sound file.

> ***How to run the hetro analysis (Win)***
> Enter the WCShell "*Util*" menu, select first "*Analysis*", then "*Hetro*". A dialog box will appear with a default command line. The program will consider the currently selected WAVE file as the input to be analyzed, and it will give the analysis file the same name as the WAVE file, but with the file extension *.het*. You can change any of the command line flags, and then click the OK button. Csound will create the required analysis file.

> ***TIPS & TRICKS (Win):*** *The analysis file can be assigned a name other than the sound file's. It is good idea not to change the file extension (.het), so that the file is easily recognized as an* hetro *analysis file.*

> ***How to launch the hetro analysis (Mac)***
> In the "*Utility preprocess*" menu, select "*HETRO*" and choose a sound file to analyze. The program will give the analysis file the same name as the sound file. If the sound file is called "*bug.aiff*", the analysis file will be called "*bug.adsyn*". If such a file already exist, enter a new filename. It is recommended, however, that any file generated with *hetro* have the extension *.adsyn*. You can specify the *beginning frequency*, the number of *partials* and the number of *breakpoints* required. You can also specify an amplitude *threshold*, and determine the particular sound file segment to analyze. The default segment duration is "the whole sound file". When you are done with these settings, just click the "*analyze*" button. Csound will generate the analysis file.

It is very important to fix the appropriate number of breakpoints. Too few would result in an oversimplified analysis, especially for sounds with rapid and complex attacks. That usually causes the loss of relevant data and is perceivable in the resynthesis. Fig.8-2 shows the amplitude profile of a "pizzicato" viola sound (top) and the amplitude envelope of the first harmonic as drawn from the analysis file *vpz30.het* (center) created with the command:

csound -U hetro -f430 -n30 -h10 vlapizz.wav vpz30.het

Observe that 30 breakpoints (-n30) are indicated. Also, fig.8-2 shows (bottom) the amplitude envelope of the first harmonic as extracted from the analysis file vpz200.het generated with the command:

csound -U hetro -f430 -n200 -h10 vlapizz.wav vpz200.het

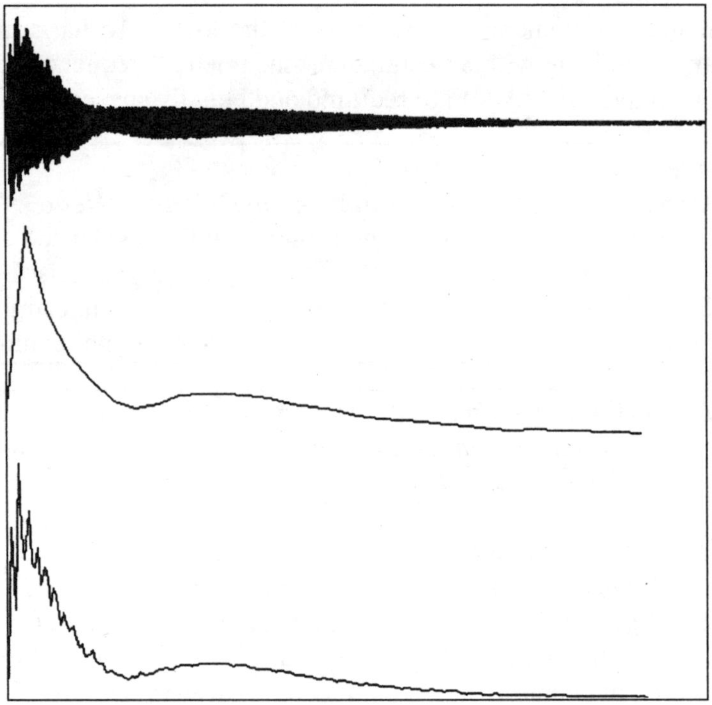

Fig. 8-2

This time, 200 breakpoints are used. Observe that a lot of details are missing in the prior analysis which appear in the latter. This difference is likely to create two very different sounds during the resynthesis process.

Because the analysis breakpoints are equally spaced, we are forced to fix an optimal number of breakpoints with respect to the most salient portions of the analyzed sound, i.e. with respect to the highest rate of variation in the sound. That may result in a temporal resolution, which is more precise than necessary for less rapidly changing portions of the sound. This is no problem, and only makes our analysis file larger.

Here are some more examples of *hetro*:

csound -U hetro -f250 -h16 -n100 -b1.1 -d2 vla.wav vla.het

This takes the "vla.wav" sound and performs the analysis on a segment beginning at 1.1 seconds (*-b1.1*) whose duration is 2 seconds (*-d2*).

csound -U hetro -f250 -h16 -n100 -l1000 vla.wav vla.het

This uses the optional internal filter with a cutoff frequency of 1000 Hz (-l1000).
Here's an example of an incorrect usage of the *hetro* command line:

csound -U hetro -f250 -h16 -n100 -l1000 vla.wav vla pizzicato.het

On Windows systems, that causes a system error by introducing blank space in the analysis file name.

8.5 *ADSYN* RESYNTHESIS

The *adsyn* opcode basically consists of an oscillator bank whose frequencies and amplitudes are controlled by the data from a .het file. The syntax is:

ar adsyn kamod, kfmod, ksmod, ifilcod

ar is the output signal
kamod is a multiplier of the overall amplitude level. 1 means no amplitude change.
kfmod is a multiplier of the frequency values. 1 means no frequency change.
ksmod is a multiplier determining the incremental step of the read pointer, thus determining changes in the duration of the analysis file read. 1 means no change.
ifilcod is the analysis file to read. It may be a number, like 12, in which case the program will try to open a file saved previously as *adsyn.12*. It may be also an explicit filename, such as "vlapizz.het". If no path is specified, Csound will look for the file in the current directory, then in the SADIR (*Sound Analysis Directory*), provided that is included in the system preferences.

Suppose we want to resynthesize a viola sound, "vlapizz.wav". First, we prepare the file analysis with *HETRO*. Then we run Csound using the following orchestra and score files:

```
;adsyn1.orc
        sr      =   44100
        kr      =   4410
        ksmps   =   10
        nchnls  =   1
        instr       1
a1      adsyn       1, 1, 1, "vlapizz.het"
        out         a1
        endin
```

```
; adsyn1.sco
i1 0 1.5
```

Observe that the note duration is the same as the file duration.

Such an orchestra does not allow us to create any sound transformation, as it can only reproduce the original sound, with higher or lower precision. Let's try a second orchestra that allows us to modify the amplitude and the frequency.

```
;adsyn2.orc
        sr     = 44100
        kr     = 4410
        ksmps  = 10
        nchnls = 1

        instr    1
ikamp          = p4                            ;amplitude multiplier
ikfrq          = p5                            ;frequency multiplier
a1      adsyn    ikamp, ikfrq, 1, "vlapizz.het"
        out      a1
        endin
```

Here's a score example for that orchestra:

```
;adsyn2.sco
;p1   p2    p3    p4     p5
;     act   dur   kamp   kfreq
i1    0     1.5   .5     1
i1    +     1.5   2      1.5
```

There the first note has half the amplitude of the original sound (p4=.5) and the same frequency (p5=1). The second has twice that amplitude (p4=2), while its pitch is shifted a fifth higher (p5=1.5).

There are more convenient ways to specify amplitude and frequency parameters, provided we know their value in the original sound. Suppose that the original amplitude is -12 dB and the original frequency is 440 Hz. We could then write:

```
;adsyn3.orc
        sr     = 44100
        kr     = 4410
```

```
        ksmps     =   10
        nchnls    =   1
        instr         1

iampor            =   ampdb(78)                 ; convert dB in absolute amplitude units
ifrqor            =   440                       ; convert pitch to Hz
ikamp             =   ampdb(p4)/iampor
ikfrq             =   cpspch(p5)/ifrqor
a1      adsyn         ikamp, ikfrq, 1, "vlapizz.het"
        out           a1
        endin
```

Here the amplitude variable, *ikamp*, is calculated by dividing the absolute value (converted earlier from dB) by the original amplitude. The frequency variable, *ikfreq*, is calculated by dividing the Hz value (converted earlier from *pitch* notation) by the frequency of the original sound, *ifrqor*. For example, if the target pitch is 8 (middle C), the pitch value is first converted to Hz (261.626) and then divided by the original frequency (440 Hz). This gives us a scale factor of 0.5946 which is finally used to transpose the original pitch to middle C.

A score example for the adsyn3 orchestra:

```
;adsyn3.sco
;p1    p2     p3     p4     p5
;      act    dur    amp    pitch
i1     0      .5     80     8
i1     +      3.5    70     8.07
```

What happens in the two output sounds? The sound signal of the first note, lasting .5 seconds, is truncated. The second note does not last the specified 3.5 seconds. It was only to be expected, since the first note reads only a shorter portion of the analysis file, while the second is longer than that of the analysis file itself. Shall we now use several analysis files, each with a different duration? We shall not. Indeed we should modify the *ksmod* argument (the *ismod* variable in the orchestra example) in such a way that the analysis file is read by *adsyn* at a faster or slower rate, and that matches the desired note duration. To do so, we have to know, in advance, the duration of the original sound.

```
;adsyn4.orc
        sr    =   44100
```

```
        kr     =  4410
        ksmps  =  10
        nchnls =  1
        instr     1
iduror         =  1.5                              ;original duration
iampor         =  ampdb(78)                        ;original amplitude
ifrqor         =  440                              ;original frequency
ismod          =  iduror/p3                        ;calculate ismod
ikamp          =  ampdb(p4)/iampor
ikfrq          =  cpspch(p5)/ifrqor
a1      adsyn     ikamp, ikfrq, ismod, "vlapizz.het"
        out       a1
        endin
```

```
;adsyn4.sco
;p1     p2      p3      p4      p5
;       act     dur     amp     pitch
i1      0       .5      80      8
i1      +       8       70      8.07
```

Now run Csound using these files. When you listen to the resulting sound, pay attention to the duration of the second note.

It sounds wrong. The attack is “stretched” and it doesn’t resemble a “pizzicato”. This happened because we modified the look-up rate for the entire analysis file. To do better, we should leave it unchanged until after the attack transient, and then have it slow down. Here’s how we can implement this:

```
;adsyn5.orc
        sr     =  44100
        kr     =  4410
        ksmps  =  10
        nchnls =  1
        instr     1
iduror         =  1.5
iampor         =  ampdb(78)                        ;original amplitude
ifrqor         =  440                              ;original frequency
ismod          =  iduror/p3
ksmod             linseg  1, .05, 1, .001, ismod, p3-.05, ismod   ; generate the ksmod signal
ikamp          =  ampdb(p4)/iampor
```

```
ikfrq           =       cpspch(p5)/ifrqor
a1      adsyn           ikamp, ikfrq, ksmod, "vlapizz.het"
        out             a1
        endin
```

Here *ksmod* is generated with *linseg*. It remains 1 as defined by the attack transient (0.05 secs), then suddenly it changes to the new rate value for the rest of note duration. (i.e. *ismod*). Notice that "suddenly" here means 1 millisecond, and that *linseg* cannot accept segment durations of 0 seconds (see fig. 8-3).

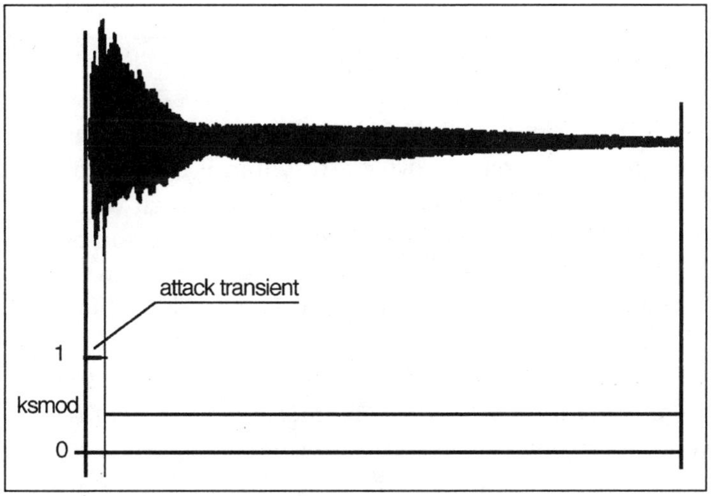

Fig. 8-3

The score example can be the same as above.

```
;adsyn5.sco
;p1     p2      p3      p4      p5
;       act     dur     amp     pitch
i1      0       .5      80      8
i1      +       8       70      8.07
```

8.6 MODELING THE VOCAL TRACT WITH *LPANAL*

The third analysis/resynthesis method we'll look at here is called LPC (*Linear Predictive Coding*). It is especially useful for speech synthesis, and in the simulation of the singing voice and other vocal sounds.

The method is an example of physical modeling, and it attempts to model the behavior of the human vocal tract as illustrated in fig.8-4. The excitation source can be *voiced* (as in the utterance of vowels) or *unvoiced* (as in the utterance of consonants).

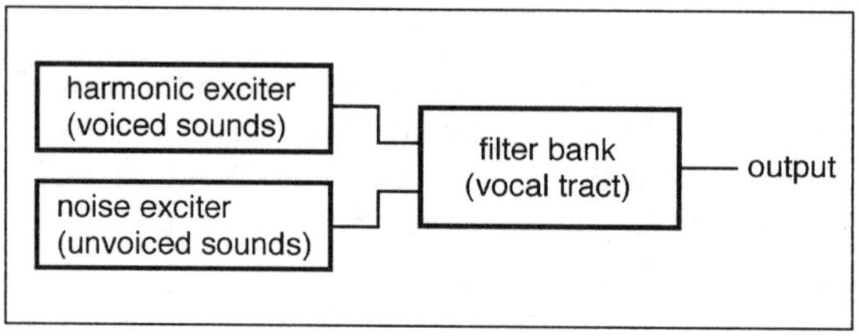

Fig. 8-4

The analysis is performed with the *lpanal* program. It generates an analysis file containing all the data necessary to drive a resynthesis filter bank. Also, the analysis is performed using equally spaced analysis windows. For each window it returns the RMS value, the estimated pitch, and the estimated error (due to the complexity of the input signal). The error estimate is useful when discriminating between voiced (small errors) and unvoiced sounds (larger errors). LPC analysis does not only render spectral data, but also returns: *a) average amplitude of the residual sound (a measure of how imperfect the resynthesis would be, assuming a voiced source); b) average amplitude of the original sound; c) ratio of the two amplitudes, i.e. a measure of the analysis error (which helps determine whether the sound is voiced or unvoiced); d) tracked pitch, or fundamental frequency.*

The syntax for *lpanal* is the following:

Csound -U lpanal [flags] sound file analysis_file

Available flags include:

-s<srate> sampling rate of input sound file. If the sound file includes a header (as in WAVE and AIFF files), the flag can be omitted. The default is 10000 Hz.

-c<channel> for stereo or quad sound files, indicates which particular channel must be analyzed. The default is 1 (= stereo left channel).

-b<begin> start time (in seconds) of the sound file segment to analyze. The default is 0.0.

- d<duration> duration (in seconds) of the sound file segment to analyze. The default is 0.0, meaning that the analysis proceeds until the end of file is reached.

-p<npoles> number of poles required (= number of analysis bandpass filters). The default is 34. The largest possible number depends on the particular Csound release being used.

-a if present, causes the filters to be stabilized and makes the program generate a file with filter pole values, instead of filter coefficients.[1]

-h<hopsize> time interval, in samples, between frames of analysis. This determines the number of frames per second (*srate/hopsize*) in the output file. The actual size of the analysis framesize is *hopsize*2*samples*. The default hopsize is 200 samples, while the largest possible size depends on the Csound release you are using.

-C<string> any text string you would like to include in the "comment" field of the analysis file header. The default is a null string (no comment).

-P<mincps> the lowest frequency (in Hz) to be considered by the program for tracking the fundamental frequency (*pitch tracking*). *P0* causes tracking to be omitted. The default is 70.

-Q<maxcps> the highest frequency (in Hz) to be considered by the program for tracking the fundamental. A narrow bandwidth (*Q-P*) results in more accurate tracking. The default *maxcps* is 200.

-v<verbosity> messages monitoring the analysis process: 0=no messages, 1=average number of messages, 2=all messages.

An example:

lpanal -p26 -d2.5 -P100 -Q400 vox.wav vox.lpc (*Win*)
lpanal -p26 -d2.5 -P100 -Q400 vox.aiff vox.lp (*Mac*)

This command line example launches the analysis of the initial 2.5 seconds (*-d2.5*) of the "vox.wav" file, and creates an analysis file "vox.lpc" containing the coefficients of a 26-pole filter (*-p26*). The analysis process will attempt to track the fundamental frequency, presumably between 100 (*-P100*) and 400 (*-Q400*) Hz.

How to launch the* lpanal *analysis (Win)
Enter the WCShell "*Util*" menu, select "*Analysis*", then "*Lpanal*". A dialog box appears with a default command line. The program will consider the currently selected WAVE file as the input for analysis, and will give the analysis file the same name as the sound file, with the file extension *.lpc*. You can change any of the available flags, and then click the OK button. Csound will create the required analysis file.

TIPS & TRICKS (Win): *It is always possible to give the analysis file a name other than the sound file. We recommend, however, to always use the file extension .lpc, so at any time you can easily recognize the file as a LPC file.*

[1] In the former case (pole values), stored in the analysis file is the center frequency of the bandpass filters. In the latter (coefficients), stored are the numerical values necessary for the prediction algorithm, i.e. values that make no sense at all in terms of frequency. This latter works better.

How to launch the* lpanal *analysis (Mac)
In the "*Utility preprocess*" menu, select "*LPANAL*" and choose a sound file to analyze. The program will give the analysis file the same name as the sound file. If the sound file is called "*timbales.aiff*", the analysis file will be called "*timbales.lp*". You can change the output file name, but we recommend that you always use the proper extension, *.lp*. You can enter the *number of poles* and the *hopsize*, as well as the lowest and highest presumed fundamental frequency values. You can also turn off the pitch tracking. By default, the analysis segment is the entire sound file, but you can change this, by selecting a particular segment. When you are done with these settings, just click the "*analyze*" button. Csound will generate the analysis file.

8.7 MODELING THE VOCAL TRACT: *LPREAD/LPREASON* RESYNTHESIS

Two distinct opcodes are required for sound resynthesis based on LPC analysis: *lpread* (reads the analysis data) and *lpreson* (implements the filter bank driven by the analysis data). The task of creating a source signal is left to the user. The *lpread* syntax is:

krmsr, krmso, kerr, kcps lpread ktimpnt, ifilcod

krmsr is the average amplitude (RMS) of the analysis residual
krmso is the average amplitude (RMS) of the input signal
kerr is the estimated error in the tracking of the fundamental frequency (ranges from 0-1)
kcps is the fundamental frequency
ktimpnt (time pointer) drives the look-up pointer across the analysis file (similar to *pvoc*, see section 8.2)
ifilcod analysis file. It may be a number, like 12, in which case the program will try to open a file which had been saved as *lp.12*. It may be an explicit filename, such as "voice.lpc". If no path is specified, Csound will look for the file in the current directory, then in the SADIR directory, provided the latter was specified as a system variable.

Suppose we have some analysis file "voice.lpc", containing the LPC data for the 3-second long "voice.wav" sound file. How do we resynthesize the original sound? The Csound instrument will have to read the data from the "voice.lpc" file, with *lpread*, and get the four variables *krmsr*, *krmso*, *kerr*, and *kcps*. Depending on the value of *kerr*, we will use either a voiced (*kerr* < .3) or unvoiced excitation source (*kerr* > .3). Somewhere in the instrument, we should include the line

```
if      kerr<.3 goto     vocal
```

so that the program jumps or doesn't jump to the *vocal* label, thus using a voiced or unvoiced source generator (see example below) respectively.

The *lpreason* syntax is:

```
ar      lpreson     asig
```

where *asig* is the excitation source signal.

Here's the full orchestra example:

```
;lpc1.orc
        sr      =   44100
        kr      =   4410
        ksmps   =   10
        nchnls  =   1
        instr       1
ktimpnt                 line 0, p3, 3           ; read the entire analysis file through
krmsr, krmso, kerr, kcps lpread  ktimpnt, "voice.lpc"

                                                ;if kerr < 0.3 then we should use a voiced (harmonic) sound
                                                ; source, else we should use an unvoiced sound source (white
                                                ; noise)

        if   kerr < 0.3 kgotovocal              ;if true jump to "vocal"
aecc    rand        krmso                       ;else generate noise excitation
        kgoto       okecc                       ;and jump to the "okecc"

vocal:
aecc    oscil       krmso, kcps, 2              ;voiced (harmonic) excitation

okecc:
aout    lpreson     aecc                        ;resynthesis
        out         aout*.01                    ;it is useful to scale the output to avoid possible saturation
        endin

;lpc1.sco
; create a function table with 20 harmonic components (for voiced excitation)
f2      0   4096    10  1 1 1 1 1 1 1 1 1 1 1 1 1 1 1 1 1 1 1 1
i1      0   3
```

To change the fundamental frequency and its amplitude, we should introduce two scaling factors only, as is shown in the next orchestra example:

```
;lpc2.orc
          sr     =  44100
          kr     =  4410
          ksmps  =  10
          nchnls =  1
          instr     1
ikamp            =  p4                         ;amplitude scaling factor
ikfreq           =  p5                         ;frequency scaling factor
ktimpnt   line      0, p3, 3
krmsr, krmso, kerr, kcps    lpread     ktimpnt, "voice.lpc"
          if        kerr<0.3   kgoto  vocal
aecc      rand      krmso
          kgoto     okecc

vocal:
aecc      oscil     krmso*ikamp, kcps*ikfreq, 2
okecc:
aout                lpreson aecc
          out       aout*.01
          endin
```

```
;lpc2.sco
; define a function table with 20 harmonic components (for voiced excitation)
f2    0   4096   10  1 1 1 1 1 1 1 1 1 1 1 1 1 1 1 1 1 1 1 1
i1    0   3   1   1
i1    3   3   2  .5
```

The first note in this score is identical with the first note in the previous example, but the second note has an amplitude two times as loud and a frequency an octave lower.

ktimpnt, too, can be modified for an effect similar to *pvoc* (see section 8.3).

We may even want to use a sound file as an excitation source, provided it has a rich spectrum (e.g. a symphonic orchestra, a shouting crowd, etc.). That creates crazy sounds such as a "speaking orchestra" and follies of that kind. We have to make sure that the Csound sampling rate is the same as the sound file's, and that the sound file duration is at least as long as the longest note required in the score (p3).

```
;lpc3.orc
            sr      =  44100
            kr      =  4410
            ksmps   =  10
            nchnls  =  1
            instr      1
ifact       =          p4                          ;scaling factor for the output sound (to fix empirically,
                                                   ;should be close to 0).
ktimpnt     line       0, p3, 3                    ; read the entire analysis file through
krmsr, krmso, kerr, kcps    lpread   ktimpnt, "voice.lpc"

aecc        soundin    "orchestra.wav"             ; external excitation source
aout        lpreson    aecc                        ; resynthesis
            out        aout*ifact                  ; scale and output
            endin

;lpc3.sco
i1  0  3  .0002
```

EXTENSIONS

8.A.1 FAST FOURIER TRANSFORM (FFT)

The Fourier Transform is the operation that allows us to turn a time-domain representation into a frequency-domain representation. Therefore, it transforms a time/amplitude signal into a frequency/amplitude spectrum (on this, see also 2.A.1).

The calculations it requires are somewhat demanding and complicated, even for the computer! When working with digital signals, however, there are ways to speed up the whole operation. That's why we speak of the *fast* Fourier Transform. The only constraint is the number of samples we can analyze. It must be a power of two (32, 64, 128. 256. 512. 1024, 2048, 4096, etc.).

The more samples, the higher the frequency precision in the analysis. In fact, if we call *n* the number of samples and *sr* the sampling frequency, the bandwidth in each analysis channel will be

bw = sr/n

For example, with *sr* = 44100 and *n* = 256, the analysis channel bandwidth is:

44100/256=172.27 Hz

which means that the analysis spectrum will include the amplitude values of the following frequencies:

172.27, 344.5, 516.8, 689, 861.3, 1033.6, etc.

Things are made a bit complicated by the fact that we are forced to use sample quantities with a power of two. In principle, the Fourier transform analyzes *one* cycle in the sound signal, and breaks it into sine and cosine terms (or sine terms plus phase values). Now, the problem is that it is rather unlikely that a sound signal has a cycle of as many samples as some power-of-two. We could simply truncate the signal and take some arbitrary chunk of the original length, but this will most probably introduce discontinuities at the beginning and the end of the analyzed signal, and cause serious distortions.

In fig.8-A-1 we see the effect of analyzing a sinusoidal signal in two different ways: in the first example (bottom) we simply take a chunk of a sinusoid and analyze it (using a *rectangular analysis window*); in the other (top) we apply some envelope to smooth out the beginning and the end of the sinusoid (in this case, we applied a *Hamming window*). You can see the difference in the results. The rectangular window, introduces many more spurious components than the Hamming window.

Many analysis windows exist, each having their own advantages and disadvantages. The choice of the particular window largely depends on the characteristics we hope to achieve in the resulting spectrum.

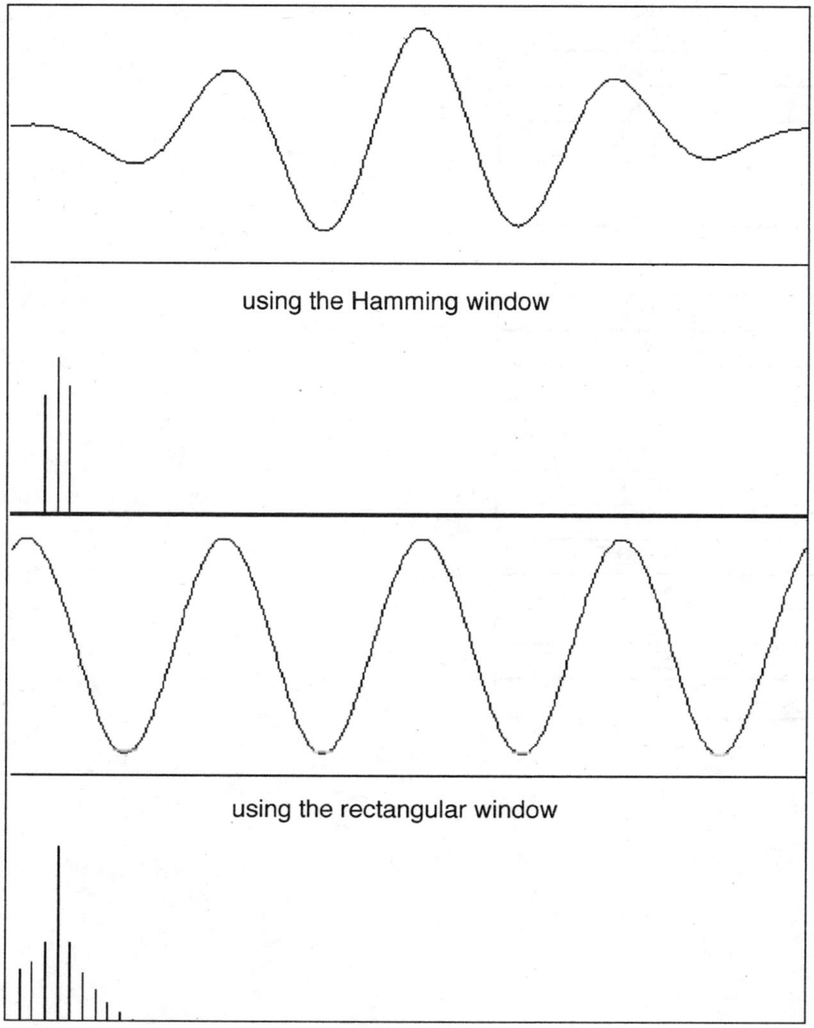

Fig. 8-A-1

Appendix - Chart of equivalences between intervals and frequency ratios

interval	frequency ratio
+12	2
+11	1.8878
+10	1.7818
+9	1.6818
+8	1.5874
+7	1.4983
+6	1.4142
+5	1.3348
+4	1.2599
+3	1.1892
+2	1.1225
+1	1.0595
0	1
-1	0.9439
-2	0.8909
-3	0.8409
-4	0.7937
-5	0.7492
-6	0.7071
-7	0.6674
-8	0.6300
-9	0.5946
-10	0.5612
-11	0.5297
-12	0.5

LIST OF OPCODES INTRODUCED IN THIS SECTION

a1 pvoc look-up_pointer, freq_scale_factor, analysis_file [, spectral_envelope_preservation_code]
a1 adsyn amp_scale_factor, freq_scale_factor, increment_scale_factor, analysis_file

krmsr, krmso, kerr, kcps lpread ktimpnt, ifilcod
krmsr average amplitude of analysis residual
krmso average amplitude of input signal
kerr estimated error in tracking fundamental frequency
kcps tracked fundamental frequency

a1 lpreson excitation_source_signal

9

USING MIDI FILES

9.1 STANDARD MIDI FILES

In 1982, the biggest music instrument manufacturers came to an agreement concerning a standard communication protocol for electronic instruments known as MIDI (Musical Instrument Digital Interface). In 1993, a standard file format was established, the Standard MIDI File (SMF) is used for storing MIDI data in a format common to many commercial software products (sequencers, notation programs, etc.). Under Windows operating systems, for example, standard MIDI files have the extension .MID and contain information needed to drive any MIDI device.

There exist two types of SMF, called Type 0 and Type 1. The only difference between them is that Type 0 has one track of MIDI data, while Type 1 can contain as many as 256 tracks. The single track in Type 0 can, however, address MIDI messages through any of the 16 MIDI channels.

Type 0 SMFs include the following information:

General header (with data such as the id file format, time patterning, metronome, tempo, musical key, etc.)
Track header (track id, etc.)
Track data (executable MIDI messages, such as note *ons* and *offs*, *program changes*, etc., separated by time lags).

Type 1 SMFs include the following:

General header
Track 1 header
Track 1 data
Track 2 header
Track 2 data
...
Track 19 header
Track 19 data.
etc.

Nearly all computer music applications can save data either in a proprietary format or the SMF format.

9.2 USING STANDARD MIDI FILES IN CSOUND

What is the use of having Csound data controlled via MIDI files? There are several answers to this. First, there are so many standard MIDI archives available (commercial CD-roms, the Internet, etc.) that it seems fairly reasonable to make them compatible with a powerful and ubiquitous system such as Csound. Second, creating a conventional music score is easier with a sequencing program or a notation program than with Csound, and usually, such programs can save the music as a standard MIDI file.

For these reasons, it is useful for us to have Csound to read and compile data from SMF. However, Csound reads only Type 0 SMFs. The reason for the restriction is quite simple. In Type 0 files, MIDI messages are parsed according to the timing of musical events, and therefore, Csound can read the MIDI data during its compilation. In Type 1, messages are distributed across several tracks, so that the entire file must be copied to memory *before* any program can read the data.

How can we make Csound read data from a SMF? We must use the flag *-F* in the Csound command line.

Win: suppose we have created some Csound code, saved as *midi1.orc* and *midi1.sco*, and suppose a standard MIDI file is available on our hard disk, called *bach.mid*. The complete command line will be:

csound -W -Fbach.mid -obach.wav midi1.orc midi1.sco

Mac: in the window, you'll find the MIDI file option box. Click on the box, and choose the name of some standard MIDI file you have on your hard disk. There is a "+" sign to visualize the whole interface.

We may ask: why use a Csound score (*midi1.sco*) here given that all necessary music data is in the *bach.mid* file? The score is needed for two reasons:

1. If the instruments in our orchestra require a table look-up (as is usually the case), the usual way to create the appropriate function tables is through the *f* statement in the Csound score.

2. Csound remains active as long as there are new score events to perform. For example, if a score has only a few *f* statements in it, such as

```
f1   0   4096   10   1    .3   .5
f2   0   4096   10   .1   1    .3
```

then Csound would create those function tables at time 0:00, and would then stop running. No sound would be generated. When using SMFs, the Csound score always has a *phantom event*, and the program remains active while all MIDI messages are processed. For example:

```
f1   0   4096   10   1    .3   .5
f2   0   4096   10   .1   1    .3

f0   3000
```

The third line here indicates a phantom event. It makes Csound run for up to 3000 seconds and creates the function number zero afterwards (f0 in actuality is void). In this way, the program reads a SMF for 3000 seconds. If the MIDI file has a duration of 3030 seconds, Csound will stop after 3000 seconds anyway, in which case, we'd better create f0 at 3030 seconds.

9.3 INSTRUMENT ASSIGNMENT

How do we translate MIDI messages into values that make sense for Csound? There are some special opcodes for that. Before examining them, let's deal with a different and more basic problem. We know that any instrument in the Csound orchestra can be called to play some *i* statement in the score. And, we know that the first argument to the *i* statement (p1) is the instrument id number. Fine. Every MIDI message comes with a channel number associated with 1 to 16. The particular Csound instrument called to play will be identified by the MIDI channel number.

Does that mean that our orchestra must include 16 instruments? What if our orchestra has only 3 instruments? Csound will look for the instrument id number corresponding to the MIDI channel number, and, if no instrument has that id number, it plays the note from the instrument with the closest (smaller) id number. For example, if our orchestra includes 3 instruments (instr 1, 2 and 3), and the standard MIDI file we want to execute has messages coming from 5 channels (1 through 5), Csound will call up the following instruments to play:

channel 1	→ instr 1
channel 2	→ instr 2
channels 3, 4 and 5	→ instr 3

9.4 MIDI VALUE CONVERTERS

Csound provides a variety of opcodes relative to input MIDI messages. They include:

ival notnum	returns a MIDI note number (0-127, 60 = middle C)
ival veloc	returns the *key velocity* (0-127)
icps cpsmidi	converts a MIDI note number to Hz
icps cpsmidib	same as above, but adding the MIDI pitch-bend
kcps cpsmidib [irange]	same as above, but scaling to the specified range
ioct octmidi	converts a MIDI note number to an *octave-pitch* value
ioct octmidib	same as above, but adding the MIDI pitch-bend
koct octmidib [irange]	same as above, but scaling to the specified range
ipch pchmidi	converts a MIDI note number to *pitch* value
ipch pchmidib	same as above, but adding the MIDI pitch-bend
kpch pchmidib [irange]	same as above, but scaling to the specified range
iamp ampmidi iscal[, ifn]	returns the MIDI *key velocity* normalized in the range 0-iscal, eventually mapped by the *ifn* function
kaft aftouch iscal	returns the MIDI *aftertouch* normalized in the range 0-*iscal*
kchpr chpress iscal	returns the MIDI *channel pressure* normalized in the range 0-*iscal*
kbend pchbend iscal	returns the MIDI *pitch-bend* normalized in the range 0-*iscal*
ival midictrl inum [, initial]	returns the value of the *inum* controller, initially set to *initial*

kval midictrl inum [, initial] returns the value of the *inum* controller, initially set to *initial*

kval midictrlsc inum [,iscal] [, ioffset] [, initial] returns the value of the *inum* controller, initially set to *initial*, normalized in the range 0-*iscal*, and shifted by some offset. For example, if *iscal* = 3000 and *ioffset* = 1000, *kval* can vary between 1000 and 4000 (i.e. between 0+*ioffset* and *ioffset*+*iscal*).

Depending on the particular Csound release, there can be other useful opcodes, such as those introduced by Gabriel Maldonado, including midic14 and midic21. These enable the linking of two or three MIDI controllers, in order to enlarge the value range of MIDI controls. While the output from a single controller is in the range 0-127 (a 7-digits binary number), the coupling of two yields the range 0-16383, and the coupling of three yields 0-2097151.

idest imidic7 ictlno, imin, imax [, ifn] returns the value of the MIDI controller number *ictlno*, normalized in the range *imin-imax*, and eventually mapped by the *ifn* function table.

kdest midic7 ictlno, kmin, kmax [, ifn] returns the value of the MIDI controller number *ictlno*, normalized in the range *kmin-kmax*, and eventually mapped by the *ifn* function table.

idest imidic14 ictlno1, ictlno2, imin, imax [, ifn] returns the value of the MIDI controller number *ictlno1* multiplied by that of MIDI controller *ictlno2*, normalized in the range *imin-imax*, and eventually mapped by the *ifn* function table.

kdest midic14 ictlno1, ictlno2, kmin, kmax [, ifn] returns the value of the MIDI controller number *ictlno1* multiplied by that of MIDI controller *ictlno2*, normalized in the range *kmin-kmax*, and eventually mapped by the *ifn* function table.

idest imidic21 ictlno1, ictlno2, ictlno3, imin, imax [, ifn] returns the value of the MIDI controller number *ictlno1* multiplied by that of MIDI controller *ictlno2* and by that of MIDI controller *ictlno3*, normalized in the range *imin-imax*, and eventually mapped by the *ifn* function table.

kdest midic21 ictlno1, ictlno2, ictlno3, kmin, kmax [, ifn] returns the value of the MIDI controller number *ictlno1* multiplied by that of MIDI controller *ictlno2* and by that of MIDI controller *ictlno3*, normalized in the range *kmin-kmax*, and eventually mapped by the *ifn* function table.

Let's examine an orchestra example:

```
;midi1.orc
        sr      =   44100
        kr      =   4410
        ksmps   =   10
        nchnls  =   1
        instr       1
ifrq    cpsmidi
iamp    ampmidi     12000
a1      oscil       iamp, ifrq, 1
        out         a1
        endin
```

Here's a score for that orchestra:

```
;midi1.sco
f1      0       4096    10      1
f0      30
```

Let's run Csound using the example above. Type in the following command line:

csound -W -Fbach.mid -obach.wav midi1.orc midi1.sco (*Win*)
csound -A -Fbach.mid -obach.aiff midi1.orc midi1.sco (*Mac*)

Csound expects the *bach.mid* file to be in your Csound folder. If it is in a different folder, you should type in the complete path, e.g.:

csound -W -F c:/midifiles/bach.mid -obach.wav midi1.orc midi1.sco

During performance, Csound will return a series of messages on screen. Here's an example:

```
midi channel 1 using instr 1
c:/csound/bach.mid: found standard midi file header
Metrical timing, Qtempo = 120.0, Qticks = 120
kperiods/tick =  18.375
tracksize = 194
audio buffered in 1024 sample-frame blocks
```

```
SFDIR undefined.  using current directory
writing 2048-byte blks of shorts to bach.WAV (WAV)
SECTION 1:
ftable 1:
new alloc for instr 1:
  rtevent          T   0.150   TT        0.150 M:    7500.0
  rtevent:         T   0.300   TT        0.300 M:    7500.0
  rtevent:         T   0.450   TT        0.450 M:    7500.0
  rtevent          T   0.600   TT        0.600 M:    7500.0
  ....
  rtevent:         T   3.000   TT        3.000 M:    7500.0
  rtevent:         T   3.150   TT        3.150 M:    7500.0
  rtevent:         T   3.300   TT        3.300 M:    7500.0
  rtevent:         T   3.450   TT        3.450 M:    7500.0
  rtevent:         T   3.750   TT        3.750 M:    7500.0
  rtevent:         T   4.050   TT        4.050 M:    7500.0
end of midi track in 'c:/csound/bach.mid'
0 forced decays, 0 extra noteoffs
B  0.000 .. 10.000  T 10.000    TT       10.000 M          0.0
end of score.            overall amps:                  7500.0
        overall samples out of range:                        0
0 errors in performance
431 2048-byte soundblks of shorts written to d:/csound/midi0.WAV (WAV)
```

The first line (midi channel 1 using instr 1) means that the program is reading data from a standard MIDI file. The next few lines show some of the data taken from the SMF header. When the synthesis process starts, Csound returns a series of *rtevent* (real-time event) messages, each corresponding to some MIDI *note on* or *off* (or any other MIDI event).

To stop the Csound compilation, we can add the flag *-T* to the command line. This stops Csound after the last MIDI event. Otherwise it will create a larger file with a few seconds of sound followed by minutes and minutes of silence! Under Windows, the process can also be stopped with the typical *ctrl-C* key sequence. On Macs, it can be stopped with the *Kill* button in the *Perfing* message box prompted upon launching the program.

When you listen to the sound file generated by this example, you will notice that notes have no envelope. We avoided using envelopes there because a different strategy must be followed for envelopes when standard MIDI files are used. Csound cannot determine, in advance, how long the duration is of each note. The SMF has no equivalent to *p3*, but only *note on* and *note off* messages. When it reads a note off message, Csound simply switches off the instrument, causing an audible click. What can we do to create an envelope for a note whose duration is unknown?

There is a special opcode, *linenr*, which allows a note to continue after the *note off* message is received, and gradually decay to zero (this was previously discussed in section 7.4). The syntax is:

kr linenr kamp, irise, idec, iatdec

Let's modify our last orchestra and introduce some envelope values:

```
;midi2.orc
        sr     =  44100
        kr     =  4410
        ksmps  =  10
        nchnls =  1
        instr     1
ifrq    cpsmidi
iamp    ampmidi   12000
kamp    linenr    iamp, .05, .5, .01 ;rise time=0.05, decay time=0.5
a1      oscil     kamp, ifrq, 1
        out       a1
        endin
```

Run Csound again. Notice that this time, notes have an appropriate amplitude envelope with a decay time that extends half a second beyond the MIDI *note off* message.

9.5 CONVERTING SCORE FILES TO SMF FILES AND VICE-VERSA

It is possible to translate any standard MIDI file (either type) into a Csound score. For this, we can use one of a number of non-commercial programs, such as *MIDI2CS*, which are available on the Internet. These programs are usually adequate, but sometimes manual corrections are necessary. This is especially true for amplitude values. While separate MIDI voices are usually played by separate tone generators, in Csound all sounds are summed together when the waveform values are written to the output sound file. So, we have to be careful that amplitudes do not exceed the dynamic range, the peak value of 32767.

On the Internet you may find programs capable of converting Csound scores to SMFs. What's their use? We can use them to import a Csound score into a notation program, (which is useful when combining acoustic instruments and computer-generated sounds), to prepare MIDI versions of any Csound-generated music.

EXTENSIONS

9.A.1 THE MIDI STANDARD

In 1983, the International MIDI User's Group (IMUG), an association of electronic instruments manufacturers, established the MIDI communication protocol for electronic music devices which established both the hardware and software standards for MIDI machines. In the official document (dating from August 5th, 1983), we can read:

"MIDI is the acronym for Musical Instrument Digital Interface" ... "it allows synthesizers, sequencers, home computers, electronic drums, etc. to be interconnected via a standard interface" ... "Every instrument equipped with MIDI contains a receiver and a transmitter port. Some may eventually feature either the receiver only, or the transmitter only. The receiver receives messages in MIDI format and execute MIDI commands [...] the transmitter generates and transmits messages in MIDI format".

Although MIDI is rather limited and not always reliable, as we will discuss below, it must be acknowledged for its uses, such as the simple exchange of complicated musical scores that can drive powerful synthesizers with personal computers. It helped, to a certain extent, the move of computer music from large centers to the composer's private workroom, and led to a phenomenon that we call *distributed computer music*.

9.A.2 FEATURES OF MIDI DEVICES

One of the advantages of MIDI, is that it works on different types of devices, as long as they meet the MIDI specifications. A MIDI device responds to messages such as *note on* and *note off*, and also to information indicating the note amplitude. In MIDI jargon, amplitude is usually called *key velocity*, and it is determined by the speed used to depress the key of an electronic keyboard. Speed can be associated with amplitude because it is proportional to the dynamics of a note played, like on a piano.

A MIDI device may also include a *pitch-bender* which is a hardware control that allows variation in pitch during the note. It is capable of receiving the corresponding real time MIDI messages. Typically, it also features a number of other controls allowing for real time modifications in the sound.

With a MIDI device, it is usually possible to choose among a number of pre-set sounds, whose timbre is stored in the internal memory. To change timbre (or *program*) there exists a special MIDI message, called *program change*.

If many receiving devices are connected to one controlling device (e.g. a computer), there must be a way for addressing different messages to different device, otherwise all devices would play the same musical line. This is accomplished by associating the different messages with different communication channels (MIDI *channel numbers*). Each device is given its own stream of information and plays its own line.

There are several ways a device can respond to MIDI messages. The different ways are called *channel modes*. In the official MIDI document, we read:

"Synthesizers have different sound-generating elements, called voices. Voice assignment is the algorithmic process by which note on/off data are mapped from the keyboard to the internal voices, such that all musical notes are played correctly and at the right moment"

"When the MIDI protocol was implemented, some precise relationship had to be established between the 16 MIDI channels available and the voice assignment of the synthesizer. That was possible by defining several mode messages, including Omni (on/off), Poly and Mono. Poly and Mono are mutually exclusive. When Omni is used, the receiver can respond to messages coming over all channels, without discrimination. When Mono is used, it forces the voice assignment to determine a single voice per channel (monophonic). When Mono is off (= Poly on), any number of voices can be allocated by the voice assignment algorithm of the receiver (polyphonic)."

9.A.3 MIDI NUMBERS

Because in MIDI everything is expressed in numbers, one must understand its conventions. For every note (or, to say it better, for every key) there is an associated number. Middle C, for example, is expressed by the number 60. C# is expressed by the number 61, D by 62, D# by 63, etc.

Permitted note numbers are within the range 0-127. However, not all MIDI devices are actually able to play the full range. If a note message is sent to a device that cannot handle that note, the pitch will be transposed by one or more octaves in order to bring it within the available range.

The dynamics, too, are represented in the range 0-127. The difference between one amplitude value and the next is logarithmic, in agreement with auditory principles, such that a linear mapping is preserved between the numerical values and the perceived amplitude change. Equal numerical intervals correspond to equally perceived amplitude differences.

The MIDI protocol permits substitutions for the equally-tempered intonation with other intonation systems. That is, however, strictly limited by the particular device. Alternatively, one can resort to the pitch-bend control and send pitch-bend values before the actual note number. This is like moving the pitch-bend wheel, which is available on many commercial synthesizers.

9.A.4 THE MIDI PROTOCOL

The hardware implementation of MIDI sound modules and controllers is inexpensive. It requires 5-pole DIN connectors, only 2 poles of which are wired to carry signals. Therefore, connectors and cables are really cheap. A major hardware restriction is that MIDI cables cannot be longer than 15 meters.

Usually, a MIDI device is equipped with three connectors: MIDI IN, to receive messages, MIDI OUT, to send messages, and MIDI THRU, to echo messages from the MIDI IN port.

The MIDI THRU is useful for driving more than one device at a time using one controller. This is shown in fig.9-A-1 (top). In practice, it is not recommended to have more than three devices in one chain. The MIDI THRU port always introduces a delay, and chaining many devices results in compounding delays, and cause a severe loss of synchronization.

The MIDI communication protocol is *serial*. It sends one data bit after another, sequentially. In order to better synchronize the connected devices, a "start bit" and a "stop bit" are included, preceding and following each data byte. So, in effect, each MIDI information unit includes 10 bits, 8 for the data and 2 for synchronizing the transmission itself (see fig.9-A-1, bottom).

MIDI messages are packed in several bytes, usually including one status byte and one or two data bytes. At the transmission rate of 31250 Baud (bit/second), the time needed to send a single MIDI byte is 320 microseconds, which means 3125 bytes/second. That may appear impressive, but actually, it is insufficient. Suppose we want to send a 16-note chord to each of the 16 MIDI channels: that means

3 bytes * 16 notes * 16 channels = 768 bytes

The complete transmission will take

768 / 3125 = 0.246 seconds

and the result will sound more like an arpeggiato chord, but what we wanted was just a normal chord with all notes starting simultaneously.

There are two kinds of MIDI messages: *channel messages* and *system messages*. The former carries a number corresponding to the MIDI channel, represented by the 4 least significant bits of the status byte. These messages are received and can be handled only by receivers set to "recognize" that MIDI channel number. The status byte of a channel message is composed in this manner:

m m m m c c c c

where m = message bit and c = channel number bit. With a 4-digit binary number it is possible to express 16 integer values (0-15). This is why there are only 16 MIDI channels.

The channel messages themselves include:

note on (= pressed key)	simulates the lowering of a key on a keyboard
note off (= released key)	simulates the release of a previously lowered key
after-touch (variation in pressure)	send a message concerning the pressure level on the particular key (available only on some synthesizers)
control change	
program change	change the timbre preset
pitch bend	determines a subtler change in intonation for those keys associated with a particular MIDI channel (this is accomplished with the pitch-bend wheel on some keyboards).

Csound is not able to handle system messages, so we do not explain them here.

LIST OF OPCODES INTRODUCED IN THIS SECTION

k1 linenr amp, rise_time, decay_time, attenuation_factor_of_decay_curve

a1 linenr amp, rise_time, decay_time, attenuation_factor_of_decay_curve

kval midictrlsc controller_number [,max_value] [, min_value] [,initial_value]

See section 9.4 for other opcodes.

10

REAL TIME MIDI CONTROLS

10.1 USING CSOUND IN REAL TIME

As the power of personal computers increases, it becomes possible to synthesize sounds in real time. The degree of complexity of the generated sounds depends on the orchestra and the number of separate musical lines we want to create (polyphony), and, to a larger extent, on the power of the computer used.[1]

Real time sound synthesis presents many musical possibilities for interaction and synchronization with vocalists and instrumentalists. It is possible to trigger some process or event with an external event or message. It is possible to adjust the synthesis timing with the timing of live instrumentalists, etc. The point here is that the machine operations now follow from human interactions, rather than the other way round (as with pre-recorded tape).

This new situation calls for real time signal processing, a possibility that in the past was reserved solely for specialized hardware and expensive computers.

Presently, the only means we have to control Csound in real time is through MIDI messages. We can send MIDI messages from any MIDI device, such as master keyboards, MIDI controllers (also known as "MIDI mixers", due to the fact that you operate them with faders, like a mixing console). But we can also send MIDI messages

[1] With "power", here we mean mainly the effective speed of floating point operations, a crucial factor for synthesis engines like Csound.

from another computer, and even from the same computer running Csound! There's no limit to MIDI connections except in our own imagination.

Clearly, if we are to take such an approach, it behooves us to exploit the computer resources in the most efficient way possible. That implies, for example, that we define the orchestra code with due attention to avoiding redundant operations (especially operations on audio- and control-rate variables) and use the slowest applicable sampling and control rates.

As an example, the line

```
a2      =       a1/2
```

should be replaced with

```
a2      =       a1*.5
```

as in fact multiplies are performed faster than divides. The line

```
aout    =   a1*kvol/4+a2*kvol/4+a3*kvol/4
```

should be replaced with the following:

```
k1      =       kvol*.25
aout    =       (a1+a2+a3)*k1
```

thereby using one variable assignment and two multiplies instead of three divides and three multiplies.

To use Csound in real time, it is necessary to replace the output file name with words such as *devaudio* or *dac* (depending on the particular computer platform and the particular Csound release), referencing the soundcard or other output audio device available on your computer.

Therefore, instead of

csound -W -oyourfile.wav yourorc.orc yourscore.sco

you want to write

csound -odevaudio yourorc.orc yourscore.sco

How to launch real time Csound (*Win*)

In the synthesis dialog box, beside the output sound file window is the *Realtime Out* button. Click on it, and you should see the sound file name change to *devaudio*. The button itself has a different label on it now, *Audio File*. Hitting this button, you can switch between real time and deferred time (sound file) output. We recommend you change the Csound buffer size when creating sounds in real time.
See section 10.3.

How to launch real time Csound (*Mac*)

It is sufficient to hit the *Audio out* button. The sound samples will be sent, then, to the computer's *Sound Manager*, which routes the audio samples to the available output device. To change the output buffer size, select *Set Buffers* from the *Preferences* menu. See section 10.3.

10.2 REAL TIME ORCHESTRAS AND SCORES

Everything that was already discussed in section 9.2 applies here, too. Csound doesn't differentiate between standard MIDI file messages and real time MIDI messages. It is even possible to use Csound in deferred time, as usual, but send it real time MIDI messages. The only problem there, is that we cannot hear what we are "playing"!

To make Csound receive real time MIDI messages, it is necessary to add the -M flag to the standard command line. Following the flag, you have to write the name of the MIDI driver for the input device. Under Windows operating systems, the name is *sbmidi*:[2]

csound -W -Msbmidi -odevaudio yourorc.orc yourscore.sco

Let's now examine a "playable" Csound orchestra. We'll assume that the orchestra can be played via a MIDI keyboard, and that the keyboard has a controller wheel (also known as modulation wheel, which in the end, is the same as the MIDI controller #1).

```
;midirt1.orc
        sr      =  22050            ;a lower sr allows for a larger number of musical lines
        kr      =  441
        ksmps   =  50
```

[2] If you have a Windows system, it is likely that your computer is equipped with one or more MIDI devices (either hardware or software). If that is the case, Csound will ask you which device should be used. Alternatively, when launching the program you can use the -+M flag followed by a device number, e.g. -+M2.

```
          nchnls =   1
          instr      1
ifrq      cpsmidi
iamp      ampmidi    12000
kamp      linenr     iamp, .05, .5, .01       ;risetime=0.05, decaytime=0.5
kindmx    midictrl   1,13                     ;highest modulation index FM:controller #1,
                                              ;max=13
kindx     linenr     kindmx, .01, .5, .01     ;dynamical control over the modulation index
a1        foscil     kamp, ifrq, 1, 1, kindx, 1
          out        a1
          endin

;midirt1.sco
f1   0    4096  10   1
f0   3600                                     ;Csound remains active for 1 hour (=3600 seconds)
```

In the next example, the orchestra is capable of filtering and panning an input sound, for example a singing voice. We assume that the orchestra can be played via a MIDI device sending not only *note on/off* messages, but also control messages equivalent to MIDI controllers 1, 2 and 3.

```
;midirt2.orc
        sr     =  22050
        kr     =  441
        ksmps  =  50
        nchnls =  2
        instr     1
kfilt   midic7    1, 100, 3000                ;controller 1: center frequency
                                              ;of bandpass filter, ranging 100 to 3000 Hz
kbw     midic7    2, 1, 300                   ;controller 2: bandwidth ranging 1-300 Hz
kste    midic7    3, 0, 1                     ;controller 3: stereo panning, 0 to 1
a1      in                                    ;real time input sound
aout    reson     a1, kfilt, kbw, 2           ;filtering
        outs      aout*(1-kste), aout*kste
        endin

;midirt2.sco
f0      3600                                  ;Csound remains active for 1 hour(=3600 seconds)
```

10.3 SOME CAUTIONS

Experimenting with real time synthesis, we could encounter some difficulties. It is most likely that at some point you will hear frequent interruptions in the output sound stream. That is caused by the fact that the computer resources cannot be completely consumed by the runtime program. The operating system constantly requires at least some part of the available computing resources, for general "housekeeping".

Obviously, it is not possible to get rid of the operating system. However, we may want to choose carefully from among several operating systems, and select the one that least interferes with the output audio stream. What can we do, then, to solve this problem? Here are some hints:

- close all active applications, including those running in background;
- turn the screen saver off;
- close all utilities accessing your hard disk periodically (such as anti-virus programs, disk defragmenters, etc.).

You should use some special command line flags which allow for a correct buffering of the output sound stream. During performance, Csound fills the audio memory buffer with a pre-determined number of samples. When the buffer is full, Csound commands the sound i/o manager program to take those samples and send them to the DAC. While the output is buffering, Csound keeps on generating new samples, writing them to a second buffer. When this second buffer is full, these samples are themselves sent to the DAC. In the meanwhile, Csound is still calculating new samples, sending them to the former buffer, and the whole process is repeated all over again. This is called *double buffering*, but we may want to use *quadruple buffering*, etc.

The flag *-b* is used to set the buffer size. Buffers that are too small may cause frequent interruptions in the sound stream, while buffers that are too large may result in a perceivable delay between the synthesis and the output. Depending on the complexity of your orchestra, as well as on the power of your computer, you should systematically choose the most appropriate buffer size. To begin with, try with *-b*4096.

The flag *-P* is used to determine, instead, the number of buffers required. It is good idea to set a buffer size equal to some integer sub-multiple of the sampling rate and of the control rate.

If you use a Windows system, a special Csound release is now available which makes use of DirectSound for real-time output.[3] That allows for very small audio i/o buffers, and hence, Csound responds quickly to MIDI commands.

[3] DirectSound (which is part of DirectX) is a system developed in order to accelerate all sound-related operations in Windows computers. See Maldonado's reading on DirectCsound in this book.

11

AMPLITUDE MODULATION AND RING MODULATION

11.1 INTRODUCTION

"Modulation is the alteration of the amplitude, phase, or frequency of an oscillator in accordance with another signal".[1] The modulated oscillator is called the *carrier*, the modulating oscillator is called the *modulator*.

Do you remember the way in which we created tremolo?

What we did was to introduce a slight **amplitude modulation** by means of a modulating signal (a control variable), and that changed the amplitude of a carrier signal. In that case, the modulator caused limited amplitude variations, and had a very low frequency in the sub-audio range (*infrasonic* frequencies). But, what happens if we use a modulator with a frequency higher than 20 Hz? The resulting sound is different, and includes new frequency components to the side of the carrier frequency. These new components are usually called *sidebands*, as they are symmetrically placed below and above the carrier frequency as we shall see in a moment.

Amplitude modulation (AM) and *ring* modulation (RM) both are based on this simple process. The difference is that the former involves a *unipolar* modulator signal while the second involves a *bipolar* one (see fig.11-1).

[1] C.Dodge & T.Jerse, *Computer Music*, Schirmer, New York, 1985, p.80.

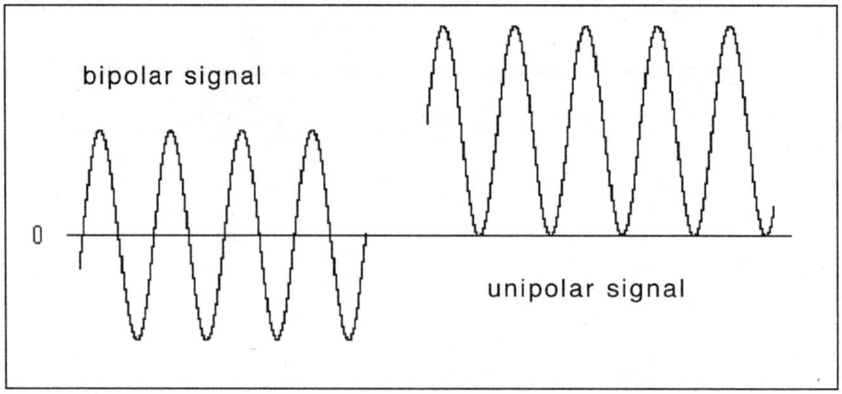

Fig. 11-1

A **bipolar** signal oscillates between positive and negative peaks:

```
a1 oscili 10000, 220, 1            ;signal oscillates between 10000 and -10000
```

A **unipolar** signal oscillates only in the positive (or negative) field. To create a unipolar signal, we have to add some constant value to a bipolar oscillation. The constant value is usually referred to as *DC offset* (direct current offset, see section 2.7). Let's consider an example of a unipolar signal oscillating in the positive field:

```
abimod     oscili 1 , 220, 1       ;abimod oscillates between 1 and -1
aunimod  = abimod+1                ;aunimod oscillates between 0 e 2, i.e.
                                   ;in the positive field
```

As you see, we simply add a constant value, 1, to the signal *abimod*, and make it oscillate only in the positive field.

In chap.5, we used both uni- and bipolar modulators with a very low, infrasonic, frequency.

11.2 AMPLITUDE MODULATION (AM)

To create a tremolo, the modulating signal can be conveniently represented as a control variable. But to implement amplitude modulation, we have to use audio variables. In fact, the modulating signal frequency this time will be within the audible range.

Example:

```
;am.orc
        sr     =  44100
        kr     =  4410
        ksmps  =  10
        nchnls =  1
        instr     1
abimod  oscili    5000, 200, 1       ;abimod oscillates between 5000 and -5000
aunimod        =  abimod+5000        ;add an offset of 5000, to get a unipolar
                                     ;modulator (aunimod oscillates between 0
                                     ;and 10000)
acar    oscili    aunimod, 800, 1    ;carrier: amplitude is controlled with the
                                     ;unipolar oscillation
        out       acar
        endin

;am.sco
f1  0   4096   10   1
i1  0   3
```

If both the carrier and the modulator have a sinusoidal waveform, two sidebands are created, one having a frequency equal to the carrier frequency plus the modulator frequency (800+200 = 1000 Hz), the other having a frequency equal to the carrier frequency minus the modulator frequency (800-200=600 Hz). The resulting spectrum will include the carrier frequency.

We call C the carrier and M the modulator. The spectrum of the output signal, *acar*, includes these frequencies:

C-M	**C**	**C+M**
600	**800**	**1000**

What about the amplitude of those components? The amplitude of the 800 Hz component will not be affected in any way by the modulation, while the amplitude of the sidebands depends on the ratio between the modulator amplitude and the DC offset value. This ratio is called the *modulation index*. If the DC offset equals the modulator amplitude, the index is 1. The amplitude level of the frequency corresponding to the carrier frequency is not affected by the modulation.

The sidebands amplitude can be calculated by multiplying the DC offset by half the index value. Therefore, if the modulation index equals 1, the amplitude of the sidebands will be half the amplitude of the carrier band. Let's examine a concrete case. Call *I* the modulation index, *DC* the direct current offset and *Aside* the sideband amplitude:

Aside = DC*I/2

With DC=x and I=1, we get
Aside = x*1/2, that is
Aside = x/2.

With DC=x and I=0.5, we get
Aside = x*0.5/2, that is
Aside = is x/4.
With I=0, we get Aside = 0.

Usually the ear easily detects the ongoing amplitude variations when the modulator is lower that 10 Hz (tremolo). The sidebands will be perceived as separate when the modulator frequency is higher than 10 Hz and exceeds one-half the critical band.

Fig.11-2 (left) shows the flow-chart of this simple AM instrument. It also shows (right) a fragment of the resulting signal and its spectrum.

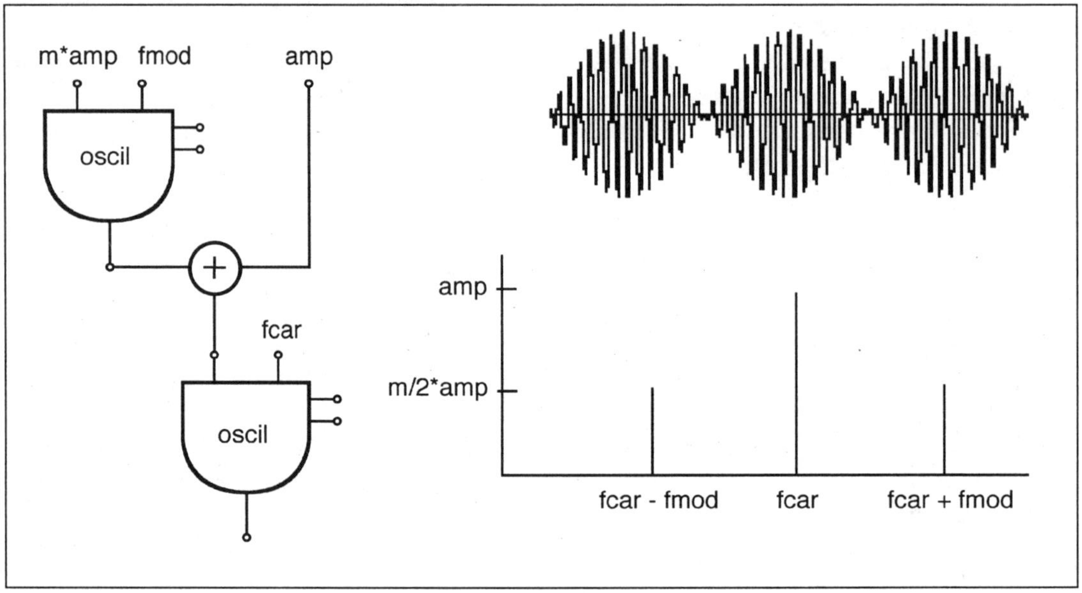

Fig. 11-2

When discussing AM, some authors describe the DC offset with a different terminology. The DC offset is referred to as "the carrier amplitude *before* the modulation". We believe the term DC offset is less confusing, as it shows that it is a direct current component.

To see what happens by gradually increasing the modulation index, from 0 to 1, let's experiment with the following orchestra and score:

```
;am2.orc
          sr     =  44100
          kr     =  4410
          ksmps  =  10
          nchnl  =  1
          instr     1
kenv      linseg    0, p3, 5000           ; the envelope curve, raising from 0 to 5000,...
mod       oscili    kenv, 1000, 1         ;...is used as the amount of modulation...
acar      oscili    5000+amod, 2000, 1    ;...(index goes from 0 to 1)
          out       acar
          endin
```

```
;am2.sco
f1   0   4096   10   1
i1   0   4
```

11.3 RING MODULATION (RM)

Now we modify our AM orchestra, using a bipolar signal as the modulator. For that aim, we have to drop the sum of *abimod* and DC offset.

```
;am3.sco
          sr     =  44100
          kr     =  4410
          ksmps  =  10
          nchnls =  1
          instr     1
abimod    oscili    5000, 200, 1          ;abimod oscillates between -5000 and 5000
                                          ;(bipolar signal)
acar      oscili    abimod, 800, 1        ;carrier: amplitude is driven by abimod
          out       acar
          endin
```

```
;am3.sco
f1   0    4096   10    1
i1   0    3
```

By using the output signal from the modulating oscillator to control the amplitude of the carrier oscillator, we obtained *ring modulation*. This is equivalent to "the multiplication of two bipolar audio signals by one another. That is, a carrier signal C is multiplied by a modulator signal M".[2] When the amplitude of the modulator is 0, then there will be no output signal at all, not even the carrier frequency. In AM, on the contrary, even when the modulator is 0 there will always be some output signal (the carrier frequency), as the carrier gets the DC offset value as its amplitude. The basic difference in AM, is that the spectrum of RM signals does not include the carrier frequency (see fig.11-3).

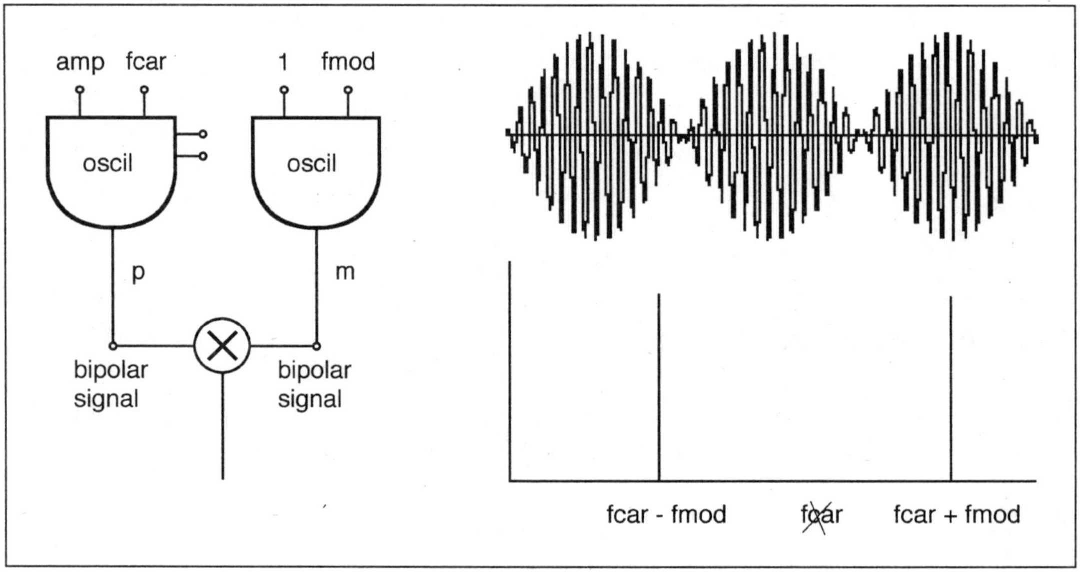

Fig. 11-3

As an example, the following instrument

```
        instr   1
abimod  oscili  100, 200, 1     ;bipolar modulator
acar    oscili  100, 800, 1     ;carrier
```

[2] C.Roads, *Computer Music Tutorial*, MIT Press, Cambridge Mass., 1996, p.216.

```
amult   =       abimod*acar   ;multiply
        out     amult
        endin
```

will output a signal made of two components (provided function 1 is a sine wave):

C-M	**C+M**
600	**1000**

We may want to multiply two complex signals. In this case, the output signal will include all the sidebands relative to each of the partial components in each of the two original signals. Therefore, if both signals are made of 6 components, we get a sound whose spectrum includes 6*6*2 components. Some of these output components could overlap each other, especially if the two multiplying signals are harmonically related.

Let's examine the following example:

```
;ring.orc
        sr      =  44100
        kr      =  4410
        ksmps   =  10
        nchnls  =  1

        instr      1
abimod  oscili     100, 250, 1              ;bipolar mod
acar    oscili     100*abimod, 800, 1       ;bipolar car
        out        acar
        endin
```

```
;ring.sco
f1   0   4096   10   3   2   1
i1   0   3
```

Here the carrier and the modulator have this spectral composition:

C	**M**
800, 1600, 2400 Hz	**250, 500, 750 Hz**

Thus the output components will be:

C+M = 1050, 1300, 1550, 1850, 2100, 2350, 2650, 2900, 3150 Hz
C-M = 50, 300, 550, 850, 1100, 1350, 1650, 1900, 2150 Hz

This is illustrated in fig.11-4 where we see the spectral analysis of the output generated with *ring.orc* and *ring.sco*.

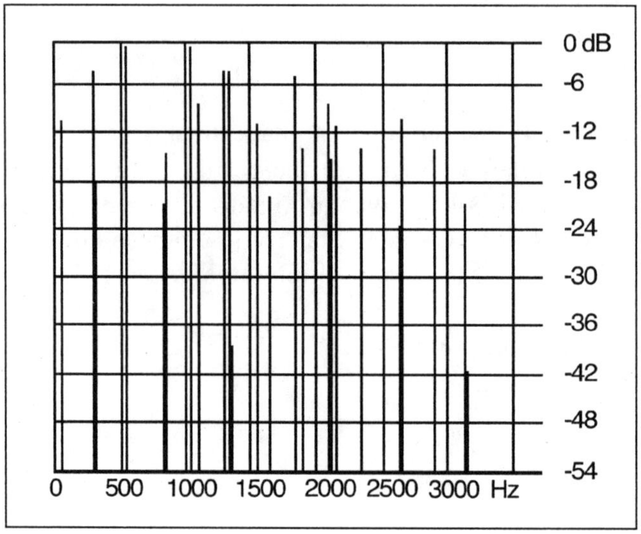

Fig. 11-4

EXTENSIONS

11.A.1 THE AM AND RM FORMULAS

Trigonometry provides us with the mathematical means by which we may understand amplitude and ring modulation. The so-called *prostapheresis* formulas state that:

$$\sin(\alpha) * \sin(\beta) = 1/2(\cos(\alpha - \beta) - \cos(\alpha + \beta))$$

which means simply that the multiplication of two sinusoidal signals, of frequencies α and β, results in a signal made of two sine (or cosine) components whose frequencies are, respectively, the difference and the sum of the two original frequencies. This corresponds to ring modulation as described in this chapter. In our examples, we assumed that the two sinusoidal signals have unit amplitude.

With amplitude modulation, the modulator, $\sin(\beta)$, has to be unipolar, thus it becomes:

$$1 + \sin(\beta)$$

The left term of the prostapheresis formula is

$$\sin(\alpha) * (1 + \sin(\beta))$$

which can be rendered as

$$\sin(\alpha) * \sin(\beta) + \sin(\alpha)$$

which, in accordance with the prostapheresis formula, is equal to

$$\sin(\alpha) * \sin(\beta) + \sin(\alpha) = 1/2(\cos(\alpha - \beta) - \cos(\alpha + \beta)) + \sin(\alpha)$$

There we see that the AM signal includes the carrier frequency.

11.B.1 HISTORICAL SKETCHES ON RING MODULATION

Just like amplitude modulation, ring modulation was initially used for radio broadcasting purposes. The idea to use it to create and transform sounds, was first developed in the WDR studio in Cologne. The name "ring modulation" stems from the fact that four diodes were required to implement an RM analog circuit and were placed one beside the other as in a ring (fig.11-A-1). The input sound passed through two of the ring vertices, the output sound passed out from the opposite two vertices.

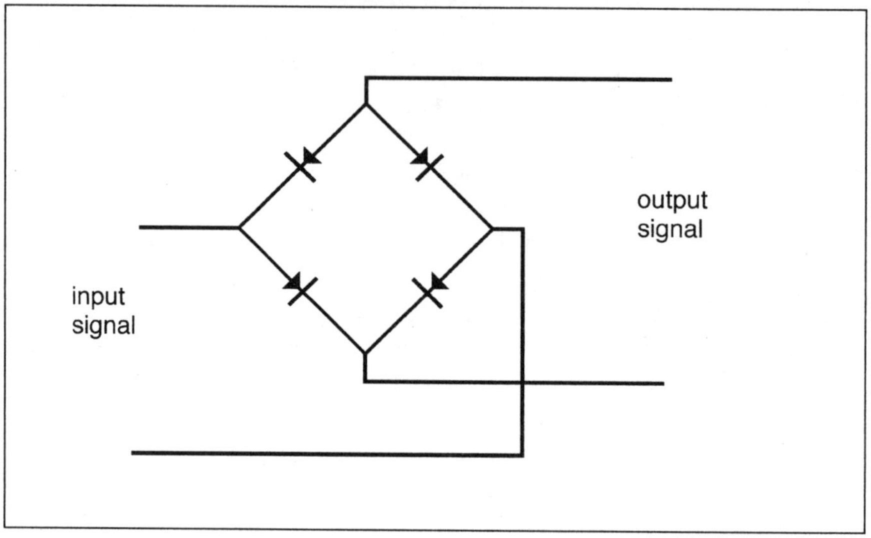

Fig. 11-A-1

Ring modulation was widely utilized through the 1950's and 1960's. It was employed to obtain complex sounds with just two oscillators, or to heavily modify the timbre of instrumental sounds. In some cases, the technique was also used to extend the limitations of the equally-tempered scale inherent to the fixed intonation of most acoustic instruments.

Karlheinz Stockhausen exploited the process of ring modulation in such pieces as *Momente*, *Mixtur* and *Mikrophonie I.* In *Mantra*, for two pianos and two ring modulators, he used the technique for all the three goals we have briefly listed above, but most prominently for timbre modifications. He wrote: "*...the metallic sound element emerges, due to the fact that the differential components determine sub-harmonic spectra finally heard together with the harmonic spectra of the sum components. And when I come back to the 13th note, at the end of the 'mantric' exposition, I actually come back to maximum consonance: the* mantra *intervals are so composed that they go away from the central tone making more and more way to deviations, micro-intervals and noise components - that we call dissonant components - and eventually come back*". [3]

[3] J.Cott, *Stockhausen. Conversations with the composer,* New York, 1973.

12

FREQUENCY MODULATION (FM)

12.1 BASIC FM THEORY

Like amplitude modulation, frequency modulation (FM), too, involves a modulating oscillator and a carrier oscillator (at least in the simplest setup). In this technique, however, the modulator drives the frequency of the carrier, not its amplitude. The flow-chart of a simple FM instrument is illustrated in fig.12-1. As you see, this is similar to the flow-chart for the vibrato instrument discussed in section 5.3.

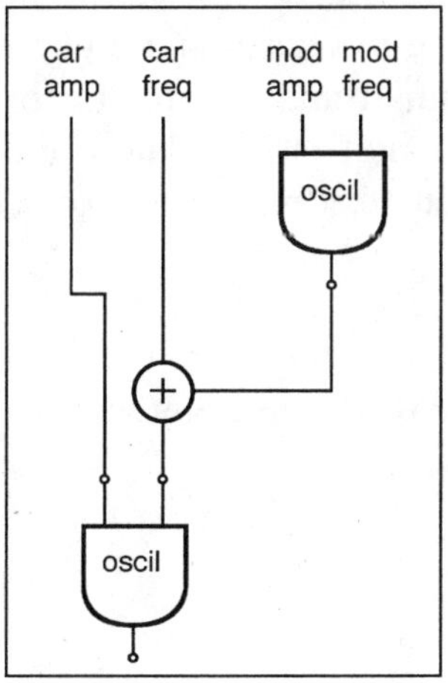

Fig. 12-1

So we have two sine wave oscillators, one called the carrier, the other called the modulator. If the modulator amplitude is 0, there will be no modulation and the output signal will be identical with the carrier signal. By increasing the modulator amplitude, we introduce frequency modulation. In effect the carrier frequency will go up and down following the waveform pattern of the modulator. When the modulating oscillation is in the positive field, the carrier frequency will raise above the base frequency. When it moves to the negative, the carrier frequency shifts below the base frequency. As we increase the modulator amplitude, the amount of deviation gets larger. The maximum deviation in the carrier is called the *peak frequency deviation*, and is measured in Hz.

In AM, a sine wave modulator + carrier coupled results in a spectrum with three components (the carrier frequency plus two sidebands). In FM, theoretically the number of sidebands can be infinite. However, the number of audible sidebands depends on the peak frequency deviation. The higher the peak, the more numerous the sidebands in the output sound spectrum.

With a carrier frequency (**C**) of 1000 Hz and a modulating frequency (**M**) of 3 Hz, the following sidebands are obtained:

1003 (C+M)	997 (C-M)
1006 (C+2*M)	994 (C-2*M)
1009 (C+3*M)	991 (C-3*M)
1012 (C+4*M)	988 (C-4*M)
1015 (C+5*M)	985 (C-5*M)
......	....

In theory, the FM sidebands are *always* infinite in number. In practice, however, the higher-order sidebands often have too weak an amplitude level to be heard, especially when the modulation index is small and the modulator frequency is in the sub-audio range. The peak frequency deviation is calculated multiplying a constant, called the modulation index (**I**) by the modulator frequency:

D = I * M

Consider the following score. We will use this score in conjunction with the orchestra illustrated in next section, *fm.orc*:

```
;fm.sco
f1   0    4096    10    1
;    start   dur    car amp    car frq    mod frq    mod indx
i1   0       2.9    10000      1000       3          10
```

i1	3	.	10000	1000	3	30
i1	6.	.	10000	1000	3	50
i1	9.	.	10000	1000	3	1000

With the first three notes, we perceive a sine tone sweeping higher and lower across the frequency range, in a glissando effect. Here the sidebands are so close to the carrier frequency (1000 Hz) that they fall in the same critical band.[1] As they are not perceptible they do not affect the overall timbre.

Things change with the fourth note. Although the modulator has the same 3 Hz as the preceding notes, the modulation index is much larger and causes the frequency deviation to be wider. The amplitude of the sidebands is sufficiently large, and we will hear something that is not quite the same as a sine wave with glissando. Let's calculate the peak deviation for this note:

D = 3*1000 = 3000 Hz.

The audible components of this sound fall within a frequency band as wide as 6000 Hz, and range from -2000 Hz (C - D = carrier frequency minus peak deviation = 1000 - 3000) to 4000 Hz (C + D = carrier frequency plus peak deviation = 1000 + 3000). Things seem to be getting more and more complicated. What happens when frequencies are negative?

Negative frequency components are identical with positive frequency components, but with inverted phase. They sum algebraically with positive components and are destructive to those components that happen to have the same frequency. The phenomenon is illustrated fig.12-2.

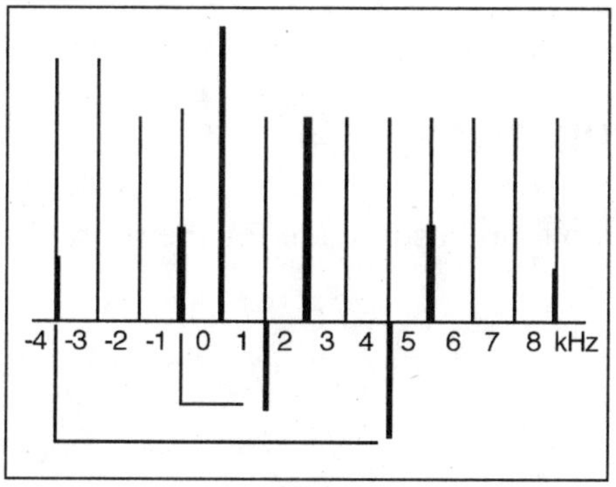

Fig. 12-2

[1] The "critical band" is defined as the smallest frequency difference between two components that allows the human ear to hear those components as separate and distinct sounds, not as a single sound.

There is a 2000 Hz carrier and a 3000 Hz modulator. In the resulting sound spectrum, the -1000 Hz and -4000 Hz components fold back into the positive frequency range and are phase-shifted, causing a loss of amplitude in the 1000 Hz and 4000 Hz components.

This is similar to the foldover phenomenon which takes place when we try to generate frequencies higher than the Nyquist frequency (*sr/2*). For example, suppose a sampling rate of 22050 Hz is used (Nyquist frequency = 11025 Hz), and a FM synthesis instrument is used with C = 5000 Hz and M = 5000 Hz and with I = 3. The sideband frequencies sweep between -10000 Hz and +20000 Hz, and that causes the folding of both the higher components (higher than 11025 Hz) and the negative components. This is illustrated in fig.12-3. You see that there are at least four components higher than the Nyquist frequency. Consider the 15 kHz one. It folds back into the audible frequency range, as a frequency of 15000-11025=3975 Hz.

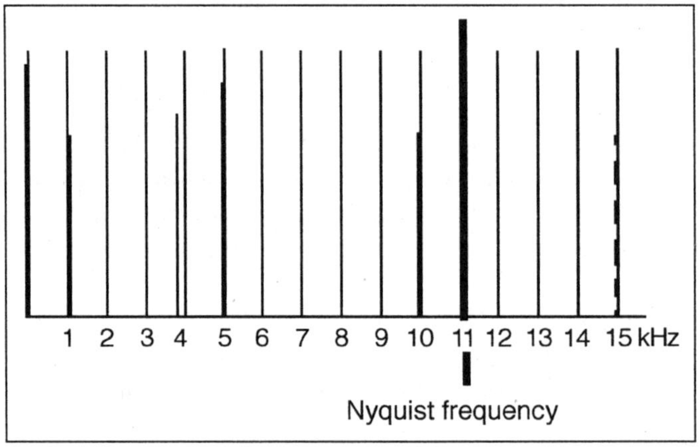

Fig. 12-3

12.2 SIMPLE FM ORCHESTRAS

Let's now write the suitable orchestra code for the score described above (fm.sco):

```
;fm.orc
        sr      =  44100
        kr      =  2205
        ksmps   =  20
        nchnls  =  1

        instr   1
```

```
icamp    =  p4                        ;carrier amplitude (0-32767)
icfrq    =  p5                        ;carrier freq(Hz)
imfrq    =  p6                        ;modulator freq(Hz)
indx     =  p7                        ;modulation index

;- - - - - - - - - - - - - - - - - - - - - - MODULATOR
amod  oscili  indx*imfrq, imfrq, 1    ;modulator amp argument = imfrq * indx
                                      ;e.g. if imfrq=1000 and indx =.5
                                      ;then modulator amp= indx*imfrq=500

;- - - - - - - - - - - - - - - - - - - - - - CARRIER
acar  oscili  icamp, icfrq+amod, 1    ;amplitude argument = icamp
                                      ;freq argument = icfrq + amod

      out     acar
      endin
```

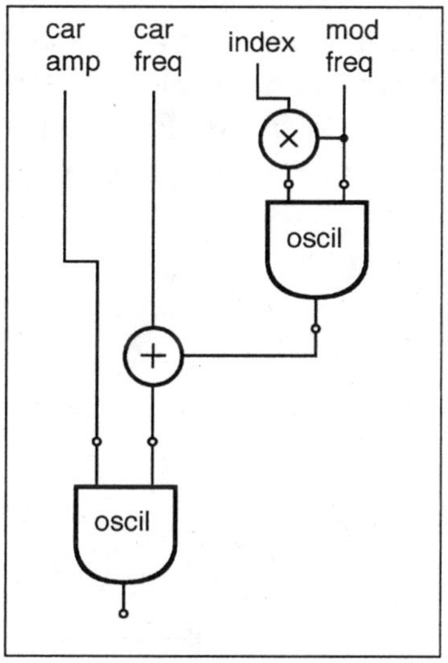

Fig. 12-4

Another way to implement this simple FM setup, is to use the special opcodes *foscil* and *foscili*. These have a built-in FM couple (carrier + modulator). Their syntax is:

ar foscil xamp, kcps, kcar, kmod, kndx, ifn[, iphs]
ar foscili xamp, kcps, kcar, kmod, kndx, ifn[, iphs]

ar	output audio variable
xamp	overall amplitude
kcps	"nominal" frequency value
kcar	carrier factor: carrier frequency is *kcps*kcar*
kmod	modulator factor: modulator frequency is *kcps*kmod*
kndx	modulation index
ifn	table function number (typically, it contains a sine wave)

Let's examine the *kcps*, *kcar* and *kmod* arguments.

If we wanted to define a carrier frequency of 200 Hz and a modulator frequency of 350, we have a number of choices:

kcps	kcar	kmod	
1	200	350	(carrier freq= 1*200=200, modulator freq=1*250=350), or
50	4	7	(carrier freq= 50*4=200, modulator freq=50*7=350), or
200	1	1.75	(carrier freq= 200*1=200, modulator freq=200*1.75=350).

These statements create the required carrier and modulator frequencies. In the third possibility, however, the C:M ratio is more clearly stated, and more easily readable (especially when comparing the sound spectra families discussed in next section).

Now, let's add a new instrument to our orchestra, instr 2, using the *foscil* opcode:

```
        instr   2

icamp   =   p4                  ;carrier amp (0-32767)
ifrq    =   p5                  ;nominal freq
ipk     =   p6                  ;carrier freq factor
imk     =   p7                  ;modulator freq factor
indx    =   p8                  ;modulation index

aout    foscili  icamp, ifrq, ipk, imk, indx, 1

        out aout
        endin
```

and test the new instrument by adding these lines to the event list in *fm.sco*:

```
;p1   p2    p3    p4      p5     p6     p7   p8
i2    12    2.9   10000   1000   1000   3    10
```

```
i2   15   .   10000   1000   1000   3   30
i2   18   .   10000   1000   1000   3   50
i2   21   .   10000   1000   1000   3   1000
```

12.3 SOUND SPECTRA FAMILIES

When the greatest common divisor (GCD) of the carrier and modulator frequencies is a value corresponding to an audible frequency, the FM output sound has a **harmonic spectrum** and a fundamental frequency which corresponds to the GCD value itself.[2] To be more precise, here we should speak of the **apparent** fundamental, as in fact, the actual fundamental tone could in principle be missing; and still, it would be re-constructed by the ear provided a sufficient number of harmonics are present in the spectrum - particularly the lower ones.

Every C:M ratio yields a variety of sounds similar in spectral composition. It represents a whole *family* of sound spectra.

For example:

Car freq		Mod freq	Fundamental	
100		100	100	
diff		sum		
0	C-M	200	C+M	
-100	C-2M	300	C+2M	(-100 Hz becomes a phase-shifted 100 Hz)
-200	C-3M	400	C+3M	
-300	C-4M	500	C+4M	
-400	C-5M	600	C+5M	
.....		.....		

Special cases are:

a. Mod freq = Car freq, generates the complete set of harmonics. For example:

```
i1   0   2   10000   200   200   2
```

b. Mod freq = 2*Car freq, generates odd harmonics only:

---

2 If such a value actually exists: indeed, when the c:m ratio is an irrational number (for example, 1/3) there is no GCD, and the spectrum will be inharmonic.

Car freq	Mod Freq
100	200

diff	sum	Fundamental
-100	300	100
-300	500	
-500	700	

Example:

```
i1  0  2  10000  100  200  2
```

c. Mod freq = 11/35*Car freq

Car freq	Mod freq	apparent Fundamental
550	700	50

Example:

```
i1  0  2  10000  550  700  1
```

In the last case, we obtain the following components:

- 150	1250
- 850	1950
-1550	2650
-2250	3350

whose GCD = 50. However, the lower harmonics are too weak for the ear to provide the apparent fundamental tone. So the spectrum is heard as a chord instead of a pitched sound).

To obtain inharmonic spectra, we should use two prime numbers as the carrier and the modulator frequencies,[3] or at least two numbers whose GCD < 20.

As a rule of thumb, the number of sidebands with audible amplitude level (levels higher than 1/100th of the fundamental's level, i.e. at least -40 dB) is approximately equal to I+1 (remember I is the modulation index value). The total bandwidth in the generated sound spectrum is approximately equal to twice the sum of the peak deviation frequency and the modulator frequency:

[3] Any two numbers are prime when they have no integer divisor in common.

Bandwidth = 2 * (D + M)

12.4 MULTIPLE-CARRIER FM

Let's build another FM instrument, with the modulator driving the frequency of three carrier oscillators, each with different amplitude and frequency values. Observe the flow-chart in fig.12-5. The resulting sound is more complex in comparison to the sound of the single-carrier FM instrument.

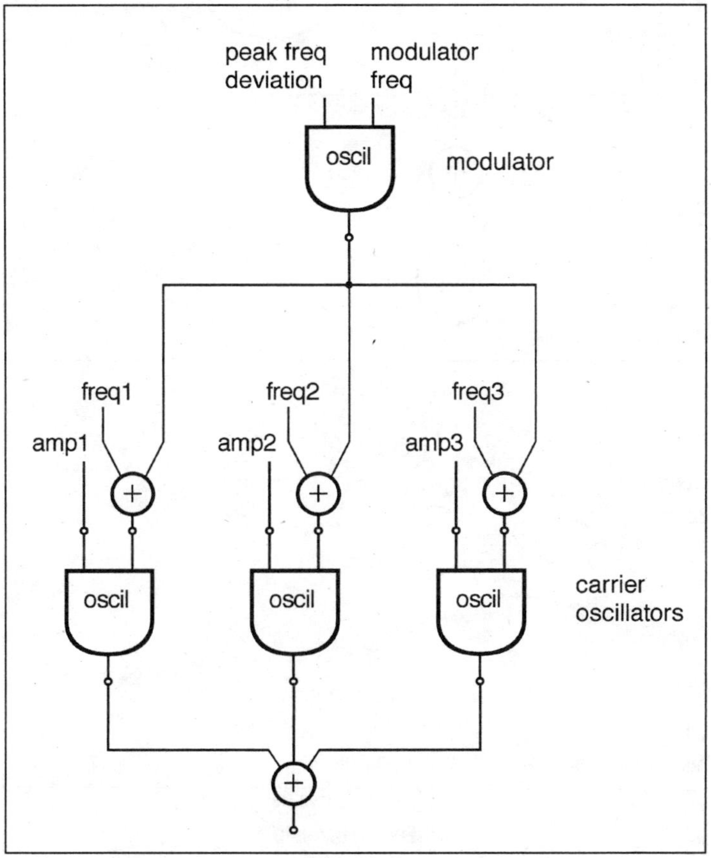

Fig. 12-5

Now let's implement this new FM setup using *foscil* following the flow-chart in fig.12-6. Here we shall drive the amplitude of the three carriers with separate envelopes (*kenvcar1, kenvcar2, kenvcar3*), and the modulation index with another envelope (*kenvindx*):

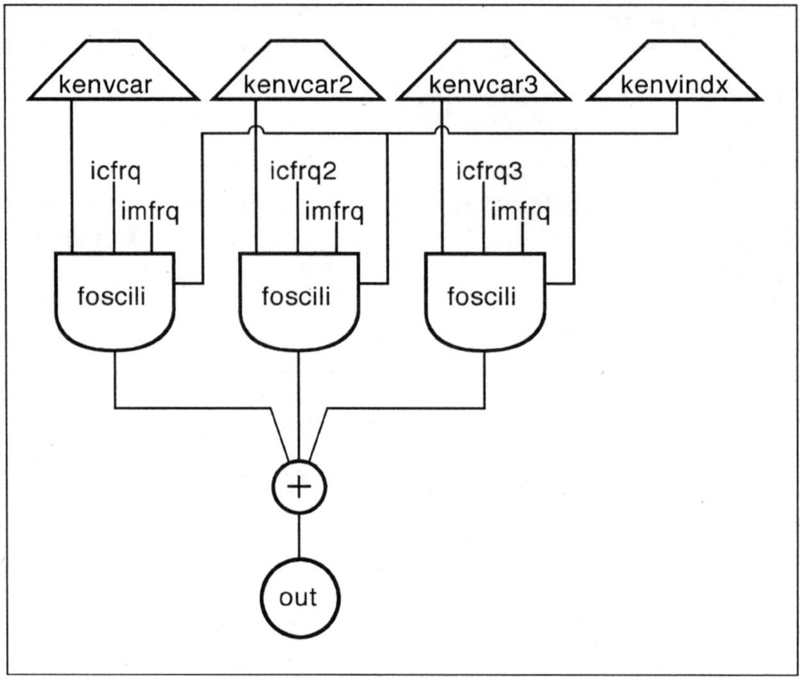

Fig. 12-6

```
;fm1.orc
        sr      = 44100
        kr      = 4410
        ksmps   = 10
        nchnls  = 1
        instr     1

icamp           = p4                        ;1st carrier amp
icfrq           = p5                        ;1st carrier freq
imfrq           = p6                        ;modulator freq
indx            = p7                        ;max index value
icamp2          = p8                        ;2nd carrier amp
icfrq2          = p9                        ;2nd carrier freq
icamp3          = p10                       ;3rd carrier amp
icfrq3          = p11;                      3rd carrier freq

kenvcar linseg  0, p3/2, icamp, p3/2, 0     ;envelope of 1st oscillator
kenvcar2 linseg 0, p3/2, icamp2, p3/2, 0    ;envelope of 2nd oscillator
```

```
kenvcar3  linseg   0, p3/2, icamp3, p3/2, 0                   ;envelope of 2nd oscillator
kenvindx  linseg   0, p3/4, indx, p3/4, 0, p3/4, indx, p3/4, 0
acar1     foscili  kenvcar, 1, icfrq, imfrq, kenvindx, 1
acar2     foscili  kenvcar2, 1, icfrq2,  imfrq, kenvindx, 1
acar3     foscili  kenvcar3, 1, icfrq3, i mfrq, kenvindx, 1
          out      acar1+acar2+acar3
          endin
```

Here's a test score for this orchestra:

```
;fm1.sco
f1  0   4096  10  1
;                 camp   icfrq  imfrq  indx   icamp2  icfrq2  icamp3  icfrq3
i1  0   6         12000  100    100    5      12000   200     8000    300
i1  7   6         12000  100    113    5      12000   258     8000    356
i1  14  6         12000  100    107    5      12000   111     8000    117
```

12.5 MULTIPLE-MODULATOR FM

To conclude, let's build an instrument with two modulators and one carrier, as in figure 12-7. Here the two modulators have separate index envelopes, and the carrier has its own amplitude envelope.

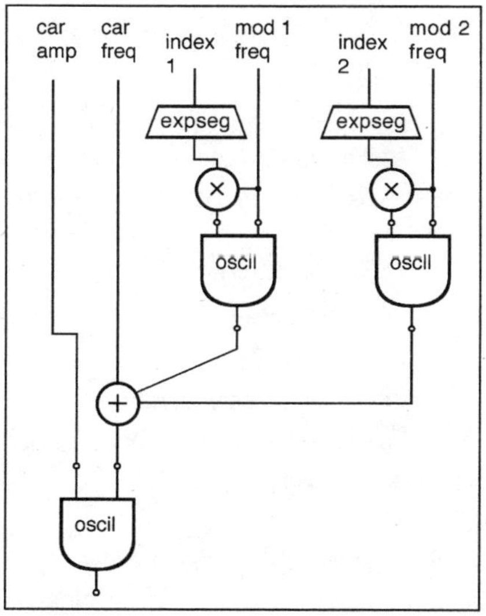

Fig. 12-7

```
;fm2.orc
        sr     =  44100
        kr     =  4410
        ksmps  =  10
        nchnls =  1

        instr     1

                                        ; 1st MODULATOR
imfrq       =  p4                       ;modulating freq
indmax      =  p5                       ;max index value
indxatk     =  p6                       ;rise time for the index envelope
indxperc    =  p7                       ;percentage of indmax for decay (in decimals:
                                        ;0.80=80%). When indmax = 100, the modulation
                                        ;index will go from 0 to 100 over indxatk seconds, then if indxperc = 0.80,
                                        ;it decays to 80. When indxperc=1 there's no decay, and the index value
                                        ;remains unchanged. Were indxperc=1.2, there would be a further increase in
                                        ;the index, up to 120. This second portion of the envelope (be it decay,
                                        ;sustain or further increase) takes place in p3-indxatk-indxrel seconds, i.e.
                                        ;in a time equal to the note duration minus attack time and release time. In
                                        ;the last envelope portion, the index goes down to 0 in indxrel seconds (we
                                        ;write 0.001 instead of 0 because the envelope is generated with expseg, see
                                        ;Chap.1).

indxrel     =  p8                       ;release time

                                        ;1st modulator index envelope
kindxenv expseg .001, indxatk,indmax,p3-indxatk, indxrel,indmax*indxperc,indxrel,.001

                                        ;2nd MODULATOR
imfrq2      =  p9                       ;modulating freq
indmax2     =  p10                      ;max index value
indxatk2    =  p11                      ;rise time for index envelope
indxperc2   =  p12                      ;percentage of indmax2 for decay (see above)
indxrel2    =  p13                      ;release time

                                        ;2nd modulator index envelope
kindxenv2 expseg .001,indxatk2, indmax2, p3-indxatk2-indxrel2, indmax2*indxperc2, indxrel2, .001
```

```
                                        ;CARRIER
icamp         =   p14                   ;carrier amp (0-32768)
icfrq         =   p15                   ;carrier freq(Hz)
iatk          =   p16                   ;rise time
iperc         =   p17                   ;percentage of icamp for decay
irel          =   p18                   ;release time

                                        ;carrier amplitude envelope
kenvc   expseg  .001, iatk, icamp, p3-iatk-irel, icamp * iperc, irel, .001

amod1         oscili  kindxenv*imfrq, imfrq, 1          ;1st modulator
amod2         oscili  kindxenv2*imfrq2, imfrq2, 1       ;2nd modulator
acar          oscili  kenvc, icfrq+amod1+amod2, 1       ;carrier

out     acar
        endin
```

A score for the new orchestra:

```
;fm2.sco
f1 0 4096 10 1
;p1  p2  p3  p4   p5  p6  p7  p8  p9   p10  p11  p12  p13  p14    p15  p16  p17  p18
i1   0   10  100  8   2   80  1   125  10   2    6    2    10000  200  .1   .90  3
```

EXTENSIONS

12.A.1 FM FORMULAS

In trigonometry, the formula for the instant amplitude of a sine wave of peak amplitude, A_0, is

$$\mathbf{A = A_0 * \sin(2\pi\omega t)}$$

where ω is the angle velocity (see A.II.4). The term 2πωt represents a frequency value, and we can replace it with a more general symbol, such as *f*. (The substitution is incorrect from a trigonometric perspective, but helps musicians understand these matters). Therefore, we write:

$$\mathbf{A' = A_1 * \sin(f_1)}$$

The FM operation involves the variation of $\mathbf{f_1}$ in accordance with another sine wave of frequency $\mathbf{f_2}$:

$$\mathbf{A' = A_2 * \sin(f_2)}$$

Therefore, the basic FM formula is:

$$\mathbf{A = A_1 * \sin(f_1 + A_2 * \sin(f_2))}$$

which is the trigonometric equation for FM.

Let's introduce another important element, the modulation index I, which is defined as

$$\mathbf{I = d/M}$$

where *d* is the peak deviation (the maximum variation in the carrier frequency) and M is the modulator frequency. We can re-write the FM equation as follows:

$$\mathbf{A = A_1 * \sin(f_1 + I * \sin(f_2))}$$

A special FM technique is the "modulated modulator" method. The equation is:

$$\mathbf{A = A_1 * \sin(f_1 + I_1 * \sin(f_2 + I_2 * \sin(f_3)))}$$

Still another technique is the multiple-modulator method, also discussed in the preceding section:

$$\mathbf{A = A_1 * \sin(f_1 + I_1 * \sin(f_2) + I_2 * \sin(f_3))}$$

where 2 modulators are added together before driving the carrier frequency.

Unfortunately, there is no clear-cut relationship between the modulation index and the resulting sound spectrum because, as the index changes, the amplitude of the sidebands themselves change *Bessel functions*, with rather complicated curves. Fig.12-A-1 shows the evolution of the first 10 components of a FM sound generated with a unit C:M ratio. In the graph, we can see frequency on the horizontal axis. Time is projected in the depth dimension. The note starts from the rear and ends in front. The index varies with time, moving from 0 to 7. You can see that at the very beginning of the sound only the fundamental is present. Then, its amplitude level decreases as the modulation index increases. The other components (sidebands) also rise as the fundamental falls. Then the overall pattern gets more and more complex. You see that the amplitude of the second harmonic rises and falls twice as the index moves from 0 to 7. It is clear that the overall temporal pattern of this spectrum is far from intuitive.

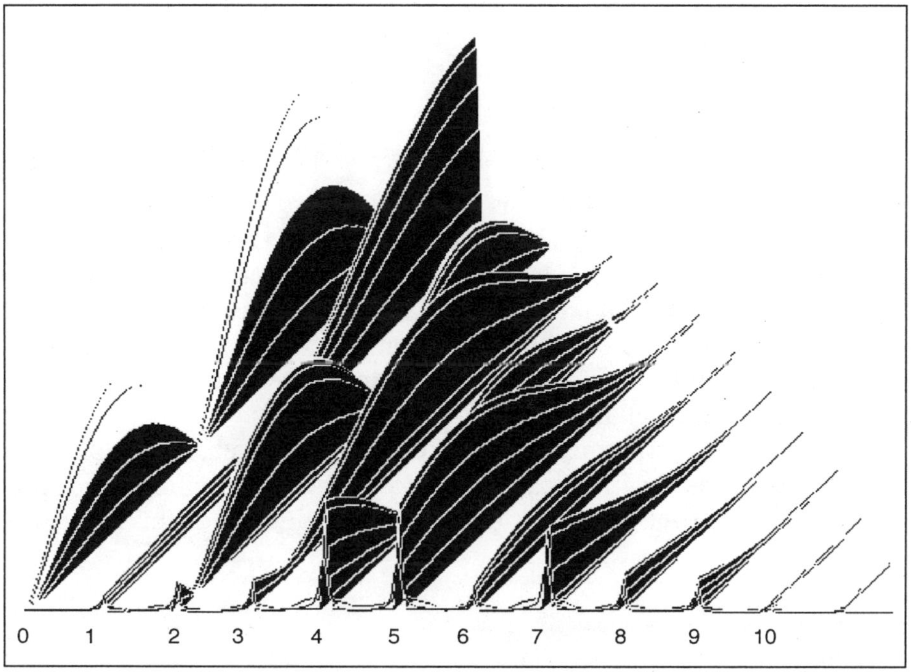

Fig. 12-A-1

Things are simpler with the FM setup on the well-known Yamaha FM synthesizers. Yamaha introduced a FM technique called *feedback* FM which allows for higher predictability and a more precise control over the sideband amplitude level variations. Feedback FM, however, is not a subject for this introductory chapter on FM.

12.A.2 SIMULATION OF INSTRUMENTAL SOUNDS

Since the inception of musical use of FM synthesis, musicians have tried to simulate instrumental sounds, with varying degrees of success. It is impossible to define general rules for instrument simulation, but a good understanding of the FM theory may provide us with some useful suggestions.

If we are to simulate the clarinet sound, we have to consider that this instrument generates almost exclusively odd harmonics. We can use a modulator with twice the frequency of the carrier. It is easy to check that such a C:M ratio generates a spectrum with only the odd harmonics. Let's call C the carrier frequency and 2C the modulator frequency:

sum frequencies	difference frequencies
C+2C=3C	C-2C=C
C+4C=5C	C-4C=3C
C+6C=7C	C-6C=5C
C+8C=9C	C-8C=7C
...	...

The resulting spectrum is a good basis for the clarinet.

Let's consider the sound of brass instruments, now. We know that their sound begins as almost a pure sinewave and soon becomes more complex and rich. We can model this kind of attack by starting with a null index value and then raise it to some higher value, e.g. 4. The release should follow the reverse path. It would be very effective to also introduce refined controls to model the peculiar "imperfections" (slight frequency deviations) found in the attack transient of brass instruments.

For the simulation of instruments with indeterminate pitch, like bells, gongs and cymbals, we should consider irrational C:M ratios, which yield inharmonic spectra. For example, given some carrier frequency, C, we can determine M in this way:

$$\mathbf{M} = \sqrt{\mathbf{2 * C}}$$

The singing voice is still more complex because it requires that we simulate vocal formants in addition. The idea is that each formant in the voice spectrum should be synthesized with a separate FM couple. In fig.12-A-2 you see the spectrum of the vowel "ee" sung by a soprano, with a fundamental of 250 Hz. Main formants lay at 250, 2000, 2500, 3250 and 4250 Hz. We can use a single modulator, M = 250 Hz, and 5 carriers whose frequencies correspond to the formant frequencies. Therefore:

Carriers	Index values
C1=250	**I1=0.2**
C2=2000	**I2=0.4**
C3=2500	**I3=0.8**
C4=3250	**I4=1**
C5=4250	**I5=0.6**

That provides an acceptable simulation, but for a more realistic result, we should introduce vibrato and tremolo.

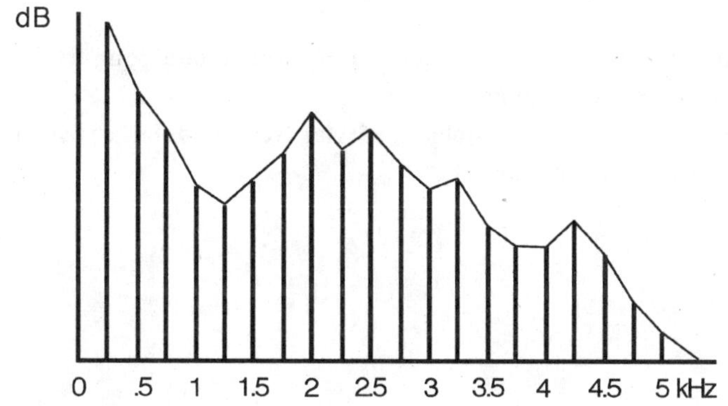

Fig. 12-A-2

The sounds of hit or plucked strings always contain some noise component from the hitting of either a hammer (piano) or a quill plectrum (harpsichord) against the string. It is important to distinguish between the initial noise burst and the string vibrations, and to model the two with two different FM groups. Conveniently, envelopes are shaped like the functions illustrated in fig.12-A-3. The top function shows the envelope for the noise component, the other shows the string vibrations.

Although it is impossible to create true white noise with FM, we can approach this to a satisfying degree by using irrational C:M ratios and largest index values.

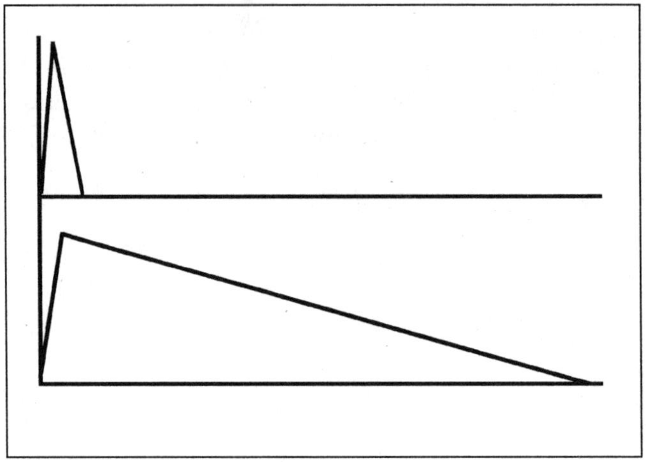

Fig. 12-A-3

LIST OF OPCODES INTRODUCED IN THIS CHAPTER

ar foscil **amplitude, nominal_frequency, carrier freq, modulating freq, index, function_number[,phase]**

ar foscili **amplitude, nominal_frequency, carrier freq, modulating freq, index, function_number [,phase]**

13

GLOBAL VARIABLES, ECHO, REVERB, CHORUS, FLANGER, PHASER, CONVOLUTION

13.1 ECHO AND REVERB

Echo and reverb are well-known "effects" utilized in sound synthesis and processing. The echo effect simulates the reflection of a sound against a surface. Itës only audible when the reflection is heard at least 1/20th of a second after the direct sound (see fig.13-1, top). If there are several reflecting surfaces, as is the case in a cube shaped room, we hear multiple echoes (fig.13-1, bottom).

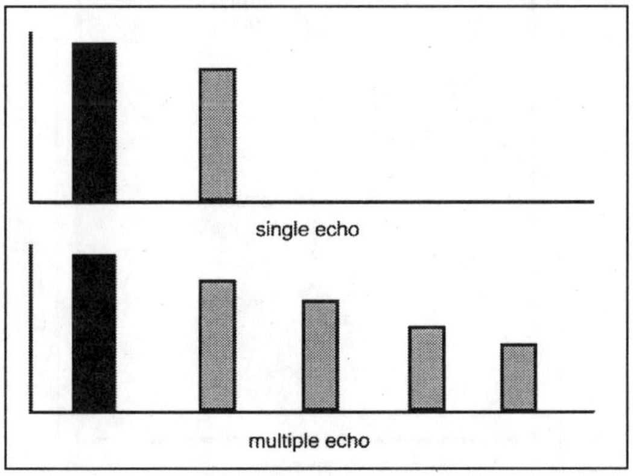

Fig. 13-1

A true reverberation is achieved when multiple echoes merge together (fig.13-2). In this case, we hear the early reflections first, a few milliseconds after the direct sound. Then we hear several echoes that fuse together and slowly decay in amplitude.

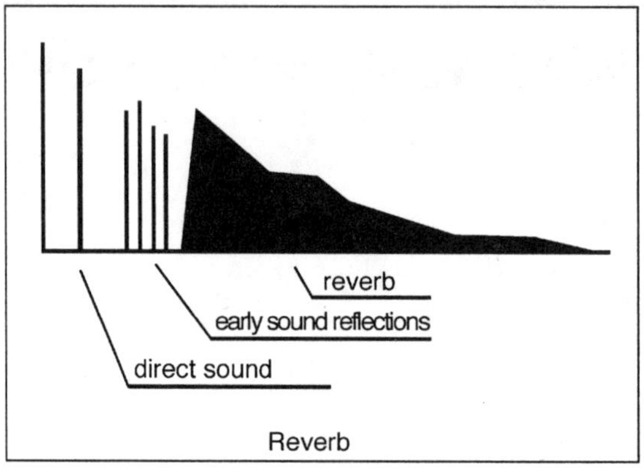

Fig. 13-2

In fig.13-3 we see the map of a rectangular room. The first sound that reaches the listener's ear is the direct signal from the sound source itself, followed next by several sound reflections. These sounds travel a longer distance to the ear, and therefore are delayed. The delays differ in the number of reflections. First we hear the echoes of a single reflection, then those of two, then three reflections, and so on. The higher the number of reflections, the softer the amplitude level of the echo, as in fact each reflection implies some loss of energy.

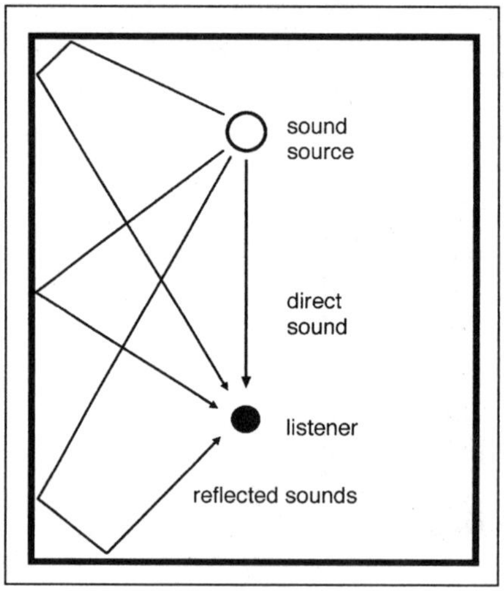

Fig. 13-3

We call *reverberation time* the time it takes for the echoes to decrease in amplitude by 60 dB. It is one of the main acoustical characteristics of a room or hall. In theory, to really understand the reverberation of a particular room, several tests are required to analyze the surface materials which have different reflecting properties at different frequency regions.

13.2 THE *DELAY* OPCODE

How do we simulate the echo effect in Csound? Let's take a look at this simple orchestra, with its score, illustrating how we do this:

```
;eco1.orc
        sr      =   44100
        kr      =   4410
        ksmps   =   10
        nchnls  =   1
        instr       1
a1      soundin     "voice.wav"         ; read samples from sound file
a2      delayr      .5                  ; create a 0.5 seconds delay line...
        delayw      a1                  ; with a1 as the input
aout    =           a1+a2               ; sum of delayed and direct signals
        aout
        endin

;eco1.sco
i1  0   5
```

There you see two new opcodes, *delayr* and *delayw*. During synthesis, they work together as a single unit called a *delay* line. Its function is to delay a signal by some predetermined time. The syntax is:

ar delayr idlt[, istor]
delayw asig

delayr reads the signal from a memory location which is *idlt* seconds long. In the orchestra code, this opcode must precede the *delayw* opcode (however, other opcodes can be placed in between them).

delayw writes in the delay line created with *delayr.*

idlt is the requested delay time in seconds. The shortest allowable delay period is equal to a single control period (= 1/kr), while the largest is restricted only by available memory space. The memory space required for *n* seconds of delay, is 4**n**sr bytes.

istor (optional) is the initial condition of the internal delay-loop memory (similar to *reson*). The default value is 0, which initializes the memory and fills it with zeros. A value of 1 causes the initialization stage to be skipped, letting currently stored data remain in the delay-loop.

Any digital delay line, including a delay line implemented with Csound, consists of an array of memory locations. The input signal is written to the first location. Then, with each successive sample, it gets shifted to the next location until it reaches the last location. The output signal is read from the last location.

It is also possible to read samples off the intermediate locations in the delay line array created with *delayr/delayw*. This is done with the *deltap* opcode, or its interpolated version, *deltapi*. The syntax for these opcodes, is as follows:

a1 deltap ktime
a1 deltapi xtime

ktime and *xtime* (expressed in seconds) represent the point in the delay line from which the signal is to be read. This value must be smaller than the *idlt* value in *delayr*. Be aware that Csound will not check these values for you! Therefore, if you use a delay time that is either less than 0 or greater than *ktime*, Csound will substitute data for the delay line! It is possible to use many *deltap* opcodes in a row:

```
a1      delayr   1.5
ad1     deltap   .2
ad2     deltap   .7
ad3     deltap   1.1
        delayw   asig
```

Examine the flow-chart printed on this page.

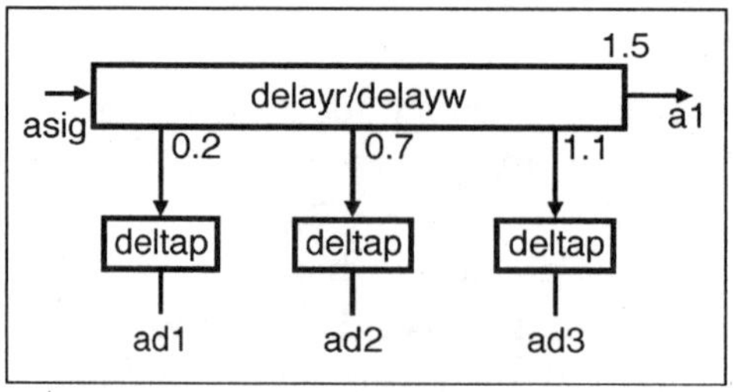

There are three *deltapi* readings for the signal from different points in the delay line prior to the last read, namely at 0.2, 0.7 and 1.1 seconds. This allows you to create multiple echoes with a single delay line. In this example, a *deltapi* time of 1.8 seconds would have been an inappropriate value (but Csound would not recognize it as an error) because the delay line itself (*delayr/delayw*) is 1.5 seconds long.

Be careful to avoid rapid variations in *ktime* and *xtime* as it might cause discontinuities (spikes) in the signal.

Another useful opcode is *delay*, which has the same arguments as the *delayr/delayw* pair.

The syntax is:

ar delay asig, idlt[, istor]

Different from *delayr/delayw*, here *idlt* has no minimum delay period.

Finally, there is still another delay line opcode, *delay1*:

ar delay1 asig[, istor]

which implements a single-sample delay. It is the same as

delay asig, 1/sr

but more economical in terms of computation time and memory occupation. It is especially useful for implementing filters.

Using the *delay* opcode, instead of the *delayr/delayw* pair, we can re-write our single-echo example orchestra as follows:

```
;eco2.orc
        sr     =  44100
        kr     =  4410
        ksmps  =  10
        nchnls =  1
        instr     1
a1      soundin   "voice.wav"          ;read samples from sound file
a2      delay     a1, .5               ;0.5 seconds delay
aout           =  a1+a2                ;sum of delayed and direct signals
out     aout
        endin
```

```
;eco2.sco
i1   0    5
```

A multiple echoes example would look like this:

```
;eco3.orc
        sr      =  44100
        kr      =  4410
        ksmps   =  10
        nchnls  =  1
        instr      1
a1      soundin    "voice.wav"
a2      delay      a1+a2*.8, .2
aout            =  a1+a2
out     aout
        endin
```

```
;eco3.sco
i1   0    5
```

If we try to run Csound using this file, it will return an error message:

```
error:  input arg 'a2' used before defined, line 8:
a2      delay   a1+a2*.8,.5
1 syntax errors in orchestra.  compilation invalid
```

It should be obvious that a variable was used before any value was assigned to it. When a variable is created, Csound allocates some memory space to store the values of that variable. You should remember that, as we have already discussed, Csound instructions are compiled from right to left. In other words, to encode a simple addition such as

2 + 2 = 4

we would write

4 + 2, 2

Which reflects the following general syntax:

result opcode argument1, argument2

Now, in the line in question

```
a2      delay       a1+a2*.8, .2
```

we are instructing the Csound compiler to use the *a2* variable as an argument to the *delay* opcode while that variable does not actually exist yet! A legal statement would be:

```
;eco3a.orc
        sr      =   44100
        kr      =   4410
        ksmps   =   10
        nchnls  =   1

        instr       1
a2      init        0                       ;initialization, to declare the a2 variable
a1      soundin     "voice.wav"
a2      delay       a1+a2*.8, .2
aout            =   a1+a2
        out         aout
        endin

;eco3a.sco
i1  0   5
```

The new line, *a2 init 0*, is performed during initialization and instructs Csound to create the *a2* variable. Now we can compile without errors, and we can finally listen to multiple echoes of the input sounds every 0.2 seconds, each with smaller and smaller amplitudes. Let's take a look at the flow-chart in fig.13-4.

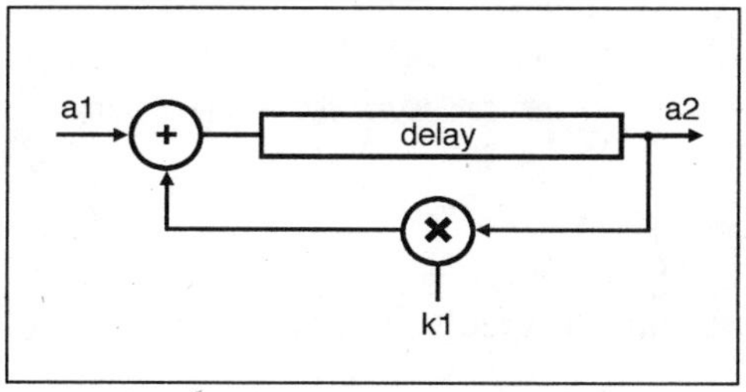

Fig. 13-4

A new concept is featured there, namely *feedback*. You have feedback whenever you store a signal to a memory location, and later add it to the current signal.

Examine the example above. The input to the delay line is called *a1*. It is summed with the delayed signal, *a2*, which is scaled by a factor *k1*. The scale factor has to be appropriate with respect to the output signal. If the output signal is summed with the input signal, scaled by a factor larger than 1, the result shows excessive amplitude values. Suppose *a1* has an amplitude of 1 (unit amplitude) and *k3* equals 3. In that case, we would have an output value of 3 after 0.2 seconds (delay time), an amplitude of 9 after 0.4 seconds, and so on. Very soon the process will return large values that can't be represented by the computer. In sound synthesis jargon, we say that the instrument "explodes". When using factors smaller than 1, the amplitude level in the output signal decreases and fades out. This is what we really want to obtain, here. Now, we can experiment further with our orchestra

```
;eco3b.orc
          sr      =  44100
          kr      =  4410
          ksmps   =  10
          nchnls  =  1
          instr      1
ifeedback =          p4                    ;feedback scale factor
a2        init       0                     ;declare variable a2
a1        soundin    "voice.wav"
a2        delay      a1+a2*ifeedback, .2
aout      =          a1+a2
          out        aout
          endin
```

```
;eco3b.sco
i1  0  5  .5          ; echoes amplitude decays rapidly...
i1  +  5  .7          ; ... less rapidly...
i1  +  5  .9          ; ... less rapidly...
i1  +  5  1.5         ; amp gets larger and larger, and finally crashes
```

13.3 REVERB

Let's turn now to reverberation effects. There are two ready-made opcodes:

ar reverb asig, krvt [, istor]

ar reverb2 asig, ktime, khdif [, iskip]

asig	is the input to the reverb unit
ar	is the output from the reverb unit
krvt (or *ktime*)	is the reverberation time in seconds (the time for the signal to decay to 60 dB down its original amplitude)
khdif	(only *reverb2*) is a decay value for higher frequencies, ranging from 0 to 1. When it is 0, all frequencies will be equally reverberated. When it is 1, higher frequencies will have a reverberation time shorter than lower frequencies.
istor (optional)	is the initial disposition of the internal memory space. A value of 0 causes a clearing of the internal space at init time. A value of 1 causes initialization to be skipped, letting currently stored data remain in the delay-loop. The default is 0.
iskip	values other than 0, cause the initialization stage to be skipped. The default is 0.

The *reverb* memory storage is proportional to the sampling rate sr: with sr = 44100, approximately 27 Kbytes of memory are required.

Let's create now an orchestra including the *reverb* opcode:

```
;reverb1.orc
        sr     =   44100
        kr     =   4410
        ksmps  =   10
        nchnls =   1
        instr      1
ifrq    =          cpspch(p5)
iamp    =          ampdb(p4)
kenv    linseg     0, .01, iamp, .1, 0, p3-.11, 0      ;triangle envelope
a1      oscili     kenv, ifrq, 1                       ;direct sound
ar      reverb     a1, 3                               ;3 seconds reverberation time
        out        a1+ar                               ;direct + reverb sound
        endin
```

Use this orchestra to play the following score:

```
;reverb1.sco
f1  0   4096  10  1
```

```
i1  0  1  80  8
i1  +  .  .   8.04
i1  +  .  .   8.07
i1  +  .  .   9
```

When listening, it is evident that there is something wrong in the sound. The reverb is truncated at the end of each note. All Csound instruments are switched off at the end of the note duration. That means *before* the reverb sound has completed its decay.

To solve this problem we take a different approach. We shall create a special instrument, whose task is to reverberate any sound. This special instrument is activated at the beginning of the score, with a duration equal to the score's duration plus the reverberation time. In the example above, we have four 1-second notes and a reverberation time of 3 seconds. The reverb instrument, then, should play for 4+3=7 seconds.

But how do we implement this reverb instrument? To answer this, we have to understand Csound's *global* variables.

13.4 LOCAL AND GLOBAL VARIABLES

When we define a variable within the body of an instrument, that variable is valid for that instrument only. It can be referenced only by the opcodes in that instrument. We can use identical variable names in two or more instruments, without causing any interference between instruments. This is illustrated in the following code example:

```
        instr   1
...
a1      oscil   k1, ifrq, 1
...
        endin

        instr   2
a1      soundin   "myfile.wav"
        ...
        endin
```

In this example, the two instances of variable *a1* will be referenced only by the particular instrument code in which they are included. Is it impossible to pass values from one instrument to another? No, it isn't, but it requires that we define variables that can be shared among instruments. In Csound, these are called *global* variables (see section 1-A-1). Global variables have names beginning with *g* (=global). There are three different types: audio global variables, control global variables and init global variables.

All have with names beginning with *ga*, *gk* and *gi*. respectively

variable type	local	global
init	i...	gi...
control	k...	gk...
audio	a...	ga...

Examples of init global variables are *girl*, *gialias* and *giout*.
Examples of control global variables are *gkytr*, *gk34* and *gkenv*.
Examples of audio global variables are *gallop*, *garbage*, *ga2* and *gaudio*.

We can now re-write our reverb orchestra, incorporating our new reverb instrument (e.g. instr 99)

```
;reverb2.orc
        sr     =  44100
        kr     =  4410
        ksmps  =  10
        nchnls =  1

garev   init 0

        instr     1
ifrq           =  cpspch(p5)
iamp           =  ampdb(p4)
kenv    linseg    0, .01, iamp, .1, 0, p3-.11, 0      ;envelope
a1      oscili    kenv, ifrq, 1                       ;signal to be reverberated
garev          =  garev+a1                            ;turn audio var to global audio var
        out       a1                                  ;output (only direct sound)
        endin

        instr     99
arev    reverb    garev, 3
        out       arev                                ;output (only reverb sound)
garev          =  0                                   ;clear garev, to avoid accumulation
        endin
```

Try that orchestra with these notes:

```
;reverb2.sco
f1   0    4096  10   1
i1   0    1      80  8
i1   +    .      .   8.04
i1   +    .      .   8.07
i1   +    .      .   9
i99  0    10
```

Let's examine the orchestra, and notice the following:

1. the line *garev init 0* lies outside of any instrument body. Its use is to declare a global audio variable.
2. instrument 1 generates the *a1* signal, which is summed with *garev*. This operation allows us to use instrument 1 polyphonically, by summing all values of *a1* for all instances of instr 1 called up to play.
3. *garev* is included in the body of instr 99, as the input argument to the *reverb* opcode.
4. after being reverberated, *garev* is zeroed, to avoid the effect of accumulating each of the values it assumes at each sample.

Good reverberation allows us to simulate sounds coming from great distance. The perception of distance is usually measured as the ratio between the level of direct sound to the level of reverberant sound. Close sound sources have a predominance of direct sound. Distant sound sources have a predominance of reverberant sound.

13.5 MORE EFFECTS USING DELAY: FLANGING, PHASING AND CHORUS.

The opcodes so far described in this chapter, *delayr/delayw*, *delay* and *delay1*, are also used to create other sound effects such as *flanging*, *phasing* and *chorus*.

The flanging effect, is created by summing up two instances of the same sound where one instance is passed through a cyclically varying delay line. In the early years of analog electronic music, this effect was created by de-synchronizing two tape recorders recording the same sound (see fig.13-5). The left reel flange of one of the tape recorders was depressed slightly (by hand), which caused the tape speed to decrease a bit (the left tape machine in fig.13-5). The output signal of one tape recorder (right) had a fixed delay (according to the distance between the recording head and the playback head) while the other (left) had a variable delay. The effect is a kind of phasing that changes with successive wave cancellations and summations in the sound. The pattern of cancellations and summations is different at different frequencies, and the final effect is a kind of sweeping filter, some frequencies are amplified while others are cancelled.

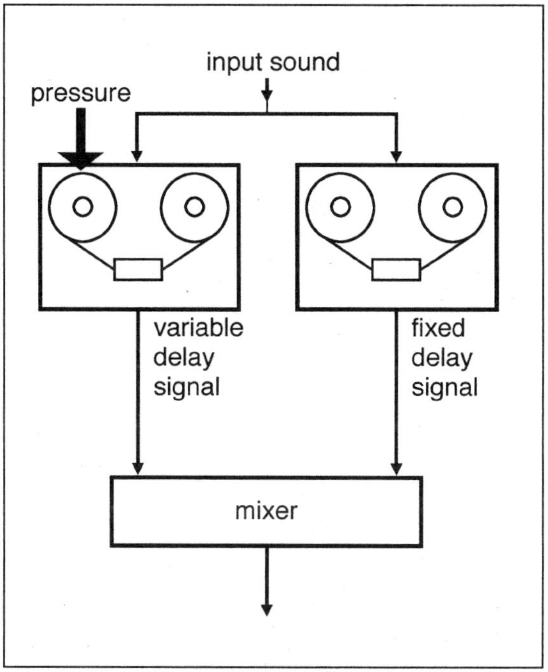

Fig. 13-5

How can we do this with Csound? We have to use two delay lines and the *deltapi* opcode, or we can also use another opcode, *vdelay* (variable delay), whose syntax is:

ar vdelay asig, adel, imaxdel [, iskip]

This creates an interpolated variable delay line, whose functionality is identical an interconnected *delayw/delayr* pair with *deltapi* reads.

imaxdel is the maximum delay period required during a given performance. It is expressed in *milliseconds* (not seconds!)

iskip, values other than 0 prevent initialization of the internal memory. The default is 0.

asig is the input signal

adel is the current delay time, in milliseconds. When *adel* changes at a very high rate, discontinuities in the output signal, could create undesired noise.

Here's an implementation of the flanging effect using delayr/delayw and deltapi:

```
;flanger.orc
        sr     =  44100
        kr     =  4410
        ksmps  =  10
        nchnls =  1
        instr     1
idel           =  .008                    ;delay time
a1      soundin   "voice.wav"             ;input  sound
k1      oscil     idel/2.5, .2, 1              ;oscillator to control the delay time

;- - - - - - - - - - - - - - - - - - - - - - - -variable delay
a0      delayr    idel
ar1     deltapi   idel/2+k1
        delayw    a1
;- - - - - - - - - - - - - - - - - - - - - - - -fixed delay
ar      delayr    idel/2
        delayw    a1
;- - - - - - - - - - - - - - - - - - - - - - - -variable+fixed
aout    =         ar+ar1
        out       aout/2
        endin

;flanger.sco
f1  0   4096   10   1
i1  0   5
```

We can write a more compact orchestra which creates the same result, with *delay* and *vdelay*:

```
;flanger1.orc
        sr     =  44100
        kr     =  4410
        ksmps  =  10
        nchnls =  1
        instr     1
idelm          =  8                       ;delay time in milliseconds
a1      soundin   "voice.wav" ;input
```

```
k1      oscil     idelm,.2,1                 ;oscillator controlling the delay time
;- - - - - - - - - - - - - - - - - - - - - - - - -variable delay
ar      vdelay    a1, idelm+k1, 1000
;- - - - - - - - - - - - - - - - - - - - - - - - -fixed delay
ar1     delay     a1, idelm/1000
;- - - - - - - - - - - - - - - - - - - - - - - - -delay + variable
aout    =         ar+ar1
        out       aout/2
        endin

;flanger.sco
f1  0   4096   10   1
i1  0   5
```

Let's see a more complex orchestra, coded by Hans Mikelson, exploiting the feedback effect. The effect is somewhat similar to an electric guitar. In fact, the electric guitar pick-ups can detect not only the string vibrations from the guitar, but also the sounds coming off the loudspeakers.

```
;feedback.orc
        sr      =  44100
        kr      =  4410
        ksmps   =  10
        nchnls  =  1

ga1     init 0

        instr      1                 ; instr 1 generates a plucked sound (see chap.16)
ifrq               =  cpspch(p5)
iamp               =  ampdb(p4)
ga1     pluck         iamp, ifrq, ifrq, 0, 1
        endin

        instr      2
kamp    linseg 0, .002, 1, p3-.004, 1, .002, 0
irate              =  p4             ;oscillator frequency for flanging effect
idepth             =  p5/10000       ;amount of flange shift
ifeed              =  p6             ;feedback level
ideloff            =  p7/10000       ;fixed delay
```

```
adel1       init    0

;the input signal gets delayed, the delay being modulated at a rate of .001
;seconds. The direct signal is mixed with the delayed, and the result
;is fed back into the feedback loop

asig1       =       ga1 + ifeed*adel1
aosc1       oscil   idepth, irate, 1
aosc1       =       aosc1+idepth+ideloff/2
atemp       delayr  2*idepth+ideloff
adel1       deltapi aosc1
            delayw  asig1
            out     ga1+adel1
ga1         =       0
            endin

;feedback.sco
f1    0     4096   10     1
;ins  act   dur    dB     pitch
i1    0     .5     80     8                          ;two arpeggiato major chords
i1    +     .      .      8.04
i1    +     .      .      8.07
i1    +     .      .      9
i1    +     .      .      8
i1    +     .      .      8.04
i1    +     .      .      8.07
i1    +     .      .      9
;ins  act   dur    rate   depth   feedb   deloff
i2    0     5      .5     10      .5      10
s                                                    ;end section

i1    0     .5     80     8
i1    +     .      .      8.04
i1    +     .      .      8.07
i1    +     .      .      9
i1    +     .      .      8
i1    +     .      .      8.04
i1    +     .      .      8.07
i1    +     .      .      9
```

```
;ins    act    dur    rate    depth  feedb   deloff
i2      0      5      .5      10     .8      20
```

***EXERCISE**: experiment with the delay parameters (be careful with the feedback level, and avoid "explosions")*

The *chorus* effect transforms a single sound source into a multitude of similar, but not identical, sources. This is similar to the many singers in a choir who (try to) sing in unison. In the following example, instrument 1 implements the chorus effect with *delayr/delayw* and *deltapi*, while instrument 2 does the same with *vdelay*.

```
;chorus.orc
        sr      =   44100
        kr      =   4410
        ksmps   =   10
        nchnls  =   1
        instr       1
idel            =   .02                     ;delay in seconds
a1      soundin     "voice.wav"
ar0     delayr      idel
        delayw      a1
;- - - - - - - - - - - - - - - - - - - - - - - - randi/deltapi pair n.1
k1      randi       idel/2, 3, 1
ar1     deltapi     idel/2+k1
;- - - - - - - - - - - - - - - - - - - - - - - -randi/deltapi pair  n.2
k2      randi       idel/2, 3.5, .5
ar2     deltapi     idel/2+k2
;- - - - - - - - - - - - - - - - - - - - - - - -randi/deltapi pair  n.3
k3      randi       idel/2, 2.9, .3
ar3     deltapi     idel/2+k3
;- - - - - - - - - - - - - - - - - - - - - - - -randi/deltapi pair  n.4
k4      randi       idel/2, 2.1, .1
ar4     deltapi     idel/2+k4
;- - - - - - - - - - - - - - - - - - - - - - - -final mix
aout            =   ar1+ar2+ar3+ar4
        out         aout/4
        endin

instr   2
```

```
idel          =        20              ;delay in milliseconds
a1    soundin   "voice.wav"
;- - - - - - - - - - - - - - - - - - - - - - - - randi/deltapi pair n.1
k1    randi     idel/2, 3, 1
ar1   vdelay    a1, idel/2+k1, 1000
;- - - - - - - - - - - - - - - - - - - - - - - - randi/deltapi pair n.2
k2    randi     idel/2, 3.5, . 5
ar2   vdelay    a1, idel/2+k2, 1000
;- - - - - - - - - - - - - - - - - - - - - - - -randi/deltapi pair n.3
k3    randi     idel/2, 2.9, .3
ar3   vdelay    a1, idel/2+k3, 1000
;- - - - - - - - - - - - - - - - - - - - - - - -randi/deltapi pair n.4
k4    randi     idel/2, 2.1, .1
ar4   vdelay    a1, idel/2+k4, 1000
;- - - - - - - - - - - - - - - - - - - - - - - - final mix
aout          = ar1+ar2+ar3+ar4
      out       aout/4
      endin

;chorus.sco
f1  0   4096  10   1
i1  0   5
i2  6   5
```

As you can see, there are four delayed sounds, each with its own delay time. Of course, you can introduce more delay lines and oscillators, in order to achieve a more intense *chorus* effect.

13.6 CONVOLUTION

Convolution was introduced in section 3-B-1. It is the multiplication of two spectra. In other words, it is the multiplication of *two signals in the frequency domain*, as distinct from the multiplication of *two signals in the time domain* (the latter process is "ring-modulation", see 11.A.1). The difference between the two is that in order to multiply A and B the time domain multiplication is the product of the samples of signal A multiplied by the corresponding samples of signal B (only 1 multiplication is performed at a time, and there are as many multiplications as there are samples). Instead, a frequency domain multiplication is the product of every single sample of A by every single sample of B. For each A sample, there will be an entire array of values, representing as many products as there are B samples. The final signal is made of the summation of all arrays, each array being shifted by one sample.

Suppose we have two time-varying signals, A and B. With the Fast Fourier Transform we can calculate their time-varying spectra, A' and B'. We can then multiply the two spectra with the convolution operation:

Z' = A' x B'

thus obtaining a third spectrum, Z'. Finally, by applying the Inverse Fast Fourier Transform (IFFT) to Z', we obtain a time-varying signal Z, which represents the convolution of A and B.

Observe figure 13-6. The signal A has a harmonic spectrum, and a 100 Hz fundamental. The sixth harmonic is missing. Signal B also has a harmonic spectrum, but a 200 Hz fundamental and a different spectral composition. The spectrum obtained by convolving A and B is called C, and includes only those frequencies which are included in both the original spectra.

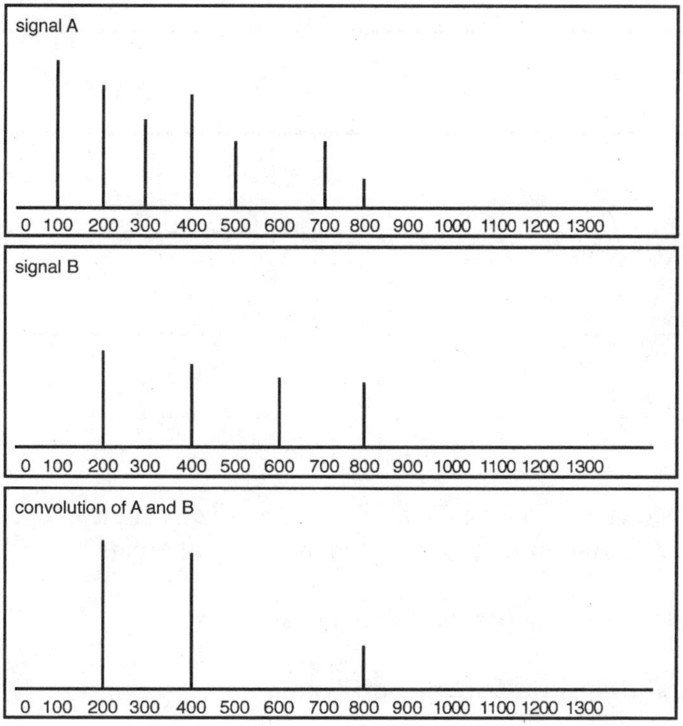

Fig. 13-6

Now, what's the use of calculating the convolution of two signals? Convolution is an essential operation in DSP (digital signal processing). It has made possible many sound effects that are well-known to experts in this field. For example, a filter effect can be created by the convolution of some input sound and the response curve of the required filter. Below, we discuss a simple instance of convolution that adds some reverberation to an input sound. However, the potential of convolution is enormous, but as of yet, it has remained largely unexplored by musicians.

Take a look at figure 13-7. On top, we see the time-domain graph of a pulse signal (unit pulse). Beneath, we see the time-domain graph of the impulse response of a bandpass filter. In fig.13-8, the two signals are represented in the frequency domain, i.e. represented are their spectra. By multiplying the spectrum of any input signal with the impulse response of a filter, and then applying the IFFT, we obtain a new signal which represents the filtered version of the original signal.

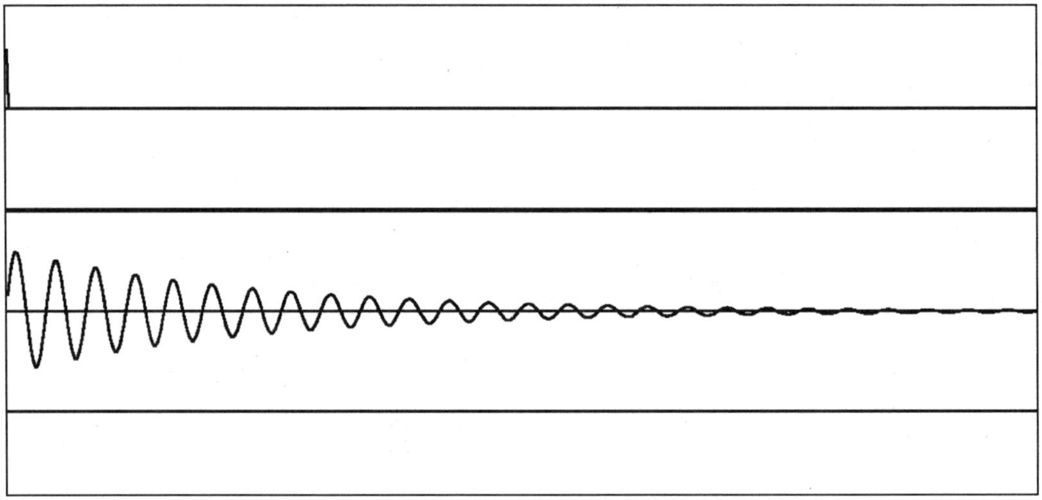

Fig. 13-7

In Csound a special opcode is available, *convolve*, which is used in conjunction with the *cvanal* command. *cvanal* prepares the analysis file to be used with *convolve*.

The *cvanal* command line has the following syntax:

csound -U cvanal [flags] infilename outfilename

Flags include:

-s<srate> sampling rate of the input sound file. If the sound file has a header (as is the case with WAVE and AIFF files), the flag can be omitted. Notice that sound file sampling rate can be different from the resynthesis sampling rate.

-c<channel> for stereo or quad sound files, this selects the particular channel to analyze. The default is 1 (= stereo left channel).

-b<begin> start time (in seconds) of the sound segment to analyze. The default is 0 seconds.

- d<duration> duration (in seconds) of the sound file segment to analyze. The default is 0 seconds, meaning that the entire sound file must be analyzed. Maximum duration is 32766 seconds.

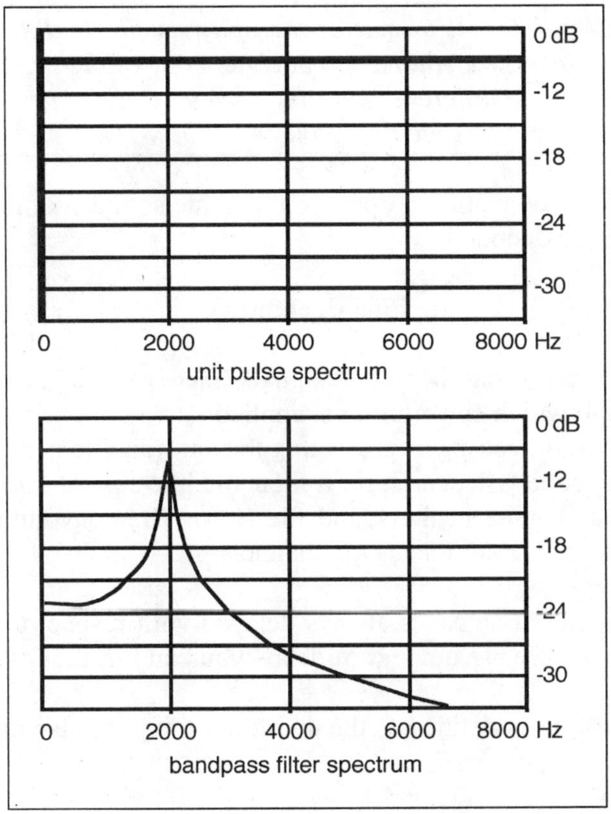

Fig. 13-8

As an example, suppose we have a sound file, "berliner.wav", containing the impulse response curve recorded in the Berliner Philarmoniker concert hall. The response curve can be thought of as the characteristic reverberation of that particular hall. In order to generate this kind of data, the most commonly used impulse-like sound is a (blank!) gun shot. We analyze this sound file with the following command:

Csound -U cvanal berliner.wav berliner.cnv

which creates the *berliner.cnv* file (Win), or the *berliner.cv* file (Mac).

TIPS & TRICKS (Win): it is possible to give the output file any name and extension, but you'd better use the .cnv extension, to make it easy to locate this kind of files in the future.

TIPS & TRICKS: the internal format of the analysis file is different under different operating systems. Make sure you have a back-up copy of the original sound file, such that in case you move to a different operating system, you can generate a new analysis file. Otherwise, you won't be able to use the previously generated analysis file.

Now, let's apply the convolution operation to some sound file, like "voice.wav". The syntax of the *convolve* opcode is:

ar1[,...[,ar4]] convolve ain, ifilcod, channel

ar1, ar2, ar3, ar4 represent the output signals (there can be 1, 2 or 4 output signals)
ain is the signal to which convolution is applied
ifilcod is a number, or a string, representing the analysis file generated with *cvanal*. If it is a number, n, Csound will search for a filename like *convolve.n*.
channel selects a channel in the sound file (0-4). The convolution is applied to the sound from that channel. Zero means *all* channels.

The convolution output signal is always delayed with respect to the input signal. In order to determine the precise amount of delay, you can use the following formulas:

If **1/kr ≤ IRDur** (IRDur is defined as the duration of the impulse response, in seconds), then

Delay = ceil (IRDur * kr) / kr

where *kr* is the control rate and *ceil(n)* returns the closest integer number greater than or equal to *n*. I.e. if *n* = 1.3, *ceil(n)* = 2.

If **(1/kr) > IRDur, then**

Delay = IRdur * ceil(1/(kr*IRdur))

Because, normally, the output signal includes both the direct and the reverberated sound signals, it is essential to calculate the amount of delay in advance. To compensate this delay, then, the direct signal should be itself delayed before getting summed up with the convolution signal.[1] Suppose our "berliner.wav" file has a duration of 1.379 seconds (IRDur = 1.379), and suppose kr = 441. We have

1/kr = 0.0023, which is ≤ **IRDur (1.379).** Hence:

Delay1 = ceil(IRDur * kr) / kr =
= ceil(1.379 * 441)/441 =
= ceil(608.14) / 441 =
= 609/441 =
= 1.38095 seconds

```
;convolve.orc
          sr       =   44100
          kr       =   441
          ksmps    =   100
          nchnls   =   1
          instr        1
imix               =   .22                       ;scale the amount of output reverb sound
idel               =   1.38095                   ;needed delay time to synchronize the two signals
adry      soundin      "voice.wav"               ;input signal
awet1     convolve     adry, "berliner.cnv"      ;apply convolution
adrydel   delay        adry, idel                ;delayed original signal
          out          adrydel+ awet1 * imix     ;sum
          endin
```

The following score includes one note, with a duration equal to the "voice.wav" sound file duration plus the delay needed for synchronization.

```
;convolve.sco
i1   0   7
```

[1] Of course, that implies that real-time convolution is not possible in Csound.

EXTENSIONS

13.A.1 HOW TO BUILD UP A REVERB UNIT

In many cases, neither *reverb* nor *reverb2* yield satisfying results. Success is defined not only by the personal taste of the composer who judges these subtle changes in the sound, but also by limitations of those opcodes. However, Csound allows you to build your own reverb unit. To do so, the basic elements youíll use are opcodes such as *comb* and *alpass*.

ar comb asig, krvt, ilpt[, istor]
ar alpass asig, krvt, ilpt[, istor]

comb is the most commonly used opcode element in complex reverb units. It has a rather "colored" sound, while *alpass*, in contrast, offers a flat frequency response. The *reverb* opcode itself is made up of four parallel *comb* units and two *alpass* units in series. The *alpass* filters the summed output of the four *comb* opcodes.

Similarly, *reverb2* is made of six *comb* opcodes in parallel, and five *alpass* opcodes in series.

asig is the input signal
krvt is the reverberation time, in seconds
ilpt is the length, in seconds, of the internal delay-loop. This determines how dense the reflections will be. With *comb*, this parameter also affects the "color" of the reverberated signal. The value of *ilpt* is only limited by the available memory. The allocated memory space will be *4*n*sr* bytes (*n*= delay line in second).
istor (optional) determines whether the internal memory will be initialized (0) or not (1). The default, as ever, is 0.

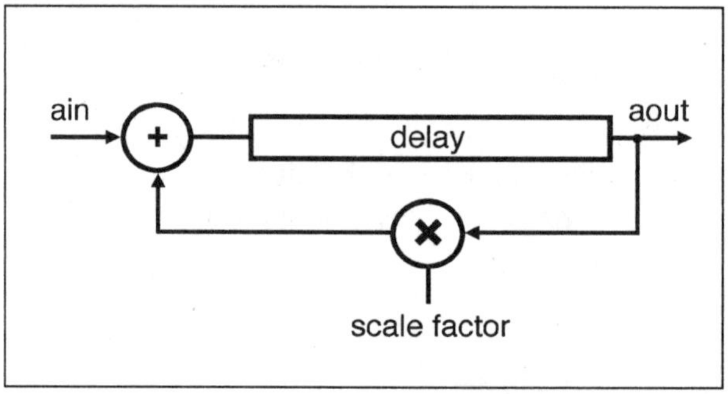

Fig. 13-A-1

The algorithm in *comb* is one of the simplest digital filter algorithms. It includes a delay line with feedback, as shown in figure 13-A-1. The feedback scale factor is automatically calculated by Csound, and is proportional to *ilpt* and *krvt*. The response curve is illustrated in figure 13-A-2, and includes a number of peaks (similar to comb teeth) equally spaced throughout the frequency range (0 to *sr/2*). The number of peaks is *ilpt*sr/2*.

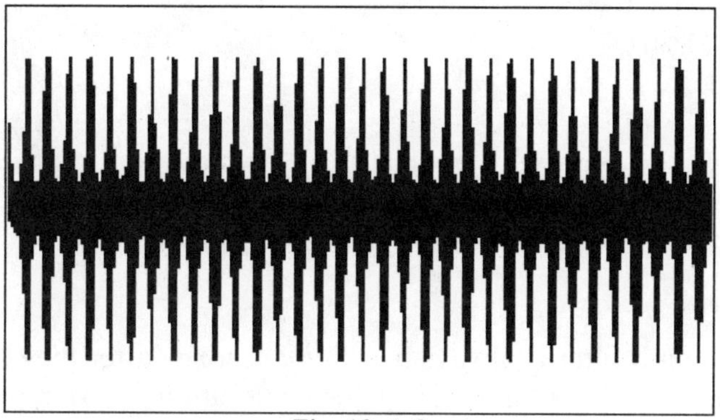

Fig. 13-A-2

The graph in fig.13-A-2 was obtained with the following orchestra, where comb filtering is implemented using *delay*. This implementation allows for both *ilpt* and feedback to be freely set up (here *ilpt* = 0.005 and *feedback* = 0.8).

```
;myrev.orc
        sr      =   44100
        kr      =   4410
        ksmps =     10
        nchnls =    1
        instr       1
a2      init 0
kfrq    line        10, p3, 10000
a1      oscili      5000, kfrq, 1
a2      delay       a1+a2*.8, .005                  ;delay implementing a comb filter
        out         a2
        endin
```

A similar effect is created in the following orchestra, using the comb code by itself:

```
;comb.orc
        sr      =   22050
```

```
        kr     =  2205
        ksmps  =  10
        nchnls =  1
        instr     1
kfreq   line      10, p3, 10000
a1      oscili    1000, kfreq, 1
acomb   comb      a1, . 5, .001
        out       acomb
        endin
```

```
;comb.sco
f1   0    4096   10   1
i1   0    5
```

The output of a comb filter is always heard *ilpt* seconds after the original sound.

Different from *comb, alpass* has no frequency coloration, but it introduces some phase shift into the signal. The shift is different at different frequencies. Indeed, all filters introduce some frequency-dependent phase shift, but in most cases that is simply a side-effect. With *alpass*, however, the phase shift is the intended effect of the filtering. When the input signal is very dynamic, and changes a lot over time (e.g. attack transients), *alpass* introduces frequency colorations which emphasize the phase variation in the signal itself.

Now that we have examined the main features of *comb* and *alpass*, let's see how we can use them to implement a custom reverberator.

```
;myrev1.orc

        instr   99

;ain = input signal
;irevt=riverberation time

a1      alpass  ain,  5, .04996
a2      alpass  a1*.72,  5, .05465
a3      alpass  a2*.961, 5, .02418
aoutl   alpass  a3*.649, 5, .01785
aoutr   alpass  a3*.646, 5, .01795
        outs    aoutl, aoutr
        endin
```

This instrument (a variation upon James A. Moorer's reverb algorithm)[2] is made of five *alpass* units connected together as shown in figure 13-A-3. Observe the *ilpt* values, on the right of each *alpass* box. It is crucial to choose the appropriate *ilpt* values, to avoid multiple resonances. It is essential that they have the least possible number of common divisors (i.e. they have to be prime numbers).

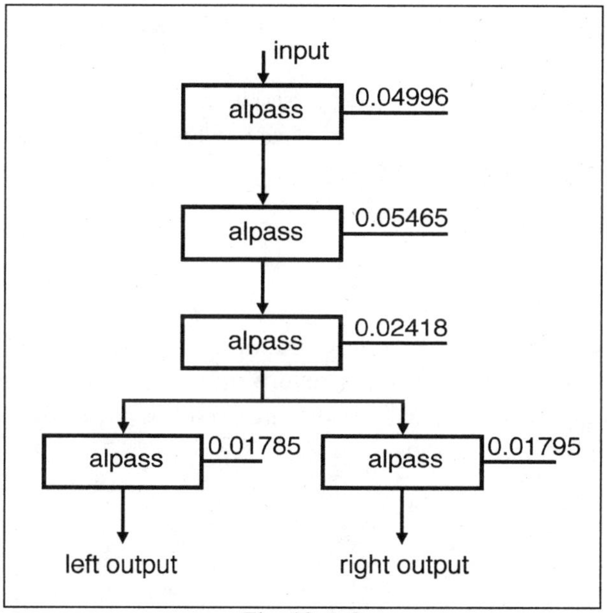

Fig. 13-A-3

Now, let's see how we build a reverb unit with *delayr/delayw* and *deltapi*. This example attempts to simulate the multiple reflections typical of the walls of a cubic room. Observe that each *deltapi* signal read is fed back into the delay line, just as any sound reflected off one wall is reflected all the other walls in the room, as well.

```
;myrev2.orc

        instr   99
                                                        ;the input signal is ga1
afeed   init    0                                       ;init feedback variable
iloop   =       1
```

[2] J.A.Moorer, "Signal processing aspects of computer music", in J.Strawn (ed.) Digital audio signal processing. An anthology, William Kaufmann Inc., Los Altos, Ca. 1985

```
ar          delayr      .2                          ;delay line must be larger than the actual
                                                    ;delay times in the deltapi below

            delayw      ga1+afeed
ar1         deltapi     .063*iloop
ar2         deltapi     .071*iloop
ar3         deltapi     .107*iloop
ar4         deltapi     .129*iloop
afeed       =           (ar1+ar2+ar3+ar4)*.2        ;sum up the reflected signals
                                                    ;and feed them back to the delay
aout        =           ar+ar1+ar2+ar3+ar4
            out         aout
ga1         =           0
            endin
```

To conclude this example, let's examine the following orchestra developed at Stanford University. It represents a more complex reverb unit than those examined earlier, and is based on *comb* and *alpass* opcodes. It also features a lowpass filter in order to attenuate the reflections of higher frequencies.

```
;myrev3.orc

            instr   99

;- - - - - - - - - - - - - - - - - - - - - - - - data definition
;ga1         =   left input, ga2=right input
irevfactor   =   p4                         ;overall reverberation time
ilowpass     =   9000                       ;cutoff freq   for the lowpass
ioutputscale=    p5                         ;scale factor for the output reverb signal

;- - - - - - - - - - - - - - - - - - - - - - - - ilpt values (for comb and alpass units)
idel1        =   1237.000/sr
idel2        =   1381.000/sr
idel3        =   1607.000/sr
idel4        =   1777.000/sr
idel5        =   1949.000/sr
idel6        =   2063.000/sr
idel7        =   307.000/sr
idel8        =   97.000/sr
```

```
idel9       =   71.000/sr
idel10      =   53.000/sr
idel11      =   47.000/sr
idel12      =   37.000/sr
idel13      =   31.000/sr

;- - - - - - - - - - - - - - - - - - - - - - - - reverb times (for comb and alpass, expressed as
; fractions of the overall reverb time)
icsc1       =   .822 * irevfactor
icsc2       =   .802 * irevfactor
icsc3       =   .773 * irevfactor
icsc4       =   .753 * irevfactor
icsc5       =   .753 * irevfactor
icsc6       =   .753 * irevfactor
icsc7       =   .7 * irevfactor

;- - - - - - - - - - - - - - - - - - - - - - - - combs for the left channel
acomb1      comb    ga1,  icsc1, idel1
acomb2      comb    ga1,  icsc2, idel2
acomb3      comb    ga1,  icsc3, idel3
acomb4      comb    ga1,  icsc4, idel4
acomb5      comb    ga1,  icsc5, idel5
acomb6      comb    ga1,  icsc6, idel6

acomball    =   acomb1 + acomb2 + acomb3 + acomb4 + acomb5 + acomb6

;- - - - - - - - - - - - - - - - - - - - - - - - alpasses for the left channel
allp1       alpass  acomball, icsc7, idel7
allp2       alpass  allp1,  icsc7, idel8
allp3       alpass  allp2,  icsc7, idel9
alow        tone    allp3,  ilowpass
allp4       alpass  alow,  icsc7, idel10
allp5       alpass  allp4,  icsc7, idel12
arevout1    =       allp5 * ioutputscale

;- - - - - - - - - - - - - - - - - - - - - - - - combs for the right channel
acomb1      comb    ga2,  icsc1, idel1
acomb2      comb    ga2,  icsc2, idel2
acomb3      comb    ga2,  icsc3, idel3
```

```
acomb4    comb   ga2,  icsc4, idel4
acomb5    comb   ga2,  icsc5, idel5
acomb6    comb   ga2,  icsc6, idel6

acomball  =   acomb1 + acomb2 + acomb3 + acomb4 + acomb5 + acomb6

;------------------------ alpasses for the right channel
allp1     alpass  acomball, icsc7, idel7
allp2     alpass  allp1, icsc7, idel8
allp3     alpass  allp2, icsc7, idel9
alow      tone    allp3, ilowpass
allp4     alpass  alow, icsc7, idel10
allp6     alpass  allp4, icsc7, idel13
arevout2  =   allp6 * ioutputscale

;------------------------ output
          outs      arevout1, arevout2

;------------------------ zeroing of the global values
ga1       =  0
ga2       =  0
          endin
```

Designing good reverb units is an art. A pleasing reverberation is crucial for most compositions realized with Csound (or any other software synthesis systems).

LIST OF OPCODES INTRODUCED IN THIS CHAPTER

ar delayr delay_time[, internal_memory_storage]
delayw input_signal
a1 deltap delay_time
a1 deltapi delay_time
ar delay input_signal, delay_time[, internal_memory_storage]
ar delay1 input_signal [,internal_memory_storage]
ar reverb input_signal, reverb_time[, internal_memory_storage]
ar reverb2 input_signal, reverb_time, high_freq_reverb_time[, internal_memory_storage]
ar vdelay input_signal, delay_time, max_delay_time[,internal_memory_storage]
ar1[,...[,ar4]]] convolve input_signal, filename, channel
ar comb input_signal, reverb_time, loop_time [,internal_memory_storage]
ar alpass input_signal, reverb_time, loop_time [,internal_memory_storage]

14

THE TABLE OPCODE. WAVESHAPING SYNTHESIS, VECTOR SYNTHESIS

To use function tables of any kind and shape for generation of signals (with *table* opcode) it is necessary to use the appropriate GEN routines introduced in this chapter.

14.1 GEN02 AND SOME OBSERVATIONS ON FUNCTIONS

GEN02 transfers the required parameter values (p-field values other than p1, p2, p3 and p4) into a memory table.

The syntax is:

fn t s 2 v1 v2 v3 ...

n	function table number
t	action time
s	table size
2	GEN routine number (if positive, the function values are normalized to peak at an amplitude of 1; if negative, normalization is omitted)
v1, *v2*, ...	values

Let's see an example:

```
f1 0 16 2 0 1 2 3 4 5 6 7 8 9 10 9 8 7 6 5
; normalized values, range = 0-1

f1 0 16 -2 0 1 2 3 4 5 6 7 8 9 10 9 8 7 6 5
; non-normalized values, range = 0-10
```

Both tables are made of 16 points. They include 16 positions, each with a value of its own. The contents of the second table, with non-normalized values, are as follows:

Index	1	2	3	4	5	6	7	8	9	10	11	12	13	14	15	16
Table values	0	1	2	3	4	5	6	7	8	9	10	9	8	7	6	5

The first table includes normalized values. The contents are as follows:

Index	1	2	3	4	5	6	7	8	9	10	11	12	13	14	15	16
Table values	.0	.1	.2	.3	.4	.5	.6	.7	.8	.9	1	.9	.8	.7	.6	.5

The values we entered in the second table do not get normalized, due to the fact that we set a negative GEN number. Here's another example, using GEN10:

```
f1 0 4096 10 2       ;values normalized (-1 to 1)
f1 0 4096 -10 2      ;values in the required range (-2 to 2)
```

Before we go through the remainder of this chapter, let's define some of the terms and concepts relative to their functions.

a. Functions

A function is a mathematical method for generating the values of one variable from another variable. The former is called the *dependent* variable. The latter is called the *independent* variable.

The general notation for a function is:

y = f(x)

where:

x=independent variable (can assume any value)
y=dependent variable (values vary with x according to the law expressed by *f*)

(consider these examples: y=2*x, y=sin(x), $y=4*x^2+3$...)

b. GEN

In Csound, a **GEN** routine represents a method, labeled with a number, for generating a series of values to be stored into a series of memory locations (= a table). Each GEN represents the implementation of a separate function.

c. Tables

A **table** is a 1-dimensional set of values (= an array), which you access by specifying some **index**. For example, given the following table, the **index** 4 returns a **value** of 7:

Index	0	1	2	3	4	5	6	7	8
Table values	1	5	7	3	7	9	56	3	12

Csound stores different tables in different memory areas. Each table is identified by a number (the total number of tables is dependent on the particular Csound release). In each table, new values can be entered to replace previously entered values. At some predetermined time, new values (perhaps generated by a new function) fill the table and replace older ones.

Here's an example:

```
f 1 0  4096 10 1
;this table is valid from 0 to 10 secs
;at 10 seconds, new values replace the older, as from the table function
;below
f 1 10 4096 10 1 .5 .4 .3 .2 .1
;this new table remains valid until it is cancelled out by the statement
;below (a negative function number causes the table function to be
;destroyed)
f -1 20
```

14.2 THE *TABLE* OPCODE

Opcodes *table* and *tablei* are useful for generating any kind of signal (audio, control or init variables), based on the a table look-up process. They are usually listed under the opcode heading "signal generators", but actually can be used for many different purposes including custom tuning systems, waveshaping synthesis, sound spatialization, etc.

```
ir    table    indx, ifn[, ixmode][, ixoff][, iwrap]
ir    tablei   indx, ifn[, ixmode][, ixoff][, iwrap]
kr    table    kndx, ifn[, ixmode][, ixoff][, iwrap]
kr    tablei   kndx, ifn[, ixmode][, ixoff][, iwrap]
ar    table    andx, ifn[, ixmode][, ixoff][, iwrap]
ar    table    andx, ifn[, ixmode][, ixoff][, iwrap]
```

indx/kndx/andx	index pointing to a particular table location
ifn	function table number (with *tablei* it is advisable to use a table of size equal to a power-of-2-plus-1; the last point in the table must contain the same value as the first - it is called *extended guard point*).
ixmode	(optional) switch between two available modes for accessing the table data: 0 = raw index (index ranges between 0 and table size); 1 = normalized index (index ranges between 0 and 1). The default is 0 (raw index)
ixoff	(optional) amount by which the index is offset. For a table with origin at the center, use tablesize/2 (raw index) or .5 (normalized index). The default is 0.
iwrap	(optional) if >0, the table will be interpreted as a circular function. Index values higher than the table size point to some table position equivalent to the value minus the table size. (wraparound). When 0 or <0, higher index values will point to the last table location. The default is 0.

The following orchestra example allows you to create non-equally tempered scales (i.e. tuning systems with variable ratio between each two pitches).

```
;scale.orc
        sr      =  22050
        kr      =  2205
        ksmps   =  10
        nchnls  =  1

        instr      1

;first separate the integer part (octaves) from the fractional part
;(semitones) of p5
```

```
ioct    =       int(p5)               ;octaves
isem    =       frac(p5)*100          ;semitones, multiplied by 100 (hence 8.01 yields 1,
                                      ;8.11 yields 11 etc). These numbers are used, then,
                                      ;as index to function table n.2, returning new
                                      ;pitch values: each tempered pitch is
                                      ;replaced by some non-tempered pitch stored in the table

isem1           table   isem, 2, 0    ;takes a value from function table 2, at the position specified by isem
                                      ;(3rd argument = 0, i.e no index scaling:
                                      ;herefore, isem=0 takes the first value,
                                      ;isem =1 takes the second, isem =3 the fourth, etc.)

ifrq    =       cpspch(ioct+isem1)    ;convert octave+semitone to Hertz
iamp    =       ampdb(p4)
a1      oscili  iamp, ifrq, 1
        out     a1
        endin

instr   2

;use table to build a non-equally tempered tuning system, with interpolation

ioct    =       int(p5)               ;octave
isem    =       frac(p5)*100          ;semitone, multiplied by 100

isem1   tablei  isem, 2, 0            ;same as instr 1, but interpolated table
                                      ;read, isem1 can be fractional.
ifrq    =       cpspch(ioct+isem1)    ;convert octave+semitone to Hertz
iamp    =       ampdb(p4)             ;convert dB values to absolute amplitude
a1      oscil   iamp, ifrq, 1
        out     a1
        endin
```

An example score:

```
;scale.sco
f1 0 4097 10 1 ;(sine for oscili)
f2  0  17 -2 0 .015 .02 .035 .04 .055 .06 .075 .08 .095 .10 .115 0 0 0 0 0
;the above GEN02 is negative, i.e. normalization is omitted
```

```
;new pitches replace the traditional pitches C-C#-D-D#...B.
;As the table has 17 locations(= a-power-of-two-plus-1), 5 void p-fields
;can be appended to the utilizable locations

i1   0   .5   80   8        ;instrument 1 has a non-interpolated table
                            ;read, therefore only integer numbers
                            ;(semitones) can be used as index to the function table
i1   +   .5   80   8.04
i1   +   .5   80   8.07
i1   +   .5   80   8.10

i2   3   .5   80   8        ;instrument 2 has an interpolated table read (tablei), therefore it is
                            ;possible to use non-integer values (smaller than semitones)
                            ;to index the function table (in this example quarter-tones are used)
i.   +   .    80   8.005
i.   +   .    80   8.01
i.   +   .    80   8.015
i.   +   .    80   8.02
i.   +   .    80   8.025
i.   +   .    80   8.03
i.   +   .    80   8.035
i.   +   .    80   8.04
i.   +   .    80   8.045
```

14.3 LINE-SEGMENTS, EXPONENTIALS, CUBIC SPLINES: GEN05, GEN07 AND GEN08

GEN05 and GEN07 generate function tables made of line segments (GEN07) or exponential curves (GEN05). Routine GEN08 generates "cubic spline" curves (cubic polynomials, representing the smoothest possible curve through a number of break-points). Each segment or curve must be given a length, expressed in table locations ("points", or "samples").

fn t s 5 val0 length0 val1 length1 val2 ...
fn t s 7 val0 length0 val1 length1 val2 ...
fn t s 8 val0 length0 val1 length1 val2 ...

n	function table number
t	action time

s	table size
5,7,8	GEN type (when positive, values are normalized; when negative, normalization is omitted)
val0	start value in the first segment
length0	length of the first segment (in table locations)
val1	end value in the first segment (same as the initial value in the second segment)
length1	length of the second segment
val2	end value in the second segment (same as the initial value in the third segment)
etc.	

With GEN05 (exponential curves), values must be non-0 and all alike in sign. The restriction does not apply to GEN07 and GEN08. Segment lengths cannot be negative. They must be integers for GEN05 and GEN07, but they can be fractions for GEN08.

Normally, the sum of all segment lengths (*length0+length1+length2...*) gives *s* (table size). But if the sum is less than the table size, the empty locations are filled with zeroes. When greater, only a portion of the required function table will be created, corresponding to *s* locations.

With GEN05 and GEN07, segment lengths of 0 determine discontinuities in the waveform, as is the case with the following example:

```
f1  0  512  7  0  256  1  0  -1  256  0
```

This line creates a single period of saw-tooth wave with a discontinuity right in the middle of the function table.

GEN08 creates cubic spline curves, each running between two points specified by the neighbors on both side. Neighboring segments agree in value and slope at their common point. The slope at both end points is forced to zero (null slope, horizontal line). The following example creates a curve with a "hump" in the middle. The curve briefly moves to negative values as it nears the end points, but becomes horizontal as it reaches end points themselves.

```
f1  0  65  8  0  16  0  16  1  16  0  16  0
```

The following creates a similar table, but includes no negative values:

```
f2  0  65  8  0  16  0  .1  0  15.9  1  15.9  0  .1  0  16  0
```

14.4 WAVESHAPING SYNTHESIS (NONLINEAR DISTORTION)

One of the most interesting applications of the *table* opcode is the implementation of shaping functions, or functions that can be easily used to transform any input signal. This is called *waveshaping synthesis*, which is a method that lends itself well to the generation of dynamical spectra. The method is also known as "nonlinear distortion".

A very simple example of nonlinear distortion is the process of *clipping* an audio signal. This was often utilized by musicians in the 1970's, and perhaps first employed by Stockhausen in his *Kontakte*. It is created by feeding an amplifier with a signal higher than can be supported. That causes the waveform peaks to be truncated, or *clipped* down to the maximum value allowed by the amplifier circuit. The input signal is thus shaped more like a square wave (hence the term *waveshaping*). Odd-numbered harmonics are introduced in the output sound as a by-product of clipping.

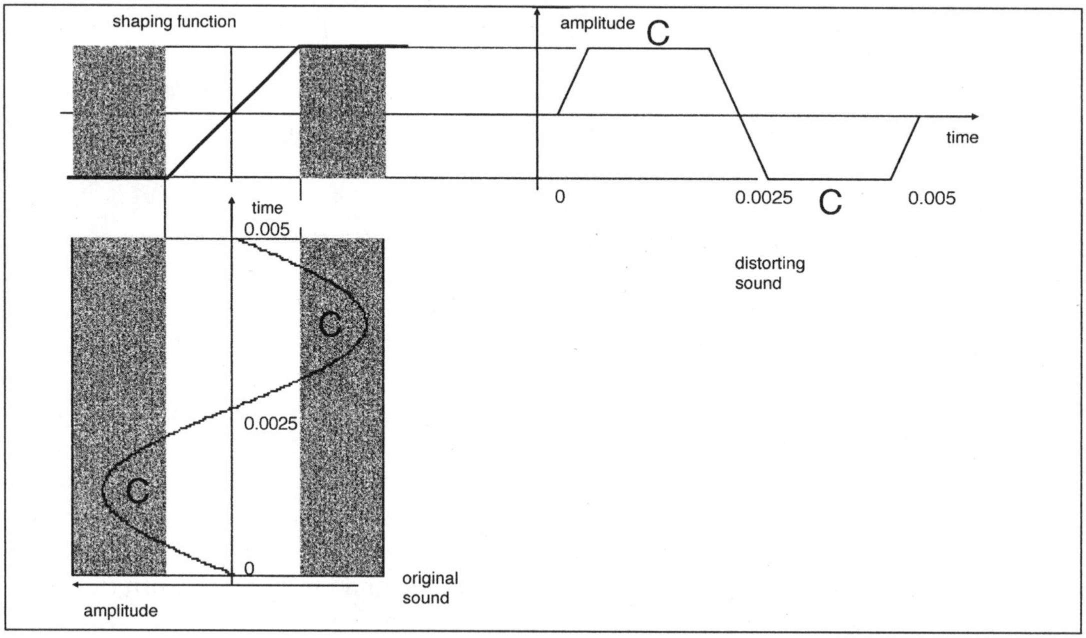

Fig. 14-1

In a more controlled implementation, waveshaping consists of a table look-up process driven by an input signal. The table contains a waveshaping function (distorting function or transform function), and the look-up index is provided by the instantaneous amplitude of the input signal. If the waveshaping function is a straight line inclined by 45 degrees, the output is identical with the input. A different inclination indicates a change in amplitude. If we want to introduce more drastic changes to the output waveform (possibly creating a different spectrum), we must resort to non-linear transform functions.

It goes without saying that the output signal waveform depends on the input signal amplitude. See figure 14-1 (the waveshaping function is shown on top-left, the input signal is on the bottom, and the output on top-right).

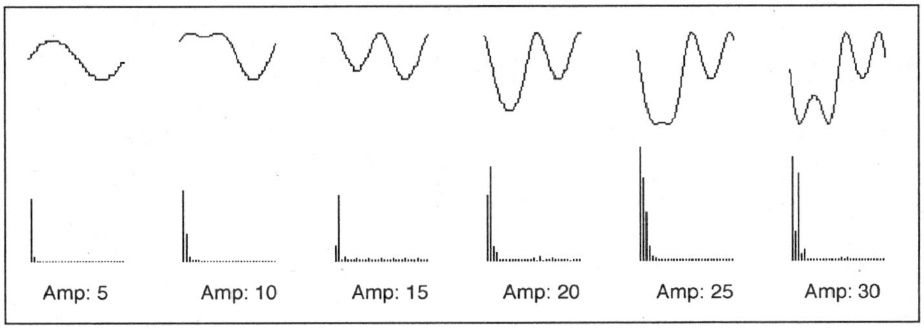

Fig. 14-2

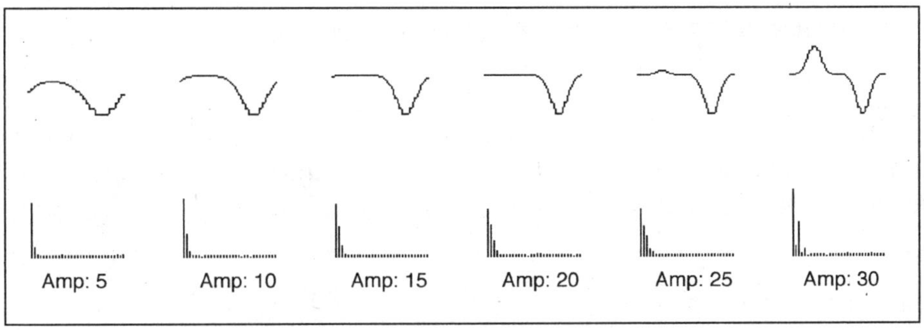

Fig. 14-3

In fig.14-2 and 14-3 you can see the effect of using two different waveshaping functions, a sinusoid (14-2) and a paraboloid (14-3). The two figures illustrate the output waveform and its spectrum for increasing input amplitudes.

Here's a waveshaping synthesis instrument:

```
;dnl0.orc
        sr      =  44100
        kr      =  4410
        ksmps  =  10
        nchnls =  1
```

```
        instr       1

; waveshaping (non-linear distortion)

        ifrq    =   p5
        iamp    =   ampdb(p4)

kenv    linseg      0, .1, .5, p3-.1, 0
a1      oscil       kenv, ifrq, 1       ;sinusoid with envelope  scaled between -.5 and .5

        a2      =   a1 + .5             ;add offset of .5, so sinusoid now oscillates between 0 and 1
        a3  table   a2, 2, 1            ;use the sinusoid signal, a2, to index table n.2 (index mode=1, normalized)
        a4      =   a3 * iamp           ;amplitude scaling
        out         a4
        endin

;dnl0.sco
f1 0 4096 10 1                              ;sinusoid
f2 0  4096  7  -1 1635 -1 827 1 1635 1      ;waveshaping function (see fig.14-4)
i1      0   3   80  200
```

Figure 14-4 illustrates the mapping of a2 (amplitude 0-1) onto the table size range. An amplitude value of 0 would point to the first table location, while a value of 0.5 would point to the 2048th location, etc.

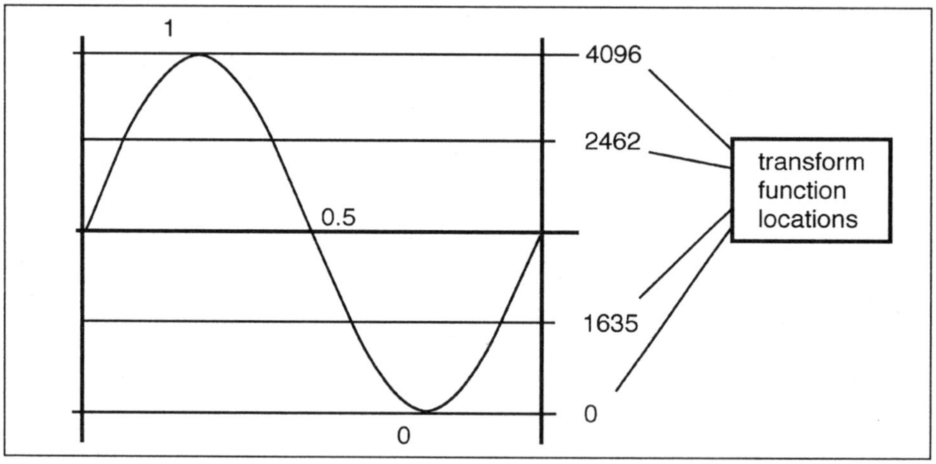

Fig. 14-4

In this example, f2 is identical to the line-segment function in figure 14-5. When the input signal points to any of the first 1635 locations in the table, the output is clipped (= -1). When the input signal points to any of the locations between 1636 and 2462, the output is the same as the input, with no clipping. When the input signal points to any of the locations between 2463 and 4096, again the output signal is clipped (=1). This process is illustrated in figure 14-1.

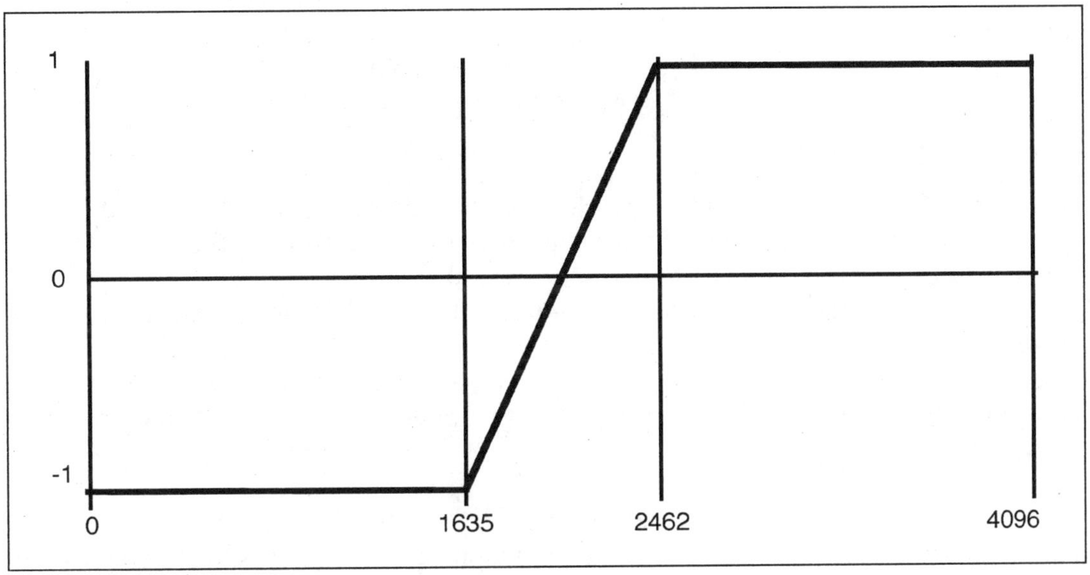

Fig. 14-5

14.5 USING CHEBYCHEV POLYNOMIALS (GEN13)

By using the so-called "Chebychev polynomials" as waveshaping functions, it becomes possible to calculate the resulting spectrum before waveshaping. Chebychev polynomials represent a whole set of functions. The first 5 elements in the set are as follows:

$$T0(x) = 1$$
$$T1(x) = x$$
$$T2(x) = 2x^2 - 1$$
$$T3(x) = 4x^3 - 3x$$
$$T4(x) = 8x^4 - 8x^3 + 1$$
$$T5(x) = 16x^5 - 20x^3 + 5x$$

...

The n-th harmonic in the output spectrum will depend on the weight (coefficient) of the n-th polynomial in the waveshaping function. For a complete description of this process, please see the references, especially [De Poli 1981].

The GEN routine for calculating Chebychev polynomials is GEN13. Each polynomial in the set can be given a different coefficient so that we can determine, by the weight of the various polynomials, the precise spectral composition of the output signal.

function number	action time	size	GEN type	minimum value for x	amplitude (max value for x)	weight of the 0th harmonic	weight of the 1st harmonic	weight of the 2nd harmonic	...	weight of the n-th harmonic
f#	time	points	13	xint	xamp	h0	h1	h2	...	h3

As usual, the table *size* must be equal to a power-of-two, or a power-of-two-plus-1.

xint defines the left and right limit values (-*xint* and +*xint*) of the interval, x, over which the polynomial is drawn. The normal xint value is 1.

xamp is a scaling factor for the sinusoid input that will be used to produce the required spectrum

h0, h1, h2... are the relative weights of partials 0 (direct current), 1 (fundamental), 2 (second harmonic), etc., as relative to an input sine wave of amplitude = *xamp*int(size/2)/xint.*

In general, as the input level increases, the resulting spectrum becomes harmonically richer. The separate harmonics appear one after another in ascending order (the relationship between the output spectral composition and the input signal amplitude is non-linear). Negative coefficients *h0*, *h1*, etc. cause a 180-degree phase shift. In order to minimize the DC offset in the output sound, we may use the following pattern of coefficients: +, +, - , - , +, +, -, -, ... (that is: +h0, +h1, -h2, -h3, + h4, +h5, ...).

For example, the following generates a table which, in a waveshaping application, will split an input sine wave into three components, a fundamental with relative amplitude 5, a third harmonic with relative amplitude 3 and a fourth harmonic with relative amplitude 1:

```
f 1 0 1025 13 1 1 0 5 0 3 0 1
```

Now, let's try the following orchestra and score:

```
;dnl.orc
```

```
        sr          =   44100
        kr          =   4410
        ksmps       =   10
        nchnls      =   1
        instr           1
        ifrq        =   cpspch(p5)
        iamp        =   ampdb(p4)
kenv    linen           .5, p3/2, p3, p3/2      ;envelope (amp ranges 0 to .5)
a1      oscil           kenv, ifrq, 1           ;sinusoid (oscillates between -.5 and .5)

;waveshaping

a2      table           a1, 2, 1, .5            ;a1=input signal
                                                ;2=waveshaping table number
                                                ;1= index mode (normalized)
                                                ;.5 offset added to the input signal
        a2          =   a2 * iamp

;besides using alternating coefficient signs, as suggested in the text,
;to avoid the DC offset we can also use a highpass filter, such that
;the DC component is eliminated (or attenuated) at the beginning and at the
;ending of the note - to that aim, cancel the semicolon in the following
;line and use aout as the output signal, not a2.

;aout   atone           a2, 30

        out             a2
        endin

;dnl.sco
f1 0 4096 10 1
;EXAMPLE 1: first 5 harmonics have the same amplitude
;           xmin/xmax xamp   coefficients
f2 0 4096 13    1    1    0 1 1 1 1 1
i1      0   3   80 7
;EXAMPLE 2: odd harmonics only, resulting in a square wave
;(graphically this is not a square wave, as the harmonics are not in phase)
f2 3 4096 13  1 1   0 1 0 .33 0 .2 0 .14 0 .11 0 .09 0 .0769 0 .067 0 .0588
i1 3 3 80 7
```

14.6 USING *TABLE* FOR DYNAMIC RANGE PROCESSING (COMPRESSORS AND EXPANDERS)

Another application of *table* is dynamic range processing effects such as created by *compressors* and *expanders*. A compressor is a signal processor which reduces the dynamic range of the input signal. An expander performs the opposite operation. Take a look at the graph in figure 14-6. The three lines illustrate three different input/output relationships. Line 1 determines no change. Line 2 determines the signal compression. For any given dynamic variation in the input signal, it reduces the amount of variation in the ouput. Line 3 shows a signal expansion. For any given dynamic variation in the input, it increases the amount of variation in the output.

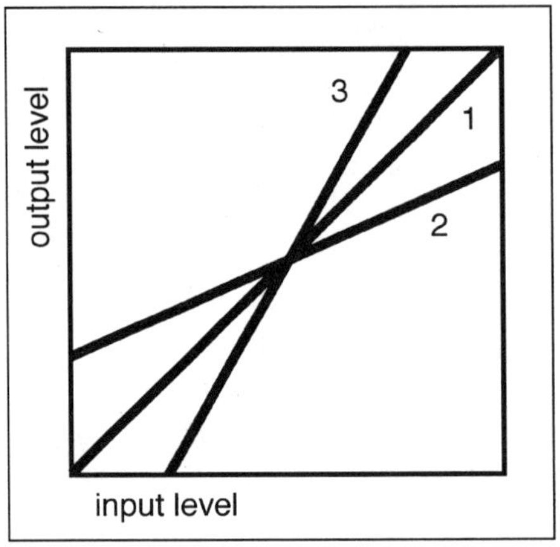

Fig. 14-6

How can we use these effects? A compressor can reduce the signal peaks and, hence, avoid saturation, without decreasing the overall amplitude. Other, more radical effects, well-known to anyone experienced in rock guitar, include heavy compression effect to smooth out of the attack of notes.

Expanders are used to extend the dynamic range of sounds with little dynamic range, and also to imbue flat or dull sonorities with a more aggressive timbral quality, not to mention distortion effects.

Used in pairs, compressor and expander can enhance the quality of sounds on analog tapes. Noise-reduction systems such as *Dolby* ™ and *dbx* ™, are based on this principle. Figure 14-7 illustrates the process of *companding* (using a compressor/expander pair). On the left is the input signal. On the right is the output signal. In the middle is the clipping area, which represents the level at which the input signal cannot be recorded without also introducing distortion. Beneath is the portion of signal which is masked by the analog tape noise. During the recording, the input signal is compressed so that it matches the tape's dynamic range. Then, during the playback, the signal is expanded to match the range of the original performance.

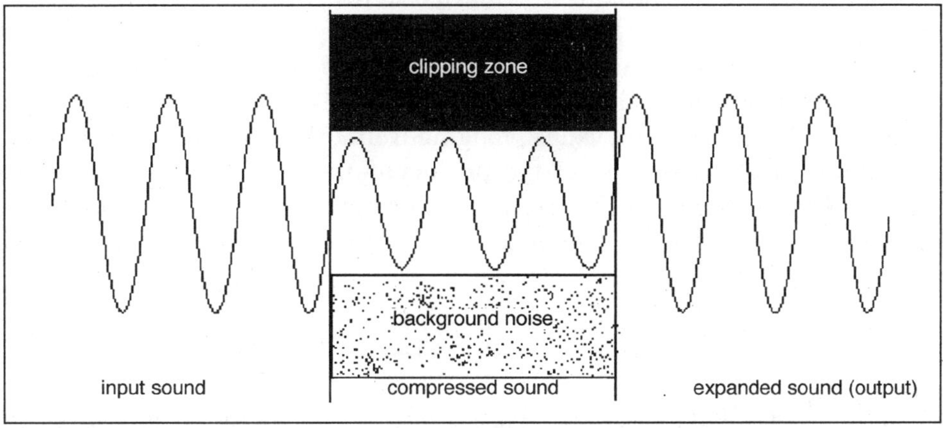

Fig. 14-7

Of course, infinitely many shaping functions can be used for interesting dynamic range processing. The following Csound example incorporates a compressor. The code also includes several interesting opcodes, such as *table*, *gain* and *rms*.

```
;compress.orc
          sr     =  44100
          kr     =  4410
          ksmps  =  10
          nchnls =  1
          instr     1
a1        soundin   "voice.wav"      ;input samples
krmsin    rms       a1               ;effective amplitude extraction
kdbin            =  dbamp(krmsin)    ;amp to dB conversion
kdbout    tablei    kdbin, 1         ;table read
krmsout          =  ampdb(kdbout)    ;dB to amp conversion
aout      gain      a1, krmsout      ;amp scaling
          out       aout             ;output
          endin

;compress.sco
f1    0    129    -7    30    128    60    1    60
```

```
i1   0   5
```

Examine this orchestra. We read samples off some "voice.wav" file, and extract the amplitude value, krmsin. That is then converted to dB, with *dbamp*(). The dB value is used as the index argument for *tablei*, which, given the particular f1 function used here, causes a transformation of the amplitude dB value. Finally, the input signal, a1, is scaled to the amplitude value retrieved from the table.

In function table n.1 the input values, ranging from 0-128, are mapped onto a smaller interval, 30-60. Figure 14-8 shows the profile of the original signal (top) and the compressed signal (bottom). The horizontal axis is time, the vertical is dB. Observe that the compressed signal is a bit flattened, its dynamic variations are smaller than the original.

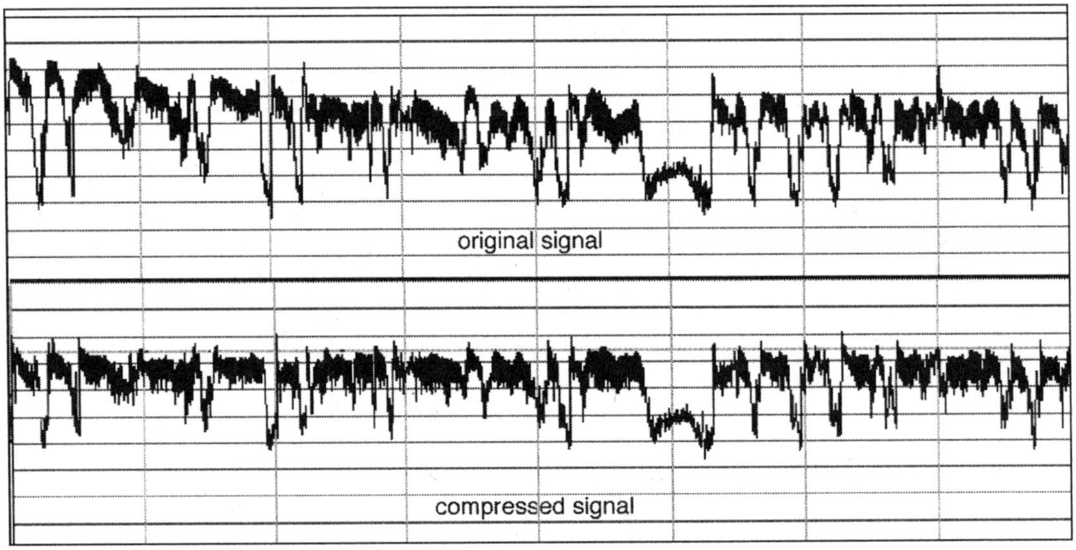

Fig. 14-8

14.7 GEN03

GEN03 generates a table with a polynomial of the x variable specified within an interval. The polynomial coefficients are entered starting from seventh p-field.

fn t s 3 xval1 xval2 c0 c1 c2 ...

n function table number

t	action time
s	size
3	GEN type
xval1	initial x value for the polynomial
xval2	final x value for the polynomial
c0, c1, c2...	polynomial coefficients (c0=coefficient of x^0, c1= coefficient of x^1, etc.).

For example, with this *f* statement

```
f1 0 1024 3 -1 1 0 3 2
```

we require the second-order polynomial (paraboloid) for x varying from -1 to 1

$$y = 3x + 2x^2$$

GEN03 may be used to create transfer functions for waveshaping synthesis, but with less predictable results than Chebychev polynomials. It may also be used to create several kinds of transfer function for dynamic range processing (compression/expansion).

14.8 TABLE CROSSFADE: VECTOR SYNTHESIS

So far, we have used individual function tables as the basic, predetermined elements for generation of audio and control signals. In this section, we discuss the process of crossfading between several tables. The goal is to achieve a smooth passage from one timbre model to another, in a kind of spectral mutation. The approach allows for the generation of unusual sounds such as a piano-like attack with an inharmonic FM spectrum, that fades out with a decay curve extracted from a real harp sound. The sound event evolves, during the note, across a number of timbre models. In contrast, using a single function table can allow the repetition of only one timbre model. For example, a sinusoid waveform repeated 440 times per second results in a 440 Hz sine tone.

It is easy to create an orchestra for crossfading tables. We have only to mix together a number of oscillators enveloped as to create the required crossfades between different sounds. We also have to define a sequence of timbre models, so that the right function table fades in and out at the proper time. This is essentially a special kind of additive synthesis. When two or more tables are used, we refer to the process as *vector synthesis*. The concept is not radically different from additive synthesis, but the implementation, perhaps, appears more complicated.

Here's an orchestra example, followed by its score:

```
;vector.orc
        sr      =  44100
        kr      =  4410
        ksmps   =  10
        nchnls  =  1
        instr      1
k1      expseg     .001, .001, 20000, 1, 20000, 3, .001
a1      loscil     k1, 220, 1, 220
k2      linseg     0, 1, 20000, 2, 20000, 2, 0
a2      foscili    1, 1, 440, 220, 3, 2
        out        a1+(a2*k2)
        endin

;vect.sco
f1      0       0       1       ´piano.wavª     0       0       0
f2      0       4097    10      1
;ins    act     dur
i1      0       5
```

LIST OF OPCODES INTRODUCED IN THIS SECTION

i1	**table**	**index, function_table [, index_mode][, offset][, wrap]**
k1	**table**	**index, function_table [, index_mode][, offset][, wrap]**
a1	**table**	**index, function_table [, index_mode][, offset][, wrap]**
i1	**tablei**	**index, function_table [, index_mode][, offset][, wrap]**
k1	**tablei**	**index, function_table [, index_mode][, offset][, wrap]**

15

GRANULAR SYNTHESIS AND FORMANT SYNTHESIS

15.1 WHAT IS GRANULAR SYNTHESIS

"When the slow variations in the sound are thought of as discrete-time functions" (as is the case with Csound control variables) "the generated sound should be described as a chain of elementary sounds, each having its own, constant characteristics. [...] The elementary sounds are called *grains*, and the technique exploiting this facility is *granular synthesis*" [De Poli, 1981].

Granular synthesis involves creating large masses of small acoustical events, called "grains", of duration ranging from 10 to 100 milliseconds. A sound grain is usually characterized by a symmetrical envelope shape. Typical grain envelopes include the bell-like Gaussian curve, the 3-segment trapezoid envelope, and the 2-segment attack-and-decay envelope (see figures 15-1 and 15-2).

In Csound, granular synthesis usually implies that a single "note" (a single *i* statement in the score) gives rise to a very complex event, sometimes including the synthesis of a few thousands grains per second. Starting with very short and simple sonic units, granular synthesis creates extremely rich and articulated sound structures. Another approach involves generating thousands of *i* statements (via some preprocessing software), each of which produces a single grain.

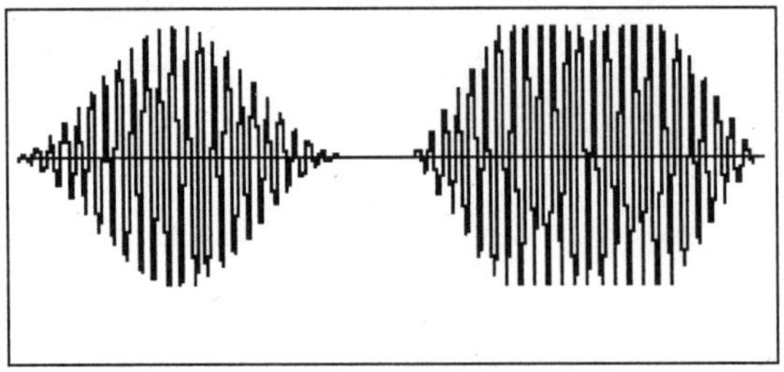

Fig. 15-1

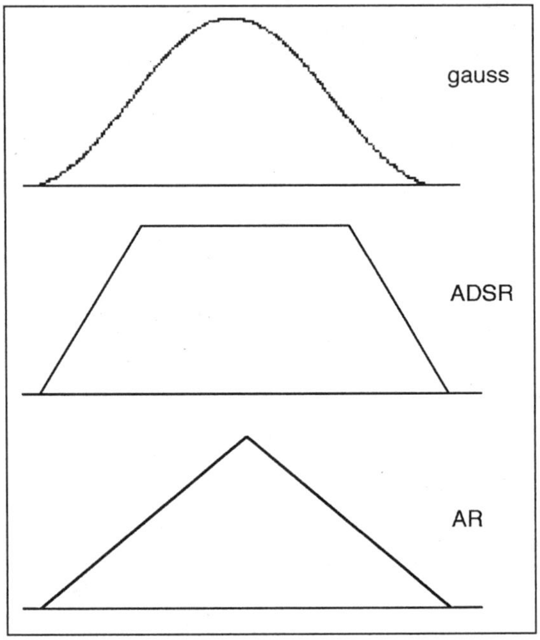

Fig. 15-2

In 1947, Dennis Gabor first discussed a granular approach in his article "Acoustical Quanta and the Theory of Hearing". Later, Norbert Wiener (1964) and Abraham Moles (1969) contributed to the approach. Iannis Xenakis, in his *Musiques Formelles* (1971), was the first composer to define a compositional theory based on sound grains. In 1975, Curtis Roads implemented a simple form of digital granular synthesis, experimenting with his own automated methods for generating massive streams of grains, and also composing his *prototype* (1975). Later he published two important articles on granular synthesis, in 1978 and 1985.

During its early stages, granular synthesis was difficult to use, due to the enormous amount of calculations required. In 1986 Barry Truax first proposed a real-time implementation using a dedicated digital signal processor called the DMX-1000. He also composed *Riverrun* (1988), a tape piece where sound grains are likened to water drops, which little by little accumulate and give rise to the powerful image of large river flow (for the implementation of Truax's method, see the discussion in Eugenio Giordani's lecture at the end of this book).

The waveform of a sound grain can be either extracted from a sampled sound or generated with another synthesis method, like FM or additive synthesis. In any case, the sound grain waveform is conveniently stored in a table. This method differs, however, in that the sound grain waveform, being so short, is already enveloped and entirely encapsulated in a function table.

A grain represents a kind of cell, a microscopic sound unit with its own parameters. Parameters include: duration, frequency, envelope, rise time, stereo location, waveform. Time delay between successive grains (inter-grain delay) is another crucial parameter.

As is clear, the generation of thousands of grains per second requires a huge number of calculations, that can be difficult to handle. A practical solution is achieved by implementing higher-level control structures, through which you adjust all data according to a global approach. Typical controls including preset values, maybe ramped or randomly scattered over a set range, according to "tendency masks" or any other approach that can generate a very large number of control values. For example, we can set the grain frequency to 220 Hz and have each successive grain change in a random manner. The amount of "randomness" can be given set boundaries. If the variation range is +/- 10 Hz (20 Hz), the frequency will change, randomly, between 210 and 230 Hz. Other grain parameters could be randomized as well, including duration (we can specify an average duration and a random variation range) and inter-grain delay. As an alternative to inter-grain delay, we could define a *density* parameter. For example, if we specify a fixed grain duration of 50 milliseconds, and a density of 15 grains per second, that automatically determines an inter-grain delay of 16.7 milliseconds (fig.15-3, top). A density of 20 grains per second would give a null (0) delay (fig.15-3, center), while a density of 30 would give a negative delay, resulting in overlapping grains (fig.15-3, bottom).

To start, let's create a granular synthesis orchestra using sine wave grains. The grain can be generated using a classic table look-up process, and can be given a symmetrical envelope (rise time = decay time). In this orchestra we use opcodes such as *timout*, *reinit* and *rireturn*, which are discussed in section 17.3.

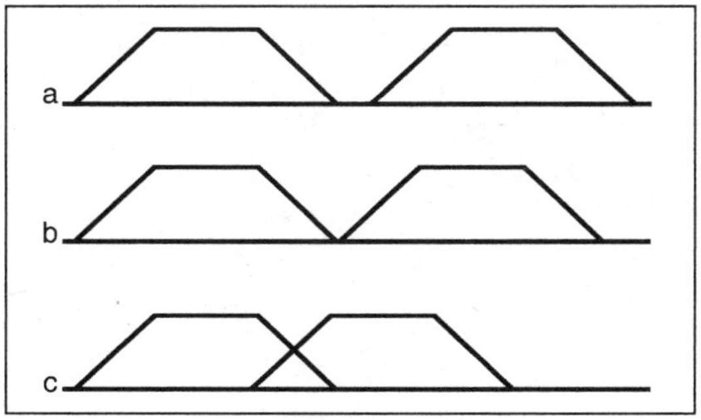

Fig. 15-3

```
;grain1.orc
        sr      =   22050
        kr      =   22050
        ksmps   =   1
        nchnls  =   1

instr   1

iskip1  init        0
iskip2  init        0
iamp            =   p4
ifrq            =   p5
ifrqrnd         =   p5/20
idur            =   p6                      ; grain duration: each grain is followed by
                                            ; a pause, itself lasting idur seconds
iatkdec         =   p7                      ; rise time and decay time (symmetrical envelopes)

label:

kenv1   linseg      0, iatkdec, iamp, idur-iatkdec*2, iamp, iatkdec, 0, idur, 0
                                            ; the grain envelope is followed by a pause, of the same
                                            ; duration as the grain duration

kfrqrnd rand        ifrqrnd, -1             ; random frequency values
a1      oscili      kenv1, ifrq+kfrqrnd, 1  ; grain signal

        timout      0, idur*2, continue     ; these opcodes "re-initialize"
                                            ; the grain envelope every
                                            ; idur*2 seconds.
        reinit       label                  ; that way, many grains are continue:
                                            ; generated for each note in the
        rireturn                            ; score (see section 17.3)

kenvt   linseg      0, p3*.25, 1, p3*.5, 1, p3*.25, 0  ;overall amplitude envelope
        out         a1*kenvt
        endin

;grain1.sco
f1 0 4096 10 1
```

```
;ins    act   note_dur    amp    frq    grain_dur    rise/dec time
i1      0     5           7000   1000   .02          .005
i1      .1    5           .      1002   .023         .005
i1      .2    5           .      1001   .018         .005
i1      .3    5           .      999    .015         .005
i1      .4    5           .      998    .011         .005
```

15.2 THE *GRAIN* OPCODE

The opcode *grain* was designed especially for granular synthesis. It makes the synthesis easy to implement, but includes a greater number of arguments than is usually required. It can be given either synthetic or sampled grain tables, but samples are not simple to handle. For granular textures of sampled sound, we are better off using another opcode, *granule* (described in next section).

ar grain xamp, xpitch, xdens, kampoff, kpitchoff, kgdur, igfn, iwfn, imgdur

xamp	grain amplitude (0-32767)
xpitch	grain frequency in Hz
xdens	density (grains per second)
kampoff	offset value, determining the upper limit to the amplitude range: if *xamp* = 10000 and *kampoff* = 3000, the grain amplitude varies between 10000 and 13000.
kpitchoff	offset value, determining the upper limit to the frequency range: if *xpitch* = 500 Hz and *kpitchoff* = 200, the grain frequency varies between 500 and 700 Hz.
kgdur	grain duration in seconds
igfn	waveform function number (the table size must be equal to a power-of-two, or a power-of-two-plus-1; a size of 0 is not permitted)
iwfn	envelope function number
imgdur	maximum grain duration, in seconds

```
;grain2.orc
        sr     =  44100
        kr     =  4410
        ksmps  =  10
        nchnls =  2

        instr     1
```

```
iamp      =  p4    ;amp
ipitch    =  p5    ;freq
idens     =  p6    ;density
iampoff   =  p7    ;p7=amp variation range
ifrqoff   =  p8    ;p8=freq variation range
igdur     =  p9    ;grain duration
;stereo   =  p10   ;(1=left, 0=right, .5=center)
igfn      =  1     ;igfn = grain envelope function
iwfn      =  2     ;iwfn = grain waveform function
imgdur    =  .5    ;imgdur = maximum grain duration
a1        grain  iamp, ipitch, idens, iampoff, ifrqoff, igdur, igfn, iwfn, imgdur
          outs   a1*p10, a1*(1-p10)
          endin
```

Here's a score for the new granular synthesis orchestra:

```
;grain2.sco
f1 0 4096 10 1
f2 0 4096 19 1 .5 270 .5
;ins  act  dur  amp    hz   dens  ampoff  frqoff  dur  st
i1    0    5    10000  500  30    10000   200     .05  .5
```

When considering models of human perception, it is convenient to approach the synthesis in terms of average frequency and duration values, and make the orchestra translate these values into the appropriate upper and lower range limits. This is the task of the following exercise.

EXERCISE 1*: create a new orchestra whose* kampoff *and* kpitchoff *determine the ranges of random variation around, respectively, an average amplitude value* iamp *(p4) and an average frequency value* ipitch *(p5) (the distance between the average value and the upper limit is equal to the distance between the average and the lower limit).*

Here's the solution:

```
sr      =  44100
kr      =  4410
ksmps   =  10
nchnls  =  2

instr   1
```

```
iamp        =   p4              ; average amplitude
ifreq       =   cpspch(p5)      ; average frequency (converted from pitch)
idens       =   p6              ; grain density
iampoff     =   p7              ; amplitude variation range
ifreqoff    =   cpspch(p8)      ; freq variation range(converted from pitch)
igdur       =   p9              ; grain duration
;stereo     =   p10             ; (1=left, 0=right, .5=center)

kamprnd     rand    iampoff/2   ; random amplitude variation +/- kampoff/2
kfrqrnd     rand    ifreqoff/2  ; random freq variation +/- kampoff/2
igfn        =   1               ; igfn = grain envelope function
iwfn        =   2               ; iwfn = grain waveform function
imgdur      =   .5              ; imgdur = maximum grain duration

a1          grain   iamp, ipitch, idens, kamprnd, kfrqrnd, igdur, igfn, iwfn, imgdur
            outs    a1*p10, a1*(1-p10)
            endin
```

***EXERCISE 2:** create a new orchestra that includes a dynamic control for kpitchoff. Use linseg as the control generator, going from 0 to some maximum value, and then back to 0.*

Solution:

```
        sr     =  44100
        kr     =  4410
        ksmps  =  10
        nchnls =  2

        instr     1
iamp           =  p4          ;amp
ifreq          =  cpspch(p5)  ;freq, in octave-point-pitch class (pitch)
idens          =  p6          ;density
iampoff        =  p7          ;amp variation range
ifreqoff       =  cpspch(p8)  ;max freq variation range (pitch)
igdur          =  p9          ;grain duration
;stereo        =  p10         ;(1=left, 0=right, .5=center)
igfn           =  1           ;igfn = grain envelope function
iwfn           =  2           ;iwfn = grain waveform function
imgdur         =  .5          ;imgdur = maximum grain duration
```

```
kfrq    linseg  0, p3/2, ifreqoff, p3/2, 0
a1      grain   iamp, ipitch, idens, iampoff, kfrq, igdur, igfn, iwfn, imgdur
        outs    a1*p10, a1*(1-p10)
        endin
```

15.3 THE *GRANULE* OPCODE

The *granule* opcode introduces a more sophisticated form of granular synthesis - at the cost of a really large number of arguments (so large that it may be difficult to manage them). In particular, *granule* provides a simple way to "granulate" sampled sounds. The syntax is:

ar granule xamp, ivoice, iratio, imode, ithd, ifn, ipshift, igskip, igskip_os, ilength, kgap, igap_os, kgsize, igsize_os, iatt, idec [,iseed] [,ipitch1] [,ipitch2] [,ipitch3] [,ipitch4] [,ifnenv]

xamp amplitude
ivoice number of voices (overlapping grains)
iratio ratio of the speed of the *gskip* pointer relative to output audio sample rate. Used to modify duration causing no frequency change. E.g. 0.5 will be half speed.
imode the grain pointer moves forward (same direction of the *gskip* pointer) when *imode*=+1; it moves randomly back and forward when *imode*=0, and moves backward (opposite direction to the *gskip* pointer) when *imode*= -1.
ithd amplitude threshold: only the portions of the signal having a greater amplitude level than *ithd* will be used, while others will be skipped.
ifn function table number of sound source
ipshift pitch shift control. If *ipshift* is 0, pitch will be set randomly up and down an octave. If *ipshift* is 1, 2, 3 or 4, up to four different pitches are added to the determined number of voices, in which case the optional parameters *ipitch1*, *ipitch2*, *ipitch3* and *ipitch4* should be used to quantify the particular shift values.
igskip initial skip from the beginning of the function table in seconds (see section 7.1).
igskip_os range of random variation of the *gskip* pointer, in seconds. 0 gives no variation
ilength length of the table to be used starting from *igskip*, in seconds.
kgap gap between grains in seconds (inter-grain delay)

igap_os range of random variation of inter-grain delay. Expressed as fractions of *kgap*. 0 gives no variation
kgsize grain duration in seconds
igsize_os range of random variation of grain duration, in fractions of *kgsize*
iatt rise time, expressed in fractions of *kgsize*
idec decay time, expressed in fractions of *kgsize*
[*iseed*] (optional) seed for the random number generator. The default is 0.5.
[*ipitch1*], [*ipitch2*], [*ipitch3*], [*ipitch4*] (optional) pitch shift parameters: up to 4 additional voices can be added (when *ipshift* = 1, 2, 3 or 4) and, that being the case, each additional voice is shifted by the corresponding shift parameter (*ipitch1*, *ipitch2*, *ipitch3*, *ipitch4*). Pitch shift parameters are expressed as ratios relative to the original pitch: 1 means no shift, 1.5 means a fifth above, etc.
[ifnenv] optional, function table number for the envelope, in case *envlpx* is used.

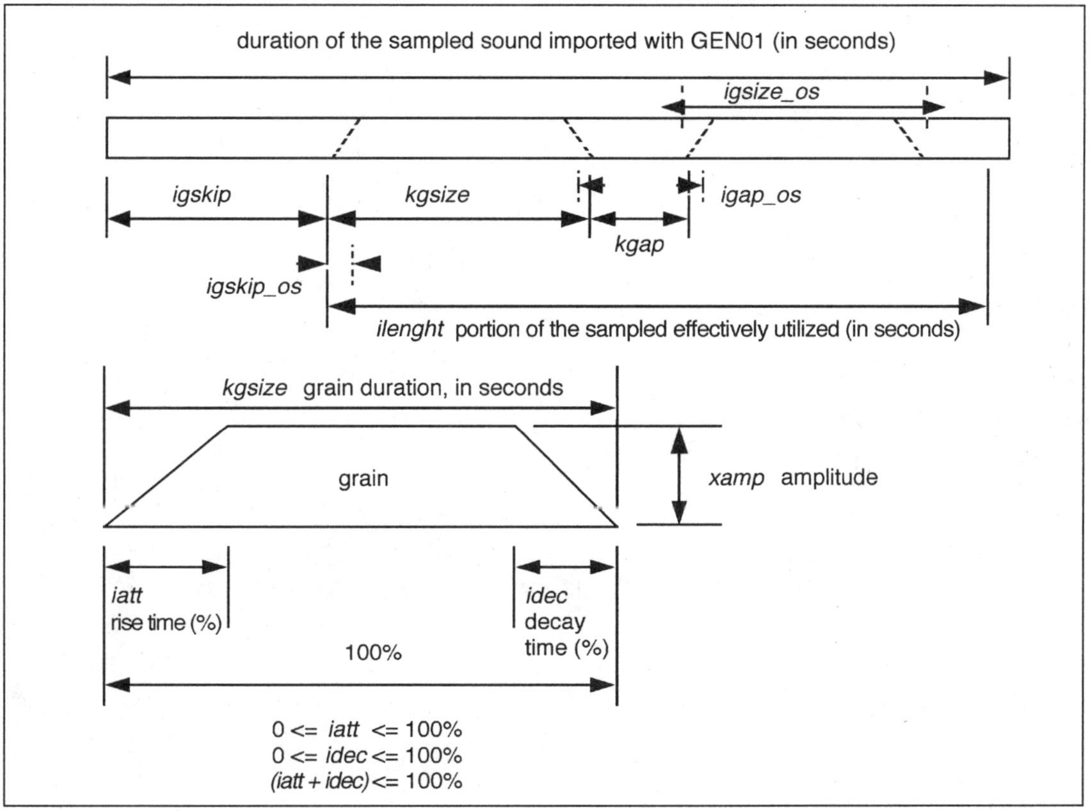

Fig. 15-4

Here's an example:

```
;granule.orc
        sr     =  44100
        kr     =  4410
        ksmps  =  10
        nchnls =  1

        instr     1

;p4 xamp
;p5 ivoice
;p6 iratio
;p7 imode
;p8 ithd
;p9 ifn
;p10 ipshift
;p11 igskip
;p12 igskip_os
;p13 ilength
;p14 kgap
;p15 igap_os
;p16 kgsize
;p17 igsize_os
;p18 iatt
;p19 idec
;p20 [iseed]
;p21, 22, 23, 24 [ipitch1], [ipitch2], [ipitch3], [ipitch4]
;p25 [ifnenv]

k1 linseg  0, 0.5, 1, (p3-p2-1), 1, 0.5, 0
a1 granule p4*k1, p5, p6, p7, p8, p9, p10, p11, p12, p13, p14, p15, p16, p17, p18, p19,p20, p21, p22, p23, p24
        out       a1
        endin

;granule.sco

f 1 0 131072 1 "voice.wav" 0 0 0
;1  2  3  4  5  6  7  8  9  10  11  12  13  14  15  16  17  18  19  20  21  22  23  24  25
```

```
i1  0 6 2000 12 .33 0 0 1 4  0 .005 2 0.01 50 0.05 50 30   30 .39 1 1.42 1.29 1.32 2
```

Practice trying different inter-grain delays (*kgap*) and speed ratios (*iratio*). Try speed ratios greater or smaller than 1.

15.4 FORMANT WAVE SYNTHESIS (*FOF*)

The synthesis process based on *FOF* (*forme d'onde formantique*) generators, allows us to create sounds featuring spectral formant characteristics. It can be seen either as a subtractive method (e.g. a pulse-train passed through a bandpass filter) or an additive method (banks of damped sinusoidal oscillations). We consider the latter first. The sound is generated by a series of damped sine waves, or FOF grains, with variable rise time and a nearly-exponential decay curve. "Since the duration of each FOF grain lasts just a few milliseconds, the envelope of the FOF grain contributes audible sidebands around the sine wave, creating a formant [...] The result of summing several FOF generators is a spectrum with several formant peaks. Each FOF generator is controlled by a number of parameters, including fundamental frequency and amplitude" (Roads, 1996, p.303). Figure 15-5 (adapted from Roads, 1996, p.304) shows the four formant parameters.

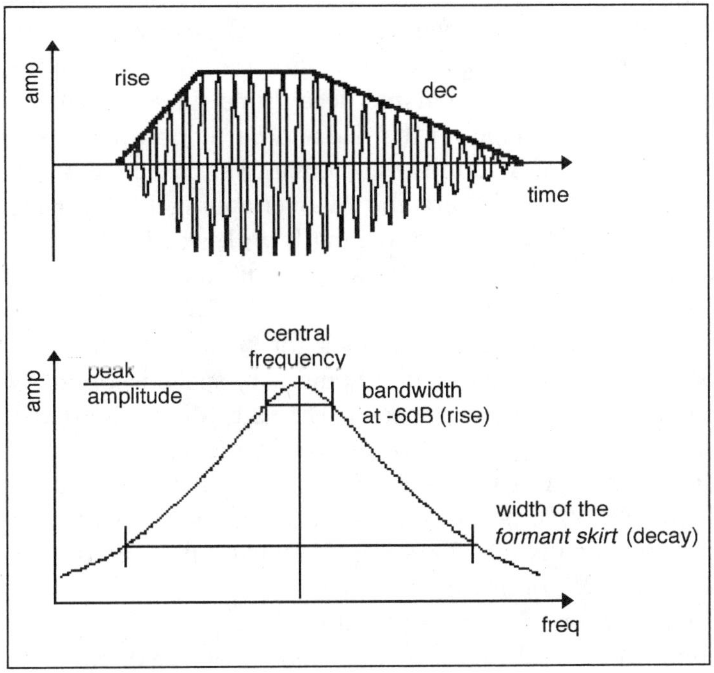

Fig. 15-5

"The center frequency of the formant, the formant bandwidth, defined as the width between the points that are -6 dB from the peak of the formant, peak amplitude of the formant, and the width of the formant *skirt* [i.e.] the lower part of the formant peak, about -40 dB below the peak [...] The skirt parameter is independent of the formant bandwidth, which specifies the breadth at the peak of the mountain" (Roads, 1996, p.303).

The *fof* syntax is as follows:

ar fof xamp, xfund, xform, koct, kband, kris, kdur, kdec, iolaps, ifna, ifnb, itotdur[, iphs][, ifmode]

xamp peak amplitude for each FOF grain bank. When the bandwidth is very large, the output amplitude can exceed *xamp*.
xfund fundamental frequency, in Hz
xform formant frequency, in Hz
koct *octaviation* index, normally set to 0. If greater than 0, causes the fundamental pitch to be transposed down by the prescribed interval (1=1 octave lower; 1.5= 1 octave + a fifth lower; 2= 2 octaves lower, etc.), in which case the odd-numbered grain banks will be attenuated.
kband bandwidth of the formant region at -6 dB, in Hz. It affects the slope of the exponential damping of the FOF grain each bank (see figure 15-5)
kris, kdur, kdec rise time, duration and decay time (in seconds) of the FOF grains. The envelope shape for the rise and decay portions is stored in *ifnb*. *kris* also affects the width of the formant skirt (see figure 15-5), while *kdur* also determines the amount of overlapping FOFs (hence it affects the computation time, and how long it will take for Csound to generate the output soundfile). For simulation of the human voice, try these values: 0.003, 0.02, 0.007.
iolaps pre-allocated memory locations for storing the data of the FOF grain banks. The maximum required memory space is *xfund*kdur*. For a single bank only 50 bytes are needed. The value does not affect the computation time, so you can set *iolaps* to a very large value.
ifna, ifnb table numbers of stored functions. *ifna* must be a sinusoid function table of at least 4096 points. *ifnb* is the shape for the rise and decay curves for the FOF grains (can be a ramp created with GEN07, a sigmoid created with GEN19, or any other shape).
itotdur total duration in seconds (usually = p3)
iphs (optional) initial phase of the fundamental, expressed as fractions of a cycle (0-1). The default is 0 (= 0 degrees).

ifmode (optional) if *ifmode*= 0, the formant frequency *xform* is fixed. Otherwise, it can change during the note. The default is 0.

Let's examine a simple case. The following orchestra and score pair generates a 600 Hz formant, other spectral components are equally spaced 200 Hz apart.

```
;fof1.orc
        sr      =   44100
        kr      =   4410
        ksmps   =   10
        nchnls  =   1
        instr       1
;       xamp, xfund, xform, koct, kband, kris, kdur, kdec, iolaps, ifna, ifnb, itotdur
a1      fof 15000, 200, 650,  0,  40, .003, .02, .007, 5,   1,   2,  p3
        out         a1
        endin
```

```
;fof1.sco
f1 0 4096 10 1
f2 0 1024 19 .5 .5 270 .5
i1 0 3
```

The output sound is very poor indeed. That was only to be expected. There is only 1 formant. For more interesting sounds (and certainly for the simulation of the human voice) several formants are required. Let's try the following:

```
;fof2.orc
        sr      =   44100
        kr      =   4410
        ksmps   =   10
        nchnls  =   1
        instr       1
iamp            =   p4
ifund           =   p5
iform           =   p6
;ar      fof  xamp, xfund, xform, koct, kband, kris, kdur, kdec, iolaps, ifna, ifnb, itotdur
a1       fof  iamp, ifund, iform, 0,  40,  .003, .02, .007,   5,   1,   2,  p3
         out        a1
         endin
```

```
;fof2.sco
f1  0  4096  10  1
f2  0  1024  19  .5  .5  270  .5
;in      act      dur      amp      fund      form
i1       0        3        15000    200       650
i1       +        3        15000    200       1300
i1       +        3        15000    100       400
i1       +        3        15000    100       1200
```

The Csound Manual and the Csound on-line *Help* file include a very well-made FOF tutorial by J.M.Clarke, illustrating the potential of formant wave synthesis.

15.5 SNDWARP

With granular sound processing algorithms, it is possible to modify the frequency of a sound without changing its duration, and vice-versa. In Csound, this process has a special opcode, *sndwarp* (or its stereophonic version, *sndwarpst*). The sound to modify is copied from a soundfile into the computer memory with GEN01. *sndwarp* divides the sound into several separate "windows", or "grains", and then re-combines them together. Here's the syntax:

asig [, acmp] sndwarp xamp, xtimewarp, xresample, ifn1, ibeg, iwsize, irandw, ioverlap, ifn2, itimemode

asig1, asig2 [, acmp1, acmp2] sndwarpst xamp, xtimewarp, xresample, ifn1, ibeg, iwsize, irandw, ioverlap, ifn2, itimemode

asig, asig1, asig2 output signal (stereo for *sndwarpst*)

acmp, acmp1, acmp2 signal complement of *asig* (or *asig1* and *asig2*): useful for adjusting the output amplitude. The output generated by *sndwarp* can have a strikingly different amplitude level, either smaller or greater than the input. Using *balance*, we can adjust the output level to match the input.

xamp amplitude scale factor

xtimewarp the meaning of this argument depends on the *itimemode* argument: When *itimemode* = 0, then *xtimewarp* is the time-scale value for the output duration as relative to the input. e.g., if *xtimewarp* = 2, the output duration will be twice as long as the input; if *xtimewarp* = 0.5, the duration will be halved. When *itimemode* is non-zero, *xtimewarp* is defined as the time

	pointer into the function table containing the input sound (this is like the *ktimpnt* argument to opcodes *lpread* and *pvoc*, see section 8.2 and 8.6). Then, it has to be controlled with another opcode, such as line, for example.
xresample	pitch transposition factor. e.g., *xresample* = 2 shifts the sound an octave higher than the original pitch.
ifn1	function table number. The table contains the sampled sound whose duration or pitch are subject to modifications (normally this table is created with GEN01).
ibeg	the first *ibeg* seconds in the sampled sound are skipped
iwsize	portion of table to actually use
irandw	range for random variations of *iwsize*
ioverlap	number of overlapping windows (density)
ifn2	grain envelope function table. Half a sine wave period works very well (= f1 0 16384 9 .5 1 0), but can be any other envelope shape
itimemode	(see *xtimewarp*, above here)

To begin, set *iwsize=sr/10*, *ioverlap=15* and *irandw=iwsize**.2*. A smaller overlap value would speed up the computation, but it would also cause audible amplitude fluctuations. It is always difficult to predict whether *sndwarp* will or will not generate a satisfying result. That depends mostly on the characteristics of the input sound.

Example 1. Let's slow down the sound stored in *ifn1*. The time-scale shift will be controlled dynamically, moving from no modification at the beginning to 10-times-slower-then-real at the end. Pitch is gradually shifted an octave higher. Notice that *itimemode* is 0.

```
;sndwrp1.orc
            sr     =  44100
            kr     =  4410
            ksmps  =  10
            nchnls =  1
            instr     1
iwindfun           =  1   ; envelope window
isampfun           =  2   ; table with sampled sound
ibeg               =  0
iwindsize          =  2000
iwindrand          =  400
ioverlap           =  10
itimemode          =  0
```

```
awarp       line        1, p3, .1
aresamp     line        1, p3, 2
kenv        line        1, p3, .1

asig sndwarp kenv, awarp, aresamp, isampfun, ibeg, iwindsize, iwindrand, ioverlap, \
iwindfun, itimemode
            out         asig*10000
            endin
;sndwrp1.sco
f1    0     16384  9        .5      1      0      ;half sine wave period
f2    0     1310721         "voice.wav"    0      0      0
i1    0     2
```

> *TIPS & TRICKS: in the orchestra above, the line with the* sndwarp *opcode includes a "back-slash" (\) to instruct the compiler that the code continues on next line. That is allowed in most Csound releases.*

Example 2. Now use *itimemode*=1, so that *xtimewarp* has the role of a time index pointer to the function table. The driving signal for *xtimewarp* is called atime, and gradually moves from 0 to 10 seconds. If p3 = 20, then the output sound will be twice as long as the original. Here *atime* is generated with *line*, but any other control signal generator can drive the time index.

```
;sndwrp2.orc
            sr     =   44100
            kr     =   4410
            ksmps  =   10
            nchnls =   2
            instr      1
iwindfun           =   1   ; envelope window
isampfun           =   2   ; function table with sampled sound
ibeg               =   0
iwindsize          =   2000
iwindrand          =   400
ioverlap           =   10
aresamp     line       1, p3, 2
kenv        line       1, p3, .1
itimemode          =   1
atime       line       0, p3, 10
```

```
asig1,  asig2   sndwarpst  kenv, atime, aresamp, isampfun, ibeg, iwindsize,\ iwindrand, ioverlap, iwindfun, itimemode
                outs     asig1*10000, asig2*10000
                endin
;sndwrp2.sco
f1      0       16384  9        .5      1       0
f2      0       262144 1        ´voice.wavª     0       0       0
i1      0       2
```

Example 3. Like example 2, but with amplitude balance.

```
;sndwrp3.orc
                sr      =  44100
                kr      =  4410
                ksmps   =  10
                nchnls  =  2
                instr      1
iwindfun                =  1    ; envelope window
isampfun                =  2    ; table with sampled sound
ibeg                    =  0
iwindsize               =  2000
iwindrand               =  400
ioverlap                =  10
aresamp     line           1, p3, 2
kenv        line           1, p3, .1
itimemode               =  1
atime       line           0, p3, 10
asig1, asig2, acmp1,acmp2   sndwarpst1, atime, aresamp, sampfun, \
            ibeg, iwindsize, iwindrand, ioverlap, iwindfun, itimemode
abal1   balance            asig1, acmp1
abal2   balance            asig2, acmp2
                outs       abal1*10000, abal2*10000
                endin

;sndwrp3.sco
f1      0       16384  9        .5      1       0
f2      0       262144 1        ´voice.wavª     0       0       0
i1      0       2
```

LIST OF OPCODES INTRODUCED IN THIS CHAPTER

ar grain amp, freq, density, amp_offset, freq_offset, waveform_table_number, envelope_table_number, max_grain_dur

ar granule amp, number_of_voices, speed_ratio, speed_mode, amp_thrshld, function_table_no, pitch_transpose , initial_skip, random_skip, duration, inter-grain_delay, random_delay, grain_dur, random_grain_dur, rise_time, decay_time [,seed] [, pitch_shift1] [,pitch_shift2] [,pitch_shift3] [,pitch_shift4] [, envelope_func_table]

ar fof amp, fundamental, formant_freq, octave_index, formant_bandwidth, fof_rise_time, fof_dur, fof_decay_time, overlap_factor, fof_function_no, envelope_table_no, duration[, initial_phase] [, frequency_mode]

asig[, acmp] sndwarp amp, dur_scale [or time_index], freq_scale, sampled_sound_table_no, start_point, size, random_size_range, overlap_windows, envelope_window, itime_mode (=switch between dur_scale and time_index)

16

PHYSICAL MODELING SYNTHESIS

16.1 INTRODUCTION

Physical modeling is a powerful tool for the production (or reproduction) of sounds that closely resemble real musical instruments. Even when it is used for the synthesis of non-imitative sounds, it retains a realistic quality. It differs from other digital synthesis techniques in that physical modeling attempts to simulate mechanical sound-generating systems, not the sounds themselves. The approach embodies the mathematical reconstruction of the physical properties of the modeled system.

There are several modeling styles:

1. Mass/spring paradigm (Hiller and Ruiz, 1971). This requires a precise description of the physical characteristics of vibrating objects: length, width, thickness, mass, elasticity, etc. Furthermore, it requires that we stipulate what physicists call *boundary conditions* which are the limits to which a vibrating object is constrained. Finally, it requires that we have a mathematical description of the excitation mechanism (a force impressed on the elastic object), so that we can study its effect on the system. This is usually represented by *difference equations*, thereby obtaining a *wave equation* that describes the resulting sound signal.

2. Modal synthesis (Calvet, Laurens and Adrien, 1990). This approach is based on the premise that a vibrating object can be represented as a collection of simpler elements (also called *substructures*), including the bridge and the bow on the violin, or the drum heads and the drum body on percussion instruments. Each substructure is characterized by its own *modes of vibration*, which are captured as a collection of *modal data*. Usually, modal data include the frequencies and the damping coefficients for the modes of vibration of the substructure under consideration. Modal data also include a set of coordinates representing the vibrating mode's shape. The peculiar advantage of this approach is the modularity of the substructures. For example, we could experiment with a drum head striking a cello string, and other such "unnatural" situations. The method was incorporated into synthesis programs like MOSAIC and MODALYSE.

3. MSW synthesis (McIntyre, Schumacher, and Woodhouse, 1983). This approach is based on a precise study of the birth and propagation of waves, and on an exact characterization of the physical mechanisms behind the sound phemomenon. The physical model is usually partitioned into two constituent elements: a *non-linear excitation* mechanism (an oscillator with a waveshaper block simulating the behavior typical of, perhaps, a reed, whose output sound features peculiar distortions) and a linear resonator (a filter of variable complexity).

4. Waveguide model (Smith, Cook, et al. 1982-1993). This is the only physical modeling approach that has been used in commercial applications. It is the basis of synthesizers manufactured by Yamaha, Korg, and Roland. The waveguide theory is quite complicated, and is far beyond the scope of this short introductory chapter. For an in-depth explanation, please refer to the scientific literature in the references.

16.2 THE KARPLUS-STRONG ALGORITHM

One of the earliest physical modeling algorithms was proposed by Alex Karplus and Kevin Strong for the simulation of plucked strings. Strictly speaking, it is not a true physical model, but it can be conveniently explained as if it were.

The basic idea is that we start with some noise burst and subject it to recursive filtering until the result approaches a sine wave. Karplus and Strong were seeking a method that could be implemented using integrated circuits (i.e. on microcomputers that were available at the time. They invented this method in the early 1980's). Therefore, they had to reduce the number of operations as much as possible. They started with a wavetable filled with random values. For each table look-up, the output sample was calculated as the average of the current and the previous sample.

In fig.16-1, we see a noise generator (active only at init-time) feeding a wavetable with random values. The wavetable is implemented with a simple delay line. After initialization, the noise generator is disconnected from the wavetable, and the signal starts circulating in the filter circuit. The current sample is sent to the output, but it also gets delayed (1 sample delay) and sign-inverted (sample value multiplied by -1). Then, the average of the delayed and the next sample is taken and written in the wavetable. The process is repeated over and over. Little by little the output sound decays and the higher components get more and more attenuated, and eventually disappear. The overall effect is a realistic plucked string sound, and the computation time is quite short. The fundamental frequency depends on the table length and the sampling rate (see section 2-C-1).

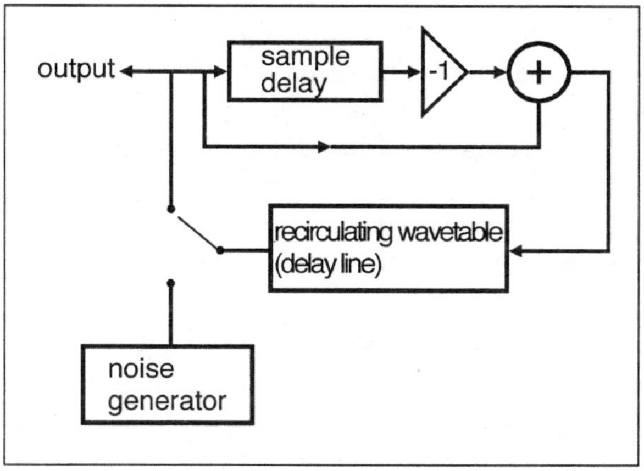

Fig. 16-1

Csound allows us to use a unique opcode, *pluck*, to implement the original Karplus-Strong algorithm. Plus, it has some useful variations. The syntax is:

ar pluck kamp, kcps, icps, ifn, imeth [, iparm1, iparm2]

kamp amplitude
kcps fundamental frequency in Hz
icps used to set up an internal buffer with 1 cycle of audio samples. Normally, it is set to the same value as kcps. If higher or lower than *kcps*, it creates particular timbral effects.
ifn function table number, used to initialize the cyclic decay buffer. When = 0, a random sequence will be used instead (as in the original Karplus-Strong)
imeth method of decay. There are six, some of which use optional arguments.

imeth = 1: simple averaging (original Karplus-Strong). No optional argument required.
imeth = 2: stretched averaging. The decay time is stretched by a factor of *iparm1* (*iparm1* must be 1 or greater)

imeth = 3: drum-like. The range from pitched to noise-like is influenced by *iparm1* ("roughness factor", 0 to 1). Zero gives the normal plucked string effect. 1 inverts the polarity of averaged values, generating a sound 1 octave lower than required, comprising only odd harmonics. 0.5 gives a good snare drum effect.
imeth = 4: stretched drum. Uses two optional arguments: *iparm1* as the roughness factor (0 to 1), and *iparm2* as the stretch factor (1 or greater)
imeth = 5: weighted averaging. Similar to method 1, but this time *iparm1* represents the coefficient for the current sample, and *iparm2* the coefficient for the previous sample. The sum *iparm1+iparm2* must be equal to, or smaller than 1.
imeth = 6: 1st order recursive filter. No optional argument required.

As the relationship between parameters and the output sound is scarcely intuitive, we recommend that you experiment with this method. Here's an example to start you off:

```
;pluck.orc
        sr     =  44100
        kr     =  4410
        ksmps  =  10
        nchnls =  1
        instr     1
ifrq           =  cpspch(p5)
iamp           =  ampdb(p4)
a1      pluck     iamp, ifrq, ifrq, 0, 1 ; true Karplus-Strong
        out       a1
        endin
```

```
;pluck.sco
i1    0    1    80    8
i1    +    .    .     8.04
i1    +    .    .     8.07
i1    +    2    .     9
```

Notice that the sound is abruptly switched off. To avoid this, you can use an envelope generator for smoother fade out:

```
kenv   linseg  1, p3*.75, 1, p3*.25, 0
```

You should multiply the audio signal by that envelope signal.

16.3 PLUCKED STRINGS

Basically, a plucked string (or an air flow) can be described with a very simple algorithmic model. Examine figure 16-2: The exciter signal, aexc, can be generated with *linseg* (control variables can be used as if they were audio, not just control signals). The exciter signal will consist of a short pulse followed by a silent pause, just as a force being briefly applied to a string (a pluck). This signal is then sent to a delay line modeling the propagation of the initial pluck across the string. The delay time determines the period for the propagation wave to reach the two end points of the string and come back to the pluck point, simulating the formation of a stationary wave. The dissipation of energy, caused by imperfections in the string materials, can be simulated with a low-pass filter, *tone*.

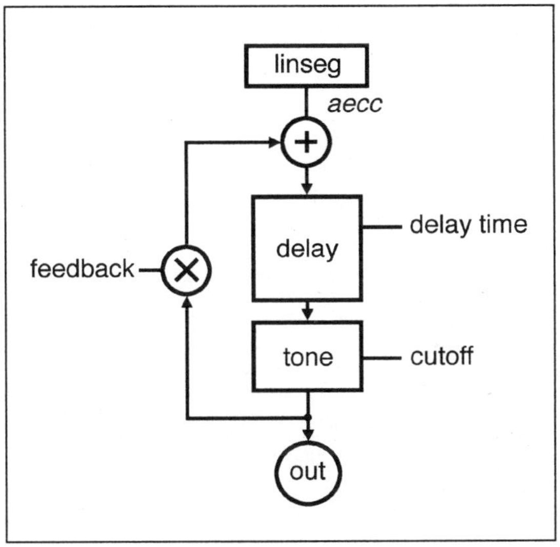

Fig. 16-2

The wave "excited" by the pluck is then sent again into the delay line, and scaled by some feedback factor. If the feedback factor is 1, no energy dissipation occurs. If it is less than 1, then dissipation occurs and the signal decays (similar to a piano damper pedal).

The following orchestra code reproduces such a process for the simulation of plucked strings (it may be modified for air flows set to vibrate by some appropriate exciter function).

```
;phmod1.orc
        sr    =   44100
        kr    =   44100
```

```
            ksmps  =  1
            nchnls =  1

            instr     1

            ifrq   =  cpspch(p5)
            iamp   =  ampdb(p4)
afilt       init      0             ;initializes the afilt variable
            ifeed  =  p6
            iexcdur = p7

aexc    linseg  1,iexcdur,0,p3-iexcdur,0
; signal decays from 1 to 0 in iexcdur seconds  then remains zero for the remainder time

 asum   = aexc+afilt*ifeed
; sum of aexc and afilt (filter output),
; feedback control is applied

; feedback delay line
adel        delay     asum,1/ifrq      ; delay time is the  inverse  of the required  fundamental freq: the higher is the
                                       ; frequency, and the shorter is the time it takes for the wave to travel across the
                                       ; string (delay time = period of fundamental frequency)
afilt       tone      adel, p7         ; afilt is the delayed signal, passed through a low-pass (the low-pass
                                       ; simulates energy dissipation)
aout        atone     afilt*iamp, 30   ; high-pass to attenuate DC offset
            out       aout
            endin
```

Notice that the filter output, *afilt*, is multiplied by the required amplitude value, *iamp*.

In general, the specification of rise time can be omitted, as the low-pass filter produces a smooth attack as a side-effect anyway (see section 3.A.1).

The following score explores the influence of the low-pass cutoff frequency on the output sound. As the cutoff frequency gets higher, the sound turns from damped to resonating, and the overall amplitude level increases and the duration gets longer (lesser and lesser energy is dissipated through the feedback loop).

```
;phmod1.sco
;ins   act   dur   dB   pitch   feed   cutoff fr.   iexcdur
i1     0     3     80   7       1      500          .01
```

```
i1   +   3   80   7   1   1000   .
i1   +   3   80   7   1   2000   .
i1   +   3   80   7   1   4000   .
i1   +   3   80   7   1   8000   .
```

A negative feedback factor causes the same effect as a 180 degree phase shift. Also, it shifts the pitch 1 octave lower than the required fundamental. To explain this effect, notice that the sign of the feedback signal is now inverted and causes the loop cycle to be twice as long (see figure on this page). The output spectrum changes accordingly, similar to a clarinet (a tube with one open end). The odd harmonics (1, 3, 5, 7, 9, etc.) are stronger, and have these amplitude levels:

harmonic	amplitude
1	-9.5 dB
3	-9.7 dB
5	0.0 dB
7	-8.9 dB
9	-21.9 dB
11	-34.2 dB
13	-51.0 dB
15	-41.0 dB
17	-31.0 dB

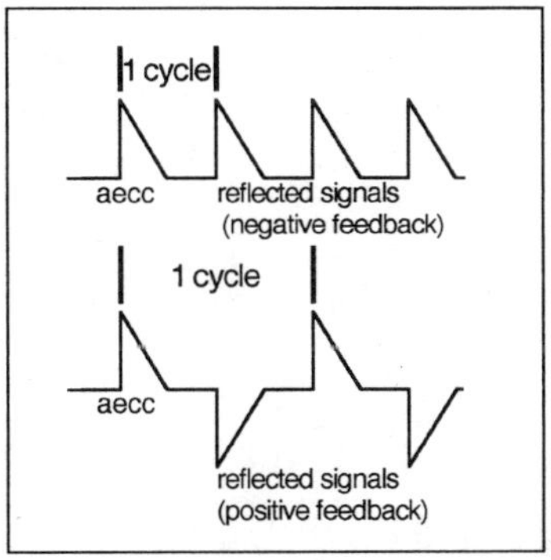

Another element influencing the character of the output sound is the duration of the exciter signal. The next score example explores the different results obtained with different exciter durations, ranging from 0.01 to 0.4 seconds (the exciter signal has a triangular wave shape). The longer the excitation, the more clearly audible the noise in the sound, just as in passing from plucked effects (short excitation) to “breathing” sounds (longer excitation).

```
;phmod1b.sco
;ins   act   dur   dB    pitch   feed   fcutoff   iexcdur
i1     0     3     80    7       -1     4000      .01
i1     +     3     80    7       -1     4000      .05
i1     +     3     80    7       -1     4000      .1
i1     +     3     80    7       -1     4000      .2
i1     +     3     80    7       -1     4000      .4
```

A relevant modification can be introduced that creates for even more realistic plucked string sounds. It consists of modulating the delay line length during the attack transient (e.g. for a duration of 0.05" from the onset of the note). The excitation of a real string usually causes the string tension to increase during the attack transients, causing a temporary change in the elasticity of the vibrating system. This is equivalent to the string being briefly shortened (95% of the normal length). To experiment with this effect, we modify the orchestra as follows (try the modified orchestra with the previous score):

```
;phmod2.orc
        sr      =   44100
        kr      =   44100  ; notice sr = kr !
        ksmps   =   1
        nchnls  =   1
        instr       1
        ifrq    =   cpspch(p5)
        iamp    =   ampdb(p4)
        ifeed   =   p6
        icutoff =   p7
        iexcdur =   p8
afilt   init        0
kenvx   linseg      1, p3-.1, 1, .1, 0
        idel    =   1/ifrq

kdel    linseg      idel*.95, .05, idel, p3-.05, idel
; kdel is the modulated delay time, going from 95% to 100% of the nominal delay time (1/ifreq), in .05 seconds

aexc    linseg      iamp, iexcdur, 0, p3-iexcdur, 0
asum            =   aexc+afilt*ifeed
a0      delayr      1             ; replace the delay opcode with delayr/delayw/deltapi
        delayw      asum
adel    deltapi     kdel          ; the adel signal is now picked-up with deltapi, variable delay time is kdel
```

```
afilt   tone    adel, icutoff
aout    atone   afilt*kenvx, 30  ; high-pass to attenuate the DC effect
        out     aout
        endin
```

It would be good idea to have the delay time modulation last for a duration proportional to pitch. In that way, when lower pitches are played, it will take a longer time for the string to reach the full length, and when higher pitches are played, it will take a shorter time. To do this, you need to change the orchestra line where *kdel* is generated.

16.4 STRUCK PLATES

Let's turn now to an algorithm featuring two delay lines instead of one. The second delay line is added in order to approach a bi-dimensional wave propagation model, with two vibrating modes following directions which are orthogonal one to the other (string simulation implies uni-dimensional propagation). As illustrated in figure 16-3, an excitation source is sent to two delay lines of different lengths (*delay1* and *delay2*).

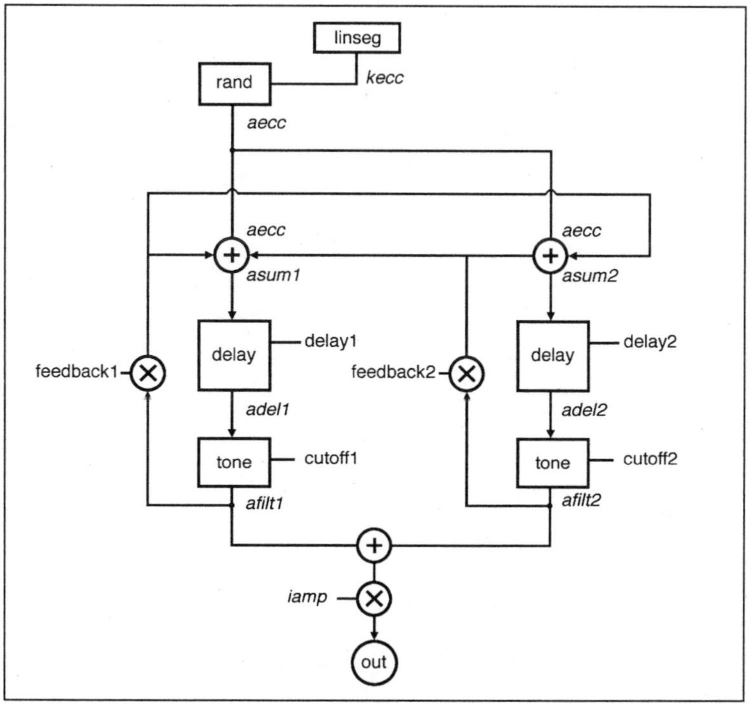

Fig. 16-3

The signals are then low-pass filtered (with *tone*), added together, and summed with the exciter signal. Finally, they are fed back into the delay loop. That process causes a complex chain of delay interactions, which results in a richer sound. For interesting percussion-like results, the two delay lines should have different lengths in non-integer ratio (otherwise, the resonances of the one would overlap with those of the other). Also, the sum of the two feedback factors should not be greater than 1, otherwise the algorithm would generate greater and greater values, and would eventually "crash". To avoid this problem, it is sufficient to negate (multiply by -1) one of the two feedback factors.

The following orchestra sounds like of metal plates being struck.

```
;phmod3.orc
        sr     =  44100
        kr     =  44100  ; NOTICE kr=sr
        ksmps  =  1
        nchnls =  1
        instr     3
        ifrq   =  cpspch(p5)
        idel1  =  1/ifrq
        idel2  =  1/ifrq*p7
        iamp   =  ampdb(p4)
afilt1  init      0
afilt2  init      0
        ifeed  =  p6
kexc    linseg    1, .01, 0, p3-.01, 0
aexc    rand      kexc
        asum   =  aexc+afilt1*ifeed+afilt2*ifeed
adel1   delay     asum, idel1
afilt1  tone      adel1, p8
adel2   delay     asum, idel2
afilt2  tone      adel2, p9
        aout   =  (afilt1+afilt2)*iamp
aout    atone     aout, 30
        out       aout
        endin
```

Observe that we calculate the second delay line period, *idel2*, as a function of the first, *idel1*. The ratio between the two is entered in *p7*. The following score illustrates the influence of different ratios.

```
;phmod3.sco
;instrument 3: STRUCK PLATE
;ins   act   dur   dB    pitch  feed   ratio   fc1    fc2
i3     0     3     86    7      .5     1.02    18000  18000
i3     +     .     .     7      .      1.07    .      .
i3     +     .     .     7      .      1.11    .      .
i3     +     .     .     7      .      1.17    .      .
i3     +     .     .     7      .      1.27    .      .
i3     +     .     .     7      .      1.47    .      .
i3     +     .     .     7      .      1.77    .      .
i3     +     .     .     7      .      1.87    .      .
i3     +     .     .     7      .      2.17    .      .
```

You can also try a ratio of 2.77, setting the low-pass cutoff frequency to 18000 Hz (for slowly decaying sounds). If you play higher notes (say, from 7.00 to 10.00 pch), that ratio will give you a rather muted sound, still reminiscent of metallic objects being struck.

By adjusting the cutoff frequency, you can achieve a vast palette of percussion-like sounds, ranging from membrane to wooden instruments (250 to 2000 Hz), and also extending to more "metallic" sounds.

For more sustained sounds, try feedback factors greater than 0.5. However, be very careful with feedback values. The following example has a value of 0.63, that you might consider to be a safe value, but actually, it causes the instrument to "explode".

```
;phmod3a.sco
;ins   act   dur   dB    pitch  feed   ratio   fc1    fc2
i3     0     3     90    7      .63    1.77    250    250
```

16.5 TUBE WITH SINGLE REED

We discuss now another physical modeling algorithm. This time, however, the two delay lines create a uni-dimensional wave propagation model. One line generates a wave traveling in one direction, the other generates a wave traveling in the opposite direction. One wave propagates as from a reed toward the open end of a tube (bell), while the other propagates in the opposite direction. This model was initially proposed by J.O.Smith (see Bibliography).

Figure 16-4 (top) shows the flow-chart for this model. The exciter is modeled with an air flow pressure function applied to a reed (*amouthp*), plus a force applied by the lips against the embouchure (embouchure offset, *kembofs*), and the lip position.

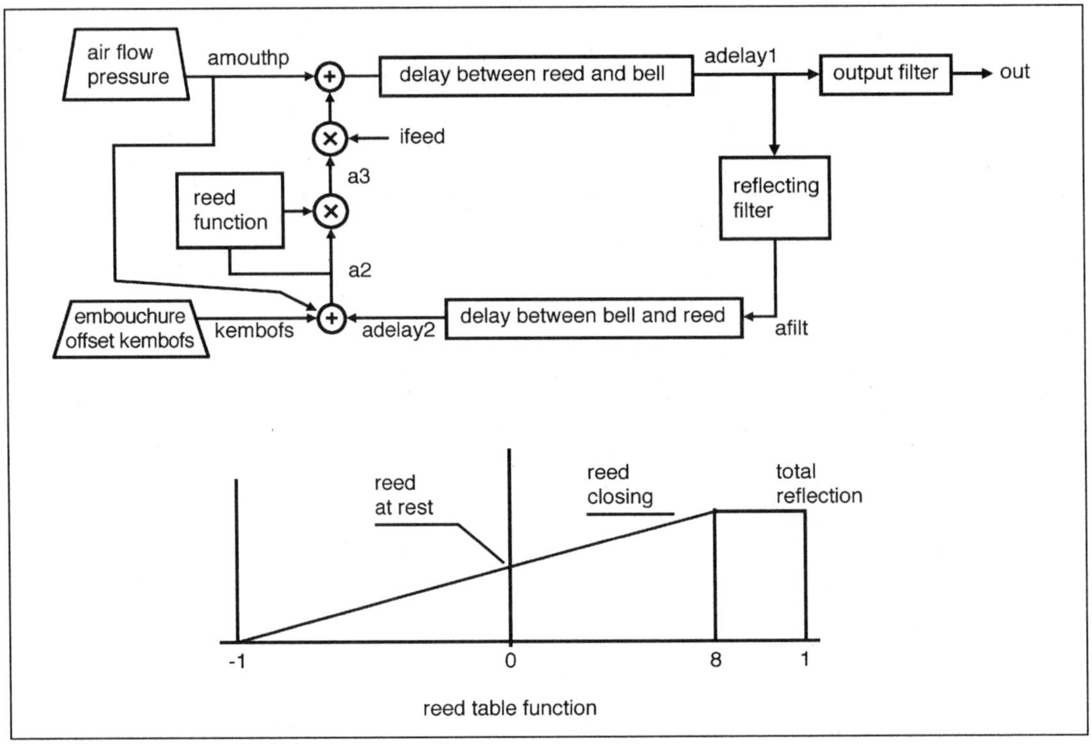

Fig. 16-4

The *amouthp* signal enters the first delay line, representing the time needed for the wave to travel from the reed to the bell. The output of that delay line, *adel1*, is low-pass filtered, to simulate the energy loss due to the bell, and then enters the second delay line, representing the time needed for the wave to travel from the bell to the reed. Obviously, the latter delay line is as long as the former. The signal from the second delay line, *adel2*, is summed with the embouchure offset, *kembofs*, and the absolute value of the result, *a2*, is used as an index to the *reed table function*. The value read off the table is multiplied with the signal *a2*. That causes a *limiter* effect, simulating a completely closed reed (a total wave reflection). The signal thus created, *a3*, is scaled by a feedback factor, *ifeed*, and is re-circulated into the delay line network by summing it with *amouthp*.

The output from the network is *adelay1*. Before being sent to the output, this signal is low-pass filtered to simulate a bell effect.

To simplify things, in the flow-chart of figure 16-4 we did not include the filter necessary to eliminate the DC component which could cause the model to crash (*atone* could be used). Nor did we include envelopes for *amouthp* and *kembofs*. Omitting these elements, however, does not harm a qualitative understanding of the delay network.

The Csound orchestra implementation of the model just described follows:

```
;phmod4.orc
        sr        =  44100
        kr        =  44100       ;NOTICE sr=kr!
        ksmps     =  1
        nchnls    =  1
        instr        1

adelay1 init         0           ; initializes the adelay1 variable
a3      init         0           ; and the a3 variable

ifrq              =  cpspch(p5) ; pitch to Hz conversion
idelay1           =  1/ifrq      ; set the delay of the 1st delay line
iamp              =  ampdb(p4)*10
iatk              =  p6          ; duration of the attack transient
ifeed             =  p7          ; feedback factor
imaxemb           =  p8          ; max value for the embouchure
icutoff           =  p9          ; cutoff freq for low-pass filter

kembofs linseg       0, .1, imaxemb, p3-.1, 0 ; pressure applied against embouchure
amouthp linseg       0, iatk, 1, p3-iatk, 1, .001, 0 ; air flow pressure
avibr   oscil        .05, 5, 1   ; oscillator for vibrato
        amouthp   =  amouthp+avibr
        a1        =  amouthp - a3 * ifeed
adelay1 delay        a1, idelay1
ahp1    atone        adelay1, 50 ; four high-pass filters ...
ahp2    atone        ahp1, 50    ; ...in series ...
ahp3    atone        ahp2, 50    ; ...equivalent to a 4th order ...
ahp     atone        ahp3, 50    ; ...high-pass
afilt   tone         adelay1, icutoff ; signal after reflection energy loss
adelay2 delay        afilt, idelay1
        a2        =  adelay2 + amouthp + kembofs
k2      downsamp     a2          ; abs value converter works only at krate!
                                 ; downsamp opcode discussed in section 17.2
ktab    table        abs(k2), 99, 2
        a3        =  a2 * ktab
kenv    linseg       1, p3-.1, 1, .1, 0
        aout      =  ahp*iamp*kenv
```

```
        out     aout
        endin
```

The appropriate function tables are:

```
f 1     0   4096   10  1
f 99    0   4096   7   0   3072   1   1024   1
```

Table 1 contains a sine wave, as is appropriate for the vibrato oscillator featured in the orchestra. Table 99 is the reed table function (fig.16-4, bottom).

Try this orchestra with the following score:

```
;phmod4.sco
; clarinet.sco:
; incipit of «Peter and the Wolf - The Cat»  by Sergey Prokofiev
f 1     0       4096    10      1
f 99    0       4096    7       0       3072    1       1024    1
t0      80
;                                       atk     feedback  embouchure  cutoff
i 1     0.      0.25    90.     8.07    0.05    1.        0.          6000.
i 1     0.5     0.25    90.     9       .       .         .           .
i 1     1.      1.      90.     9.04    .       .         .           .
i 1     2.      0.25    90.     9       .       .         .           .
i 1     2.5     0.25    90.     8.07    .       .         .           .
i 1     3.      1.      90.     8.06    .       .         .           .
i 1     4.      0.25    90.     8.07    .       .         .           .
i 1     4.5     0.25    90.     9       .       .         .           .
i 1     5.      0.25    90.     9.04    .       .         .           .
i 1     5.5     0.25    90.     9.07    .       .         .           .
i 1     6.      1.25    90.     9.05    .       .         .           .
i 1     7.5     0.25    90.     9.04    .       .         .           .
i 1     8.      0.25    90.     9.07    .       .         .           .
i 1     8.5     0.25    90.     9.05    .       .         .           .
i 1     9.      0.25    90.     9.04    .       .         .           .
i 1     9.5     0.25    90.     9.02    .       .         .           .
i 1     10.     0.25    90.     9.05    .       .         .           .
i 1     10.5    0.25    90.     9.04    .       .         .           .
i 1     11.     0.25    90.     9.02    .       .         .           .
```

```
i 1     11.5   0.25   90.    9      .     .     .     .
i 1     12.    0.25   90.    9.04   .     .     .     .
i 1     12.5   0.25   90.    9.02   .     .     .     .
i 1     13.    1.     90.    8.11   .     .     .     .
i 1     14.    1.     90.    9      .     .     .     .
e
```

By adjusting the embouchure offset value, several spectral modifications can be obtained. Fig.16-5 shows the spectra of offset values from 0 to 0.3 (the vertical axis, amplitude, is divided in steps of 6 dB).

17

CSOUND AS A PROGRAMMING LANGUAGE

17.1 CSOUND IS A PROGRAMMING LANGUAGE

In every respect, Csound is a computer programming language. Although it is heavily oriented towards sound synthesis (it was specially designed for that purpose), nothing really prevents us from using it for any other kind of calculation. Try running the program from the following orchestra and score:

```
;calcul.orc
        sr     =  100
        kr     =  1
        ksmps  =  100
        nchnls =  1

        instr     1
        i1     =  log(10) ; assign the natural logarithm of 10 to the i1 variable
        print     i1      ; display i1 (see section 17.5 on print)
        endin

;calcul.sco
i1      0   .01
```

This example simply prints the value 2.303 (the logarithm of 10) on screen. In this piece of code, you will have surely noticed some oddities, like *sr* = 100 Hz. In truth, that sampling rate is too large. No sound file is generated here. The control rate is quite low (1 Hz!). As a matter of fact, no control variable is featured in the orchestra, so any control rate would be fine. The "duration" is 1 centisecond, but could be any other.

Just like any other programming language, Csound is very powerful for certain tasks (sound synthesis) while not particularly suited to others (data management and manipulation, etc.). However, we should also add that it allows us to create "intelligent" programs, capable of changing their behavior upon input data changes.

17.2 PROGRAM FLOW MODIFICATIONS. VARIABLE TYPE CONVERTERS

Normally, Csound opcodes are executed sequentially, from the first to the last one. However, it is possible to change the program flow. For example, some opcodes could be executed only when some condition is satisfied.

The most important program control statements include the *unconditioned branch* statements:

```
igoto   label
kgoto   label
goto    label
```

igoto is an unconditioned branch to the statement labeled by *label* (initialization time only, see section 1.A.1).
kgoto is identical, but works at control rate statements.
goto works both at initialization time and control rate.

Notice that no program control statements apply at audio rate.

Special statements allow for the modification of the program flow dependent upon the occurrence of some other event.

These are called *conditioned branches*, including:

```
if   ia COND ib   igoto   label
if   ka COND kb   kgoto   label
if   ia COND ib   goto    label
```

Here *ia* and *ib* are expressions, while COND is a general name for relational operators such as:

- \> (greater than)
- < (lesser than)
- \>= (either greater than and equal to)
- <= (either lesser than and equal to)
- == (equal to)
- != (other than)

Notice that the symbol "=" means a value assignment (e.g. *a1* = *12*), while "==" is a relational operator (*13==13* is TRUE, *12==13* is FALSE).

As an example, consider the following code:

```
...
        if      i1>i2   goto jump
a1      rand    iamp
        goto    alright

jump:
a1      oscil   iamp, ifrq, 1

alright:
...
```

There the program control branches to the line labeled *jump*, and continues thereafter, only if *i1* is greater than *i2*. The branch causes the *a1* variable to be generated with *oscil* rather than *rand*. If the conditional branch does not occur, the program executes *rand* and skips to the *alright* label, such that *oscil* is not executed. The program flow is illustrated in figure 17-1.

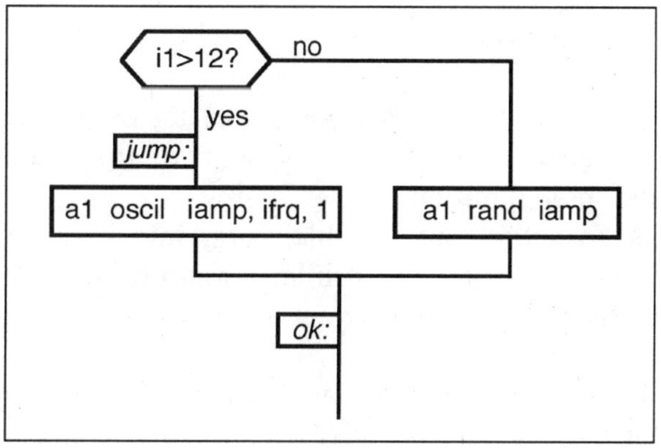

Fig. 17-1

For efficiency reasons, no conditional branches are available at audio rate. Therefore, in Csound a line such as the following is not permitted:

```
if    a1<a2    goto  joe
```

But what if we really need a branch conditioned by audio rate variables? The only way out of that problem is to set the control rate as high as the audio sampling rate, and use special opcodes for variable type conversions:

```
        sr     =  44100
        kr     =  44100
        ksmps  =  1
        nchnls =  1
        instr     1
a1      oscil     10000, 440, 1
a2      oscil     10000, 458, 1
k1      downsamp  a1
k2      downsamp  a2
        if        k1<k2  goto    joe
        ...
```

Csound variable type converters include:

```
i1   =           i(ksig)
i1   =           i(asig)
k1   downsamp    asig[, iwlen]
a1   upsamp      ksig
a1   interp      ksig[, istor]
```

i(ksig) and *i(asig)* return init-time variables equal to, respectively, control rate and audio rate variables. In a sense, they take a "snapshot" of either control or audio signals and hold it for the entire note duration.

downsamp converts an audio rate variable, *asig*, into a control rate variable, *k1*. *upsamp* and *interp* do the opposite. But, while *upsamp* samples and holds the current *ksig* value, *interp* linearly interpolates between the current *ksig* value and the previous one.

iwlen is the length in samples of an internal window over which the signal is averaged to determine a downsampled value. The maximum length is *ksmps*. Values 0 and 1 imply no averaging. The default is 0.

17.3 RE-INITIALIZATION

Another way to change the program flow is by multiple initialization passes during a note event. Suppose we want to repeat a given note every 10th of a second, changing the frequency as in the pattern illustrated in figure 17-2.

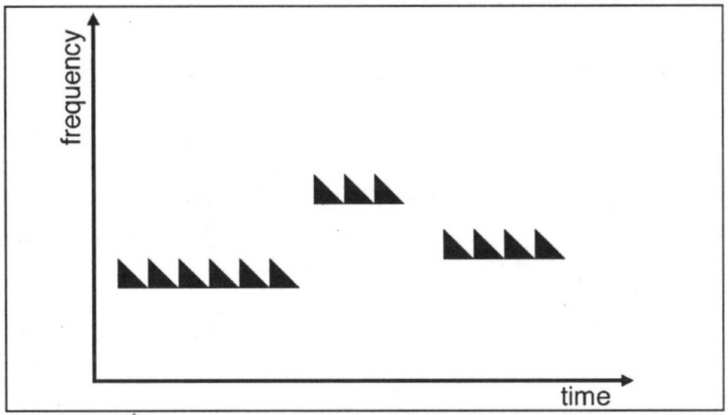

Fig. 17-2

Probably we would type in the following code:

```
;reinit.orc
        sr     =  44100
        kr     =  4410
        ksmps  =  10
        nchnls =  1
        instr     1
        iamp   =  ampdb(p4)
        ifrq   =  cpspch(p5)
kenv    linseg    0, .01, iamp, p3-.01, 0
a1      oscili    kenv, ifrq, 1
        out       a1
        endin

;reinit.sco
f1      0      4096    10     1
i1      0      .1      80     8       ; repeat 6 times
i1      +      .       .      .
i1      +      .       .      .
i1      +      .       .      .
```

```
i1    +     .     .     .
i1    +     .     .     .
i1    .7    .1    80    9       ; repeat 3 times
i1    +     .     .     .
i1    +     .     .     .
i1    1.1   .1    80    8.04    ; repeat 4 times
i1    +     .     .     .
i1    +     .     .     .
i1    +     .     .     .
```

Couldn't we simply determine the total duration for each of the three separate events, and have the computer repeat successively shorter notes at the appropriate time? That is done by using two special opcodes:

reinit label
rireturn

reinit causes the program performance to be temporarily stopped to allow a new initialization pass. The re-initialization starts from the line labeled by *label.* Then, with *rireturn* (as well as *endin*) performance is resumed. In other words, *rireturn* terminates a re-initialization pass begun with *reinit.* We specify *when*, during the Csound performance, it should happen, using *timout*:

timout istrt, idur, label

Basically, *timout* determines a branch conditioned by the elapsed note time. The branch to *label* will take place after *istrt* seconds, and will remain effective for *idur* seconds. We can re-initialize *timout* many times over the course of a note.

Our previous orchestra, then, can be re-written as follows:

```
;reinit1.orc
        sr     =  44100
        kr     =  4410
        ksmps  =  10
        nchnls =  1
        instr     1
        iamp   =  ampdb(p4)
        ifrq   =  cpspch(p5)
        idur   =  .1                ; re-initialization takes place every .1 secs.
```

```
from_here:

kenv    linseg    0, .01, iamp, .09, 0
        timout    0, idur, contin  ; jump to the "contin" label, unless time  has come for re-initialization
        reinit    from_here        ; re-initialize all previous opcodes included below the "from_here" label

contin:
        rireturn                   ; exit re-inizialization pass
a1      oscili    kenv, ifrq, 1    ; generates the sound
        out       a1
        endin

;reinit1.sco
f1   0     4096   10   1
i1   0     .6     80   8      ; repeat first note 6 times
i1   .7    .3     80   9      ; repeat second note 3 times
i1   1.1   .4     80   8.04   ; repeat third note 4 times
```

17.4 PROLONGING THE NOTE DURATION

It is possible to indefinitely prolong the note duration regardless of the actual p3 value. This is done with

ihold

which transforms a finite-duration note event into a "held" note (the same is obtained with a negative p3 value). To stop a "held" note, then, it is sufficient to use the opcode

turnoff

A "held" note is turned off, anyway, when a new note by the same instrument begins. That implies that instruments featuring *ihold* cannot play polyphonically, unless one uses fractional instruments numbers.

turnoff can be used independent of the presence of *ihold*. As an example, let's create an instrument which stops itself as a control signal, *kfreq*, reaches a value greater than the Nyquist frequency (*sr*/2):

```
k1      expon   440,  p3/10, 880        ;an exponential glissando curve
```

```
        if   k1 < sr/2 kgoto contin     if greater than Nyquist
        turnoff                         ;instrument turns off
contin:
a1      oscil    a1, k1, 1              ;otherwise keeps playing
```

17.5 DEBUGGING

In Csound, debugging is done mainly in an on-screen data display and by saving data files to disk. A simpler method requires usage of the *print* opcode:

print iarg[, iarg,...]

iarg is an init-time variable whose value is printed on the screen at initialization time and at each re-initialization pass requested by *reinit*. Here's an example:

```
...
ifrq    =   cpspch(p5)
iamp    =   ampdb(p4)
print       ifrq,  iamp
...
```

This prints the values *ifreq* and *iamp*, for each note event in the score. During performance, Csound displays something like the following (the *printed* data are in bold):

```
new alloc for instr 1:
instr 1:  ifrq = 261.626  iamp = 9999.996
B  0.000 ..  0.100 T  0.100 TT  0.100 M:          0.0
instr 1:  ifrq = 130.813  iamp = 3162.277
B  0.100 ..  0.200 T  0.200 TT  0.200 M:          0.0
instr 1:  ifrq = 277.167  iamp = 1000.000
B  0.200 ..  0.300 T  0.300 TT  0.300 M:          0.0
instr 1:  ifrq = 293.657  iamp = 6309.571
B  0.300 ..  0.400 T  0.400 TT  0.400 M:          0.0
instr 1:  ifrq = 311.101  iamp = 12589.249
B  0.400 ..  0.500 T  0.500 TT  0.500 M:          0.0
instr 1:  ifrq = 329.609  iamp = 31622.764
B  0.500 ..  0.600 T  0.600 TT  0.600 M:          0.0
end of score.            overall amps:     0.0
         overall samples out of range:     0
```

Debugging also includes:

display **xsig, iprd[, iwtflg]**
dispfft **xsig, iprd, iwsiz[, iwtyp][, idbouti][, iwtflg]**

display draws the signal *xsig* (amplitude vs time graph) every *iprd* seconds. *dispfft*, instead, draws the FFT spectrum of the signal *xsig* every *iprd* seconds. The *dispfft* arguments are:
iwsiz FFT analysis window size in samples
iwtyp (optional) windows type: 0 = rectangular, 1 = Hanning. The default is 0.
idbout (optional) units of output for the Fourier coefficients: 0 = absolute values, 1 = dBs. The default is 0.
iwflag (optional) wait flag: if non-zero, each display is held until the you press any key. The default is 0, no wait.

In almost all versions of Csound, the graphs created with *display* and *dispfft* are approximated with ascii (or ansi) characters.

The following opcodes are available only in certain versions:

printk **itime, kval [, ispace]**
printk2 **kval [,ispace]**

printk prints the value of kval every *itime* seconds, adding *ispace* blank spaces after each print.
printk2 prints *kval* only when it changes in its value, adding *ispace* blank spaces after each print.

The first print takes place during the first control rate period. With *printk*, you get a new print at each control rate period, by setting *itime*=0.

17.6 MATHEMATICAL AND TRIGONOMETRIC FUNCTIONS

The Csound instruction set includes a number of mathematical and trigonometric functions. Some functions are used for the purpose of converting values from one kind of unit to another, others are for more general purposes.
Value converters include:

ftlen(ifno) returns the number of samples of a stored function *ifno*

Example:

```
if2    =  ftlen(2)
```

This returns the size, in samples, of some table #2 (be aware that *ftlen()* cannot be used with tables created with GEN01 having the length 0).

int(kx) returns the integer part of a control or init-time variable.

Example:

```
i1     =  int(4.32)
```

the variable *i1* is assigned the value 4.

frac(kx) returns the fractional part of a control or init-time variable.

Example:

```
i1     =  frac(4.32)
```

the variable *i1* is assigned the value 0.32.

dbamp(kx) returns a decibel value equivalent of the raw amplitude *kx*.
i(kx) converts a control variable into a init-time variable (see section 17.2).
abs(x) returns the absolute value of *x*.

Example:

```
i1     =  abs(-3.1)
```

the variable *i1* is assigned the value 3.1.

```
i1     =  abs(2.5)
```

the variable *i1* is assigned the value 2.5.

exp(x) returns the exponential value of any variable (e^x)
log(x) returns the natural log of *x* (*x* must be positive)

sqrt(x) returns the square root of *x* (*x* must be non-negative)
sin(x) returns the sine of *x* (*x* must be expressed in radians)
cos(x) returns the cosine of *x* (*x* must be expressed in radians)
ampdb(x) returns the absolute amplitude value equivalent of the decibel value *x*.

Exponentiation can also be performed with the following opcodes:

ir pow iarg, kpow
kr pow karg, kpow, [inorm]
ar pow aarg, kpow, [inorm]

iarg, *karg* and *aarg* represent the base and *kpow* represents the exponent.
inorm (optional) is a scale factor, whose value defaults to 1 (no scale).

Here's a couple of examples:

```
i2raisedto3 pow     2, 3
```

The init-time variable *i2raisedto3* is assigned the value 8.

```
i2raisedto3 pow     2, 3, 4
```

This time, instead, the variable is given the value 2 (= 2^3 / 4).

Starting with Csound 3.50 release, exponentiation can be operated directly on variables of any kind (*i,k,a*), using the operator ^. Hence, the code

```
i2raisedto3 pow isig, 3
k1       line 0, p3, i2raisedto3
```

can be replaced with a single line, such as:

```
k1       line 0, p3, isig^3
```

17.7 CONDITIONAL VALUES

There is a particularly efficient way to perform value assignments conditionally, depending on the result of some other expression. Depending on the particular condition to test, we can write:

(a > b ? v1 : v2)
(a < b ? v1 : v2)
(a >= b ? v1 : v2)
(a <= b ? v1 : v2)
(a == b ? v1 : v2)
(a != b ? v1 : v2)

where *a*, *b*, *v1* and *v2* can be either constants, variables or expressions (no audio rate variables allowed).

Csound first compares *a* with *b* (is *a* greater than *b*? is *a* lesser than *b*? is *a* greater than or equal to *b*? is *a* lesser than or equal to *b*? is *a* equal to *b*? is *a* different from *b*?). If the test is TRUE, then the output variable *ia* assigned the value *v1*. If it is FALSE, then the output variable is assigned the value *v2*.

Example:

```
k0      =  (k1 < p5/2 + p6 ? k1 : p7)
```

First the expression *p5/2+p6* is calculated, and then, if the result is a number smaller than *k1*, *k0* is given the value *k1*. Otherwise it is given the value contained in *p7*.

EXTENSIONS

17.A.1 DESIGNING COMPLEX EVENTS

In a typical Csound score, a line beginning with an *i* statement corresponds to a single note event. In some cases, however, with just a single *i* statement a compounded event can be generated, such as a tune, a scale, etc...

In section 17.3 we studied how to re-initialize an instrument so that they to have multiple envelopes over the course of a note. In this section we turn toward more complex tasks.

Suppose we want to design an instrument playing ascending chromatic scale segments comprised between any two notes specified in the score. The score appears as follows:

```
;chromscale.sco
f1     0      4096   10     1      .3     .3     .2     0      .4
;p1    p2     p3     p4     p5     p6
;ins   act    dur    dB     start  end
i1     0      3      80     8      8.07
```

The scale segment must begin with the pitch specified in p5 (8.00) and must end with the pitch in p6 (8.07). Here's the orchestra playing such a score:

```
;chromscale.orc
        sr        =  44100
        kr        =  4410
        ksmps     =  10
        nchnls    =  1
        instr        1
        iamp      =  ampdb(p4)
        ipitch    =  p5              ;start pitch
        ioctst    =  int(p5)         ;octave of start pitch
        ioctend   =  int(p6)         ;octave of end pitch
        isemist   =  frac(p5)*100    ;start pitch class
        isemiend  =  frac(p6)*100    ;end pitch class
        isemirng  =  (ioctend-ioctst)*12+(isemiend-isemist)+1
                                     ;total number of pitches to play
        idur      =  p3/isemirng     ;duration for each partial event

from_there:
```

```
        ifrq     =    cpspch(ipitch)              ;pitch to Hz conversion
kenv    linseg        0, .01, iamp, idur-.01, 0   ;envelope
        timout        0, idur, contin             ;re-init instrument every
;idur seconds
        ipitch   =    ipitch+.01                  ;and increment pitch for next event

reinit from_there
contin:
        rireturn
a1      oscili        kenv, ifrq, 1               ;sound synthesis
        out           a1
        endin
```

What have we done exactly? First we stored the start pitch of the required chromatic segment in a temporary variable, *ipitch*. Then we assigned the octave for the first pitch in *ioctst*, and the octave for the end pitch in *ioctend*. The values were obtained using *int()*. Also, we assigned the pitch class for the start pitch in *isemist*, and the pitch class for the end pitch in *isemiend*. These values were obtained with *fract()*. At that point, we calculated the total number of semitone steps to perform. That was done by subtracting the start octave from the end octave, multiplying the result by 12, plus the result obtained by subtracting the end pitch class from the start pitch class. Finally, we also added 1 to get the right result.

Then we divided p3 by the total number of pitches to play and got the duration for each partial event. The envelope for every partial event is the triangle shape generated in the *kenv* variable.

Finally, we created a re-initialization loop (lines between *from_there* to *reinit*), each time through the loop incrementing the pitch value by 1 semitone (i.e. 0.01). That increases the pitch a semitone higher for each successive event.

As another example, suppose you want to create a mass of small sound particles, with frequencies and durations randomly taken from preset ranges.

```
;masses.sco
f1    0     4096   10    1          .3          .3        .2       0    .4
;p1   p2    p3     p4    p5         p6
;ins  act   dur    dB    min.freq   max.freq    min.dur   max.dur
i1    0     3      80    400        600         .1        .2
```

As you see, the minimum frequency value is defined in p5, the maximum in p6. The minimum duration is defined in p7, the maximum in p8.

```
;masses.orc
        sr        =   44100
        kr        =   4410
        ksmps     =   10
        nchnls    =   1
        instr         1
        iamp      =   ampdb(p4)
        ifrmin    =   p5
        ifrmax    =   p6
        ifrrng    =   ifrmax-ifrmin       ;frequency range
        idurmin   =   p7
        idurmax   =   p8
        idurrng   =   idurmax-idurmin     ;duration range

from_there:
;- - - - - - - - - - - - - - - - - - - - - - - - - - - - - - - - - - - get a freq value
kfrq    rand          ifrrng, -1          ; second argument (seed) is set to -1
                                          ; not to get identical random patterns
        kfrq      =   abs(kfrq)
        ifrq      =   ifrmin+i(kfrq)
;- - - - - - - - - - - - - - - - - - - - - - - - - - - - - - - - - - - get a duration value
kdur    rand          idurrng, -1
        kdur      =   abs(kdur)
        idur      =   idurmin+i(kdur)
;- - - - - - - - - - - - - - - - - - - - - - - - - - - - - - - - - - - envelope
kenv    linseg        0, .01, iamp, idur-.01, 0
;- - - - - - - - - - - - - - - - - - - - - - - - - - - - - - - - - - - re-initialization
        timout        0, idur, contin
        reinit        from_there
contin:
        rireturn
;- - - - - - - - - - - - - - - - - - - - - - - - - - - - - - - - - - - synthesis
a1      oscili        kenv, ifrq, 1
        out           a1
        endin
```

Examine this orchestra:

First we calculated the frequency and duration ranges (*ifrrng=p6-p5* and *idurrng=p8-p7*) .

Then we generated a random number in the range -*ifrrng* to +*ifrrng*. Actually, we got the absolute value of the random number, using *abs()*. The value thus obtained, *kfrq*, converted to a init-time variable, was then summed to *ifrmin*, which finally determined *ifrq*, i.e. the frequency of a single sound particle in our complex event. In a way similar, we determined the duration for the sound particle, *idur* (ranging p7 to p8). The latter value is used in the generation of the appropriate envelope, and the envelope is applied to an oscillator having *ifrq* as the frequency.

Observe that the instrument is re-initialized every *idur* seconds. As we have seen, *idur* is not fixed, as it gets re-initialized at each re-initialization pass. So, re-initialization takes place at a randomly selected time interval.

Listening to the output sound, we notice that the very last sound particle is truncated. Indeed, it may well be the case that the sum of randomly calculated shorter durations is not identical with the overall duration, p3. We have to modify the instrument to prevent the generation of the very last partial event. This is done by checking if the time left until the end of the overall event is or is not less than *idur*. The solution is (check the code lines in bold characters):

```
;masses1.orc
        sr          =   44100
        kr          =   44100
        ksmps       =   1
        nchnls      =   1
        instr           1
        iamp        =   ampdb(p4)
        irem        =   p3                  ;remainder time
        ifrmin      =   p5
        ifrmax      =   p6
        ifrrng      =   ifrmax-ifrmin       ;freq range
        idurmin     =   p7
        idurmax     =   p8
        idurrng     =   idurmax-idurmin     ;dur range

from_there:

        kfrq    rand    ifrrng/2, -1
        kfrq        =   abs(kfrq)
        ifrq        =   ifrmin+i(kfrq)
        kdur    rand    idurrng/2, -1
        kdur        =   abs(kdur)
```

```
        idur    =   idurmin+i(kdur)
        irem    =   irem-idur            ;get the remainder time
        if  irem<idur goto nosound       ;if remainder time is not enough
                                         ;then no sound is generated
                                         ;(jump to the “nosound” label)
kenv    linseg      0, .01, iamp, idur-.01, 0
        timout      0, idur, contin
        reinit      from_there
contin:
        rireturn
a1      oscili      kenv, ifrq, 1

nosound:
        out         a1
        endin
```

LIST OF OPCODES INTRODUCED IN THIS SECTION

	igoto	label		
	kgoto	label		
	goto	label		
	if	ia COND ib	igoto	label
	if	ka COND kb	kgoto	label
	if	ia COND ib	goto	label
i1	=	i(control-rate_variable)		
i1	=	i(audio_rate_variable)		
k1	downsamp	audio_variable [, window_size]		
a1	upsamp	control_variable		
a1	interp	control_variable [, memory_initialization_flag]		
	reinit	label		
	rireturn			
	timout	init_time, duration, label		
	ihold			
	turnoff			
	print	init-time_variable_1 [,init-time_variable_2,...]		
	display	variable, time [, wait_flag]		
	dispfft	variable, time, window_size [,window_type][, amp_units] [, wait_flag]		
	printk	time, control_variable [, number_of_blanks]		
	printk2	control_variable [, number_of_balnks]		
ir	pow	basis, exponent		
kr	pow	basis, exponent, [scale_factor]		
ar	pow	basis, exponent, [scale_factor]		

APPENDIX 1

WCSHELL

A1.1 WHAT IS WCSHELL?

WCShell is a program created by Riccardo Bianchini to simplify using Csound on Windows95/98/2000/NT computers. It is the next generation of a previously designed MS-DOS application called CShell. The present WCShell release (5.4.1) was developed from a number of preceding releases created for Windows 3.x.

WCShell includes a command console enabling you to select among available disk units and folders, and to load orchestra, score and sound files. It also includes a text editor to write the orchestra and score code, and a number of buttons to launch Csound and listen to sound files. Also included with WCShell is a number of utility programs.

WCShell was written in Microsoft™ VisualBasic© 5.00. The current release works under Windows95/98/2000 and WindowsNT. It is a shareware product, and can be freely copied and circulated.

A1.2 THE MAIN PAGE

The main page of WCShell is printed in figure A-1-1. It includes:

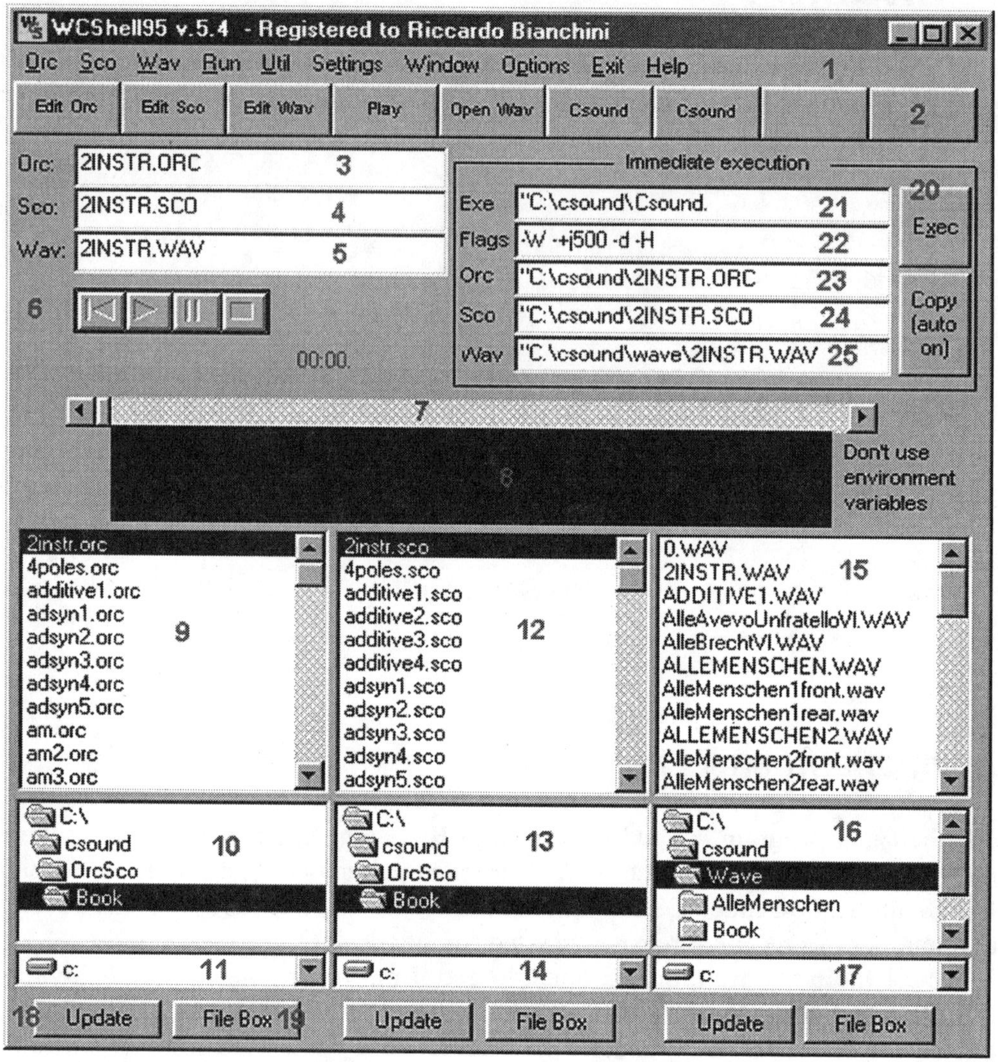

Fig. A-1-1

1. menu bar
2. command buttons
3. filename of currently selected orchestra
4. filename of currently selected score
5. filename for the output sound file
6. tape-recorder buttons (play, stop, rewind, pause)
7. a scroll bar to browse across the current sound file

8. the waveform (amplitude/time graph) of the currently selected sound file
9. orchestra file list-box (available orchestras in current orchestra folder)
10. orchestra folder list-box (available folders on current disk drive)
11. orchestra disk drive
12. score file list-box (available scores in current score folder)
13. score folder list-box (available folders on current disk drive)
14. score disk drive
15. sound file list-box (available sound files in current sound file folder)
16. sound file folder list-box (available folders on current disk drive)
17. sound file disk drive
18. update buttons (update contents of file, directory and disk drive list-boxes, as relative to orchestras, scores or sound files)
19. explore resource buttons (to launch the file manager facility currently installed on your computer)
20. start button (to run Csound from selected files)
21. currently selected Csound executable file
22. Csound command line flags
23. filename for the Csound sound output
24. orchestra file pathname
25. score file pathname

Most important are the main menu bar, the command buttons (for quick access to commands also accessible from the menu), and three text boxes with the filenames of currently selected orchestra, score and sound file. Also important are the playback buttons (similar to a cassette tape recorder), a scroll-bar to move across the sound file, three separate list boxes (for orchestra, score and sound files) with the respective folder and disk-drive. These latter allow you to browse the hard disks on your computer and locate the files.

A.1.3 INSTALLATION FROM CD

It is quite simple to install WCShell from the free CD-ROM packaged with this book. Before you proceed, however, we recommend that you read the readme.txt file for information concerning updates and changes. To install WCShell, do the following:

1. Close all applications currently in use
2. from the Start button, choose the "Run" dialog box and enter the following path and file name: "D:\WCSHELL\SETUP.EXE" (replace drive D with any other drive letter, as necessary). As an alternative, you can browse the CD-ROM drive

and locate the *setup.exe* file. Now run the setup program. During the installation, we recommend that you choose “C:\CSOUND” as the destination folder.

3. When you’re done with the installation, run WCShell and select the “Settings”. That opens a dialog box where you can enter the settings for correct use of the program. See figure A-1-2.

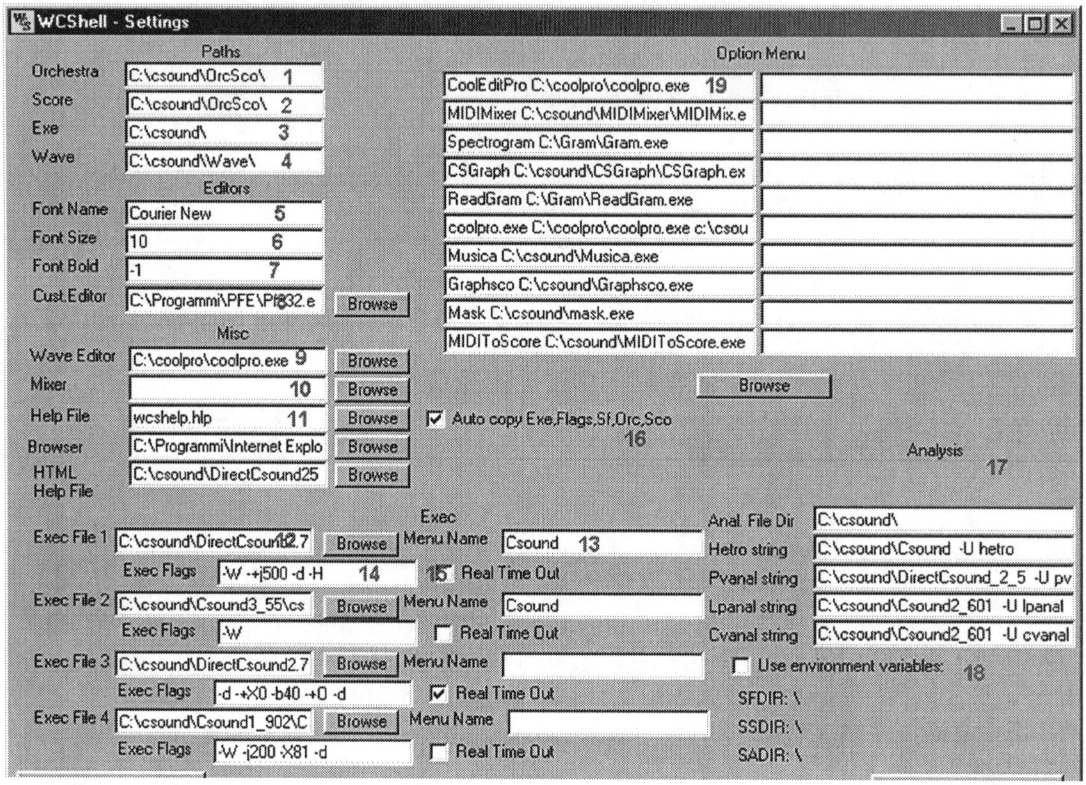

Fig. A-1-2

A.1.4 INSTALLATION FROM INTERNET

To install WCShell from your Internet browser, follow these steps:

1. create a temporary folder, such as C:\TEMP on your hard drive
2. download the *wscshell.zip* file, or *wcshellXX.zip* if available (for example *wcshell51_a.zip*, or *wcshell51_b.zip* would be subsequent versions of the 5.1 release).
3. unzip the downloaded file, and save the extracted files to the same temporary folder as the zip file

4. locate and run *setup.exe*, then follow the same instructions as in the preceding section (2 and 3).

A.1.5 WCSHELL STARTER

The first thing to do is to tell WCShell the folder where it should load and save files during your work sessions. Select "Settings" from the main menu. In the appropriate text boxes, enter the folder pathname for orchestra files (1), score files (2), executable files (3) and sound files (4). Enter the folder where WCShell should locate the Csound executable (normally c:\csound\csound.exe) (12). Enter the string "Csound" (13) that will then appear on the start synthesis button. Enter the flag "-W" as the sole *Exec Flag* (14). Output sound files will be saved in Wave format.

Now click *Write Settings* and *Exit*.

At this point, we can really start a WCShell session. Select Orc and then *New Orc* to launch the orchestra text editor. Write your orchestra code and save it with *File/Save as...*, then close the editor with the *File/Exit* command. Create your score code first selecting *Sco/New Sco*, then following the same procedure you used to create the orchestra file.

As soon as you exit the score editor, you can launch Csound by clicking the start button (now indicated by the button name "Csound"). You'll see a dialog box where you can enter more command line flags, change the output filename, etc. If no change is necessary, click the *OK* button. Csound is now running. Provided no syntax errors are found, the synthesis terminates without problems. Close the synthesis monitor window by pressing Enter. Click the *Play* button (or press F3) to listen to the newly generated sound file. Quite simple, isn't it?

To modify the orchestra, click the *Edit Orc* button or press F1. To modify the score, click the *Edit Sco* button or press F2.

A.1.6 THE ORCHESTRA EDITOR

The orchestra editor option menu includes the following:

FILE

New	remove the current contents from the editor window. If the file was not saved, the program asks for your confirmation.
Open	open an existing file
Save	save file
Save as...	save file with a new name

Insert load the contents of another file and paste them to the cursor position
Append load the contents of another file and paste them to the end of current file
Print send the editor contents to the printer
Exit leave editor. If the file was not saved, the program asks for your confirmation.

EDIT

Copy copy selection to the clipboard
Paste paste the contents of the clipboard to the cursor position
Goto line... move cursor to line number...
Goto Tag <CsOptions> jump to the first command line flag in a csd file
Goto Tag <CsInstruments> jumps to the beginning of the orchestra code in a *csd* file
Goto Tag <CsScore> jump to the beginning of the score code in a *csd* file

FONTS open a dialog box to choose a character type, size and attributes

FIND

Find find a text string
Find next find next occurrence of the text string
Find Insno... find instrument number... (for this to properly work, the instr opcode and the instrument number must be separated by a tab)

OPTIONS

Header allows you to automatically insert any of the following standard headers:
22050 Hz Mono
22050 Hz Stereo
44100 Hz Mono
44100 Hz Stereo
48000 Hz Mono
48000 Hz Stereo
Conversions allows you to insert any of standard value converters

WINDOWS

Strip Windows strip the edit windows one on top of the other, horizontally
Tile Windows arrange the edit windows one next to the other, vertically

Close Editors close editors in use
Main bring the main WCShell window in foreground

CSD TAGS

<CsoundSynthesizer>	insert the <CsoundSynthesizer> tag
</CsoundSynthesizer>	insert the </CsoundSynthesizer> tag
<CsOptions>	insert the <CsOptions> tag
</CsOptions>	insert the </CsOptions> tag
<CsInstruments>	insert the <CsInstruments> tag
</CsInstruments>	insert the </CsInstruments> tag
<CsScore>	insert the <CsScore> tag
</CsScore>	insert the </CsScore> tag

SPECIAL

Reread the line feed	reread a UNIX file (*line feed* without *carriage return*)
OVERWRITE ON/OFF	switch between "insert" and "cancel" editing modes

A.1.7 SCORE EDITOR

The score editor option menu includes the following options:

FILE

New	remove the current contents from the editor window. If the file was not saved, the program asks for your confirmation.
Open	open an existing file
Save	save file
Save as...	save file with a new name
Insert	load the contents of another file and paste them to the cursor position
Append	load the contents of another file and paste them to the end of current file
Print	send the editor contents to the printer
Exit	leave editor. If the file was not saved, the program asks for your confirmation.

EDIT

Copy	copy selection to the clipboard

Paste paste the contents of the clipboard to the cursor position
Comment selected allows you to insert a comment string for the selected text (semicolons ";" are automatically inserted to separate code lines from comments)
Uncomment selected cancels all semicolons ";" from selected text

FONTS open a dialog box to choose a character type, size and attributes

FIND

Find find a text string
Find next find next occurrence of the text string

OPTIONS

Insert Sine Function automatically insert the line *f1 0 4096 10 1* at the beginning of score
Draw Function open a special window where you can draw functions (the function table will be generated with either GEN07 or GEN08, see next section)
View Selected Function allows you to view a function table created with GEN07; the corresponding *f* statement line must be previously selected and copied into the clipboard

WINDOWS

Strip Windows strip windows one on top of the other, horizontally
Tile Windows arrange windows one next to the other, vertically
Close Editors close editors in use
Main bring the main WCShell window in foreground

SPECIAL

Reread the line feed reread a UNIX file (*line feed* without *carriage return*)
OVERWRITE ON/OFF switch between "insert" and "cancel" editing modes

A.1.8 DRAWING FUNCTIONS

The *Draw Function* option in the Score Editor opens a windows like the one in fig.A-1-3. It allows you to graphically render a function with GEN07 and GEN08.

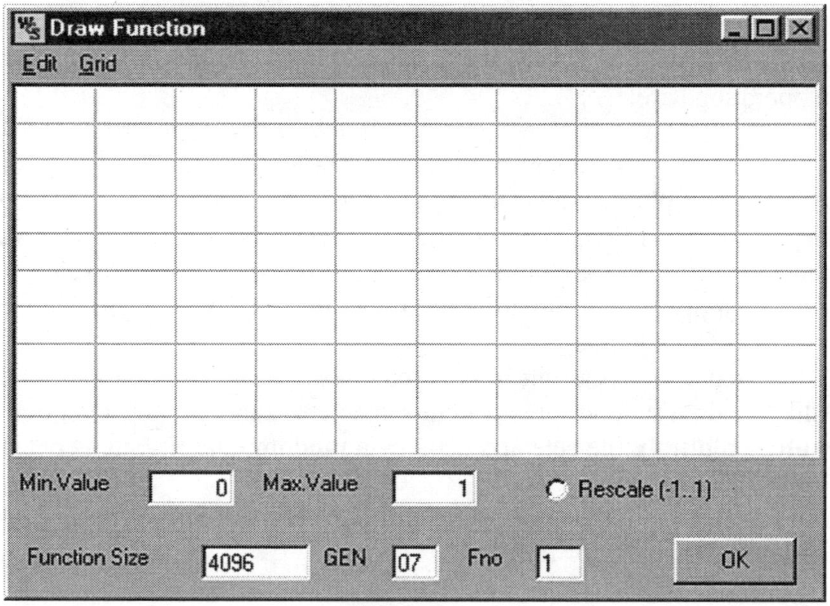

Fig. A-1-3

You can define a value range by entering the appropriate values in the *Min Value* and *Max Value* text boxes (the default is 0 and 1). Also, you can define a table size (default is 4096), the particular GEN to use (default is GEN07), and the table id number (default is 1). Finally, you can decide whether the function table should or should not be normalized (re-scaled).

To draw a function, you move the cursor to the desired horizontal/vertical coordinates and click. That creates the first break point in your function. Each new click will create a straight line linking the new break point to the previous one. Trying to move back in the horizontal direction makes no sense.

From the option menu you can choose *Grid* to create a grid with any number of vertical and horizontal lines, which provide a visual aid to help you draw functions.

The *Edit* option allows you to undo previously drawn line segments (you can undo as many segments as were created since you started drawing).

A.1.9 SCORE PROCESSING

From within WCShell you can call up and run *Scorex*, an application designed to convert a Csound score (with p-fields separated either by tabs or blanks) to a spreadsheet, similar to the old *Visicalc* ™ or the newer *Excel* ™ applications. In the spreadsheet editor, rows correspond to notes or functions, columns correspond to p-fields. It is then possible to perform calculations or to modify a single cell in a row or any number of selected cells in rows and columns.

Featured operations are:

Add	add a given quantity to selected cells
Mult	multiply the selected cells by a given quantity
Lin Interp	perform linear interpolation between first and last selected cells
Exp Interp	perform exponential interpolation between first and last selected cells
Func	apply a given function (exp, log, int, frac, sine, cosine, tangent, abs) to selected cells
Fill	enter a text string in selected cells
Rand Add	add a random quantity, in a specified range, to selected cells
Rand Mult	multiply the selected cells by a random quantity, in a specified range.

When you call any of these operation, a dialog box prompts you and asks you to specify the required quantity or ranges.

WCShell and *Scorex* provide many other useful options, that you can learn on your own by consulting the on-line help.

APPENDIX 2

MATHEMATICS AND TRIGONOMETRY

A.2.1 FREQUENCY VALUES FOR THE EQUALLY-TEMPERED CHROMATIC SCALE

octaves	0	1	2	3	4	5	6	7
C	32.7032	65.4064	130.8128	261.6256	523.2511	1046.5023	2093.0045	4186.0090
C#	34.6478	69.2957	138.5913	277.1826	554.3653	1108.7305	2217.4610	4434.9221
D	36.7081	73.4162	146.8324	293.6648	587.3295	1174.6591	2349.3181	4698.6363
D#	38.8909	77.7817	155.5635	311.1270	622.2540	1244.5079	2489.0159	4978.0317
E	41.2034	82.4069	164.8138	329.6276	659.2551	1318.5102	2637.0205	5274.0409
F	43.6535	87.3071	174.6141	349.2282	698.4565	1396.9129	2793.8259	5587.6517
F#	46.2493	92.4986	184.9972	369.9944	739.9888	1479.9777	2959.9554	5919.9108
G	48.9994	97.9989	195.9977	391.9954	783.9909	1567.9817	3135.9635	6271.9270
G#	51.9131	103.8262	207.6523	415.3047	830.6094	1661.2188	3322.4376	6644.8752
A	55.0000	110.0000	220.0000	440.0000	880.0000	1760.0000	3520.0000	7040.0000
A#	58.2705	116.5409	233.0819	466.1638	932.3275	1864.6550	3729.3101	7458.6202
B	61.7354	123.4708	246.9417	493.8833	987.7666	1975.5332	3951.0664	7902.1328

A.2.2 LOGARITHMS

The logarithm of a number, *a*, is defined as that number which, raised to the logarithm base, *b*, gives *a*. Accordingly, if **$c=\log_b a$** then **$b^c = a$**.
The logarithm basis can be any number. In music calculations, most often used are logarithms base 2 and 10. Base 2 is often used for measuring pitch:

pitch = $\log_2$ (frequency / reference frequency)

(as the reference frequency consider C_0). Conversely

frequency = (reference frequency) * 2^{pitch}

The following defines the pitch of a 440 Hz tone:

pitch = $\log_2$ (440 / 32.703) = A3

Vice-versa, the following defines the Hz value for the A3 pitch:

frequency(A3) = 32.703 * $2^{3.75}$ = 440 Hz

A.2.3 DECIBELS

As observed in section 1.3, the ear is particularly sensitive to intensity variations. To avoid dealing with large numbers, we can use exponential notations to deal with such scales.
In exponential notation, the number

0.00000000000001

is re-written as

$1 * 10^{-14}$

If we isolate the exponent, we have a 2-digit number (14) representing a 15-digit one (0.00000000000001). Which is a very handy way to express large magnitude variations. The unit for measuring intensity variations is called the **deciBel** (1/10 of a **Bel**), named for Alexander Graham Bell. DeciBel values (**dB**) are calculated using the formula

$$\mathbf{dB = 20 * \log (A) / \log (A_0)}$$

where A is the value being measured and A_0 is a reference magnitude. The latter is considered as a conventional zero. As a unit the deciBel is not used for measuring absolute magnitudes, like *Hz* or *feet*. It is a *relational value*: it measures the *ratio between two magnitudes*. Normally, dB values are used in acoustics to express amplitude or acoustic power. However, nothing would prevent us from using it to express frequency ratios etc.

Here's a chart of equivalence between dB values and absolute amplitude values.

dB	value	dB	value	dB	value	dB	value
0	1	-30	.032	-60	.001	-90	.000032
-2	.794	-32	.025	-62	.00079	-92	.000025
-4	.631	-34	.02	-64	.00063	-94	.00002
-6	.501	-36	.016	-66	.0005	-96	.000016
-8	.398	-38	.013	-68	.0004	-98	.0000126
-10	.316	-40	.01	-70	.000316	-100	.00001
-12	.251	-42	.008	-72	.00025		
-14	.200	-44	.006	-74	.0002		
-16	.158	-46	.005	-76	.00016		
-18	.126	-48	.004	-78	.000125		
-20	.1	-50	.0032	-80	.0001		
-22	.079	-52	.0025	-82	.000079		
-24	.063	-54	.002	-84	.000063		
-26	.05	-56	.0016	-86	.00005		
-28	.01	-58	.00125	-88	.00004		

A.2.4 TRIGONOMETRY. ANGLE MEASURES

Any angle can be measured using one of two different units: degrees (1 degree is defined as the 360th part of a round angle) or radians (1 radian is defined as the angle whose arc equals the ray - see fig. A-2-1, where AB = OA). This angle (1 radian) is the equivalent of

$$\mathbf{1\ rad = 57.2988°}$$

and can be also calculated starting with the round circumference:

$2 * \pi * r = 3.1415927 * r$

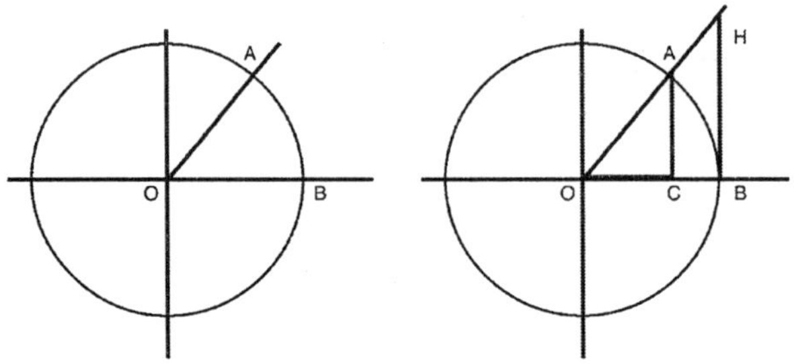

Fig. A-2-1

If r = 1 then the angle whose arc is itself equal to 1 is

$360°/\pi = 360°/3.1415927 = 57.2988°$

A.2.5 TRIGONOMETRIC FUNCTIONS

Given an angle α (see fig.A-2-1), the ratio of AC to r (= OA) is called the sine of the angle, sin(α). The ratio of OC to r is called the cosine of the angle, cos(α). The ratio of AB to r (which is identical with the ratio of HB to OH) is called the tangent of the angle, tg(α).

For r = 1, the following values are obtained for the three trigonometric functions:

degrees	sin(α)	cos(α)	tg(α)	degrees	sin(α)	cos(α)	tg(α)
0	0	1	0	180	0	-1	0
5	.2588191	.9659258	.2679492	195	-.2588191	-.9659258	.2679492
30	.5	.8660254	.5773503	210	-.5	-.8660254	.5773502
45	.7071068	.7071068	1	225	-.707107	-.7071066	1.000001
60	.8660254	.5	1.732051	240	-.8660256	-.4999999	1.732052
75	.9659258	.2588191	3.732051	255	-.9659259	-.258819	3.732052
90	1	0	∞	270	-1	0	-∞
105	.9659258	-.2588191	-3.732051	285	-.9659259	.258819	-3.732051
120	.8660254	-.5000001	-1.732051	300	-.8660256	.5	-1.732051
135	.7071068	-.7071068	-1	315	-.707107	.7071067	-1
150	.5000001	-.8660254	-.5773504	330	-.4999998	.8660256	-.5773499
165	.2588189	-.9659259	-.2679491	345	-.2588188	.9659259	-.267949

A.2.6 IN RADIANS

With reference to section A.2.4, a 360° angle coincides with the full circumference, 2π. Therefore:

$$\mathbf{360° = \frac{2 * \pi * r}{r}\ rad = 2 * \pi\ rad}$$

Following are the radian values (in fractions of ?) equivalents of important degree values:

degrees	rad	degrees	rad	degrees	rad	degrees	rad
0	0	90	π/2	180	π	180	3/2π

A.2.7 LINK TO THE TIME CONTINUUM

It is possible to graphically project the previously described trigonometric functions simply by representing them on the circle (fig. A-2-1). The function values correspond to equally-spaced steps of the θ angle.

Also, if we establish that the ray of the θ angle rotates anti-clockwise, at constant speed, it is possible to create a link between the trigonometric functions and time. Given a constant speed, ω, that is the angle covered in 1 second by the rotating ray, the angle covered in any time, t, is:

$$\theta = \omega * \mathbf{t}$$

If the ray covers the full circumference length f times per second, the angle covered in 1 second is:

$$\theta = \mathbf{2} * \omega * \mathbf{f} * \mathbf{t}$$

where f is defined precisely as the frequency of harmonic motion.

By choosing a ray of arbitrary length A, then this A is the maximum amplitude of the harmonic motion. The notation for the instantaneous amplitude (the amplitude at any moment in time) is:

$$\mathbf{I = A * sin\ (2*\pi*f*t\ )}$$

This is the equation of sinusoidal harmonic motion.

READINGS

CSOUND AND LINUX

by Nicola Bernardini

1 INTRODUCTION: WHAT IS LINUX?

Linux is a fully 'open-source' operating system for Intel hardware platforms (486, Pentiums and later) and currently it is also available for DEC Alpha, PowerMac (PowerPC) and Sun SPARC platforms [1]. It's 'open source' status means that:

• All source code that is comprises the system kernel is available to anybody on the Internet [2]

• It may be found in several Internet sites in various forms (binary executables for all platforms; the entire system in source code; documentation in several forms, etc.); furthermore, it is available commercially in as a CD-ROM for a reasonable price.

• The availability of the source code transfers functional control over programs to the user who are able to make modifications that satisfy individual requirements.

• This flexibility makes it attractive to a considerable number of hackers and software specialists (Linux users range in the millions) because it allows for very quick development and debugging which compliments the pace of hardware development. Furthermore, the resulting software is generally of high quality and evolves very rapidly;

• Since Linux does not attempt to compete as a commercial operating system, it is possible to continue using older versions and releases without experiencing compatibility problems (changes to new versions are generally bug fixes and new extensions or hardware support). Known bugs are well documented.

There is a strong trend in current development Linux for compatibility with major, commercially available, operating systems (Windows, DOS, MacOS, OS/2, various flavors of Unix, etc.) De facto standards (both commercial and research-oriented) are frequently adopted by the Linux community of developers; Linux can thus read most file systems, network through many different networking standards and imitate (?) most operating systems.

---

[1] The list of hardware platforms supporting Linux, however, is growing by the day

[2] This entails (among other things) that the system is completely free of charge; it is not a demo or what is commonly termed by shareware: no money is ever required for its use

On top of all this, Linux is a full-fledged Unix system [3]. It is a multi-tasking and multi-user system that it allows several programs to run in parallel and several users to work on the same machine by means of different (possibly graphic) terminals.

2 CSOUND AND LINUX

Since Csound was initially created on a Unix operating system, developing the Linux version has been trivial. Several binary versions are available on the Internet (addresses are listed at the end of this chapter). To support the multimedia hardware currently available on many personal computers, Linux has the options for using half- or full-duplex cards [4]. So, the system may be used as a real-time, digital signal processor when the computation load permits it.

Through the dynamic linking of various programs within the CSound Suite, composers are able to build extremely small sized executables files (ranging from about 5-10 kilobytes) with a shared library that is a few hundred Kilobytes in size.

2.1 Pros

There are several good reasons to use Linux as a working platform for Csound:

• First, Csound is (currently) oriented towards non-real time batch processing. That means orchestras and scores are written in text files before CSound processing. This compilation can last for quite a long time and it is efficient, therefore, to work on an operating system that supports multi-tasking (running different applications simultaneously). At the very least, one should be able to control the progress of the Csound processing itself. All Unix systems are inherently very efficient at multi-tasking which promotes an optimal use of hardware resources (disk, DMA, CPU, etc.). On medium-sized Linux systems several CSound processes can share resources without substantial performance degradation.

• The availability of all application source code (Csound included) coupled with the sophisticated development system (compilers, libraries, tools for almost all existing languages) featured on most Linux systems enable courageous hackers to attempt modify and create new Csound modules with optimal tools. Furthermore, the high quality and the availability of these tools is rapidly leading to their adoption as the standard — thus increasing the prevalence, portability and re-usability of modules;

---

3 In fact, the name Linux was created to avoid copyright systems over the Unix trademark (and also after the first name of the finnish project founder and leader Linus Torvalds)

4 Which feature, respectively, alternative record or playback or simultaneous record or playback

• But the foremost reason is tightly connected to the intrinsic, textual nature of Csound. Orchestras and scores, the interface to the program, are text files. This characteristic is a key feature of Csound that lends itself particularly well to musical and compositional practices (which are, traditionally, connected to 'writing texts'). Obviously, text manipulation can become extremely tedious without proper tools. However, the contemporary computer interfaces complete reliance on graphical interfaces has pushed users away from textual tools. All Unix systems, which were created when the high resolution monitor was unknown feature several core tools for manipulating interactive and batch text ("text filters"). These components are so important that we have devoted a separate paragraph to them. (Of course, there are very sophisticated graphic interfaces on Unix systems nowadays as can be seen below, but they are deeply integrated in an environment which still possesses extensive text-based capabilities.

• In particular, the ubiquitous Linux's user interface, Bash, is run through a powerful shell. Although other interfaces are available, Bash lends itself especially well to complicated operation sequences distributed over time.

• Finally, the standard graphical interface for Unix, called X windows (or also X11), is also available for Linux, and is a distributed interface which allows one to launch an application on a machine while controlling its graphics output or processing via another machine connected by an ethernet network (TCP/IP). This creates a completely transparent, parallel distributed network of computers which is particularly useful for applications like Csound where optimization of hardware resources is important.

2.2 Cons - and a small digression

Considering these advantages, an obvious question emerges: how come a system like Linux - free, sophisticated and complete - is not the accepted standard for all computing applications? There are several answers to this question. These may be considered the 'cons' of this operating system. Incidentally, with minor modifications these answers may well be applied to the following question, as well: how come Csound is not the standard synthesis system for musical applications?

• First of all, even though the Linux system is relatively easy to use, it is a highly sophisticated system with many flexible features. This means that setup for proper operation is fairly complicated. There is, of course, a lot of documentation on all aspects of the system (and it is well organized). But, the reading of such a large corpus of information can become a daunting task for most non-computer literate people. This limits the user base.

• Developed in a university environment for university users, Linux (like all public-domain software) is oriented toward scientific applications. Word processing applications are less widespread and the ones that do exist present few valid alternatives to commercial packages and operating systems(with the notable exception of file and network servers — see below). [5]

• Last but not least, public domain applications do not benefit from colossal advertising campaigns because the product is free. Furthermore, in the software field, where monopolies are the rule rather than the exception, the press and other media (both specialized and popular) are often dependant on advertising commercial products and do not profit from reviewing the sophisticated software existing in the public domain (after all, public domain does not pay for advertising, as we said).

All these considerations notwithstanding, there are many elements that indicate changes in the software market towards public domain venues in general, and in particular, of Unix solutions and hence Linux.

• The increased importance of networks (both local area and global), sets Unix systems (which continue to be the network servers of choice) as the operating system standard. In this field, Linux has an increasingly relevant place due to its unique features

• Several 'plug-and-play' Linux distribution packages are available which simplify installation and maintenance. As with the rest of applications, these packages are available for free on the Net or (since they are often quite big) they can be purchased on CD-ROM

• The NeXTStep operating system, created by NeXT system programmers for the now defunct cube was entirely based on (Unix-like)public domain systems and tools.

• Apple Computer has initiated a turnaround, adopting the NeXTStep system and producing the new-generation PowerMac system (named Mac OS X), which is supposed to be completely `open source' [6]

• The few non-public domain segments of the NeXTStep interface (the display postscript in particular) are being rewritten from scratch and in the public domain under the name of GNUStep [7].

---

5 This problem is rapidly disappearing; since 1998 several important and competitive office automation packages have appeared

6 It must be noted that in the past, because of its aggressive and sectarian attitude, Apple was always boycotted by developers of public domain software — so the change is particularly noteworthy

7 The GNU prefix (a recursive acronym which stands for GNU's Not Unix) is used in all public domain produced by FSF (Free Software Foundation), the first and larger coalition of programmers dedicated to free software production

• Other than FSF, there is a proliferation of other initiatives devoted to the creation of public domain computer tools and in particular to the 'open-source' replication by reverse-engineering of commercial tools considered useful (as for example the Hungry Programmers which are replicating the Motif interface and the Word word-processor, Cygnus has built an interface layer with GNU development tools on Windows95/NT, DJ Delorie has ported all GNU development tools on MsDOS/Windows platforms, etc.)

Thus, the idea of a future freed from commercial impositions by software monopolies is not so remote. That public domain, or at least the free distribution on the Net, produces enormous leverage in commercial terms. (Take as an example Netscape Navigator, which became 'open source' in 1998).

3 USAGE

Csound is very similar on all platforms. At the command line it is sufficient to type

```
bash$ csound [options] <file.orc> <file.sco>
```

where bash$ is a possible prompt of a Linux shell. Csound will parse the options, then the orchestra and score files, and finally produce a sound file in the current directory or in a directory specified in the SFDIR environment variable (similarly, sound files opened for reading will be searched in the current directory first then the path contained in the SSDIR — if set — then by the path contained in the SADIR variable, while searching the analysis files in the current directory, then the path contained in the SADIR environment variable).

When an X Windows server is running and no -d option is set, Csound opens a graphical window for internal tables, plus a window for each display instruction in each instrument. When the -i devaudio and/or the -o devaudio options are set (the hardware input and the hardware output respectively) Csound inputs and outputs the data in real time as advertised in the official documentation (but this is not always true for all platforms and all hardware audio cards). Everything else works on Linux exactly as it does in other Csound implementations.

4 TOOLS AND UTILITIES

Linux features many tools and utilities that can prove to be very useful in many situations.

4.1 Specific tools

There are some tools that are considered to be specific audio and CSound tools, among which:

1. *Cecilia* and *Cybil*
2. *Midi2cs*
3. *Mup*
4. *DAP*, *snd* and *MixViews*

• ***Cecilia* and *Cybil*** Written in tcl/tk by Jean Piché and Alexandre Burton at the University of Montreal, *Cecilia* and *Cybil* are two public-domain graphics utilities for assisting composition using Csound.

Cecilia is an orchestra and score manager that allows one to write these in a single editor window and to simplify writing all operations with efficient conventions (color-coded opcodes, tables, centralized management of global parameters, etc.). One very important addition of *Cecilia* is the inline contextual help on all aspects of Csound which is frequently updated with subsequent versions.

Cybil is a Csound score preprocessor that tries to reduce the complexity of writing scores for Csound-generated sound events. It is a full-fledged little language which allows composers to create sophisticated and complex scores with minimal indications.

Cecilia and *Cybil* may run on all platforms that support the tcl language with tk (graphic) extensions.

• ***midi2cs*** *midi2cs* is a MIDI file to Csound score file converter that runs on many different platforms (DOS/Windows95, SunOS, NeXTStep etc.) and, the Linux version does not differ from the other ones.

Converting MIDI files into Csound score files is easier said than done. In fact, *midi2cs* goes a long way to address all problems connected to a primitive protocol like MIDI and is able to produce a musically appropriate output in most cases.

• ***mup*** *mup* stands for Music Publishing and is a shareware application devoted to musical score printing and available on several Unix platforms (among which Linux) and on DOS/Windows 95. This is a work in progress and there are still some obvious missing features, but the output quality is already quite good and, most importantly, the source code is available allowing collaboration on this important project.

Some details of interest of mup:

1. The score data is solely text (in pure ASCII). Thus it can be incorporated (through the use of the generic tools discussed below) with texts from various sources (for ex. Csound scores that generate *mup* files or vice-versa)

2. The output is in Postscript file format and is therefore completely device independent [8]

3. *mup* produces MIDI files directly. Hence it can, by using the *midi2cs* application, produce Csound scores in an efficient way

Even though these functions do not take full the advantages of the versatility of Csound (using it, in practice, as a dumb sequencer) they are very useful in creating `musical drafts' and rapid prototypes.

• ***DAP*, *snd* and *MixViews*** *DAP*, designed by Richard Kent, *snd* written by Bill Schottstaedt at Stanford University's CCRMA and *MixViews*, created by Douglas Scott, are three public domain graphic sound editing programs which run on Linux and X Windows among other Unix platforms.

As with many other applications for Linux, these programs are still considered 'works in progress' even though they have already proved to be very useful, working tools.

4.2 Generic Tools

All of these tools may be found, in various different forms on all computer platforms.

The real winning feature of all Unix systems, however, is the practically infinite cornucopia of tools for in-line processing of ASCII characters and text (commonly called text filters).

These are extremely useful for the preparation of Csound scores because they allow, as we shall see, one to reduce the complexity of writing scores.

Furthermore, being completely generic these tools cannot (and do not) impose a 'compositional vision' or 'aesthetics' as with most CAC (Computer Assisted Composition) packages. The composer may now work with her/his tools of choice and modeled them according to her/his personal musical needs. And if a given tool does not adapt well to these needs, she/he will always find one that will satisfy the requirements in a better way.

Finally, instead of large integrated applications — which are generally slow, huge, hard to master and always missing something anyway — the composer deals with a toolbox of small and fast instruments whose scope is simple and well-defined. These can be combined in series in an infinite number ways through the pipe mechanism (a well-

[8] The public-domain application Ghostscript allows the conversion of a postscript file into hardware commands for most printers and output devices.

known Unix universal tool which allow to take the output of an application and redirect it to the input of another program, and so on).

It is hard if not impossible to produce an exhaustive list of all such tools. We will choose just a few of them as examples, dividing them in the following categories:

1. text filters
2. data processors
3. interpreters
4. miscellaneous

It is interesting to note how these instruments, created for Unix systems, have been adopted (more or less officially) on most platforms. Currently, public domain implementations exist for these tools running on most operating systems.

• **Text filters** Another pervasive feature on Unix systems is regular pattern matching. Regular expressions are an extension of the meta-character concept (for example, the so-called jolly characters as the '*' or the question mark '?' characters), and they constitute a powerful mechanism to defined simple and/or sophisticated collections (classes) of characters. As an example, the regular expression string [A-Za-z_][A-Za-z0-9_]* uses 4 meta-characters ([, -,] and *) and means "all strings with at least one character, which can be any alphabetic character or the character '_', followed by zero or more characters which may be: any alphanumeric character or the character '_'". This regular expression corresponds to the collection of characters allowed to define a symbolic variable in the C language. Applied in a search command it may be able to find all valid symbolic variables in a C source text. This is only an example and a very simple one, too, just to give an idea of the power of regular expressions.

Most text filters are built on the regular expression mechanism, and they may be subdivided as follows:

1. simple tools: for ex., regular expression search engines (pattern matchers) as the *grep* family of commands, up to the in-line editor sed which allows to process automatically a given text

2. composite tools: as *awk* and its successor *perl*, two full-fledged interpreters that allow us to generate specific actions when matching given regular expressions and/or logical expressions based upon combinations of regular expressions. *awk*'s syntax is very close to the C language and handles only pure ASCII texts (no special characters), while *perl* handles a mixture of C, Basic and *awk*. It possesses all characteristics of a

system language (pointers, hash tables which may work as data structures, etc.), a large group of core system calls and an ever-growing set of libraries which allow it to connect to any network, manage device drivers, etc.

• **Data Processors** Another typology of programs concerns the generation, the analysis and the visualization of data sets. With these tools it is possible to create and/or visualize tables based on many common mathematical functions and on experimental formulas. Among these, *gnuplot* allows 2D and 3D visualization in many formats, while *octave* (which is by all means a public domain replacement for *Matlab*) is dedicated to vector computation and to all numeric applications known today. Given its compatibility with *Matlab*, *octave* may use most of function libraries written for *Matlab*.

Among their other uses, it is possible to verify the functionality of Csound algorithms in conjunction with the dumpk algorithm family, analyzing thus the control variable curves, etc. with these instruments.

• **Interpreters** There is more to interpreters than just awk and perl, of course. Linux is the ideal platform for software development and you will be able to find public domain implementations of 99 % of programming languages currently in use.

It is interesting for musicians to consider the several flavors of the lisp and the prolog languages, object-oriented languages like *Eiffel* and dedicated musical variants like *Common Music* and *Nyquist* with functions and libraries particularly suited to music composition.

These languages extend indefinitely the approaches and potential combination (with text filtering) of methods for well-defined musical creation and manipulation (as well as some 'ill-defined' ones...) - spanning from inferential expert systems to intelligent systems to Csound scores.

Another type of languages and interpreters are the shells, that is the command line managers. Far from being simple interfaces to the system, there are a wide variety of shells on Unix systems including (the already-mentioned) bash and *tcl* (pronounced ti-kl as in tickle) which is a dynamically extensible shell. The biggest extension of tcl is the *tk* library which is a graphical extension that together with the X Windows system allows *tcl* to become a full-fledged graphics interpreter (competitive with Visual Basic, etc.) while still maintaining all its standard shell features (job control, pipes, stream re-direction, etc.) Shells allow the creation of complex sequences of commands. These may be executed either by interactive, user action or in parallel with other activities (batch jobs).

• **Miscellaneous** Besides tools there is myriad of multimedia tools for format conversion, CD-R and CD-ROM mastering, recording/playback using the standard Linux device drivers, etc.

As an example, we will mention another UNIX utility which has been ported to most platforms. It is used for revision of source files. It is the *RCS* package (which stands for Revision Control System) and it allows one to maintain a unique administration file for all versions of each source file. Thus it is possible to create different versions or releases, insert automatic version identifiers, recover old versions, analyze differences, etc. This package may be very useful in the administration of Csound source files whose syntax and conceptual idiosyncrasies often lead to difficult debugging sessions which can span several versions of the same file.

5 INTERNET REFERENCES FOR CSOUND AND LINUX

Csound sources and, where specified, Linux binaries may be found in the following sites:

http://mitpress.mit.edu/e-books/csound/frontpage.html
• This is the official site of the version 2 of Csound (the so-called 'american' version); while this is the original address, this site contains versions which may now be considered 'old', while

ftp://ftp.maths.bath.ac.uk/pub/dream/
• This site holds the latest versions (also known as the 'english' versions), ported on most current operating systems (in particular, the newest sub-directory holds the most recent source and binaries)

ftp://musart.dist.unige.it/CSOUND
• This is a site kindly hosted by AIMI (Italian Computer Music Association) to hold and maintain unofficial versions of Csound optimized for Linux (furthermore, in a sub-directory named 'win95' the site hosts Gabriel Maldonadoís version of Csound called DirectCsound, specially optimized for real-time processing under Windows9x)

• the unofficial Linux versions are also available via `anonymous CVS' (a form of distributed source control which allows to access the latest software enhancements of a given package, and that is very widespread in the Linux world); the instructions to access the repository can be read at
http://aimi.infomus.dist.unige.it/AIMICSOUND/AIMICSOUND_home.html

• last but not least, the Quasimodo project, developed by Paul Barton-Davis, is worth mentioning; Quasimodo seeks to use Csound opcodes and modules to build an application that simulates a modular synthesizer; its orchestra definition is backward-compatible with Csound orchestras; the project is very rapidly evolving and to learn more about it we suggest to connect to Paul Barton-Davis' site
http://www.op.net/~pbd/quasimodo/

The Linux operating system and its applications are everywhere on the Internet. The main sites are:
www.sunsite.unc.edu
and
www.tsx-11.mit.edu

On these sites (and on their mirrors) it is possible to download all recent versions of the operating systems, all applications, tools, etc. Also, all versions of the LDP (Linux Documentation Project) may be downloaded there — the LDP is an independent project and provides valuable sources of information on just about anything concerning Linux.

Dave Phillips site
http://www.bright.net/~dlphilp/index.html
contains references and pointers to all musical Linux applications and their availability: as such, its importance is invaluable to Linux music users. It is also well maintained and kept up to date, so the information contained is reliable (and often unexpected, as there are so many projects for Multimedia Linux that keeping track of all of them is a daunting task).

(Translated from the Italian by the author)

GENERATING AND MODIFYING SCORES WITH GENERAL PURPOSE PROGRAMMING LANGUAGES

by Riccardo Bianchini

1. CHOOSING A PROGRAMMING LANGUAGE

If we want to generate or modify a Csound score by means of a general purpose programming language, we first have to choose a particular language to use. More robust and less robust languages exist; easy to learn languages, and languages that require a long time of study and practicing; languages which exist in all platforms, and languages specific to a single platform.

Interesting results can be achieved by using Artificial Intelligence languages (LISP, Prolog etc.), as these allow to define generating rules in a form that is close to human language.

We shall use, instead, BASIC, as it is easy to learn and is available on a large variety of computers and operating systems. The particular dialect we shall use is Microsoft Visual Basic.

2. WHAT SHELL WE NEED?

A programming language such as Visual Basic has a very large set of instructions and keywords. But we shall use only a little subset of these: the ones which deal with reading from and writing into a text file, the output format capability, some control structures (FOR... NEXT, WHILE... WEND and DO... LOOP WHILE), mathematical and logical expressions.

We shall launch Visual Basic, and in the Form/Load section we shall write the code. This event will occur when our application starts. As we shall not interact directly with thc application, this is all wc nccd.

3. LET'S WRITE A SCALE

Our first program simply generates a chromatic scale. Let's see it:

```
Private Sub Form_Load()                   `this is provided by Visual Basic itself
Act   =  0                                `zeroing the variable which will contain action time
Dur   =  1                                `assigning the value 1 to duration
Amp   =  80                               `assigning the value 80 to amplitude
Open "score1.sco" For Output As #1        `open a file for writing, file id = 1
```

```
For i = 0 To 11                                         `For...Next loop beginning
        Pitch = 8 + i / 100                             `assign the pitch depending of the number of the note (i)
        Print #1, "i1 "; Act; " "; Dur; " "; Amp; " "; Pitch   `write into the file
        Act = Act + Dur                                 `update the action time
Next i                                                  `For...Next loop end
Close #1                                                `close the file
End Sub                                                 `this is provided by Visual Basic itself
```

This little program will generate a score file named «score1.sco», the content of which will be:

```
i1   0    1   80   8
i1   1    1   80   8.01
i1   2    1   80   8.02
i1   3    1   80   8.03
i1   4    1   80   8.04
i1   5    1   80   8.05
i1   6    1   80   8.06
i1   7    1   80   8.07
i1   8    1   80   8.08
i1   9    1   80   8.09
i1   10   1   80   8.1
i1   11   1   80   8.11
```

Can we do better? Sure we can! Writing into the file, we separated each p-field with a blank space. Let's try separating the p-fields with tabs (in Basic, chr$(9)):

```
Private Sub Form_Load()                                 `this is provided by Visual Basic itself
Act   =  0                                              `zeroing the variable which will contain action time
Dur   =  1                                              `assigning the value 1 to duration
Amp   =  80                                             `assigning the value 80 to amplitude
Open "score1.sco" For Output As #1                      `open a file for writing, file id = 1
For i = 0 To 11                                         `For...Next loop beginning
        Pitch = 8 + i / 100                             `assign the pitch depending of the number of the note (i)
        Print #1, "i1 "; Act; chr$(9); Dur; chr$(9); Amp; chr$(9); Pitch   `write into the file
        Act = Act + Dur                                 `update the action time
Next i                                                  `For...Next loop end
Close #1                                                `close the file
End Sub                                                 `this is provided by Visual Basic itself
```

Our score will be much better looking:

```
i1	0	1	80	8
i1	1	1	80	8.01
i1	2	1	80	8.02
i1	3	1	80	8.03
i1	4	1	80	8.04
i1	5	1	80	8.05
i1	6	1	80	8.06
i1	7	1	80	8.07
i1	8	1	80	8.08
i1	9	1	80	8.09
i1	10	1	80	8.01
i1	11	1	80	8.11
```

What if we want a chromatic scale with an accelerando? And what if the amplitude of each note decreases by 2 dB? Let's rewrite our program for this:

```
Private Sub Form_Load()                              `this is provided by Visual Basic itself
Act   =  0                                           `zeroing the variable which will contain action time
Dur   =  1                                           `assigning the value 1 to duration
Amp   =  80                                          `assigning the value 80 to amplitude
Open "score1.sco" For Output As #1                   `open a file for writing, file id = 1
For i = 0 To 11                                      `For...Next loop beginning
        Pitch = 8 + i / 100                          `assign the pitch depending of the number of the note (i)
        Print #1, "i1 "; Act; chr$(9); Dur; chr$(9); Amp; chr$(9); Pitch   `write into the file
        Act = Act + Dur                              `update the action time
        Dur = Dur * 0.9                              `for each new note, let's diminish the duration
        Amp = Amp - 0.2                              `for each new note, let's diminish the amplitude
Next i                                               `For...Next loop end
Close #1                                             `close the file
End Sub                                              `this is provided by Visual Basic itself
```

The generated score will be:

```
i1	0	1	80	8	i1	1	0.9	79.8	8.01
i1	1.9	0.81	79.6	8.02
i1	2.71	0.729	79.4	8.03
i1	3.439	0.6561	79.2	8.04
```

i1	4.0951	0.59049	79	8.05
i1	4.68559	0.531441	78.8	8.06
i1	5.217031	0.4782969	78.6	8.07
i1	5.6953279	0.43046721	78.4	8.08
i1	6.12579511	0.387420489	78.2	8.09
i1	6.513215599	0.3486784401	78	8.1
i1	6.8618940391	0.31381059609	77.8	8.11

What did we do? Simply, we did not tell Visual Basic to format the output properly, in such a way as to limit the number of decimal digits. Let's correct our program once more:

```
Private Sub Form_Load()                                   `this is provided by Visual Basic itself
Act    =   0                                              `zeroing the variable which will contain action time
Dur    =   1                                              `assigning the value 1 to duration
Amp    =   80                                             `assigning the value 80 to amplitude
Open "score1.sco" For Output As #1                        `open a file for writing, file id = 1
For i = 0 To 11                                           `For...Next loop beginning
        Pitch = 8 + i / 100                               `assign the pitch depending of the number of the note (i)
        Print #1, "i1 "; Format(Act,»##0.###»); chr$(9); Format(Dur,»###.###»); chr$(9); Format(Amp,»###.#»); chr$(9);
Format(Pitch,»###.##») `write into the file
        Act = Act + Dur                                   `update the action time
        Dur = Dur * 0.9                                   `for each new note, let's diminish the duration
        Amp = Amp - 0.2                                   `for each new note, let's diminish the amplitude
Next i                                                    `For...Next loop end
Close #1                                                  `close the file
End Sub                                                   `this is provided by Visual Basic itself
```

which will generate this score:

i1	0	1	80.	8.
i1	1	.9	79.8	8.01
i1	1.9	.81	79.6	8.02
i1	2.71	.729	79.4	8.03
i1	3.439	.656	79.2	8.04
i1	4.095	.59	79.	8.05
i1	4.686	.531	78.8	8.06
i1	5.217	.478	78.6	8.07
i1	5.695	.43	78.4	8.08

```
i1     6.126  .387    78.2    8.09
i1     6.513  .349    78.     8.1
i1     6.862  .314    77.8    8.11
```

4. LET'S COMPOSE A PIECE

What does *algorithmic composition* mean? Basically, it means the invention of a set of rules, and the composition of music which is generated by following these rules.

If rules are expressed in a language that the computer can «understand» (i.e. a *program*), the program can compose the piece by itself.

Let's begin with a random piece. Visual Basic function *Rnd* generate a pseudo-random number in the range 0 ... 1. We shall use this function to determine the action time, the duration, the amplitude and the pitch of each note in our piece, limiting the random generation between some minimum and some maximum.

If in Visual Basic we write

x = Rnd

the variable x can assume any value between 0 and 1. Then we could write:

x = 8 + Rnd * 0.11

and the variable x can assume any value between 8 and 8.11, as 8 is a fixed part, to which a random number between 0 * 0.11 and 1 * 0.11 is added.

We can now write the program:

```
Private Sub Form_Load()                          `this is provided by Visual Basic itself
Open "c:\score1.sco" For Output As #1
Act    =  0                                      `zeroing the variable which will contain action time
For i = 1 To 20                                  `For...Next loop beginning
        Dur = 0.1 + Rnd * 0.4                    `generate a random duration between 0.1 and 0.5
        Amp = 60 + Rnd * 30                      `generate a random amplitude between 60 and 90
        Pitch = 8 + Rnd * 0.11                   `generate a random pitch between 8 and 8.11
        Print #1, "i1 "; Format(Act, "##0.###"); Chr$(9); Format(Dur, "###.###"); Chr$(9); Format(Amp, "###.#"); Chr$(9);
Format(Pitch, "###.##") 'write into the file
        Act = Act + Dur                          'update the action time
Next i
Close 1
End Sub
```

And we shall obtain the following score:

```
i1    0.     .382   76.    8.06
i1    0.382  .216   69.1   8.09
i1    0.598  .106   82.8   8.09
i1    0.704  .384   61.4   8.05
i1    1.087  .445   83.7   8.04
i1    1.532  .485   86.1   8.01
i1    2.017  .48    70.9   8.06
i1    2.497  .407   61.6   8.07
i1    2.904  .287   68.9   8.07
i1    3.191  .359   67.9   8.03
i1    3.55   .432   84.7   8.06
i1    3.982  .494   87.3   8.02
i1    4.477  .378   89.4   8.03
i1    4.855  .314   63.2   8.11
i1    5.168  .37    60.5   8.06
i1    5.539  .14    63.1   8.09
i1    5.679  .214   61.4   8.03
i1    5.893  .253   69.    8.1
i1    6.145  .492   72.    8.03
i1    6.637  .164   64.9   8.07
```

Let's add a function table definition, e.g. a sine wave, and run Csound with a simple orchestra

```
sr              =    44100
kr              =    4410
ksmps           =    10
nchnls          =    1
        instr   1
ifrq            =    cpspch(p5)
iamp            =    ampdb(p4)
kenv    linseg  0, .01, iamp, p3-.01, 0
a1      oscil   kenv, ifrq, 1
        out     a1
        endin
```

and we can listen to a simple piece, in a style that could be defined «cagean».

A simple modification to the program will produce a polyphonic score. We can omit the line in which the program updates the action time, and have the computer generate a random action time:

```
Private Sub Form_Load()                              `this is provided by Visual Basic itself
Open "c:\score1.sco" For Output As #1
Act     =  0                                         `zeroing the variable which will contain action time
For i = 1 To 20                                      `For...Next loop beginning
        Act = Rnd * 20                               `generate a random action time between 0 and 20 secs
        Dur = 0.1 + Rnd * 0.4                        `generate a random duration between 0.1 and 0.5
        Amp = 60 + Rnd * 30                          `generate a random amplitude between 60 and 90
        Pitch = 8 + Rnd * 0.11                       `generate a random pitch between 8 and 8.11
        Print #1, "i1 "; Format(Act, "##0.###"); Chr$(9); Format(Dur, "###.###"); Chr$(9); Format(Amp, "###.#"); Chr$(9);
Format(Pitch, "###.##") 'write into the file
Next i
Close 1
End Sub
```

5. LET'S MODIFY AN EXISTING SCORE

A slightly more complex task is to modify an existing score, as we have to read it from a file, distinguish between the p-fields, modify it according to some rule, and finally write a new file.

If the required modification are local to each single note, (i.e. they do not depend on preceding or proceeding notes), we can read a note at a time, modify it and write it down into a new file. If this is not the case, we shall read the whole score, store all the p-fields in a multi-dimensional array, modify the notes and write them into the new file.

Suppose we want to alter all the amplitudes of a piece stored in the file ′score1.sco[a], reducing them by 20%, and to write a new file called «score2.sco»;

```
Private Sub Form_Load()                              `this is provided by Visual Basic itself
Open "c:\score1.sco" For Input As #1                 `open source file for reading, file id = 1
Open "c:\score2.sco" For Output As #2                `open destination file for writing, file id = 2
While not Eof(1)
        Input #1, a$                                 `read «i1» and discard it
        Input #1, Act                                `read the action time
        Input #1, Dur                                `read the duration
        Input #1, Amp                                `read the amplitude
        Input #1, Pitch                              `read the pitch
```

```
        Amp = Amp * 0.8                                 `reduce the amplitude by 20%
Print #2, "i1 "; Format(Act, "##0.###"); Chr$(9); Format(Dur, "###.###"); Chr$(9); Format(Amp, "###.#"); Chr$(9);_
Format(Pitch, "###.##") 'write into the new file
Wend
Close 1
Close 2
End Sub
```

(Translated from the Italian by the author)

DYAD CONTROLLED ADDITIVE SYNTHESIS

by James Dashow

The rather dramatic increase in computational power of the newest CPUs for personal computers breathes new life into additive synthesis as a practical means for the generation of complex time-varying electronic sounds. To be effective, additive synthesis will often require a large number of oscillators, or in more advanced languages, the use of a multiple oscillator unit that does the work of internally summing several oscillators via an optimized loop structure.

There still remains the problem of controlling each oscillator with its own amplitude envelope and frequency variance, requiring that the composer prepare and manipulate a large amount of data: separate amplitude, pitch and function tables, if desired, for each oscillator.

The composer can, of course, design a high level score data routine that automatically adjusts these parameters based on global input variables; the group of oscillators and associated amplitude envelopes can be considered as a single unit with a small amount of data as input which is elaborated by the score routine into all the specific information necessary for the additive synthesis instrument to execute as desired. Even then, the composer will have to specify the individual frequency components in some way, and while additive synthesis offers what amounts to infinite variety of frequency combinations, this very infinity can prove an obstacle for sustained compositional use.

The method suggested here considers several oscillators as a single unit while the frequency of each oscillator is determined by the application of mathematical procedures that produce a set of results (here interpreted as frequency components) as a function of a very small number of variables (no more than 5, often less). There is, in this approach, no separate amplitude control over the individual components, only an amplitude re-scaling of the final output sum of the several oscillators. That is, one of the constraints of this concept is to accept equal amplitudes (numerically equal, not necessarily perceived as equally loud) of the separate frequencies as a characteristic of the generated sound, in the same way we accept the constraints of the partial amplitudes that make up the sound of the oboe or the flute as being simply those instrumentsí characteristic timbre. It will become clear that this particular limitation hardly puts us at any disadvantage with respect to the variety of sound obtainable from this method. Nevertheless, an adventurous user can easily apply separate amplitude controls to each oscillator, or group the oscillators into frequency zones (by filtering or by programmed logic) and apply amplitude envelopes to those zones rather than to each oscillator.

One standard use of additive synthesis is to declare certain frequencies, or even a single frequency, along with others that might have particular relationships (elaborated under program control) to the principle frequencies; these derived frequencies would be the timbral context for the principle frequencies. Further timbral manipulation can be achieved varying the function table(s) being used for the various oscillators making up the spectrum as a whole. The composer could conceivably design combinations of frequencies, harmonic and, especially, inharmonic, in order to characterize specific musical intervals, such that each interval has its set of characteristic timbres. Musical development of this notion would be through the mutual exchanging, sharing or excluding of timbral components while various combinations of intervals are being played.

The approach suggested here is based on dyads, specific intervals (in this case the intervals of the Western chromatic scale) that are made to generate sets of frequencies, often inharmonically related to each other, as the result of algorithmic procedures. The dyads, or intervals, needn't be limited to the chromatic scale, of course, but since the resultant frequency collections are generally inharmonic, it is hardly necessary to think in terms of intervals outside the well-tempered system. The advantage in this case is that the sounds have at least two frequencies, the dyad, that can in one way or another be picked up timbrally by live traditional instruments. Needless to say, any interval, Western-chromatic or non, can be used as input to the algorithms described below.

The composer chooses or invents an algorithm that will generate a set of frequencies. The equations of the algorithm are re-arranged so that it is the interval, or what will be called also the «generating dyad», that determines the way the algorithm generates the frequency components. The interval itself determines the frequency content produced by algorithm execution, and hence it is the interval that determines its own timbre. The two frequencies of the dyad are always present as two of the components of the generated frequency set. As we shall see, for any generating dyad there are a variety of frequency sets available (depending also on the type of algorithm), such that we can get many different groups of frequencies generated by the same dyad; and since the frequencies of the dyad are always two of the components we have a method not only for generating varieties of timbres, but also for structurally relating timbres by means of frequencies in common, the generating dyad itself. Using the same generating dyad with different algorithms yields a wide variety of electronic sounds all of which have at least the generating dyad in common among their frequency components.

This represents a very useful reduction of data that the composer has to worry about. Once the sound synthesis process has been programmed with the algorithm, the composer interfaces with the additive synthesis in terms of musical information rather than numeric: the generating dyad (as a musical interval or as a pair of pitches) and the necessary subsidiary «orchestrational» data: where in the spectrum the generating dyad is to be produced (register) and the timbral quality as influenced by no more than two additional factors (the function table and/or a timbral factor for the algorithm). The composer does not need to know all the frequencies generated by the procedure, on the contrary, at this point what counts is the varieties of sound, of timbre, that a generating dyad can be made to produce: work for the ears.

The first and easiest of these algorithms to implement is a set of frequencies generated by the following equation:

f(N) = f(0)+N*A [1] for N = 1,2,3....

This reads: the Nth frequency f(N) is generated by a starting frequency f(0) plus N times some factor A. If the starting frequency f(0) = 100 and A = 75, then

frequency 0 f(0) = 100 + 0 * 75 = 100 (the starting hz) frequency 1 f(1) = 100 + 1 * 75 = 175 frequency 2 f(2) = 100 + 2 * 75 = 250 frequency 3 f(3) = 100 + 3 * 75 = 325 etc.

Note the intervallic relationships between the frequency components. Between the starting frequency f(0) and f(1) the interval is 175/100 = 1.75; between f(2) and f(1), the interval is 250/175 = 1.4286; between f(3) and f(2), 325/250 = 1.3; the intervals get smaller the higher the N. This algorithm generates frequencies with equal differences between components which means the intervals will always get smaller the higher the N. This is, of course, the same frequency relationship for the upper sidebands of FM synthesis. Here, however, there is no algorithmic dependent time-varying dynamic change of the amplitudes or phases of the components as with FM, except what the composer wishes to add with the appropriate envelope controls. And these controls can be freely designed and manipulated, again, in contrast to the fixed necessary evolution of sidebands with FM.

To use the generating dyad idea, we say: let any two of the frequencies generated by equation (1) be the two frequencies of the dyad. For example, lets use an interval of an octave and a minor third, which has a ratio of 2.3784; if the f(0) is 100 Hz, the component an octave and a minor third above it is 237.84 Hz. We can have then the octave and a minor third as component f(2) or as f(3) or as f(4) or any. Let's put it on f(2). Then since we know the frequency for f(0) (100) and for f(2) (237.84), we get:

f(0) = 100 = 100 + 0 * A
f(1) = ? = 100 + 1 * A
f(2) = 237.84 = 100 + 2 * A

and we can calculate the A factor from the expression for f(2):

A = (237.84 - 100) / 2
= 68.92

Now we can generate a set of frequencies f(N) = 100 + N * 68.92 that will yield 100 as f(0) and 237.84 as f(2):

f(0) = 100 = 100 + 0 * 68.92 f(1) = 168.92 = 100 + 1 * 68.92 f(2) = 237.84 = 100 + 2 * 68.92 f(3) = 306.76 = 100 + 3 * 68.92 etc.

We can do the same thing if 100 Hz is f(0) and 237.84 is f(5):

f(5) = 237.84 = 100 + 5 * A
A = (237.84 - 100) / 5 = 27.568

And the frequency set f(N) with the generating dyad at position 0 and 5 (f(0) and f(5)) in the spectrum is produced by applying general equation (1) with A and f(0) set appropriately,

f(N) = 100 + N * 27.568.

This will get us a different set of frequencies but with the 100 and 237.84 components in common. A different timbre is produced but maintains a continuity between them, that of the common generating dyad.

Note, however, that the way we calculated A was by dividing the difference between the two frequencies of the generating dyad by the difference between their position numbers. So we can generalize by writing that the A factor is:

A = (UP - LP) / (NU - NL) [2]

where UP (or Upper Pitch) and LP (Lower Pitch) are the frequencies of the two members of the generating dyad, and NU (Upper component Number) and NL (Lower component Number) are the positions of the dyad (their «register» in more musical terms) in the frequency set, or spectrum.

In these two examples, we've always called for the LP, the bottom pitch of the dyad, to be generated as f(0), the starting frequency of the spectrum. This not need be the case. We can just as easily call for LP = 100 Hz on f(1) and UP = 237.84 Hz on f(3). In that case we get:

f(0) = f(0) + 0 * A
f(1) = 100 = f(0) + 1 * A
f(2) = ? = f(0) + 2 * A
f(3) = 237.84 = f(0) + 3 * A

Now we have two unknown quantities in the f(3) expression, but with a little algebra we can eliminate one of them: subtract

f(3) - f(1) = (f(0) + 3 * A) - (f(0) + A)
f(3) - f(1) = 2*A

since f(3) and f(1) are the generating dyad frequencies,

237.84-100 = 2*A

A = 68.92

and to find f(0), we can go back to f(1):

f(1) = 100 = f(0) + 68.92
f(0) = 100 - 68.92 = 31.08

So the frequency set f(N) for the generating dyad at positions 1 and 3 will be

f(N) = 31.08 + N * 68.92,

and the general expression for f(0) is then

f(0) = LP - NL*A,   [3]

or, the beginning Hz of the frequency set is the lower pitch of the generating dyad minus it's position number times the constant difference factor between frequencies in the set. If NL is 0, then f(0) = NL, as we saw in the first examples.

So for any dyad, any interval, any pair of frequencies, equations [2] and [3] provide values for A and for f(0), which are then plugged into repeated uses of equation [1] to generate a set of frequencies f(N) that will have the dyad at the declared positions in the spectrum. Changing the position of the dyad frequencies changes the f(0) and A values and thereby changes the timbre. But the dyad is always there. You can play as many other frequencies above and sometimes below the generating dyad members as you like depending on the desired timbre. If the generating dyad is on components 3 and 7, for example, then you might decide to play frequencies f(2) through f(8) or f(0) through f(11), depending on the sound quality required for the musical context.

Additional timbral variety is obtained by using complex wave tables for the oscillators. This method accepts the constraint that all oscillators playing use the same wave table; the sum of oscillators is considered a unit instrument here, to keep the score data within more practical dimensions. Again, the composer can specify a different wave table for each oscillator, and together with time-varying amplitude control or the re-generation of the wave table during performance, achieve a high degree of transformational control over the timbral evolution.

In this instance, we not only can generate a wave table with different harmonic partials starting with the first partial, say the sum of the first 4 odd partials (using gen10: 1,0,0.333,0,0.2,0,0.167), we can also generate an arbitrary set of partials that have inharmonic relationships between themselves, for example using gen09: 6 1 0 11 0.3 0 19 0.15 0. Here the wave table contains the 6th, 11th and 19th partial (with diminishing amplitudes) whose ratios 11/6, 19/6 and 19/11 are not those of the equal tempered scale.

To use this wave table in the additive synthesis instrument, the composer decides which of the 3 partials will actually play the frequency assigned to each oscillator, and then divide that frequency by the chosen partial number. The other two partials will play that frequency (the f(N) divided by the chosen partial number) at the ratios between the partials generating inharmonic frequency relationships >for each frequency f(N) in the additive synthesis set<. If we call for 5 frequencies, f(0) through f(4), and play each frequency with the wave table containing the partials 6^{t},11 and 19, then the additive synthesis sound will be consist of 15 frequencies, not just five, with complex inharmonic and harmonic relationships between them. Timbral variety is assured.

In the first example above, if we decide to play all each frequency in each oscillator on the 6th partial, the lowest in this wave table, we can adjust the f(N) set of frequencies by dividing each one by 6, or f(N) = f(N)/6. But to save computation time, it's more efficient to divide the generating dyad's frequencies by 6 (the chosen partial number) before beginning the f(N) calculations. We can also play the f(N) frequencies on the 11th or the 19th partial (perhaps adjusting the amplitude of the latter a bit) as well, dividing the generating dyad frequencies by 11 or 19; this will produce frequencies below the f(N) frequency (the frequency generated on the 6th partial will be 6/11 lower than that generated by the 11th partial (etc.) which can yield some very rich and musically useful timbres. Designing various wave tables for a single dyad and a single algorithmic realization yields a rich variety of timbres all generated around the same two frequencies, the generating dyad.

We can make a small Csound instrument out of this equation with the following code; here the maximum size is 6 oscillators, but you can easily expand this.

```
sr      =  44100
kr      =  44100  ;<- note sr=kr!!!!
ksmps  =  1
nchnls  =  1
```

```
        instr    1
; p4     = amplitude, in absolute values
; p11    = overall re-scale after reducing
;   amplitude by number of oscillators playing
; p11 is in the range 1.3 to 1.6
; p5     = UP, p6 = LP, p7 = NU, p8 = NL, p9 = partial number, p10 = wave table number
        iup     =   cpspch(p5)/p9
        ilp     =   cpspch(p6)/p9
        iafac   =   (iup-ilp)/(p7-p8)
        if0     =   ilp - iafac*p8
        inf     =   p10;
; p11 = highest oscil num;  p12 = lowest oscil num;  1 thru 6 here
        inum    =   p11 - p12 + 1
; now rescale the amplitude by the number of oscils playing
        iamp    =   p4 * inum * p11
; now calculate the components for num Hz as init, and play in perf
        kcount      init inum    ; p-time always reset
        atotsig =   0            ; audio variable that accumulates the sum of oscili outs for
                                 ; each sample
        if  p11 == 0  goto   x0
        if  p11 == 1  goto   x1
        if  p11 == 2  goto   x2
        if  p11 == 3  goto   x3
        if  p11 == 4  goto   x4
x5:
; this is the algorithm, equation (1) with specific
;  values for the f(5), the sixth Hz component
        if5     =   if0 + 5*iafac
        asig5       oscili   1, if5, inf, iphs
        atotsig =   asig5;
;   FIRST entry point doesn't need counter as there are always at least 2
;     oscili's playing
x4:
        if4     =   if0 + 4*iafac     ; this is the algorithm (1) generating f(4)
        asig4       oscili   1, if4, inf
        atotsig =   atotsig + asig4
        kcount  =   kcount - 1
        if  kcount == 0  goto xend
x3:
```

```
        if3     =  if0 + 3*iafac    ; etc.
        asig3      oscili   1, if3, inf
        atotsig =  atotsig + asig3
        kcount  =  kcount - 1
        if   kcount == 0  goto xend
x2:
        if2     =  if0 + 2*iafac
        asig2      oscili   1, if2, inf
        atotsig =  atotsig + asig2
        kcount  =  kcount - 1
        if   kcount == 0  goto xend
x1:
        if1     =  if0 + iafac
        asig1      oscili   1, if1, inf
        atotsig =  atotsig + asig1
        kcount  =  kcount - 1
        if   kcount == 0  goto xend
x0:
        asig0      oscili  1, if0, inf
        atotsig =  atotsig + asig0
xend:
;  here you can rescale the atotsig and control it with an amplitude envelope.
        atotsig =  atotsig * iamp   ; etc.
        out        atotsig
        endin
```

Perhaps with a score like this, using an interval of an octave and a minor seventh. Note the differences in timbre between f1 and f2:

```
f1   0   4096   9    6    1    0    11   1   0   19   1   0
f2   0   4096   9    7    1    0    11   1   0   18   1   0\
         26     10

;1   2   3      4    5      6     7    8    9      10    11     12
;ins act dur    amp  up     lp    nu   nl   parts  fno   hiosc  loosc
i1   0   5      100  10.00  8.02  4    1    6      1     6      1
i1   +   5      100  10.00  8.02  4    1    7      2     6      1
```

Since this algorithm can be expressed also in the form

$f(N) = f(N-1) + A$ [1b]

you can program the Csound instrument in a somewhat more computationally efficient fashion avoiding the multiply for each f(N).

You can also use small frequency values, like 1.1 Hz, to get interesting phasing and chorus effects. You must always divide by the partial number being used in the wave table, even with these small Hz values.

Or, you can use *linseg* or a data table to control a succession of intervals based on the same LP; the variables f1, f2, f3, f4 etc. would be controlled by the *linseg* output in k-time or re-initialized (*reinit*) with new values for each interval read off a data table. Other variants can easily be invented.

A closely related algorithm is one which produces frequencies that are equal proportions away from each other, not equal distances, or

$f(N) = f(0) * M^N$ [4a]

which can also be written in the form

$f(N) = f(N-1) * M,$ [4b]

where M is a constant multiply factor.

Using form [4b] in the instrument avoids having to do an exponential operation for each f(N) calculation, not an efficient procedure by any means.

This equation is the prototype for the equal-tempered scale, or for that matter, any scale whatsoever. For the Western chromatic scale, the keys on the piano are tuned according to

$f(N) = f(0) * 1.0594631^N$

or $f(N) = f(N-1) * 1.0594631$

the multiply factor M is simply the 12th root of 2, the semitone. If we use the generating dyad approach we are in effect generating «scales» that have inharmonic intervals as «scale steps». The procedure is substitute the known values for the generating dyad, UP and LP, along with their (composer chosen) position, NU and NL, in the f(N) collection, or spectrum, do a little algebra and derive expressions, as before, for the f(0) and M values that are plugged into equation [4b] which is programmed into the Csound instrument.

UP = f(0) * M^NU
LP = f(0) * M^NL

now we eliminate the f(0) variable by dividing

UP/LP = M^NU/M^NL = M^(NU-NL)

and solve for M (ln is the natural logarithm, to the base e):

M = exp(ln(UP/LP) / (NU-NL)). [5]

Then we can find

f(0) = LP/M*NL [6]

In the Csound instrument above, where we've written Afac and f(0), equations [2] and [3], substitute

```
imfac = exp(log(iup/ilp))/(p7-p8))
if0 = ilp/(imfac^p8)
```

and change every reference to *iafac* in the program to *imfac.*

Finally where the algorithm [3] is written specifically for each f(N) in the instrument, substitute [4a] - or substitute [4b] for [1b] if you've worked that version out -

```
if5 = if0 * pow(imfac^5)
```

etc.

There are many many more algorithms that can be explored. For example, try an adaptation of the «partial stretching» algorithm suggested by Steve MacAdams. The equation for the harmonic partial series is

f(N) = f(0) * N.

MacAdams developed the notion of stretching the partials by writing the equation as

f(N) = f(0) * N^S [7]

where S is the «stretch factor». Setting S to various values will generate a group of frequencies whose relationships quickly become inharmonic, producing some interesting timbres, especially if each f(N) is played by a complex wave table.

The relevant generating dyad equations are worked out as follows:

UP = f(0) * NU^S
LP = f(0) * NL^S

UP/LP = NU^S / NL^S = (NU/NL)^S

S = ln(UP/LP) / ln(NU/NL) [8]

and then f(0) = LP / NL^S. [9]

Again, in the Csound instrument, you substitute [8] and [9] for [2] and [3], and in the body of the instrument substitute the appropriate form of [7] for [1b], the calculation of the algorithm for each specific frequency.

You can work with more than one extra variable; one series of algorithms use a multiply, add procedure as the basis, another series uses add, multiply as the basis. These algorithms have both a Multiply and an Add factor, which requires the composer to specify not only the generating dyad and the position of the dyad frequencies in the sound, but either an Add factor, and the algorithm finds the Multiply factor, or the reverse - the Multiply factor and the algorithm finds the Add factor.

The simplest Multiply, Add algorithm is

f(N) = f(0)*M^N + N*A [10]

while the simplest Add, Multiply is

f(N) = M^N * (f(0) + N*A) [11]

Now there are two generating dyad equations for [10] and for [11], depending on whether the composer supplies the M factor or the A factor. Equation [11] can be solved for «given A, find M» mode only if the lowest pitch of the dyad, LP, is also the f(0), the bottom frequency of the spectrum. Note that in almost all of these cases, where you might specify the Lower Pitch, LP and the Upper Pitch, UP, of the generating dyad at positions 1 through whatever, where 1 is the lowest frequency in the spectrum, you must refer to the bottom position as 0 in order for the mathematics to work properly, that is, you should subtract 1 from the given NU and NL values (unless you are already working with 0 through N-1 to indicate 1 through N).

For (10): given M (the multiply factor) find A (the Add factor), the dyad equations for the Csound instrument are («mx» is a temporary work variable):

```
mx   =    M^(NU-NL)

A = ( UP - (mx*LP) ) / ( NU - (mx * NL) )
```

or given A find M mode, algorithm (10) equations are:

```
mx = log( ( UP - (A * NU) ) / ( LP - (A * NL) ) )

M = exp( mx / (NU - NL) )
```

and in both modes solve for f(0):

```
f0 = LP;
if (NL != 0.0) {
      div = pow(M,NL);
      f0 = (LP - (A * NL) )/ div;
        }
```

For (11): given M find A mode, the equations are (again it is useful to use couple of extra work variables, uxpn and lxpn):

```
uxpn = M^NU
lxpn = M^NL
A = ( (UP / uxpn) - (LP / lxpn) ) / (NU - NL);
```

in given A, find M mode, the equations can be resolved only with LP being declared the f(0) frequency, NL = 0 for these equations:

```
mx = log( UP / ( LP + (A * NU) ) );
M =  exp(mx/NU);
```

and in both modes you solve for f(0):

```
f0 = LP;
```

```
if (NL != 0.0)  /* true only for given M find A mode */
f0 = (LP / lxpn) - (A * NL);
```

As a final specific example, another equation for a frequency set generator has proved extremely flexible:

f(N) = M * f(N-1)^2 / f(N-2)   [12]

This reads: the current frequency N in the spectrum is the product of some multiplier, or scalar factor, M times the preceding frequency in the set squared divided by the next-to-last frequency in the set. If M = 1, the ratio between the first and second frequencies, f(0) and f(1) determines the ratio between all succeeding frequencies. If that ratio is 1.0594631, we get the standard chromatic scale, for example.

If M is less than 1 then the ratios between frequencies get progressively smaller by exactly that value M for each frequency in the set, or a contracting interval series. If M is greater than 1, however, the reverse happens and we get an expanding interval series, which is quite unusual, and very useful for creating different kinds of timbre. In fact, even with M > 1, if the NU and NL are in the middle of a spectrum, say 5 and 3, respectively, it is easy to generate a frequency set whose lower f(N) frequencies have intervals that compact going toward the LP of the generating dyad and which then expand going beyond the UP of the generating dyad. In short, the M factor determines the character of the interval pattern in a way that offers the composer greater control over the evolution of the frequency set than in many other algorithms.

The program is a little more involved, as the first two frequencies, f(1) and f(2), of the set have to be derived from the generating dyad and the M factor. Note in this case we don't use f(0), or NL = 0, rather the lowest frequency in the set is N = 1.

```
mx = NU - NL;
lxpn = mx - 1.0;
if (lxpn == 0.0)
flp1 = UP;  /* in Csound, use if  go construct */
else {
expM = pow(M, (mx*lxpn*0.5));
lpxp = pow(LP, lxpn);

/* flp1 is the f(NL+1) */
flp1 = pow( (lpxp*UP/expM), (1.0/mx) );
      }
/* now find the first two frequencies in the spectrum set, f1 and f2  */
```

```
if ( NL == 1.0) {  /* if true, then LP is the bottom hz f1 */ f1 = LP; f2 = flp1;
        }
else  {
/* cycle through down progressively lower Hz until you get to f1
where each next f(L-1) = M * LP^2/flp1 */
MmU = LP;   /* initialize another auxiliary variable */ f2 = flp1;
for ( j = NL-1; j > 0; j—) {
f1 = M*MmU*MmU/f2;
f2 = MmU;
MmU = f1;
}  /* end of for loop */
}  /* end of else */
```

When you get here you have values for f1 and f2 which are the first two frequencies f(1) and f(2) in the spectrum; you then calculate f(3) on up to as many as desired using equation (12), the first few times would look like this:

```
f(3) = M * f(2)^2/f(1);
f(4) = M * f(3)^2/f(2);
f(5) = M * f(4)^2/f(3);    etc.
```

if the generating dyad frequencies were declared at NU = 5 and NL = 3, you would produce them as f(3) and f(5), above.

Other versions of Multiply, Add and Add, Multiply suggest themselves. In working out the generating dyad usage for these algorithms, I found that many have a wide range of possibilities, while others are more «temperamental» working better with certain intervals in specific frequency ranges and conditions (close NU and NL positions, or very wide NU NL positions, very small M factors, or very large Add factors, etc.).

In the generating dyad mode, some of these equations do not have solutions for «given Add, find Multiply», while others, like [11] above, have solutions for «given Add, find Multiply» only if f(0) is LP, i.e. the starting pitch is also the low pitch of the generating dyad, effectively eliminating one of the variables. These are marked in the list below.

It has also been found extremely useful to write a separate C program, independent of Csound, that displays on screen the f(N) results of any configuration of any of these algorithms. It helps to see where an f(0) frequency is a sub-audio value, say .003 Hz (but the algorithm produces interesting frequencies in the f(2) through f(7) range), or where some of the generated values are in the hundreds of thousands. For this reason the

Csound instrument parameters p11 and p12 allow you to avoid some of the frequency values that are useless, often the first ones or last ones in the array of values.

A compiled c-routine and its source code (inhntrvl.c inhntrvl.exe inhnmenu.man), that does exactly as described for PC can be downloaded from the writer's web site. The routine contains the generating dyad equations for these algorithms which can be easily adapted to the prototype Csound instrument illustrated above.

MULTIPLY then ADD

f(N) = f(N-1)*M^N + A*N -> ONLY in given M find A mode;
(the add and multiply version, f(N) = f(N-1)*(M^N + A*N),
yields virtually identical spectra)

f(N) = f(0)*N^M + A*N -> Stretch Factor, no restrictions;
these next two work correctly ONLY with NL > 1 and xx & yy > 0;
xx & yy can be fractions
f(N) = f(0)*M^N + A*X -> X = N+xx/N+yy

f(N) = f(0)*M^N + A*N^X -> X = N+xx/N+yy

f(N) = f(0)*M^N + A*N^M -> ONLY in given M find A mode;

ADD then MULTIPLY

for the next two, in «given A find M» mode, NL can ONLY be 1 (i.e. f(0) is LP). to avoid overflow errors, your init routines should default NL to 1 automatically in this mode. There are no restrictions for «given M find A» mode.

f(N) = M^N*(f(0) + A*N)
f(N) = N^M*(f(0) + A*N) -> Stretch Factor proc
f(N) = f(0)*(M + A*N) -> all OK, but watch the range of M & A for small LP and large NU, A can become negative and generate useless frequency values.
f(N) = f(N-1)*(M + A*N) often generates a set of expanding intervals going up..

the above is limited to NU = NL + 1 ALWAYS, i.e. 2 and 3, 4 and 5, 5 and 6. using A find M gets huge Hz values; use VERY small A and small intervals. also very effective with smallish M (1.1 to 1.8 range). Small intervals in the gen dyad work very well here also.

f(N) = M^N*(f(0) + A*N^M) -> ONLY in given M find A mode

these work correctly ONLY with NL > 1 and xx & yy > 0,

xx and yy can be fractions. can be used only in «given M find A» mode.
f(N) = M^N*(f(0) + A*N^X) -> X = N+xx/N+yy
f(N) = M^N*(f(0) + A*X)   -> X = N+xx/N+yy
f(N) = M^N*(f(0) + A^X)   -> X = N+xx/N+yy
f(N) = N^M*(f(0) + A^X)   -> X = N+xx/N+yy

There are many others.

SOUND SYNTHESIS BY ITERATED NONLINEAR FUNCTIONS

by Agostino Di Scipio

1. INTRODUCTION

The iteration of nonlinear functions is part of the branch of mathematics called "chaos theory". In 1991, I set out to investigate the possibility of using it in the field of digital sound synthesis. It was soon clear that the approach was to open up a world of unique sounds of its own, many with turbulent and noisy components (aperiodicity), and some with more familiar harmonic sound spectra (periodicity).

This present overview is a survey of iterated function synthesis based on Csound examples that the reader can analyze and modify for him/herself (readers willing to go into the theoretical and mathematical details are referred to the references). If you try to extend the examples provided here, it will be evident that even slight changes in the synthesis parameters give rise to dramatic differences in the sound, such that often the audible result can hardly be foreseen at the outset. Which suggests that the best way to deal with iterated nonlinear functions is with a kind of empirical, explorative and open-ended attitude. Indeed, the sound synthesis approach described here is a "non-standard" approach. It is not grounded on any model of scientifically proven and verified acoustical relevance.

Rather, it represents a somewhat arbitrary, procedural model which is properly understood as an interesting way of creating sequences of numbers such that, by sending these numbers to a digital-to-analog converter, sounds may eventually emerge having properties that are useful for music and sound-design.

2. GENERAL DESCRIPTION

To iterate a function is to apply some transformation, f, to a datum, $x(0)$, and to apply the transformation again to the first resulting value, and then again to the second resulting value, ... and so on, n times again:

$$\mathbf{x(n) = f\,(x(n-1))}$$

We call $x(n)$ the nth "iterate" obtained by applying f to $x(0)$. If f is nonlinear (e.g. a sine, a line broken in several segments, or any high-order polynomial) the process will determine different sequences of results. The particular sequence is dependent on the initial datum, $x(0)$ and on the parameters of the function f. In most cases, it is impossible to predict the output series of values.

To translate this general procedure into a digital sound synthesis method, we can follow these steps:

a - initialize *x(0)* and *f'* parameters
b - take the *n*th iterate, *x(n)*, and save it as the current digital sample
c - update *x(0)* and *f'* parameters
d - repeat b and c as many times as the samples required.

In other words, the output stream of samples is the series of the *n*th iterations of *f* upon changing values in *x(0)* and *f*. If we call *i* the sample order index (discrete time index), the synthesis technique can be represented as a simple recursive formula:

x(n,i) = f(i) (x(n-1,i))

This model framework represents a class of synthesis techniques rather than a single technique. The aspect that is peculiar to all particular cases in the class is the fact that the stream of samples is calculated as the sequence of the *n*th iterations of some function. To implement a particular technique, we must select a particular nonlinear function and run a given number of iterations.

As an example, think of the technique known as *waveshaping* (often called *nonlinear distortion* in Europe). It involves the transformation of an input signal by a waveshaping function (usually a Chebychev polynomial, but can be a sine wave or something else). If the operation is repeated, feeding the output sample back into the waveshaper, we get a special case of iterated function synthesis.

Obviously, every nonlinear function determines a peculiar process of its own. However, in the literature on theory of deterministic chaos, many have stressed that the numerical sequences obtained with iterated functions are more heavily dependent on the iteration itself, rather than on the function. It is the iteration that allows coherent or chaotic patterns to emerge, not the nonlinear function being iterated.

3. IMPLEMENTATION

The Csound examples illustrated below illustrate the following iteration:

x(n) = sin (r*x(n-1))

i.e. the mapping of the sine function onto itself in the interval [-1,1]. The parameters in play include: *r* (or *control* parameter) and *x(0)* (initial datum). As a general rule, the control parameter ranges from 0 to 4, but as a matter of fact only values between 3.14

and 4 are of practical relevance for us (smaller values cause the process to move towards a "fixed-point attractor", yielding a straight line as a result). The initial datum can be assigned any value from the interval [-1,1] (but in theory it can be any real number).

What is the effect of the parameters? The control parameter, r, determines the overall timbral quality in the output sound. On the other hand, *x(0)* determines the particular series of output sample values, and is somewhat akin to the seed of a random numbers generator. Indeed, you can think of this synthesis process as a generator of "structured noise" that we can control in its internal process. The achievable results, anyway, are far more varied and rich than the results obtained with white noise generators (such as Csound's *rand* and *randh* opcodes).

To create some sound, either *x(0)* or *r* (or both) have to move across their value range. This can be done by driving them with an envelope generator or with an oscillator. By varying *x(0)* during the note and keeping *r* fixed, we obtain several sounds (several different output signals) of very similar timbral properties. The reverse is also true. By varying *r* and keeping *x(0)* constant, we obtain different sounds starting from identical initial data. By varying both *r* and *x(0)*, we obtain sounds with highly dynamic properties.

Another crucial parameter is the particular number of iterations utilized as the digital sample. In general, the higher is the iterate order, *n*, and the more chaotic and turbulent the output sound. Too high a number of iterations would generate something very close to white noise, but internally articulated and not as static. Too low a number of iterations would probably generate some silence.

Now, what would be a good way of changing *r* and/or *x(0)* in time? If we use ramps, i.e. series of linearly increasing or decreasing values, we obtain acoustical turbulences, sometime having a wind-like, or even water-like quality to the ear. If you look at the waveform of such sounds, you will notice phase- or frequency-modulation effects, which are sometimes heard as distinct gestures separated by silent pauses (the pauses are chunks of direct current signal, with either a positive or negative offset). That happens especially when a small number of iterations are used, and when *r* is close to 3.14. These strange rumbles are like the "natural state" of the mathematical model. By simply ramping either *r* or *x(0)*, we are "visiting" the whole field of possibilities implicit to the iterated function. Some of the Csound examples below, *Ex1.sco* through *Ex6.sco* (all to play with the *IFS1.orc* orchestra), illustrate this basic behavior. They show the dependency of the results on the two parameters. They also show that the timbral characteristics in the output sound are dependent on the note duration as well. Different durations imply differently quantized iterated processes, and therefore a different resultant bandwidth.

The remaining examples, *Ex7.sco* through *Ex10.sco*, illustrate the possibility of controlling *x(0)* by means of oscillating signals. This approach forces the overall process towards more regular, periodic patterns, either in the infra-audible (rhythm) or the audible (frequency) range. These examples may eventually reveal that *r* can be considered a bit like the modulation index of FM synthesis. Indeed, in theory it would be possible to explain "feedback FM" (the output of the modulation is fed back into the system to modulate itself) as a kind of iterated nonlinear function synthesis.

The *IFS1.orc* orchestra includes three instruments, each representing a different implementation (see comments in the orchestra code). It should be used in conjunction with scores *Ex1.sco* through *Ex8.sco*. The *IFS2* orchestra introduces some slight modifications in instr 2 (mathematical details), and should be used in conjunction with the last two score examples, *Ex9.sco* and *Ex10.sco*.

```
; IFS1.orc
; sound synthesis by functional iterations
; sin(r*x) [sine map]
;
; the basic technique is instr 3
; instr 1 and 2 offer more refined controls:
; by exploiting the deterministic aspect of the process
; they also introduce some periodicity in the signal
;
;-----------------------------------------------------------
        sr      =   22050
        kr      =   22050
        ksmps   =   1
        nchnls  =   2

; why sr = kr?
; Everything happens at audio rate (something even at "superaudio" rate, i.e. sr*p7).
; However, some opcodes can only work at control rate (e.g. the program control
; statements and value converters).

        instr 1

; p4 = initial value for the control parameter (r)
; p5 = final value for the control parameter (r)
; p6 = initial value for x(0)
; p7 = iterate number
; p8 = stereo location (0,1)
; p9 = increment step for x(0)
```

```
; p10 = global amplitude

ar        init   p4                     ; initialize control parameter
irstp     init   (p5-p4)/(sr*p3)        ; initialize increment step for control parameter
ixstp     init   p9                     ; initialize increment step for x(0)
asam      init   0                      ; initialize output sample variable
kcnt      init   0                      ; initialize counter
ax        init   frac(p6)               ; initialize the initial datum, x(0)
kaxnew    init   frac(p6)               ; temporary storage variable

label:
kcnt   =   kcnt+1                       ; update counter
ax     =   sin(ar*ax)                   ; iteration x=sin(rx)

      if kcnt < p7 kgoto label ; iterate loop

asam   =        ax                      ; sample is the p7-th iterate
kcnt   =        0                       ; reset counter
ar     =        ar + irstp              ; increment control parameter
kaxnew =        frac(kaxnew+ixstp)      ; update x(0), must be a k-variable, due to frac
ax     =        kaxnew                  ; reset the initial datum, x(0)

asig   =        p10*asam                ; amplitude scaling
asig   linen  asig, .05, p3, .05        ; fade in, fade out, to avoid clicks
       outs   asig*p8, asig*(1-p8)      ; stereo panning

       endin

       instr 2

; same pfields as above

ar        init   p4                     ; initialize control parameter
irstp     init   (p5-p4)/(sr*p3)        ; initialize increment step for control parameter
asam      init   0                      ; initialize output sample variable
kcnt      init   0                      ; initialize counter

aph       oscili 1,p9,1                 ; oscili determines the initial datum for next iteration
ax        =      (p6*2)*((aph+1)/2)     ; update initial datum, x(0)
```

```
label:
kcnt     =      kcnt+1                    ; increment counter
ax       =      sin(ar*ax)                ; iteration x=sin(rx)

if kcnt < p7 kgoto label                  ; iterate loop

asam     =      ax                        ; sample is the p7-th iterate
kcnt     =      0                         ; reset counter
ar       =      ar + irstp                ; increment control parameter

asig     =      p10*asam                  ; amplitude scaling
asig     linen  asig, .05, p3, .05        ; fade in, fade out, to avoid clicks
         outs   asig*p8, asig*(1-p8)      ; stereo panning

         endin

         instr 3

; same pfields as above, but p9 void

ar       init   p4                        ; initialize control parameter
irstp    init   (p5-p4)/(sr*p3)           ; initialize increment step for control parameter
ixstp    init   (1-p6)/(sr*p3)            ; initialize increment step for x(0)
asam     init   0                         ; initialize output sample variable
kcnt     init   0                         ; initialize counter
ax       init   p6                        ; initialize initi value
axnew    init   p6                        ; temporary storage variable

label:
kcnt     =      kcnt+1                    ; increment counter
ax       =      sin(ar*ax)                ; iteration x=sin(rx)

    if kcnt < p7 kgoto label ; iterate loop

asam     =      ax                        ; sample is the p7-th iterate
kcnt     =      0                         ; reset counter
ar       =      ar + irstp                ; increment control parameter
axnew    =      axnew+ixstp
ax       =      axnew
```

```
asig    =       p10*asam                        ; amplitude scaling
asig    linen   asig, .05, p3, .05              ; fade in, fade out, to avoid clicks
        outs    asig*p8, asig*(1-p8)            ; stereo panning

        endin

; SCORES FOR IFS1.ORC
;
;  p4 = initial value for the control parameter (r)
;  p5 = final value for the control parameter (r)
;  p6 = initial value for x(0)
;  p7 = iterate number
;  p8 = stereo location (0,1)
;  p9 = increment step for x(0)
;  p10 = global amplitude
;
; EX1.SCO
; dependency of the output signal on the initial datum x(0)
; other parameters being constant (dur, r, iter)
;
;   start dur   rstart  rend    x(0)    iter    stereo  xstep   ampl
i1 0     1      4       3.9     .1      10      .5      0       30000
i1 2     1      4       3.9     .11     10      .5      0       30000
i1 4     1      4       3.9     .2      10      .5      0       30000
i1 6     1      4       3.9     .3      10      .5      0       30000
i1 8     1      4       3.9     .4      10      .5      0       30000
i1 10    1      4       3.9     .6      10      .5      0       30000
i1 12    1      4       3.9     .8      10      .5      0       30000
i1 14    1      4       3.9     .9      10      .5      0       30000
s
; EX2.SCO
; two simultaneous processes start from nearly identical initial data
; and diverge in time
;
;   start dur   rstart  rend    x(0)    iter    stereo  xstep   ampl
i1 0     10     4       3       .3      10      0       0       30000
i1 0     10     4       3       .305    10      1       0       30000
s
; EX3.SCO
```

```
; dependency of the bandwidth on r
; all other parameters being constant (dur, x, iter)
;
; start dur   rstart  rend  x(0)  iter  stereo xstep  ampl
i3 0    1     2.5     2.5   .3    10    .5     0      30000
i3 2    1     2.6     2.6   .3    10    .5     0      30000
i3 4    1     2.7     2.7   .3    10    .5     0      30000
i3 6    1     2.8     2.8   .3    10    .5     0      30000
i3 8    1     2.9     2.9   .3    10    .5     0      30000
i3 10   1     3.0     3.0   .3    10    .5     0      30000
i3 12   1     3.1     3.1   .3    10    .5     0      30000
i3 14   1     3.2     3,2   .3    10    .5     0      30000
i3 16   1     3.3     3,3   .3    10    .5     0      30000
i3 18   1     3.4     3.4   .3    10    .5     0      30000
i3 20   1     3.5     3.5   .3    10    .5     0      30000
i3 22   1     3.6     3.6   .3    10    .5     0      30000
i3 24   1     3.7     3.7   .3    10    .5     0      30000
i3 26   1     3.8     3.8   .3    10    .5     0      30000
i3 28   1     3.9     3.9   .3    10    .5     0      30000
i3 30   1     4.0     4.0   .3    10    .5     0      30000
s
; EX4.SCO
; same as EX3.SCO, but with different x(0)
;
; start dur   rstart  rend  x(0)  iter  stereo xstep  ampl
i3 0    1     2.5     2.5   .1    10    .5     0      30000
i3 2    1     2.6     .     .     .     .      .      30000
i3 4    1     2.7     .     .     .     .      .      30000
i3 6    1     2.8     .     .     .     .      .      30000
i3 8    1     2.9     .     .     .     .      .      30000
i3 10   1     3.0     .     .     .     .      .      30000
i3 12   1     3.1     .     .     .     .      .      30000
i3 14   1     3.2     .     .     .     .      .      30000
i3 16   1     3.3     .     .     .     .      .      30000
i3 18   1     3.4     .     .     .     .      .      30000
i3 20   1     3.5     .     .     .     .      .      30000
i3 22   1     3.6     .     .     .     .      .      30000
i3 24   1     3.7     .     .     .     .      .      30000
i3 26   1     3.7     .     .     .     .      .      30000
```

```
i3 28   1    3.9    .     .     .     .     .     30000
i3 30   1    4.0    .     .     .     .     .     30000
s
; EX5.SCO
; dependency of the bandwidth on duration
; (i.e. on the number of samples off the control parameter interval)
;
;  start dur  rstart rend  x(0)  iter  stereo xstep ampl
i3 0    1    3.5    3     .1    10    .5     0     30000
i3 2    2    3.5    3     .1    10    .5     0     30000
i3 5    3    3.5    3     .1    10    .5     0     30000
i3 9    4    3.5    3     .1    10    .5     0     30000
i3 14   5    3.5    3     .1    10    .5     0     30000
i3 20   6    3.5    3     .1    10    .5     0     30000
i3 27   7    3.5    3     .1    10    .5     0     30000
i3 35   8    3.5    3     .1    10    .5     0     30000
s
; EX6.SCO
; dependency of the output signal on the number of iterates
; all other parameters being constant
;
;  start dur  rstart rend  x(0)  iter  stereo xstep ampl
i3 0    1    3.5    3     .1    12    .5     0     30000
i3 2    1    3.5    3     .1    11    .5     0     30000
i3 4    1    3.5    3     .1    10    .5     0     30000
i3 6    1    3.5    3     .1    9     .5     0     30000
i3 8    1    3.5    3     .1    8     .5     0     30000
i3 10   1    3.5    3     .1    7     .5     0     30000
i3 12   1    3.5    3     .1    6     .5     0     30000
i3 14   1    3.5    3     .1    5     .5     0     30000
i3 16   1    3.5    3     .1    4     .5     0     30000
s
; EX7.SCO
; periodicity introduced by cycling x(0) with a sine wave
;
f 1 0 512 10 1
;
; with constant r
```

```
; start dur   rstart rend x(0) iter stereo xfreq ampl
i2 0    4     3.2    3.2  .1   6    .5     2     30000
i2 +    .     3.2    3.2  .1   6    .5     4     30000
i2 +    .     3.2    3.2  .1   6    .5     8     30000
i. +    .     .      .    .    .    .      16    30000
i0 16 2
s
; with decreasing r (spectrum goes from complex to simple)
i2 0    1     3.2    1    .1   6    .5     32    30000
i. +    .     .      .    .    .    .      64    .
i. +    .     .      .    .    .    .      128   .
i. +    .     .      .    .    .    .      256   .
i. +    .     .      .    .    .    .      512   .
s
i2 0    .25   3.2    1    .1   6    .5     755   30000
i. +    .     .      .    .    .    .      713   .
i. +    .     .      .    .    .    .      663   .
i. +    .     .      .    .    .    .      626   .
i. +    .     .      .    .    .    .      591   .
i. +    .     .      .    .    .    .      558   .
i. +    .     .      .    .    .    .      527   .
i. +    .     .      .    .    .    .      498   .
i. +    .     .      .    .    .    .      470   .
i. +    .     .      .    .    .    .      444   .
i. +    .     .      .    .    .    .      419   .
i. +    .     .      .    .    .    .      400   .
s
; EX8.SCO
; compare the periodicity achieved by instr 1
; with that achieved by instr 2
;
f 1 0 512 10 1
;
i1 0    10    3.2    2    .1   8    .2     .0008   30000
i1 0    10    3.2    2    .21  8    .8     .000803 30000
i2 10   10    3.2    2    .1   8    .2     20      30000
i2 10   10    3.2    2    .21  8    .8     20.01   30000
e
*****************************************************
```

```
; IFS2.orc
; synthesis of sound by functional iterations
; sine map [x=sin(rx)]
;
        sr      =  22050
        kr      =  22050
        ksmps   =  1
        nchnls  =  2

        instr 2

; modification of IFS1's instr2
; to study optimal variations in x(0) [-3.14,+3.14], not [-1,1]

asam    init    0
kcnt    init    0
ifrq    init    1/p3

kar     oscili  p4-p5, ifrq, p12, 0         ; envelope for the control parameter
kar     =       kar + p5
ampx    line    p11, p3, p6                 ; envelope for x(0)
aph     oscili  ampx, p9, 1, 0              ; cycling of x(0)
ax      =       (aph+1)/2                   ; update x(0)

label:
kcnt    =       kcnt+1                      ; increment counter
ax      =       sin(kar*ax)                 ; iteration

        if kcnt < p7 kgoto label    ; iterate loop

asam    =       ax                          ; sample
kcnt    =       0                           ; reset counter

asig    =       p10*asam                    ; amp scaling
asig    linen   asig, .05, p3, .05          ; fade in fade out

        outs asig*p8, asig*(1-p8)

        endin
```

```
; SCORES FOR IFS2.ORC
;
; p4 = initial value for the control parameter (r)
; p5 = final value for the control parameter (r)
; p6 = max value for x(0)
; p7 = iterate number
; p8 = stereo location (0,1)
; p9 = increment step for x(0)
; p10 = global amplitude
; p11 = min value for x(0)
; p12 = table function envelope for the control parameter(r)
;
; EX9.SCO
; dynamical control over x(0) (values between p11 and p6)
; envelope on r values
;
f   1   0   2048   10   1
f   2   0   2048   5    .01   250   1   1900   .001
;
; varying x(0), fixed r
;
;                       xstart          xend
i2  0   3   3   3   0   5   .5  50  30000   .2  2
i2  +   .   3   3   0   5   .5  50  30000   .4  2
i2  +   .   3   3   0   5   .5  50  30000   .6  2
i2  +   .   3   3   0   5   .5  50  30000   .8  2
i2  +   .   3   3   0   5   .5  50  30000   1   2
s
;
; fixed x(0), varying r
;
i2  0   3   3   2   .3  5   .5  50  30000   .3  2
i2  +   .   3.2 2   .3  5   .5  50  30000   .3  2
i2  +   .   3.4 2   .3  5   .5  50  30000   .3  2
i2  +   .   3.6 2   .3  5   .5  50  30000   .3  2
i2  +   .   3.8 2   .3  5   .5  50  30000   .3  2
s
; EX10.SCO
; similar with EX9.SCO
```

```
;
i2  0    2   3     3  0   5   .19  50    10000   .2   2
i2  1    .   3     3  0   5   .95  51    10000   .21  2
i2  1.1  .   3     3  0   5   .25  50.1  10000   .23  2
i2  1.9  .   3     3  0   5   .75  50    10000   .38  2
i2  2.1  .   3     3  0   5   .15  49.3  10000   .4   2
i2  3    .   3     3  0   5   .85  50.1  10000   .46  2
i2  3.2  .   3     3  0   5   .15  50    10000   .48  2
i2  4    .   3     3  0   5   .95  49.3  10000   .56  2
s
i2  0    2   3     2  .2  5   .45  50    10000   .2   2
i2  1    .   3.2   2  .2  5   .55  50    10000   .2   2
i2  1.1  .   3.24  2  .2  5   .15  50    10000   .2   2
i2  1.8  .   3.3   2  .2  5   .85  50    10000   .2   2
i2  3.1  .   3.4   2  .2  5   .35  50    10000   .2   2
i2  3.4  .   3.6   2  .2  5   .65  50    10000   .2   2
i2  4    .   3.68  2  .2  5   .55  50    10000   .2   2
i2  4.9  .   3.75  2  .2  5   .45  50    10000   .2   2
e
```

BIBLIOGRAPHICAL REFERENCES

A. Di Scipio "Caos deterministico, composizione e sintesi del suono", *Proc. of the 9th Colloquium on Musical Informatics*, AIMI/DIST, Genova, 1991

A.Di Scipio & I.Prignano "Functional iteration synthesis. A revitalization of non-standard synthesis", *Journal of New Music Research*, vol.25, 1996

I.Prignano "Sintesi di eventi sonori complessi per mezzo di Iterazioni Funzionali", *Proc. of the 11th Colloquium on Musical Informatics*, AIMI/DAMS, Bologna, 1995

(Translated from the Italian by the author)

GSC4: A CSOUND PROGRAM FOR GRANULAR SYNTHESIS

by Eugenio Giordani

1. Introduction

The notion of a Granular Synthesis Csound patch was initially stimulated by the work of Barry Truax. During the Italian seminar, Musica/Complessità, held in the summer 1988, he presented material concerning his research and musical compositions based on real-time granular synthesis. One of the most didactically inexpensive yet powerful synthesis software packages available at the time was Csound. So, I decided to challenge the Music-N dualism of orchestra and score that is the typical feature of this type of programming language, try to write a simple program for this complex sound synthesis.

Since Granular Synthesis creates many acoustic events (grains) per unit of time, it is not a practical to generate each grain using one note score statements. My goal was to realize an automated process for grain generation processed at the micro-level while preserving control over the synthesis process and overall parameters, as well.

The recent releases of Csound, now include the granulation process (see the opcodes *grain* and *granule*) but at the time this patch was written, no granulation unit was available in the Csound opcodes. The goal of this lecture is to serve as a practical exercise for implementation of a complete sound synthesis algorithm in this language - from the conception of an idea to a working program.

2. General structure of the algorithm and synthesis parameters description

Using GSC4 is possible to generate four independent stereo streams of sonic grains. The number four derives from the demand of minimum vertical grain density and real-time capabilities of personal computers.

According to this scheme, the *orchestra* set up includes four grain generation instruments plus one instrument for the control and one instrument for sound mix and scale:

instr 1, 2, 3, 4	:	grain generators instruments
instr 11	:	control instrument
instr 21	:	sound mix, out and scale instrument

In order to generate a complex sound event, we need to switch on six instruments at the same start time (p2) with the same duration (p3).

The majority of the parameters (up to p13) are utilized by the control instrument, whereas the others instruments each contains only four parameters (p1 to p4).

Control of the granulation process is determined by control functions that describe the evolution in time of the synthesis parameters. Those parameters refer to instrument 11 and are:

1)	center grains duration in ms	p4
2)	random grains duration in ms	p5
3)	center inter-grain delay in ms	p6
4)	random inter-grain delay in ms	p7
5)	grain envelope ramp scale factor in non-dimensional units	p8
6)	center waveform-file frequency in Hz	p9
7)	random waveform-file frequency in Hz	p10
8)	center waveform-file phase or file pointer (normalized)	p11
9)	random waveform-file phase or file pointer (normalized)	p12
10)	overall amplitude (normalized)	p13

Each of these parameters states the function number assigned for the relative parameter. So, during the instrument activation, ten functions (created by some GENi method) must exist inside the score. Referring to the score file included in the Appendix, we can summarize the meaning of those synthesis parameters:

f11 :
the average (center) grains duration is defined by a linear function (GEN 7) with initial value of 10 ms that after 256/512 of p3 (the total event duration) reaches the value of 20 ms, keeps costant for 128/512 and moves to the final value of 16 ms after 128/512 of p3.

f12:
the peak random duration value of the grains is defined by a linear function (GEN 7) with initial value of 4 ms that after 256/512 of p3 reduces itself to 1 ms and after 256/512 goes to the final value of 0 ms (no random deviation).

f13:
the inter-grain delay is defined by a linear function (GEN 7) with initial value of 10 ms that after 256/512 of p3 raises to 20 ms and after 256/512 reaches the final value of 5 ms.

f14:
the peak random inter-grain delay value of the grains is defined by a linear function (GEN 7) with initial value of 0 ms (no random deviation) that after 128/512 of p3 stays constant to 0 ms; after 256/512 raises to the value of 2 ms and after 128/512 reaches the final value of 0 ms (no random deviation).

f15:
grain envelope ramp scale factor is defined by a linear function (GEN 7) with initial value of 2 that after 256/512 of p3 rises to 4 and after 256/512 reaches the final value of 2. Practically, the grain envelope shape change gradually from a triangle at the beginning towards a trapezium and back to triangle. When the envelope shape looks like a triangle, the duration of both the attack and decay ramp is equal to half duration of the whole envelope (no sustain). When the envelope shape looks like a trapezium, the duration of both the attack and decay ramp is equal to one quarter of the whole envelope, so the sustain duration is equal to two quarter of the whole envelope.

f16:
the frequency of the granulated waveform is defined by a linear function (GEN 7) with initial value of 220 Hz that stays constant during the whole event. Ins the score there is a comment line referring to the values of control frequency (from 1.345 to 3.345 Hz) in the case of a granulated sampled waveform (sample.wav) of 32768 samples size instead of a single cycle wave. In this case, the initial value of 1.345 derives from the ratio 44100/32768 and represents the original pitch of the waveform.

f17:
the peak random frequency of the granulated waveform is defined by a linear function (GEN 7) with initial value of 0 hz (no random deviation) that after p3 reaches the final value of 110 hz (50% of frequency modulation).

f18:
the phase (or file pointer) of the granulated waveform is defined by linear function (GEN 7) with initial value of 0 that stays constant over the whole event.

f19:
the peak random phase (or file pointer) of the granulated waveform is defined by linear function (GEN 7) with initial value of 0 that stays constant over the whole event.

f20:
the overall amplitude waveform is defined by a linear function (GEN 7) with initial value of 0 that after 128/512 of p3 rises to 1, stays constant for 256/512 and reaches 0 after 128/512 of p3.

f1:
the granulated waveform is defined by a simple Fourier additive function (GEN 10).

It is important to notice that, except in functions f1 and f20, the parameter p4 is always negative because the function breakpoints must represent their values in an absolute scale. For the four generation instruments (i1,i2,i3,i4), is sufficient to specify (besides the 3 obligatory parameters p1,p2 and p3) the function number (f1 in this case) and for instrument 21 the output scale factor.

For the audio waveform is possible to specify a single cycle wave or a sampled sound using a GEN1 function. In the first case, the value of the parameter p4 of the instrument 21 must contain the maximum output value (in the range 0 , 32767) whereas in the second one, the value is defined in the range 0, 1. The reason of this fact is that the sampled audio signal is not post-normalized during the table reading (GEN -1).

As stated before, is important to point out that the audio signal may be both a single cicle wave or a sampled sound.

Although there is no functional differences in the two cases, it is better to pay attention in the frequency specification.

In the first case, the frequency value and the relative random deviations are simply the desired values.

In the second case, the nominal value of the *natural frequency* (Fn) of the oscillator (by that we mean the frequency value to reproduce the audio signal at the original pitch) is derived from the ratio of the sampling rate (*sr*) and the length (in samples) of the table that contains the sampled waveform (Fn = sr / table length).

For example, if the length of an audio waveform sampled at 44.1 kHz is 64k samples (about 1.486 seconds) , the natural frequency will be 44100 / 65536 = 0.672 Hz.

In general, since the effective duration of the audio signal hardly ever equivalent to a powers of two, we have to provide a table to store the values in excess of the waveform size minus the nearest power of two.

If the total duration of the audio signal sampled at 44.1 kHz is 1.2 seconds, to be effective, the table should be 44.1 x 1.2 = 52920 samples. This implies one should choose a table size of 64 k-samples. However, the natural frequency will still be 0.672 Hz because the Csound oscillator modules work with tables whose length is equivalent to a power of two. The only difference, in this case, is that the phase parameter ranges from 0 and 0.807. The value 0.807 is obtained from the ratio 52920/65536.

It is also important that the random frequency fluctuation must be congruent with the corresponding deterministic value.

For example, with a natural frequency value of 0.672 Hz and a fluctuation of 10 percent the corresponding fluctualtion is about 0.06 Hz.

The concept of *natural frequency* is very important in this context because we can granulate a single cycle of a waveform or a whole sample of sound. From the point of view of the oscillator there is no difference. We can generalize this with the equation:

Fn = I x SR/ L

where :

Fn = oscillator natural frequency
SR = sampling rate
I = increment (table reading step)
L = table length (samples)

With respect to the previous example, if we want to granulate a 1.2 sec stored sound sampled at 44.1 kHz and reproduce it at the original pitch, we have to specify something like

```
f16  0  512  -7  0.672  512  0.672
```

When the granulation is applied only to sampled sounds, it is a good idea to multiply the variable *ifreq* with the expression *sr/ftlen(ifun)*, where *ftlen(x)* is a function that returns the table length in samples. Hence, the score line controlling the frequency will be:

```
f16  0  512  -7  1  512  1
```

In this way, the sound's pitch is handled as a ratio with respect to the natural frequency, and we avoid computing the real values of the frequency itself. For example, to create a continuos pitch glide of the granulated sound, starting from its original frequency and moving up to the natural fifth above (interval ratio of 3:2=1.5), the following score line is required

```
f16  0  512  -7  1  512  1.5
```

The same control is possible for random frequency deviation.

If the audio function is a single cycle of a periodic wave, the phase parameter of the oscillator has an influence on the acoustic result. But if the audio function is a sampled sound, its role is crucial. In fact, in this case, the phase parameter becomes the *table pointer*, allowing us to granulate different sections of the sampled sound.

When you want to granulate the whole sample, from the beginning to the end of sound, we can use a linear function (GEN 7) that moves from 0 to 0.999:

```
f18  0  512  -7  0  512  0.999
```

Here, the sampled sound is granulated without time warp. By exchanging two values, it is possible to reverse the sound. Following this approach, we can achieve different and interesting acoustic results.

For example, in the next score line, during the first half of the event (p3/2), the granulated sound is reversed starting from its middle point (0.5) to the origin, and in the second half, the sampled sound is forward time compressed:

```
f18 0 512 -7 0.5 256 0 256 0.999
```

In any case, the total event duration (p3) may be kept the same as the duration of the original sampled sound or it maybe increased or reduced.

To increase the time transformation of the original sound, one can use a more complex control function (i.e. non-linear) and add an additional random control with the function 19 (see code listing).

3. Origins of the synthesis algorithm

The basic algorithm is based on the model proposed by Barry Truax and implemented on the DMX-1000 real time processor controlled by a host microcomputer. Fig. 1 shows the basic process of the granulation technique in this early implementation. Here, the synthesis generation probably used two programming sections: a background section for the envelope generator bank running on the processor and managed by an interrupt logic (i.e. using a 1 ms timer), and a control section running on the host computer.

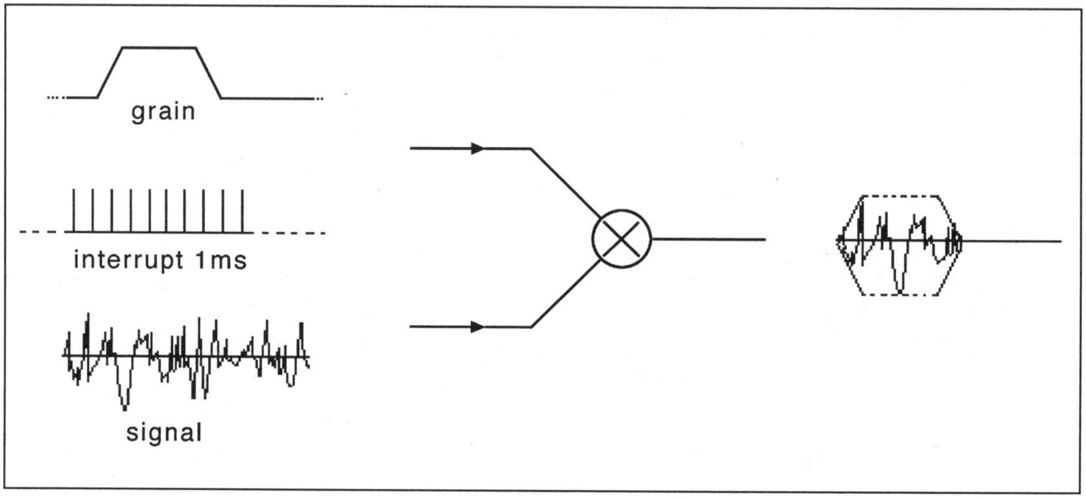

Fig. 1

Since this Csound instrument for the granulation process was implemented in 1989 (an era with few real-time applications for general purpose computers) the main goal of its development was to make a basic strategy for implementing this innovative synthesis technique in a non real-time environment.

Given the inherent necessity to generate a great amount of micro-events per units of time, it was not practical to pursue a note by note generation approach. An alternative solution would have been the utilization of a pre-processing front-end program for the generation of the innumerable lines of notes, each one corresponding to a single grain.

4. The Csound implementation of Granular Synthesis (GSC4)

GSC4 attempts to generate sequences of large number of grains (micro-events) in the high level macro-events that corresponds to single note statement in the Music-N languages. The major difficulty is how to integrate the low-level activity and the control process of the synthesis into a single level. In other words, we need an automated procedure to manage the two different levels. The most useful Csound opcode for this purpose is surely the *timout* statement. It was around this that the whole program algorithm was developed We remember that the syntax of timeout (included in the **program control statement** class) is:

timout istrt, idur, label

During P-time (performance time), a branch to the specified *label* will synthesize depending on the elapsed note time. The branch will be realized at time *istrt* and will remain so for just *idur* seconds. It is very important to note that *timout* can be re-initialized for multiple activations for a single note.

This is equivalent to a program time-counter that produces an interrupt at the end of the countdown. As a consequence, during the re-initialization process it is possible to update a predefined set of i-type variables. The core of the program is then based on this following control structure:

```
;- - - - - - - - - - Interrupt simulation section - - - - - - - - - -
;
;timeout work as an interrupt logic. It is loaded with the current grain duration and automatically decrement to zero

timout 0, igrain, cont          ;if the current value of the timer
                                ;is not zero,branch to the program section labelled with cont

reinit loop                     ;otherwise jump to re-init pass
```

The variable *igrain* contains, at each re-initialization, the current duration value of the next grain. Until this duration is not zero, the program continuously transfers the control to the *cont* label. When the timer reaches zero, the program flow is interrupted and forced by the statement *reinit* to enter a re-initialization section of the program. The label *loop* is a pointer to this section.

The basic structure of the *orchestra* consists of three fundamental blocks:

1) *Grains generator* : it corresponds to an individual instrument that contains, besides the timeout-reinit process, the re-initialization section, the updating of the synthesis parameters and the waveform reading.

2) *Grains control* : it corresponds to another instrument that provides to the control functions generation.

3) *Rescale, Mix&Out*: self determining instrument.

These three blocks are shown in figure 2. The user can easily duplicate those three fundamental blocks in order to expand the total number of voices.

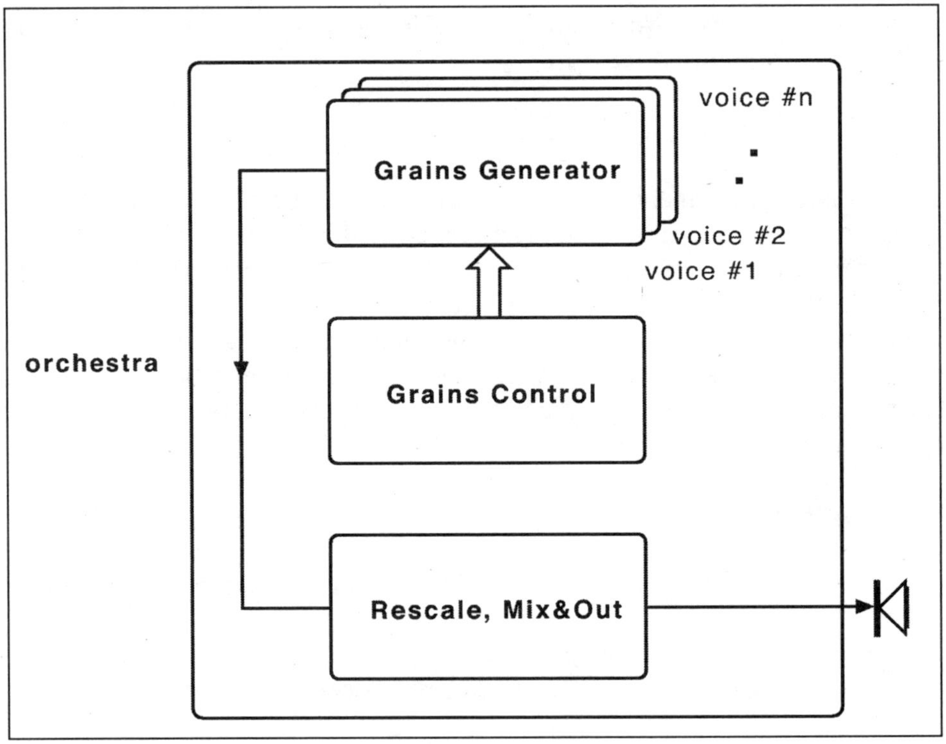

Fig. 2

As shown in figure 2, it is possible to notice a signal flow that connects the various blocks. This fact reveals the use of global variables that send and receive shared parameters.

For each grain, the synthesis parameters are updated on the timeout branch to the re-initialization section.

```
instr 1
;===================== GRAINS GENERATOR (VOICE #1)=======================

ifun    = p4            ;audio function
;


;
;Grains parameters update (re-initialization)
;   ______________________________________________
loop:
idu     = i(gkdur)      ;the current value of gkdur is sampled
                        ;from the corresponding generator in instr 11
                        ;and i-rated into a i-type variable

idurr   = i(gkrnd1)     ; the current value of gkrnd1 is ......

itrpz   = abs(0.001* (idur + idurr));compute the trapezoid duration

iramp   = i(gkramp)+ 0.1         ; the current value of gkramp (plus a magic)is ..

idel    = i(gkdel)      ; the current value of gkdel is....
idelr   = i(gkrnd1y)    ; the current value of gkrnd1y is ....
idely   = abs(0.001 * (idel + idelr)) ;compute the total delay

ifreq   = i(gkfreq)     ; the current value of gkfreq is ....
ifreqr  = i(gkran)      ; the current value of gkran is ....
iphase  = i(gkphase)    ; the current value of gkphase is ....
iphaser = i(gkrnd1p)    ; the current value of gkrnd1p is ....
iamp    = i(gkamp)      ; the current value of gkamp is ....
```

Each grain consists of a trapezoid envelope plus a delay. The trapezoid in its turn includes an attack ramp (irise), a sustain (isus) and a decay ramp (isus) as showed in figure 3.

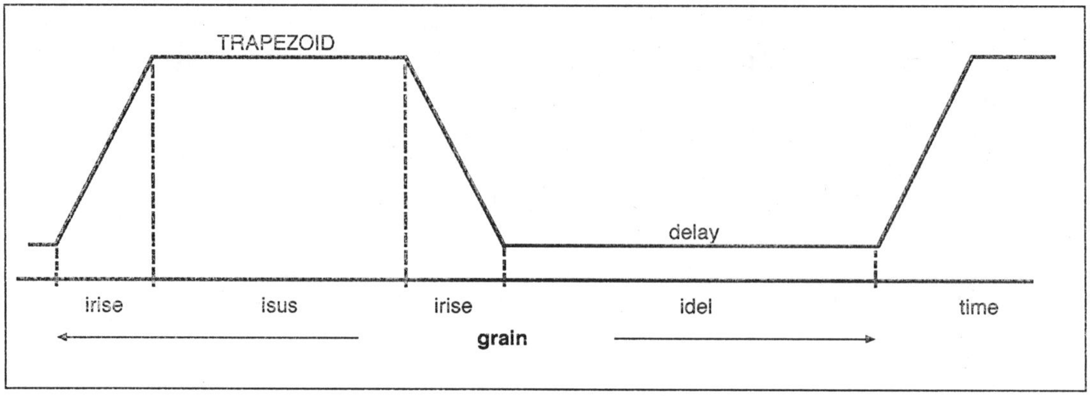

Fig. 3

The sum *irise+isus+irise+idel* represents the total grain duration (variable *igrain*). The attack and decay time of the two ramps, are computed as a fraction of the trapezoid duration (variable iramp).

For example, if *iramp* = 5, the attack (decay) time is equal to 1/5 of the trapezoid duration. The lower limit of this variable is 2. Infact, when *iramp* = 2, the trapezoid degenerates in the triangle.

This fact implies that the duration of stationary segment (*isus*) is equal to the difference between the current trapezoid duration minus the duration of the two ramps. The effective duration of each grain is calculated taking in account the random variations produced by a random generator within the Grain Control block (variable *idurr*).

```
irise   = itrpz/iramp            ;calculate the attack time of the trapezoid
isus    = itrpz - (2 * irise)    ;calculate the sustain time of the trapezoid
igrain  = itrpz + idely          ;calculate the trapezoid+delay duration
iph     = abs(iphase + iphaser)  ;calculate the phase (deterministic + randomic)
ifq     = ifreq + ifreqr         ;calculate the freq. (deterministic + randomic)
```

In substance, duration, delay, phase and frequency are always the sum result of a deterministic and aleatoric component.

The connection between the Grain Control Block and the Grain Generation Block is realized by the use of the *i(x)* function. This statement returns an Init-type equivalent of the argument, thus permitting a K-time value to be accessed ("frozen") in at init-time o reinit-time, whenever valid.

The deterministic and aleatory components of the grain parameters, are continuously updated (K-time) within the Grain Control Block. These values are then sampled by the Grain Generation Block at the end of the *timeout* cycle. Both the generation and control processes are performed in asynchronous way so that the user can specify the control variables of the synthesis at hi-level.

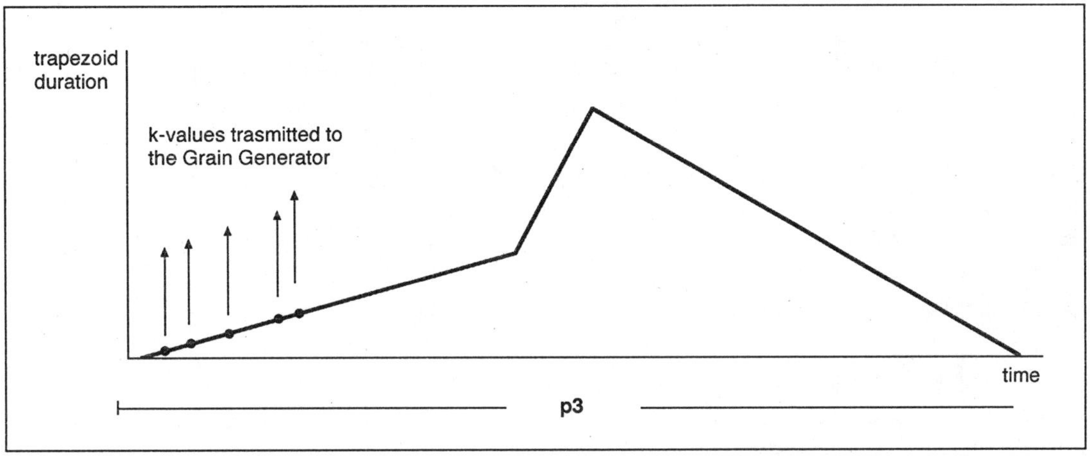

Fig. 4

In fig. 4 is shown an example of the diagram of a control function for the trapezoid duration over the note duration (p3). Inside the instrument 11 (Grain Control) are concentrated the major parts of modules for the deterministic and aleatory control parameters (see next code listing).

```
;============================== GRAIN CONTROL BLOCK ========================
instr 11
;NOTE: all the global variables are transmitted to the  instr 1, 2, 3, 4
;
gkdur      oscil1    0, 1, p3, p4    ;control generator for    idur
gkdurr     oscil1    0, 1, p3, p5    ;                         idurr
gkdel      oscil1    0, 1, p3, p6    ;                         idel
gkdelr     oscil1    0, 1, p3, p7    ;                         idelr
gkramp     oscil1    0, 1, p3, p8    ;                         iramp
gkfreq     oscil1    0, 1, p3, p9    ;                         ifreq
gkfreqr    oscil1    0, 1, p3, p10   ;                         ifreqr
gkphase    oscil1    0, 1, p3, p11   ;                         iphase
gkphaser   oscil1    0, 1, p3, p12   ;                         iphaser
gkamp      oscil1    0, 1, p3, p13   ;                         iamp

krnd1   rand 1 , 0.1                 ;random generator  (VOICE #1)
```

```
krnd2  rand    1 , 0.9          ;          (VOICE #2)
krnd3  rand    1 , 0.5          ;          (VOICE #3)
krnd4  rand    1 , 0.3          ;          (VOICE #4)

;The instantaneous values of the random generators are re-scaled to obtain the ;appropriate values of frequency, duration, delay and phase.

gkran  = krnd1 * gkfreqr/2     ;random frequency re-scale (VOICE #1,2,3,4)
gkrnd1 = krnd1 * gkdurr/2      ;random duration re-scale  (VOICE #1)
gkrnd2 = krnd2 * gkdurr/2      ;                          (VOICE #2)
gkrnd3 = krnd3 * gkdurr/2      ;                          (VOICE #3)
gkrnd4 = krnd4 * gkdurr/2      ;                          (VOICE #4)

gkrnd1y = krnd1 * (0.05 + gkdelr /2) ;random delay re-scale(VOICE #1)
gkrnd2y = krnd2 * (0.05 + gkdelr /2) ;               (VOICE #2)
gkrnd3y = krnd3 * (0.05 + gkdelr /2) ;               (VOICE #3)
gkrnd4y = krnd4 * (0.05 + gkdelr /2) ;               (VOICE #4)

gkrnd1p = krnd1 * gkphaser/2   ;random phase re-scale (VOICE #1)
gkrnd2p = krnd2 * gkphaser/2   ;                      (VOICE #2)
gkrnd3p = krnd3 * gkphaser/2   ;                      (VOICE #3)
gkrnd4p = krnd4 * gkphaser/2   ;                      (VOICE #4)
endin
```

Referring to the previous listing code, the global variable *gkdur* is the output of the ìone-shotî oscillator *oscil1* that read a control function (parameter *p4*) defined within the score. Four independent random generators were used to generate all the aleatory, control parameters.

All variables that include the aleatory component, produce complex control function that generate ideal *tendency masks* as represented in fig. 5b. Referring to the figure 4 and 5, it is possible to visualize the combination of the deterministic and random component of the trapezoid duration as a function of time: the effective value of the trapezoid duration is represented by the shaded area of figure 5b. The variables with deterministic and aleatory components are:

a) grain duration (independent aleatory component for each voice)
b) grain delay (independent aleatory component for each voice)
c) phase (independent aleatory component for each voice)

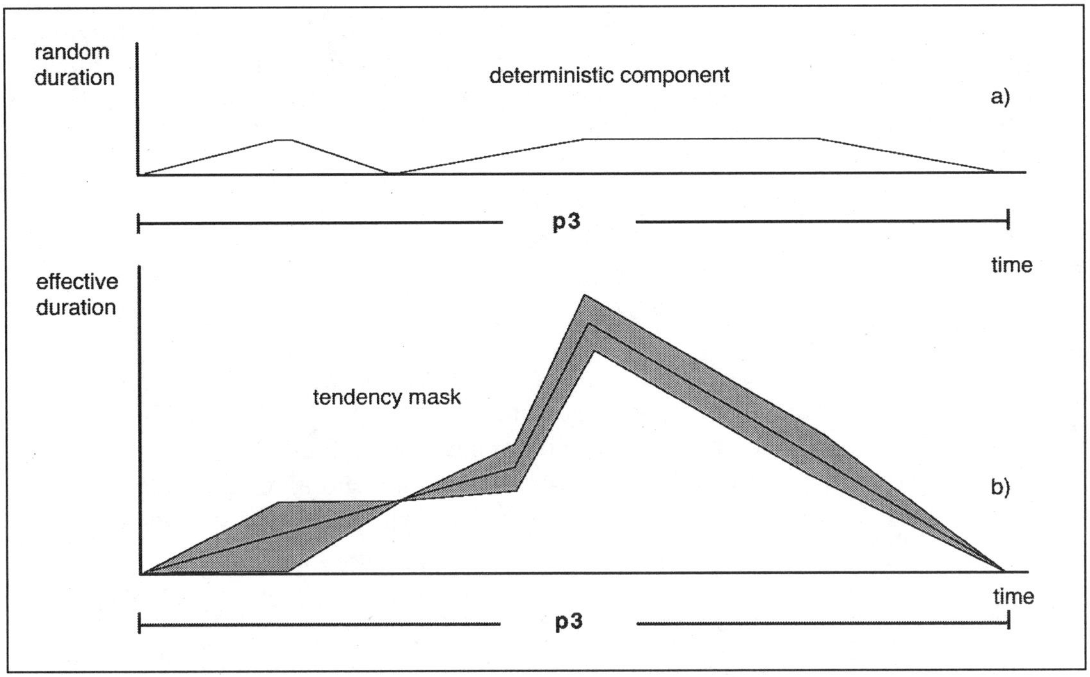

d) frequency (same aleatory component for all voices)

Fig.5

After the grains parameters are updated (at re-initialization time), the grain envelope is generated usig the simple *linseg* opcode, whose parameters are *irise*, *isus*, *idel*, *iamp* (see fig. 3):

```
cont:
k1 linseg 0, irise, iamp, isus, iamp, irise, 0, idel, 0  ;generate grain envelope

ga1 oscili k1, ifq, ifun, iph                            ;generate voice 1

endin
```

The same envelope function is used to control the amplitude (*kl*) of an interpolated oscillator (*oscili*).

The frequency input of this oscillator is controlled by the i-variable *ifq*. This includes the respective deterministic and aleatory component. The same for the phase (*iph*) whereas the variable *ifun* points to the audio function to be granulated.

The complete algorithm includes three further instruments (instr 2,3,4) that provide to the generation of additional de-correlated sequences of grains, in order to achieve a minimum sound texture. The de-correlation of the four instruments is audible only when the respective aleatory components are not zero.

```
krnd1  rand 1 , 0.1      ;random generator    (VOICE #1)
krnd2  rand 1 , 0.9      ;                    (VOICE #2)
krnd3  rand 1 , 0.5      ;                    (VOICE #3)
krnd4  rand 1 , 0.3      ;                    (VOICE #4)
```

The only difference in the previous code lines consists of different seed number in the random generation process (in the above example 0.1, 0.9, 0.5, 0.3), so the resulting sound is much more rich and ìchorusedî. When the amount of all the aleatory components is zero, the four voices are synchronized, thie ìchoralî effect is canceled and the sound is not so interesting as before. For that reason, an offset value (0.05) is permanetely added to the random generator.

5. Conclusions and future expansions

A Csound implementation of Granular Synthesis was implemented starting from the model proposed by Truax. The program structure consists of a basic group of six instruments controlled by a score, in which are specified all the synthesis parameters. It is possible to granulate any periodic waveform or a sampled sound. Starting from this basic version, it is easy to expand the synthesis process to a greater number of voices. We suggest, also, that you experiment with the granulation of different sampled sound and with different grain envelope shapes and realizing a real-time control of all the synthesis parameters. We have developed an experimental real-time C version of this program that allows up to sixteen full stereo voices. This version is integrated in a custom version of Csound.

APPENDIX (GSC4 - ORCHESTRA)

```
;gsc4.orc
;
;
;                    GRANULAR SYNTHESIS
;                  -----------------
;                        Ver 2.1
;                    Eugenio Giordani
;
;
;-----------------------------------------------------------------
;This orchestra implements Granular Synthesis based on the model proposed by B. Truax.
;
;----------------- ORCHESTRA HEADER -----------------;
;
        sr     =  44100
        kr     =  22050
        ksmps  =  2
        nchnls =  2
;----------------- Global control variables initialization -----------------
;
gkdur     init 0     ;average grains duration
gkdurr    init 0     ;random grains duration
gkdel     init 0     ;average grains delay
gkdelr    init 0     ;random grains delay
gkramp    init 0     ;ramp ratio
gkfreq    init 0     ;average audio frequency
gkfreqr   init 0     ;random audio frequency
gkphase   init 0     ;average phase
gkphaser  init 0     ;random phase
gkamp     init 0     ;overall amplitude

gkran     init 0     ;instantaneous random frequency

gkrnd1    init 0     ;instantaneous random grains duration  (VOICE #1)
gkrnd2    init 0     ;                                      (VOICE #2)
gkrnd3    init 0     ;                                      (VOICE #3)
```

```
gkrnd4     init 0          ;                                    (VOICE #4)

gkrnd1y    init 0          ;instantaneous random grains delay   (VOICE #1)
gkrnd2y    init 0          ;                                    (VOICE #2)
gkrnd3y    init 0          ;                                    (VOICE #3)
gkrnd4y    init 0          ;                                    (VOICE #4)

gkrnd1p    init 0          ;instantaneous random grains phase   (VOICE #1)
gkrnd2p    init 0          ;                                    (VOICE #2)
gkrnd3p    init 0          ;                                    (VOICE #3)
gkrnd4p    init 0          ;                                    (VOICE #4)
;
;- - - - - - - - - - - - - - - - - - - - - - - - - - - - - - - - - - - - - - - - - - - -
instr 1
;===================== GRAINS GENERATOR (VOICE #1)========================
ifun    = p4               ;audio function
;

;Grains parameters update (re-initialization)

;- - - - - - - - - - - - - - - - - - - - - - - - - - - - - - - - - - - - - - - - - - - -
loop:
idur    = i(gkdur)         ;current value of gkdur is sampled from
                           ;the corresponding generator in instr 11
                           ;and converted in a i-type variable

idurr   = i(gkrnd1)        ; current value of gkrnd1 is ......

itrpz   = abs(0.001* (idur + idurr))  ;calculates the trapezoid duration

iramp   = i(gkramp)+ 0.1   ;current value of gkramp (plus a magic) is ..

idel    = i(gkdel)         ; current value of gkdel is....
idelr   = i(gkrnd1y)       ; current value of gkrnd1y is....
idely   = abs(0.001 * (idel + idelr)) ;calculates the total delay

ifreq   = i(gkfreq)        ; current value of gkfreq is ....
ifreqr  = i(gkran)         ; current value of gkranis ....
iphase  = i(gkphase)       ; current value of gkphase is ....
```

```
iphaser = i(gkrnd1p)         ; current value of gkrn1p is ....
iamp    = i(gkamp)           ; current value of gkamp is ....

irise   = itrpz/iramp        ;calculates the trapezoid attack time
isus    = itrpz - (2 * irise) ;calculates the trapezoid sustain time
igrain  = itrpz + idely      ;calculates the sum trapezoid+delay duration
iph     = abs(iphase + iphaser);calculates the phase(deterministic + random)
ifq     = ifreq + ifreqr     ;calculates the freq.(deterministic + random)

;- - - - - - - - - - - - - - - - - Interrupt simulation section - - - - - - - - - - - - - - - - - -
;
;timeout work as an interrupt logic. It is loaded with the current grain ;duration and automatically decrements to zero

timout 0, igrain, cont       ;if the current value of the timer
                             ;is not zero,branch to the program section labelled with cont

reinit loop                  ;otherwise jump to re-init pass

cont:
k1 linseg 0, irise, iamp, isus, iamp, irise, 0, idel, 0  ;generate grain envelope

ga1 oscili k1, ifq, ifun, iph                 ;generate voice 1


endin

;- - - - - - - - - - - - - - - - - - - - - - - - - - - - - - - - - - - - - - - - - - - - - - - -
instr 2
;======================== GRAINS GENERATOR (VOICE #2)--------------------------
ifun  =  p4                  ;audio function
;

;Grains parameters update (re-initialization)

;- - - - - - - - - - - - - - - - - - - - - - - - - - - - - - - - - - - - - - - - - - - - - - - -
loop:
idur    = i(gkdur)           ;current value of gkdur is sampled from
                             ;the corresponding generator in instr 11
                             ;and converted in a i-type variable
```

```
idurr   = i(gkrnd2)                      ;current value of gkrnd2 is ......

itrpz   = abs(0.001* (idur + idurr))     ;calculates the trapezoid duration

iramp   = i(gkramp)+ 0.1                 ;current value of gkramp (plus a magic) is ..

idel    = i(gkdel)                       ; current value of gkdel is....
idelr   = i(gkrnd2y)                     ; current value of gkrnd2y is....
idely   = abs(0.001 * (idel + idelr))    ;calculates the total delay

ifreq   = i(gkfreq)                      ; current value of gkfreq is ....
ifreqr  = i(gkran)                       ; current value of gkranis ....
iphase  = i(gkphase)                     ; current value of gkphase is ....
iphaser = i(gkrnd2p)                     ; current value of gkrn2p is ....
iamp    = i(gkamp)                       ; current value of gkamp is ....

irise   = itrpz/iramp                    ;calculates the trapezoid attack time
isus    = itrpz - (2 * irise)            ;calculates the trapezoid sustain time
igrain  = itrpz + idely                  ;calculates the sum trapezoid+delay duration
iph     = abs(iphase + iphaser)          ;calculates the phase(deterministic + random)
ifq     = ifreq + ifreqr                 ;calculates the freq.(deterministic + random)

;- - - - - - - - - - - - - - - - Interrupt simulation section - - - - - - - - - - - - - - - -
;
;timeout work as an interrupt logic. It is loaded with the current grain ;duration and automatically decrements to zero

timout 0, igrain, cont                   ;if the current value of the timer
                                         ;is not zero,branch to the program
                                         ;section labelled with cont

reinit loop                              ;otherwise jump to re-init pass


cont:
k1 linseg 0, irise, iamp, isus, iamp, irise, 0, idel, 0  ;generate grain envelope

ga2 oscili k1, ifq, ifun, iph            ;generate voice 2

endin
```

```
;- - - - - - - - - - - - - - - - - - - - - - - - - - - - - - - - - - - - - - - - - - - - - - - - - -
instr 3
;===================== GRAINS GENERATOR (VOICE #3)=======================
ifun     = p4                         ;audio function
;

;Grains parameters update (re-initialization)

;- - - - - - - - - - - - - - - - - - - - - - - - - - - - - - - - - - - - - - - - - - - - - - - - - -
loop:
idur     = i(gkdur)                   ;current value of gkdur is sampled from
                                      ;the corresponding generator in instr 11
                                      ;and converted in a i-type variable

idurr    = i(gkrnd3)                  ;current value of gkrnd3 is ......

itrpz    = abs(0.001* (idur + idurr)) ;calculates the trapezoid duration

iramp    = i(gkramp)+ 0.1             ;current value of gkramp (plus a magic) is ..

idel     = i(gkdel)                   ; current value of gkdel is....
idelr    = i(gkrnd3y)                 ; current value of gkrnd3y is....
idely    = abs(0.001 * (idel + idelr)) ;calculates the total delay

ifreq    = i(gkfreq)                  ; current value of gkfreq is ....
ifreqr   = i(gkran)                   ; current value of gkranis ....
iphase   = i(gkphase)                 ; current value of gkphase is ....
iphaser  = i(gkrnd3p)                 ; current value of gkrn3p is ....
iamp     = i(gkamp)                   ; current value of gkamp is ....

irise    = itrpz/iramp                ;calculates the trapezoid attack time
isus     = itrpz - (2 * irise)        ;calculates the trapezoid sustain time
igrain   = itrpz + idely              ;calculates the sum trapezoid+delay duration
iph      = abs(iphase + iphaser)      ;calculates the phase(deterministic + random)
ifq      = ifreq + ifreqr             ;calculates the freq.(deterministic + random)

;- - - - - - - - - - - - - - - - - Interrupt simulation section - - - - - - - - - - - - - - - - -
;
;timeout work as an interrupt logic. It is loaded with the current grain ;duration and automatically decrements to zero
```

```
timout 0, igrain, cont               ;if the current value of the timer
                                     ;is not zero,branch to the program
                                     ;section labelled with cont

reinit loop                          ;otherwise jump to re-init pass


cont:
k1 linseg 0, irise, iamp, isus, iamp, irise, 0, idel, 0  ;generate grain envelope

ga3 oscili k1, ifq, ifun, iph        ;generate voice 3

endin
;- - - - - - - - - - - - - - - - - - - - - - - - - - - - - - - - - - - - - - - - - - - - - -
instr 4
;====================== GRAINS GENERATOR (VOICE #4)========================
ifun    = p4                         ;audio function
;

;Grains parameters update (re-initialization)

;- - - - - - - - - - - - - - - - - - - - - - - - - - - - - - - - - - - - - - - - - - - - - -
loop:
idur    = i(gkdur)                   ;current value of gkdur is sampled from
                                     ;the corresponding generator in instr 11
                                     ;and converted in a i-type variable

idurr   = i(gkrnd4)                  ;current value of gkrnd4 is ......

itrpz   = abs(0.001* (idur + idurr)) ;calculates the trapezoid duration

iramp   = i(gkramp)+ 0.1             ;current value of gkramp (plus a magic) is ..

idel    = i(gkdel)                   ; current value of gkdel is....
idelr   = i(gkrnd4y)                 ; current value of gkrnd4y is....
idely   = abs(0.001 * (idel + idelr)) ;calculates the total delay

ifreq   = i(gkfreq)                  ; current value of gkfreq is ....
```

```
ifreqr   = i(gkran)                    ; current value of gkranis ....
iphase   = i(gkphase)                  ; current value of gkphase is ....
iphaser  = i(gkrnd4p)                  ; current value of gkrn4p is ....
iamp     = i(gkamp)                    ; current value of gkamp is ....

irise    = itrpz/iramp                 ;calculates the trapezoid attack time
isus     = itrpz - (2 * irise)         ;calculates the trapezoid sustain time
igrain   = itrpz + idely               ;calculates the sum trapezoid+delay duration
iph      = abs(iphase + iphaser)       ;calculates the phase(deterministic + random)
ifq      = ifreq + ifreqr              ;calculates the freq.(deterministic + random)

;- - - - - - - - - - - - - - - - - Interrupt simulation section - - - - - - - - - - - - - - - - -
;
;timeout work as an interrupt logic. It is loaded with the current grain ;duration and automatically decrements to zero

timout 0, igrain, cont                 ;if the current value of the timer
                                       ;is not zero,branch to the program
                                       ;section labelled with cont

reinit loop                            ;otherwise jump to re-init pass


cont:
k1 linseg 0, irise, iamp, isus, iamp, irise, 0, idel, 0  ;generate grain envelope

ga4 oscili k1, ifq, ifun, iph          ;generate voice 4

endin

;=============================== GRAIN CONTROL BLOCK =========================
instr 11
;NOTE: all the global variables are transmitted to the  instr 1,2,3,4
;
gkdur      oscil1  0, 1, p3, p4        ;control generator for   idur
gkdurr     oscil1  0, 1, p3, p5        ;                        idurr
gkdel      oscil1  0, 1, p3, p6        ;                        idel
gkdelr     oscil1  0, 1, p3, p7        ;                        idelr
gkramp     oscil1  0, 1, p3, p8        ;                        iramp
gkfreq     oscil1  0, 1, p3, p9        ;                        ifreq
```

```
gkfreqr    oscil1  0, 1, p3, p10     ;                  ifreqr
gkphase    oscil1  0, 1, p3, p11     ;                  iphase
gkphaser   oscil1  0, 1, p3, p12     ;                  iphaser
gkamp      oscil1  0, 1, p3, p13     ;                  iamp

krnd1      rand 1 , 0.1              ;random generator  (VOICE #1)
krnd2      rand 1 , 0.9              ;                  (VOICE #2)
krnd3      rand 1 , 0.5              ;                  (VOICE #3)
krnd4      rand 1 , 0.3              ;                  (VOICE #4)

;The instantaneous values of the random generators are re-scaled to obtain the ;appropriate values of frequency, duration, delay and phase.

gkran      = krnd1 * gkfreqr/2       ;random frequency re-scale (VOICE #1,2,3,4)
gkrnd1     = krnd1 * gkdurr/2        ;random duration re-scale  (VOICE #1)
gkrnd2     = krnd2 * gkdurr/2        ;                          (VOICE #2)
gkrnd3     = krnd3 * gkdurr/2        ;                          (VOICE #3)
gkrnd4     = krnd4 * gkdurr/2        ;                          (VOICE #4)

gkrnd1y    = krnd1 * (0.05 + gkdelr /2) ;random delay re-scale  (VOICE #1)
gkrnd2y    = krnd2 * (0.05 + gkdelr /2) ;                       (VOICE #2)
gkrnd3y    = krnd3 * (0.05 + gkdelr /2) ;                       (VOICE #3)
gkrnd4y    = krnd4 * (0.05 + gkdelr /2) ;                       (VOICE #4)

gkrnd1p    = krnd1 * gkphaser/2      ;random phase re-scale     (VOICE #1)
gkrnd2p    = krnd2 * gkphaser/2      ;                          (VOICE #2)
gkrnd3p    = krnd3 * gkphaser/2      ;                          (VOICE #3)
gkrnd4p    = krnd4 * gkphaser/2      ;                          (VOICE #4)
endin

;====================== RESCALE, MIX & OUT ======================

instr 21
iscale     = p4                      ;read scale factor
outs1 (ga1/2 + ga2/2 ) * iscale      ;outputs voices 1 - 2
outs2 (ga3/2 + ga4/2 ) * iscale      ;outputs voices 3 - 4


endin
```

(GSC4 - score)

```
;gsc4.sco
;
;- - - - - - - - - - - - - - - - - Grains duration control function - - - - - - - - - - - - - - - - -
;
f11 0  512 -7 10 256 20  128 20 128 16

;- - - - - - - - - - - - - - - - - Random grains duration control function - - - - - - - - - - - - - - - - -
;
f12 0 512 -7 4 256 1 256 0

;- - - - - - - - - - - - - - - - - Grains delay control function - - - - - - - - - - - - - - - - -
;
f13 0 512 -7 10 256 20 256 5

;- - - - - - - - - - - - - - - - -  Random grains delay control function - - - - - - - - - - - - - - - - -
;
f14 0 512  -7 0 128  0 256 2 128 0

;- - - - - - - - - - - - - - - - - Ramp proportion control - - - - - - - - - - - - - - - - -
;
f15 0 512 -7 2 256 4 256 2

;- - - - - - - - - - - - - - - - - Frequency control function - - - - - - - - - - - - - - - - -
;
;f16 0 512 -7 1.345 512 3.345
f16  0 512 -7 220 512 220

;- - - - - - - - - - - - - - - - - Random frequency control function - - - - - - - - - - - - - - - - -
;
f17 0 512 -7  0  512  110

;- - - - - - - - - - - - - - - - - Phase control function  (Audio file pointer) - - - - - - - - - - - - - - - - -
;
f18 0 512 -7 0 512 0

;- - - - - - - - - - - - - - - - -  Random phase control - - - - - - - - - - - - - - - - -
f19 0 512 -7 0 128 0 256 0 128  0
```

```
;- - - - - - - - - - - - - - - - - Overall amplitude control function - - - - - - - - - - - - - - - - -
;
f20 0 512  7 0 128 1 256 1 128 0

;=====================   Audio functions   ==============================;
;f1 0 32768 -1 "sample.wav" 0 0 0
f1 0 1024 10 0.6 0.8  1   0.5  0.3  0.5  0.7
;==========================================================================
;p1  p2  p3   p4   p5    p6   p7    p8    p9    p10    p11    p12
;- - - - - - - - - - - - - - - - - - - - - - - - - - - - - - - - - - - - - - - - - - - - - ;
;           ifun
i1  0   40  1
i2  0   40  1
i3  0   40  1
i4  0   40  1
;- - - - - - - - - - - - - - - - - - - - - - - - - - - - - - - - - - - - - - - - - - - - -
;                        dur    durr   del    delr   ramp   freq   freqr  phase    phaser   amp
i11   0       40     11     12     13     14     15     16     17     18       19       20
;- - - - - - - - - - - - - - - - - - - - - - - - - - - - - - - - - - - - - - - - - - - - -
;              scale
i21     0   40  20000
e
```

References

Gabor,D. 'Acoustical Quanta and the Theory of Hearing.' *Nature* May 3,1947

Truax,B. 'Real-Time Granular Synthesis with a Digital Signal Processor.' *Computer Music Journal* 12(2)

Truax,B. 'Real-Time Granular Synthesis with the DMX-1000' *ICMC 86 Proceedings*

Roads,C. 'Granular Synthesis' from *The Computer Music Tutorial* (MIT Press)

Roads,C. 'Granular Synthesis of Sound.' *Computer Music Journal* 2(2)

Roads,C. 'The Realization of nscor' from *'The Computer Music and Digital Audio Series'* C.Roads Editor

Truax,B. 'Handbook for Acoustic Ecology' B.Truax Editor

Vercoe,B. 'Csound User Manual' Media Lab MIT

(Translated from the Italian by the author)

DIRECTCSOUND AND VMCI:
THE PARADIGM OF INTERACTIVITY

by Gabriel Maldonado

1. INTRODUCTION

Csound was initially thought of as a deferred-time synthesis language as were all the other synthesis languages, like MUSIC V, available at that time. That view of synthesis languages remained essentially unchanged from the beginning of '60s to recent times. This paradigm still continues to satisfy many composers' needs. And although this approach still has several important advantages over its real-time successors, it is impossible to ignore that the absence or real-time synthesis impedes composers' direct and immediate relationship with their sonic material.

In its original version, Csound couldn't be used in live performances because the processing speeds of the standard computers of that time (the 1980's) were insufficient for real-time synthesis. Consequently, the original Csound language didn't include any live-control functions. During the early 90's, Barry Vercoe (the creator of Csound) added some MIDI oriented opcodes to use for real-time control. At that time, the only machines capable of running Csound in real-time were Silicon Graphics machines and expensive UNIX workstations.

Nowadays, PCs with Intel processors have become fast enough to run Csound in real-time. DirectCsound, a real-time version of Csound, has filled a lot of the gaps in the original CSound interactive functionality by adding opcodes that allow live control of parameters. In this version, many new features have been implemented, such as control of MIDI input/output (which enables Csound to connect with external world). Also, there has been a reduction of the latency problems which appeared unsolvable when the first real-time versions of Csound were released.

The new functionality allows total control over synthesis parameters, all of which can be defined by the user in a very flexible way. This flexibility, together with unlimited synthesis power, makes DirectCsound superior to any hardware MIDI synthesizer available now. Just a few years ago, owning a workstation with real-time synthesis processing power at home was unthinkable. Such features were available only to machines costing hundreds of thousands of dollars.

But DirectCsound is free, and it is sufficient to have run it on a cheap PC with audio card. This minimal set up enables users to compose music interactively, and also, use CSound for live performances. It is now possible to think of Csound as a universal musical instrument.

The newest features of Csound will be explained in the following sections through several examples.

In last section, we will demonstrate some functions of VMCI (Virtual Midi Control Interface, a program that emulates several types of MIDI controllers). VMCI has been designed in order to provide a software tool which enables users to control DirectCsound in real time. It can even be used with other hardware/software MIDI stuff.

2. SPECIFIC FEATURES OF DIRECTCSOUND

2.1 Inputs and Outputs

With DirectCsound, a musician can use both MIDI IN and MIDI OUT ports to send and receive data. This feature allows real-time control of any synthesis parameter.

Regarding audio outputs, the user can choose two different types of *drivers*:

1. old *MME* (*Multi Media Extensions*) driver, which was introduced with Windows 3.1, and
2. new *DirectX* driver (*DirectSound APIs*), which allows very low latency, practically achieving the total absence of any perceptible delay in real musical situations. This allows to us to trigger DirectCsound from a MIDI keyboard, and thus retain the interactivity of any hardware MIDI synthesizer.

DirectCsound automatically recognizes all installed MIDI ports, as well as *DirectX* and *MME* audio ports.

DirectCsound can activate both audio DAC output and file writing of samples, allowing hard-disk recording of a real-time performance.

As for the number of audio channels, at the present time, DAC output can only handle mono and stereo. Whereas the new opcode ***fout*** allows composers to write to files with any number of channels. Notice that the ***fout*** opcode is totally independent from the ***out*** opcode. So, it is possible to record a real-time session to a multi-track file with four, eight, twelve tracks, etc. (Obviously, this is possible only if the hard-disk is fast enough. Otherwise it is possible to use a RAM-disk by copying the recorded file to the hard-disk at the end Csound real-time session). Presently, only monophonic or stereophonic monitoring is possible during live performance, but there is always the potential to play the multi-channel pre-generated files afterwards, and record them to another real-time multi-track format (like a digital 8 track recorder).

At last, DirectCsound permits a console window with up to 2050 lines of text (standard DOS windows only allow 25 lines). This makes orchestra and score errors faster to find.

2.2 Orchestra opcodes

DirectCsound has several opcodes which haven't been implemented in the standard version of Csound as of yet. (Most of them have already been ported to canonical Csound, and others will be ported soon). Below is a list of the opcodes that I've implemented so far (only some have been ported to the canonical version). For further information about each opcode, see the manual.

MIDI controllers
midic7, midic14, midic21, ctrl7, ctrl14, ctrl21
initc7, initc14, initc21
slider8, slider16, slider32, slider64, slider8f, slider16f, slider32f, slider64f, s16b14, s32b14 - return a signal according to incoming MIDI control-change messages.

Micro-tuning together with MIDI
cpstmid - enables definition of micro-tone scales. This opcode is designed to be used with MIDI.

MIDI generators
noteon, noteoff, ondur, ondur2 - send note-on and note-off messages to the MIDI-out port.
moscil, midion - send streams of note-on and note-off messages to the MIDI-out port.
All the MIDI-message generating process is controllable by input arguments.
outic, outkc, outic14, outkc14, outipb, outkpb, outiat, outkat, outipc, outkpc, outpiat, outkpat - send the corresponding MIDI CHANNEL messages.
mclock, mrtmsg - send the corresponding MIDI SYSTEM REAL-TIME messages

General MIDI in/out message handling
midiin, midiout, midion2, nrpn - handle byte-level MIDI messages
mdelay - MIDI delay

MIDI note duration extension
xtratim, release - allows the extension of duration in MIDI-activated notes. It extends the note-off time.

Subroutine call
call, calld, callm, callmd - allows an instrument to call an another instrument. Equivalent to subroutine calls available in other programming languages such as Basic or C.
parmck, parmtk, parmca, parmta, rtrnck, rtrntk, rtrnca, rtrnta - allows the passing of arguments to the called subroutines as well as receiving return arguments, as in structured programming languages.

Signal wrapping
wrap, mirror - wrap input signal in two different ways (see manual).

Interpolators
ntrpol - linearly interpolates between two signals.

***WaveGuide* algorithms**
wguide1, wguide2 - Plucked string and struck-plate physical models
flanger - a flanger which can be totally configured by the user.

Exponential segment envelope generator
expsega - similar to expseg, but more precise with audio signals

16-bit tables related opcodes (save half RAM space)
loscil2 - similar to loscil, but can handle 16-bit samples stored into a table (together with GEN22), halving computer RAM needs.
fof3 - similar to fof2 but it can handle 16-bit samples and gives a better audio quality because of linear interpolation
lposcint - oscillator that allows the variation of the starting point and ending point of a table during reading operations at *k-rate*. Optimized to work with 16-bit sample tables.

Signal visualization
printk2 - prints k-rate signal (only when they vary).

High-precision oscillators
poscil - similar to oscili but allows a very high frequency resolution.
lposcil - oscillator that allows to vary the starting point and ending point of a table during reading operations at k-rate.
lposcint - like the previous opcode, but for 16-bit tables.

FM oscillator
foscili2 - similar to foscili, but allows different function tables for carrier and modulator.

Filters
lowres - resonant low-pass filter.
lowresx, tonex, atonex, resonx - banks of serially-connected filters (to obtain a steeper curve).
vlowres - bank of variable resonant low pass filters, serially connected.
resony - bank of variable second-order band-pass filters, connected in parallel.

Fast power of two
powoftwo, logbtwo - power of two or logarithm base two (faster than standard *pow* opcode)

Information about sample-tables
ftlen2 - returns the length of a table generated by GEN01 or GEN22, using deferred allocation.
nsamp - returns the number of samples actually loaded into a table from a file.
ftsr - returns sampling frequency of an audio file loaded into a table.

New GEN functions
GEN22 - loads a file of samples into a table, similar to GEN01, but it stores samples using 16-bit integers instead of 32-bit floating-points, halving computer RAM need.
GEN23 - reads values from an external text file and stores it into a table.
GEN24 - reads values of another table and scales them according to minimum/maximum limits defined by the user.

Trigger
trigger - generates a boolean true value (1 = true), when a signals meets a threshold defined by the user. In any other case, trigger generates false (0 = false). Value 1 (true) can be used by other opcodes to start any kind of events.

Multi-track file writing
fout - write an arbitrary number of audio signals to a multi-track file.
foutk - same as above, at *k-rate.*
fouti - same as above, at *i-rate.*
foutir - same as above, but takes care of duration of the corresponding note.
fiopen - create a file and enable it for reading or writing.
vincr - accumulator, increment an audio variable of an arbitrary value.
clear - clear an audio variable (set it = 0).

Multi-track file reading
fin - read signals from a multi-track file at a-rate.
fink - some as above, at *k-rate*
fini - some as above, at *i-rate*

Artificial foldover
fold - generates artificial foldover on an input signal.

2.3 Score opcodes and operators

New score opcodes
{ } - Loops with the possibility of nesting
F - score tables

Nested macros

New macro syntax that allows nesting.

Nesting means having more than one loop, one inside the other. For example, if we have four composed blocks called A,B,C,D and we want to repeat 4 times the first block, 3 times the second, 2 times the third and no repetitions for the fourth; in this case we will have a sequence of the following type:

A-A-A-A-B-B-B-C-C-D.

The first four repetitions of block A can be generated by a loop of 4 iterations; likewise the 3 repetitions of B and the 2 repetitions of C. But, suppose to wish to repeat the entire construction for four times, we will have the following sequence:

A-A-A-A-B-B-B-C-C-D-A-A-A-A-B-B-B-C-C-D-A-A-A-A-B-B-B-C-C-D-A-A-A-A-B-B-B-C-C-D.

This sequence can be easily generated by an external loop with four iterations that nests the three internal loops. If using nested loop for a verbatim repetition seems impractical because of the initial difficulty of learning this technique, remember that one can find many compositional situations in which the parameters of each iteration should be varied according to user-defined algorithms. In these cases, parameters must be different for each iteration. So, calculating each parameter by hand could be far more complex and boring than the previously described technique. It is more convenient to use nested loops because they create a more synthetic and readable score writing.

New macro operators
T - returns an element contained by a score table, by giving the corresponding index.
R - returns a random number
^ - power operator
% - remainder operator (modulus)

3. USING DIRECTCSOUND IN REAL-TIME

In this section some MIDI-controlled orchestra examples are analyzed.

In order to use DirectCsound in real-time, it is necessary to start it with the appropriate flags. Thes are not present in the canonical version at the present time.

DirectCsound is capable of handling both incoming and outgoing MIDI data. With regards audio, there is the option of using old *MME* drivers or new low-latency *DirectX* drivers. However, conflicting flags can't be used at the same time. The audio buffer is unique in the *DirectX* driver while it is possible to specify a number of buffers when using old MME driver. Notice that non-standard flags have characters '-+' as prefix, whereas the standard ones only have '-'.

User must use the following flags in order to run the examples:

-b <number> set buffer length (standard flag)
-+p < number > set buffer number of MME driver (don't use with -+X)
-+X activate DirectX (don't use with -+q)
-+q activate MME (don't use with -+X)
-+K activate MIDI IN port
-+Q activate MIDI OUT port
-+j < number > set the maximum number of lines of text visualized in DirectCsound console (useful for debug)

When more than one MIDI port is available, the DirectCsound console window will show a list of all the port names, and ask the user to select the required port.

In the following examples, a basic knowledge of MIDI protocol is taken for granted.

3.1 A simple example: sine.orc

This is the simplest example. It consists of an oscillator whose frequency is controlled by a MIDI note number sent by a MIDI keyboard.

```
; sine.orc
        sr     =  44100
        kr     =  441
        ksmps  =  100
        nchnls =  1
gi1     ftgen     1, 0, 1024, 10, 1

        instr     1
ifreq   cpsmidi
iamp    ampmidi   10000
```

```
a1      oscili  iamp, ifreq, 1
        out     a1
        endin
```

This is the score:

```
; sine.sco
f0 3600
```

This example must be activated with the following command line if the user has already installed DirectX on his computer:

csound.exe -+X -+K -b200 sine.orc sine.sco

...otherwise he must use old MME driver with the following command line:

csound.exe -+q -b500 -+p8 -+K sine.orc sine.sco

DirectCsound will prompt the user to enter the audio out port number, as well as, the MIDI out port number in the console window.

After the user has typed in that data, it is possible to play notes on a master-keyboard (connected via a MIDI-IN port) and to listen to sinusoids with frequency that corresponds to the pressed key. The timbre will not be interesting, but this orchestra is useful to verify if the system is set up correctly. If sound interruptions are present, it is necessary to increase buffer length by changing the number following flag *-b*.

In this case, the opcodes handling MIDI are standard, i.e. *cpsmidi*, and return the frequency of the pressed key. *ampmidi*, returns the amplitude.

Notice that score only contains the *f0 3600* statement. That allows Csound to compile in real-time for 3600 seconds. Actually, the audio table containing the sinusoid is generated directly inside the orchestra, by *ftgen* opcode. It is possible to terminate the Csound session at any moment by pressing CONTROL-C (after being sure that the console window has got the *focus*).

Adding an amplitude envelope to sine.orc

Let's modify instrument 1 of the previous orchestra as follows:

```
        instr   1
ifreq   cpsmidi
```

```
iamp   ampmidi   10000
kenv   linsegr   0, .1, 1, .3, .5, .2, 0
a1     oscili    iamp, ifreq, 1
       out       1*kenv
       endin
```

Notice, the *linsegr* opcode is used. This opcode handles the release stage when a current note receives a MIDI note-off message. The resulting action will extend normal note duration for the time the user has assigned to the corresponding parameter (that is second to last argument of line containing *linsegr*. The last argument contains the level value that *linsegr* returns at the end of release).

linsegr automatically extends note duration, and release stage consists of only one (exponential) segment. Notice that linsegr must be used only with MIDI. Otherwise it doesn't produce any extension of note duration.

What if a complex envelope is needed in the release phase consisting of more segments? (For example, a crescendo followed by a diminuendo.)

The next example will show how to implement it by means of two new opcodes: *xtratim* and *release*.

3.3 Extending the life of a MIDI-activated note: *xtratim* and *release*

In this example we suppose that the user wants a more complex envelope in the release phase of a MIDI-activated note.

Now, it is necessary to make a distinction between two types of orchestra instruments: those which are activated by the score and those which are activated by a MIDI note-on message. The reason we need this distinction is that sometimes some opcodes operate correctly only on instruments designed to be activated by MIDI. Most opcodes, however, can operate on both score-activated instruments and MIDI-activated instruments.

Actually, extending a note in a score-activated instrument is very easy. Duration is defined by the *p3* parameter of the i-statement of the score. To extend it, it is sufficient to assign a starting value to *p3* plus a value referring the wanted extension of duration, expressed in seconds:

```
p3     =   p3+1    ;adds 1 second to the duration of current note
```

This is true for score-activated instruments.

In MIDI-activated instruments, *p3* is meaningless because corresponding notes remain active until a note-off message is received.

The only ways to extend the duration of these notes is by

• using MIDI-oriented envelope opcodes (those terminating with an 'r', *linenr*, *linsegr*, *expsegr*, the 'r' being for 'release'), or
• by using two opcodes, specially designed to accomplish this task: *xtratim* and *release*.

Look at the following example:

```
        instr   1
inum    notnum
icps    cpsmidi
iamp    ampmidi   4000
;############## complex MIDI envelope #################
        xtratim 1                  ; extra-time, i.e. release duration
krel    init    0
krel    release                    ; outputs release-stage flag (0 or 1 values)
if      (krel > .5) kgoto  rel     ; if in release-stage goto release section
;************ attack and sustain section ***********
kmp1    linseg  0, .03, 1, .05, 1, .07, 0, .08, .5, 1, .2, 50, .2
kmp     =       kmp1*iamp
        kgoto   done
;************ release section **********************
rel:
kmp2    linseg  1, .05, 4, .7, 0
kmp     =       kmp1*kmp2*iamp
done:
;####################################################

a1      oscili  kmp, icps, 1
        out     a1
        endin
```

This instrument appears complex, but it isn't. The purpose of the *xtratim* opcode is to add extra time to the duration of instr 1. The extra-time amount is defined by the input argument (one second in the example). Notice that *xtratim* has no output. The purpose of the *release* opcode is to indicate when the corresponding note is in the normal stage and when it in at the extra time stage (the release time). In this case, there are two envelopes, performed in succession. Notice one important detail. In most cases, the sustain envelope isn't performed in its entirety because it is impossible to foresee how much time the performer leaves the key pressed. So, the last value of variable *kmp1* could not be equal to the initial value of *kmp2*. In order to avoid discontinuities in the sound («tics»), it is necessary to multiply last value of *kmp1* by *kmp2*. (*kmp2* must set to value 1 at the beginning, in order to leave initial output argument of *linseg* unmodified.) The release-stage envelope acts as a multiplier for the last value from the envelope of the previous stage. In the example, initially we have an ascending release which after a second after descends toward zero.

3.4 Continuous controllers: varying amplitude and frequency of vibrato while playing notes.

```
;vibrato.orc
          instr     1
ifreq     cpsmidi
iamp      ampmidi   10000
kfrqvib   midic7    1, 0, 1
kampvib   midic7    2, 0, 1
kvib      oscili    kampvib, kfrqvib, 1
kenv      linsegr   0, .1, 1, .3, .5, .2, 0
a1        oscili    iamp, ifreq*powoftwo(kvib), 1
          out       a1*kenv
          endin
```

This example allows one to play a note on the master-keyboard, and varying both the frequency and the amplitude of vibrato simultaneously. Vibrato is generated by an oscillator (performing at k-rate),that generates a control signal which is multiplied by the base frequency of the audio signal oscillator. The frequency and amplitude of the oscillator generating vibrato can be varied continuously by means of MIDI control-change messages. The opcode used to handle these messages is *midic7* which allows scaling of the 7-bit raw values (incoming by the MIDI in port with a 0-127 range) into a minimum-maximum range defined by the user.

There are three *midic7* input arguments plus an optional one: MIDI control message number (for example 1 is corresponding to modulation-wheel, 2 to breath-control etc.), minimum and maximum values, used to re-scale the output.

Notice the use of *powoftwo()* function, which gives a multiplier varying exponentially instead than linearly: if we used a direct sum of vibrato signal and the note base frequency, the vibrato would generate large frequency variations in the low frequency range and little variations in high frequency range. In this case, multiplying by an exponent enables us to express the variation in octaves instead of cps. Although the mathematical reasoning behind this concept isn't too complex, it is beyond the scope of this chapter. Assuming that the range of the second instance of *midic7* opcode (which controls vibrato amplitude) is expressed in octaves, variations in the range of 0 to 1 octaves are sufficient.

3.5 More complex vibrato, delay and tremolo, controllable in real-time

The previous example is not optimized for speed. If the performer plays more than one note at the same time, several instances of *midic7* opcode are activated that generate an identical signal. This is a useless waste of processing time.

It is necessary to think a little about how Csound instruments and opcodes work.

A Csound instrument is a template used by Csound when it activates the corresponding note.

When this happens, an '*instance*' of that instrument, together with its data, is generated. Csound instruments are polyphonic. So, more than one note of the same instrument can be activated with different parameters at the same time. Each of these notes is actually an *instance* of the corresponding instrument.

In a similar way, multiple instances of the same opcode can be called by the same instrument (in the previous example this happens with *midic7* opcode). So, we have a hierarchy of instances. Several notes of the same instruments generate several instances of that instrument, each containing more instances of the same opcode. Csound variables represent signals which can be control signals, audio signals or initialization parameters (the last choice remains constant for all note duration). It is important to notice that the variables contained inside an instrument are local. This means that variables with the same name, placed in different instruments, are different in all respects. Furthermore, even considering the same instrument, variables with the same name are different in each new instance of that instrument, and they contain different but independent values for each parameter that correspond to activating notes.

Let's return to the previous example. When the performer activates a chord consisting of 3 notes, the two instances of *midic7* contained by instr 1 are actually multiplied by three, creating a total of 6 instances, which are useless because they all produce the same values. This is a waste of processing time. It is better to use the MIDI-control opcodes in a separate instrument which is activated only once, and remains active for the duration of current Csound session. These instruments are activated by the score instead of by a MIDI controller.

In order to make signal produced by such an instrument visible to other devices (and in particular by the MIDI activated instrument which needs to access the values produced by controllers), it is necessary to use *global variables*. Global variables have orchestra scope, not instrument scope. This means that they are common and visible by all instruments of the orchestra. Furthermore, unlike local variables, they are common to all instances of all currently active instruments.

Let's look at the example below:

```
;orchestra

        sr     =  44100
        kr     =  441
        ksmps  =  100
        nchnls =  1

gi1 ftgen 1, 0, 1024, 10, 1, .2, 0, 0, .1, 0, 0, .05        ; audio table
gi1 ftgen 2, 0, 129, 7, 0, 4, -1, 64, -1, 4, 0, 56, 0       ; tremolo table

;## vibrato functions
gi1 ftgen   50, 0, 513, 10, 1 ;sine
gi1 ftgen   51, 0, 513, 7,  1, 511, -1 ; falling saw tooth
gi1 ftgen   52, 0, 513, 7,  -1, 511, 1 ; rising saw tooth
gi1 ftgen   53, 0, 513, 7,  0, 128, 1, 256, -1, 128, 0 ;triangle
gi1 ftgen   54, 0, 513, 7,  1, 256, -1, 255, 0 ;square
gi1 ftgen   55, 0, 513, 7,  0, 170, 0, 0, 1, 170, 1,  0, -1, 170, -1, 0, 0 ;three steps
gi1 ftgen   56, 0, 513, 7,  0, 128, 0, 0, 1, 128, 1, 0, 0, 128, 0, 0, -1, 128, -1, 0, 0 ;4 steps
gi1 ftgen   57, 0, 513, 7,  1, 128, 1, 0, 0, 128, 0, 0, -1, 128, -1, 0, 0, 128, 0 ;4 steps 2
gi1 ftgen   58, 0, 513, 7,  -1, 128, -1, 0, 0, 128, 0, 0, 1, 128, 1, 0, 0, 128, 0 ;4 steps 3
; fourth, fifth and octave
gi1 ftgen   59, 0, 513, 7, 0, 128, 0, 0, 5, 128, 5, 0, 7, 128, 7, 0, 12, 128, 12
; octave, fourth, fifth and unison
gi1 ftgen   60, 0, 513, 7, 12, 128, 12, 0, 5, 128, 5, 0, 7, 128, 7, 0, 0, 128, 0
;4 glissando
gi1 ftgen   61, 0, 513, 7,  -1, 90, -1, 38, 0, 90, 0, 38, 1, 90, 1, 38, 0, 90, 0, 38, -1

gi1 ftgen 100, 0, 8193, 5,  .001, 8193, 1    ; exponential curve for slider mapping

gk1     init        0
gk2     init        0
gk3     init        0
gk4     init        0
gk5     init        0
```

```
gk6     init      0
gk7     init      0
gk8     init      0
gaout   init      0

;///////////////////////////
        instr     1
;///////////////////////////
kvib    oscili    gk1, gk2, i(gk3)+.5
atrem   oscili    gk4, gk5, 2
ifreq   cpsmidi
iamp    ampmidi   10000
aenv    linsegr   0, .05, 1, .2, .2, 10, .2, .2, 0
a1      oscili    aenv*iamp*(1+atrem), ifreq*powoftwo(kvib),1
        vincr     gaout, a1
        endin

;///////////////////////////
        instr     100
;///////////////////////////
        initc7    1, 3, (50-50)/(61.5-50)
gk1     ctrl7     1, 1, 0, 1              ; vibrato amplitude
gk2     ctrl7     1, 2, .5, 20, 100       ; vibrato frequency
gk3     ctrl7     1, 3, 50, 61.5          ; vibrato table
gk4     ctrl7     1, 4, 0, 1              ; tremolo depth
gk5     ctrl7     1, 5, 2, 20, 100        ; tremolo frequency
gk6     ctrl7     1, 6, 0, 1              ; wet/dry ratio
gk7     ctrl7     1, 7, 0, 1              ; delay feedback
gk8     ctrl7     1, 8, 1, 1000           ; delay time
gk8     tonek     gk8,2
a8      interp    gk8
a1      init      0
a1      vdelay    gaout+a1*gk7,a8,1000
        out       a1*gk6+gaout*(1-gk6)
        clear     gaout
        endin

;score
i100 0 3600
```

As you can see, the score doesn't need the *f0* statement because the duration of the real-time session is already set to 3600 seconds by the only note activating ëglobal' instr 100. We will see the purpose of instr 100 later.

Instrument 1 has three oscillators. The first and the second oscillator generate vibrato and tremolo, whereas the third one generates the audio signal. Some remarks about instr 1 follow.

1. Vibrato amplitude is defined externally from instr 1, as well as, vibrato frequency, vibrato table number, tremolo depth and tremolo frequency. These parameters are supplied to the oscillators by means of the global variables *gk1, gk2, gk3, gk4* and *gk5*. We will see the storage locations of these variable later.
2. *out* opcode is not present inside instr 1, because its output is assigned to the *gaout* global variable. The reason we use a global variable and do not send the output signal directly to the *out* opcode is that the signal is reused by another instrument that adds an effect (a delay) and balances the wet/dry ratio before it is assigned it to the *out* opcode. When sending an audio signal to the *gaout* global variable, simply assigning it is not sufficient because a global variable is common to all orchestra instrument instances. So, if instr 1 is polyphonic and its output is assigned directly to *gaout*, the signal generated by any concurrent instances of instr 1 would be replaced by the one immediate instance. In that case, when *gaout* is connected to the *out* opcode (in instr 100), the signal would be monophonic (not polyphonic) because it would contain only the output of last instance of instr 1 (last voice). In order to avoid this drawback, we have to mix output of instr 1 with the content of *gaout* instead of simply assigning the raw value directly. Here this operation is accomplished with the *vincr* opcode.
   vincr does this:
   ```
   gaout = gaout + a1
   ```
   ...but is faster. It is an accumulator, especially designed to sum a signal and a mixing line. After connecting *gaout* to the *out* opcode (placed in instr 100), it is necessary to clear *gaout* by setting it to zero. Otherwise, the variable will 'explode' because values would continue accumulating endlessly.
   To set *gaout* to zero, the following line would be sufficient:
   ```
   gaout = 0
   ```
   ...but the *clear* opcode is used instead. It is designed specifically to complete this task quickly (in this example the increasing in speed is not particularly evident, but it is apparent, in complex mixing lines when several variables have to be zeroed at the same time. See manual).

Instrument 100 is called by the score only once per Csound session. This instrument has three functions:

1. MIDI control messages handling, by filling global variables. Such variables have the following purposes:
   gk1 - vibrato amplitude
   gk2 - vibrato frequency
   gk3 - select vibrato table number
   gk4 - tremolo depth
   gk5 - tremolo frequency
   gk6 - wet/dry delay ratio
   gk7 - delay feedback (to allow echo)
   gk8 - delay time

2. generation of a delay effect (that is unique for all notes of all instruments)

3. master output control.

Let's examine this instrument more closely. Noticed that there is no *midic7* instance in instr 1. In fact, the MIDI control-change messages are controlled by several instances of *ctrl7*, an opcode similar to *midic7* but with the flexibility to choose the MIDI channel. Consequently, it can be used in score-activated instruments. Assigning *midic7* to a score-activated instrument causes CSound to crash. (The *midic7* channel is implicitly implied and has the same MIDI channel number as the instrument that activates it.)

Notice that global variables are initialized before any instruments are declared in the header section of orchestra. If global variables are not declared first errors appear caused by using variables before they are initialized.

The purpose of *initc7* opcode is to initialize the first output value of the corresponding MIDI control-change handling opcode (works both with *midic7* and *ctrl7*, see manual).

3.6 Non-linear distortion, micro-tuning and slider banks

Let's analyze the following orc/sco pair:

```
;**** distortion.orc
          sr      =  44100
          kr      =  441
          ksmps   =  100
          nchnls  =  2

ga1       init       0
gk12e4    init       882
```

```
;////////////////////////////////////////////////
        instr       1
;////////////////////////////////////////////////
kbend   pchbend     -1,1
i1      cpstmidi(gk12e4)
k2      linsegr     0, 1.5, 1, 6, .15, 1, .15, 1.2, 0
a1      oscili      k2, i1*powoftwo(kbend), 1
        vincr       ga1, a1
        endin

;////////////////////////////////////////////////
        instr       2
;////////////////////////////////////////////////
gk12e1,gk12e2,gk12e3,gk12e4,gk12e5,gk12e6,gk12e7,gk12e8  slider8f 1,\
\;      ctl     min     max     init    func    icutoff
        1,      .1,     5,      .1,     0,      5,      \;1- distortion
        2,      2,      500,    20,     92,     5,      \;2- filter cutoff
        3,      .05,    8,      1,      92,     5,      \;3- filter resonance
        4,      880,    888.5,882,      0,      10000,\;4- micro-tuning table
        5,      0,      8,      0,      0,      5,      \;5- amp. of dist.modulation
        6,      .1,     10,     1,      92,     5,      \;6- freq. of dist.modul.
        7,      0,      200,    0,      0,      5,      \;7- amp. of filter modulation
        8,      .1,     10,     1,      92,     5        ;8- freq. of filter modulation
gk12e9 ctrl7    1, 9,   870,    878.5                    ;9- distortion table

kosc    oscili      gk12e5,gk12e6,879
kosc    tonek       gk12e1+kosc,5
aosc    interp      kosc

amod    tableikt    ga1*aosc, int(gk12e9),1, .5, 0

kfilt   oscili      gk12e7, gk12e8, 879
kfilt   tonek       gk12e2+kfilt, 5
kres    tonek       gk12e3, 1.5

amod    lowres      amod, kfilt, kres
amod    =           amod*6400
adel    delay       amod,.3
        outs        amod, adel
```

```
        clear       ga1
        endin
;///////////////////////////////////////////////
;***** distortion.sco

;## audio table ##
f1 0 1024 10 1 ;sinusoid

;## exponential slider mapping ##
f92  0  4097  5  .01 4096 100

;## distortion tables ##
f870 0 4097 9 .5 1 90 ;sigmoid
f871 0 4097 8 8 2032 1 32 -1 2032 -8 ; cubic spline 1
f872 0 4097 8 0.3 1024 1 2048 -1 1024 -0.3 ; cubic spline 2
f873 0 4097 8 0 256  1 3584 -1 256  0 ; cubic spline 3
f874 0 4097 8 -1 512 1 512 -1 2048 -1 512 1 512 -1
f875 0 4097 8 -1 512 1 512 -1 2048 1 512 -1 512 1
f876 0 4097 8 -1 512 6 512 -4 2048 1 512 -1 512 1
f877 0 4097 8 7 128 8 128 6 128 7 128 5 128 6 128 4 128 5 128 3
          128 4 128 2 128 3 128 1 128 2 128 0 128 1 128 0
          128 -1 128 0 128 -2 128 -1 128 -3 128 -2 128 -4 128 -3
          128 -5 128 -4 128 -6 128 -5 128 -7 128 -6 128 -8 128 -7
f878 0 4097 8 12 128 8 128 6 128 7 128 5 128 6 128 4 128 5 128 3
          128 4 128 2 128 11 128 1 128 2 128 0 128 6 128 0
          128 -6 128 0 128 -2 128 -1 128 -3 128 -2 128 -4 128 -3
          128 -5 128 -4 128 -6 128 -5 128 -7 128 -13 128 -8 128 -12

;## positive sinusoid ##
f879 0 1024 19 1 1 0 1

;## tuning tables ##
;# equal temperament  #
;          numgrades       freqbase          scaleRatio (eq.temp.)
;                   interval        basekeymidi
f880 0 16 -2    12       2       261       60
             1                        1.059463094359     1.122462048309     1.189207115003
             1.259921049895     1.33483985417      1.414213562373     1.498307076877
             1.587401051968     1.681792830507     1.781797436281     1.887748625363
```

```
;# diatonic pure #
f881 0 16 -2    12    2    261.62    60  1  1.04166667  1.125  1.171875  1.25  1.3333  1.40625  1.5  1.5625
1.66666  1.777777777777  1.875

# harmonic progression   1( 36 steps )#
f882 0 64 -2   36  2   30.5    24   1  2  3  4   5  6  7   8   9    10 11  12 13 14  15 16  17 18 19  20  21   22 23
24 25 26  27 28  29 30 31  32  33   34 35  36

;# harmonic progression 2( 24 steps)#
f883 0 32 -2   24   2   30.5   24   2  3   4  5   6  7  8   9   10   11 12  13 14 15  16 17  18 19 20  21  22   23 24  25

;# harmonic progression 3( 24 steps)#
f884 0 32 -2   24   2   15.25   24   4  5   6  7   8  9  10  11  12   13 14  15 16 17  18 19  20 21 22  23  24   25 26  27

;# harmonic progression 4( 12 steps)#
f885 0 16 -2    12  2    61    60   4  5   6  7   8  9  10  11  12   13 14  15

;# harmonic progression 5( 12 steps)#
f886 0 16 -2    12  2   61    60   8  9   10 11  12 13 14  15  16   17 18  19

;# harmonic progression 6( 24 steps)#
f887 0 16 -2   12   2    61    60   16 17  18 19  20 21 22  23  24   25 26  27 28 29  30 31  32 33 34  35  36   37 38  39

;# 'detuned' scale #
f888 0 16 -2    12  2   261.62    60    1  1.111111111 1.142857143 1.25 1.285714286 1.388888889 1.428571429
1.5 1.607142857 1.666666667 1.714285714 1.928571429

;## note ##
i2 0 3600
e
```

This is an example of non-linear distortion with a shaping-table unique for all voices of polyphony. This produces an electric-guitar-like, chord effect.

Let's start with instr 1.

pchbend opcode controls MIDI pitch-bend messages. In this example, the output values of this opcode cover a range of -1 to 1. This corresponds to pitch shifts down or up an octave as defined by the *powoftwo( )* function.

cpstmid opcode controls table parameters containing user-defined tuning systems. *cpstmid* is similar to *cpsmidi*, because both are designed for use with MIDI-activated instruments and require a table number as the input argument. The table is filled with parameters and a set of frequency ratios (for more information see the manual). This example shows different tuning systems can be selected by means of MIDI control-change messages during the performance. In fact the *gk12e4* global variable is sampled and held in the initialization stage *(i( )* function). So, its value is available as input argument to *cpstmid*, and can change for each notes. (It remains constant for the entire duration of one single note.) Notice that the *gk12e4* variable is initialized in the header section of orchestra. As mentioned earlier, an error appears if a variable is used before it is defined.

linsegr opcode defines the amplitude envelope of a sinusoidal oscillator, and the output of such oscillator is then distorted by instr 2. Oscillator output increments global audio variable *ga1*, which is reused by instr 2. *ga1* had been defined in the header section - before it is called.

Instrument 2 starts with the *slider8f* opcode, that generates a bank of 8 sliders, giving the possibility to set MIDI channel (a unique channel for all controllers), MIDI control number, minimum and maximum values, starting value, an optional mapping table number (if not used, set the corresponding argument to zero), and cutoff frequency of a low-pass filter placed before the output, in order to smooth discontinuities due to low resolution of 7-bit MIDI data. Such parameters must be defined for each controller, for this reason the argument of slider8f opcode are split into eight text lines by using '\' character, interpreted by Csound as line continuation. Notice that after the "\" character it is possible to put comments starting with "";" character.

As controllers needed in this orchestra are nine, and *slider8f* opcode can handle only eight of those, another line containing *ctrl7* opcode is added.

Variables interpreting the MIDI messages are:

gk12e1 - amount of distortion (corresponding to the amplitude of the signal generated by the oscillator)
gk12e2 - cutoff frequency of the low pass resonant filter, used to make distorted signals more musically, resulting very harsh to hearing otherwise
gk12e3 - filter resonance
gk12e4 - select the number of micro-tuning table (read by instr 1)
gk12e5 - amplitude of distortion-amount-modulating oscillator

gk12e6 - frequency of distortion-amount-modulating oscillator
gk12e7 - amplitude of cutoff-frequency-modulating oscillator, connected to resonant low pass filter
gk12e8 - frequency of cutoff-frequency-modulating oscillator, connected to resonant low pass filter
gk12e9 - select the number of table containing the wave-shaping function

The next oscillator is used as an amplitude-modulator for the *ga1* signal (generated by instr 1). This is equivalent to modulating the amount of distortion. The oscillator output is summed with the output of the slider controlling the level of distortion (*gk12e1*). The resulting value is then filtered to smooth the stepped shape of the output caused by the low resolution of MIDI. This filtering stage prevents 'tics'.

Filter output (*k-rate* signal) is then converted to a-rate (*aosc* variable) with the *interp* opcode. It linearly interpolates between current *kosc* value and the previous one, again, smoothing the signal.

Then, we can see *tableikt* opcode, which is similar to *tablei* (linearly-interpolated table reading), but changes to the table number at *k-rate*. This opcode distorts the input signal (which is *ga1* in this example) in accordance with the corresponding waveshaping table. In this example, this table can be changed during the performance of a note which allow us to hear how the sound output changes according to the type of functions used by current waveshaping table. Notice that the level of distortion modulates with the *aosc* signal as it is multiplied by the *ga1* signal.

Next oscillator modulates cutoff frequency of the lowpass resonant filter (wah-wah effect). *kfilt* signal, generated by such oscillator, is then summed to an offset (*gk12e2* signal, controlled by a slider), and filtered by a low pass filter in order to avoid tics. The signal that controls the amount of resonance (*gk12e3*) is filtered, too.

Then, the output of the waveshaping function (*amod* variable) is sent to the resonant low pass filter (*lowres* opcode) which is controlled in frequency and in resonance amount by *kfilt* and ***kres***. At last, the signal going to right channel is delayed of 0.3 seconds, in order to enrich output sound.

clear opcode zeroes *ga1* variable in order to avoid new values to continue being summed endlessly.

3.7 Granular synthesis

In this section a granular synthesis example will be presented, which allows real-time control of almost every parameters.

```
; granular.orc
sr      =   32000
kr      =   320
ksmps   =   100
nchnls  =   2

garev1  init 0
gaout1  init 0
gaout2  init 0

;- - - - - - -

;//////////////////////////////////////
        instr   100
;//////////////////////////////////////

gk_1, gk_2, gk_3, gk_4, gk_5, gk_6, gk_7, gk_8,\
gk_9, gk_10, gk_11, gk_12, gk_13, gk_14, gk_15, gk_16  slider161,\
\;      ctl     min     max     init    func
        1,      1,      20.5,   1,      0,      \;1 audio table number
        2,      0,      13.5,   1,      0,      \;2 play speed
        3,      .5,     5,      3,      0,      \;3 grain repeat speed
        4,      0,      2,      1,      0,      \;4 phase scanning speed of current sample
        5,      0,      1,      0,      0,      \;5 end frequency of glissandos
        6,      .005,   4,      .5,     100,    \;6 total duration of grains
        7,      1/15,   1,      .3,     0,      \;7 attack time of grains
        8,      1/15,   1,      .3,     0,      \;8 decay time of grains
        9,      0,      .12,    0,      0,              \;9 reverb send level
        10,     300,    8000,   3200,   0,      \;10 reverb low pass filter
        11,     0,      2,      0,      0,      \;11 random amount of grain frequency
        12,     0,      3,      0,      0,      \;12 random amount of grain duration
        13,     0,      .2,     .05,    0,      \;13 left/right channel phase difference
        14,     0,      .5,     0,      0,      \;14 random amount of starting grain phase
        15,     0,      3,      0,      0,      \;15 octaviation factor
        16,     .05,    2,      1,      0       ;16 global volume

gk_17, gk_18, gk_19, gk_20, gk_21, gk_22, gk_23, gk_24     slider8  1,\
\;      ctl     min     max     init    func
        17,     102,    105.5,  102,    0,\;17 harmonic tuning table number
```

```
        18,   0,    8.5,  0,    0,    \;18 amount of random changes in harmonic tuning table
        19,   1,    1.5,  1,    0,    \;19 left/right deviation of grain repetition speed
        20,   0,    1,    0,    0,    \;20 stating phase offset of grains
        21,   0,    15,   0,    0,    \;21 random amount of grain starting time
        22,   0,    1,    0,    0,    \
        23,   0,    1,    0,    0,    \
        24,   0,    1,    0,    0

;************ REVERB and OUTPUT *************
arevb   tonex   garev1, gk_10,3
arev    reverb2 arevb, 9, .05
        outs    gaout1 + arev, gaout2 + arev
        clear   gaout1, gaout2, garev1
        endin

;////////////////////////////////////////
        instr   1
;////////////////////////////////////////
ifmidi  cpsmidi
iamp    ampmidi   1

ifna        =   int(i(gk_1))        ;** left channel sample table
ifna2       =   ifna                ;** right channel sample table
imemlen     =   ftlen(ifna)         ;** length of allocated table
ilen        =   nsamp(ifna          ;** number of samples contained into the table
ilnDmem     =   ilen/imemlen        ;** sampling length/table length ratio
ifsr        =   ftsr(ifna)/sr       ;** sampling frequency of audio sample up sr
isrDmem     =   sr/imemlen          ;** necessary to calculate actual frequency
isrDdur     =   ftsr(ifna)/ilen      ;** sampling frequency of audio sample up number of samples

krdharm         linrand gk_18       ;** random harmonic variation amount
krdharm2        linrand gk_18
krdharm         table   krdharm, i(gk_17)
krdharm2        table   krdharm2, i(gk_17)
kform           table   gk_2, 151
kform       =   (ifmidi/127*.98) *kform*isrDmem*ifsr
krndpch         trirand gk_11        ;**  random pitch variation of grains
krndpch2        trirand gk_11
kform1      =   kform*powoftwo(krndpch)*krdharm   ;** right chan. freq.
```

```
kform2       =     kform*powoftwo(krndpch2)*krdharm2 ;** left chan. freq.
krnd               trirand  gk_21
kfund        =     2^(gk_3+krnd)      ;** speed of grain repeats

kphsrate     =     gk_4*isrDdur

krndphs            linrand  gk_14     ;** random phase amount

kphs      init     0
kphs      phasor   kphsrate
kphs         =     (kphs+krndphs+gk_20) * ilnDmem
kphs      wrap     kphs, 0, ilnDmem

kphs2     init     0
kphs2     phasor   kphsrate, i(gk_13)  ;** right channel phase can be varied for stereo effect
kphs2        =     (kphs2+krndphs+gk_20)*ilnDmem
kphs2     wrap     kphs2, 0, ilnDmem

kgliss       =     gk_5            ;** grain glissando
krnddur   linrand  gk_12           ;** random amount of grain duration
kdur         =     (1+krnddur) * gk_6
kris         =     kdur * gk_7
kdec         =     kdur * gk_8
iolaps       =     10

kampenv   linenr   iamp*gk_16, 0,.1,.03

;**          xfund       koct    kris     kdec      ifna    itotdur    kgliss
;**     xamp        xform    kband    kdur     iolaps    ifnb       kphs
;**    ------------------------------------------------------------------------
a1      fof3   kampenv, kfund,  kform1, gk_15, 0, kris, kdur, kdec, iolaps, ifna, 101, 3600, kphs, kgliss
a2      fof3   kampenv, kfund*gk_19, kform2, gk_15, 0, kris, kdur, kdec, iolaps, ifna2,101, 3600, kphs2, kgliss

        vincr  gaout1, a1 * (1 - gk_9) ;** left main output
        vincr  gaout2, a2 * (1 - gk_9) ;** right main output
        vincr  garev1, (a1 + a2) * gk_9   ;** reverb send
        endin

;*********** Granular.sco ****************
```

```
f1  0 262144  -22  "c:\csound\icmc\voceGabEng.aif" 0 0 1
f2  0 524288  -22  "c:\csound\icmc\aiff\fm15 a(tema 2).aif" 0 0 1
f3  0 524288  -22  "c:\csound\icmc\aiff\fm15 m(arrich spett arm acute).aif" 0 0 1
f4  0 524288  -22  "c:\csound\icmc\aiff\fm15 t(arricchimento spettrale).aif" 0 0 1
f5  0 1048576 -22  "c:\csound\icmc\aiff\fm15 z(grave con arr spettr).aif" 0 0 1
f6  0 524288  -22  "c:\csound\icmc\aiff\fm15-f(iperarmonici).aif" 0 0 1
f7  0 131072  -22  "c:\csound\icmc\aiff\Gest9 (ottava gliss bassa).aif" 0 0 1
f8  0 524288  -22  "c:\csound\icmc\aiff\GestB (trilli glissati).aif" 0 0 1
f9  0 65536   -22  "c:\csound\icmc\aiff\GestD (batterie glissate).aif" 0 0 1
f10  0 65536   -22  "c:\csound\icmc\aiff\GestF (acciaccature).aif" 0 0 1
f11  0 524288  -22  "c:\csound\icmc\aiff\gyuto1 flang2 (pizzicati e raschiati).aif" 0 0 1
f12  0 262144  -22  "c:\csound\icmc\aiff\gyuto1 uuuamiu.aif" 0 0 1
f13  0 524288  -22  "c:\csound\icmc\aiff\Pigmei A(voce e flauto).aif" 0 0 1
f14  0 524288  -22  "c:\csound\icmc\aiff\Vid Nooo (E3).aif" 0 0 1
f15  0 262144  -22  "c:\csound\icmc\aiff\Vid uuuu(dissonanza).aif" 0 0 1
f16  0 262144  -22  "c:\csound\icmc\aiff\Clar PigmeiTema alto.aif" 0 0 1
f17  0 262144  -22  "c:\csound\icmc\aiff\Clar coppia temi paralleli3.aif" 0 0 1
f18  0 262144  -22  "c:\csound\icmc\aiff\Clar Tema2 retrogrado.aif" 0 0 1
f19  0 262144  -22  "c:\csound\icmc\aiff\Clar coppia temi veloce4.aif" 0 0 1
f20  0 131072  -22  "c:\csound\icmc\aiff\Clar coppia temi veloce6 cromatica2.aif" 0 0 1


f100 0 8192    5  .001 8192 1     ;** exponential curve for slider mapping
f101 0 8192    19  .5 1 270 1     ;** sigmoid curve

;**           unis / third / fifth / Min7th / octave / oct+3rd / oct+5th / oct+7th / double oct
f102 0 32  -2  1    1.25    1.5    1.75    2    2.5    3    3.5    4

;**           unis / -4 / 5  / -8  / 8  / -8 -4  / 8 +5  / -2oct / 2oct
f103 0 32  -2  1  .75  1.5  .5  2  .375   3   .25   4

;**        major just scale
f104 0 32  -2  1  1.125  1.25 1.33333 1.5 1.66666 1.875  2 2

;**        harmonic progression
f105 0 32  -2  1  1.125  1.25 1.375 1.5 1.625 1.75 1.875 2

;**     frequency table
f151   0 32  -2  .5  1  .625 .75 .875  1  1.125  1.25   1.375   1.5   1.625   1.75   1.875  2
```

```
i100 0 3600
e
```

The orchestra is quite complex. So, we'll work backwards, starting from the audio output located at the bottom of instrument, up to controller's inputs located at the top.

NOTE: We recommend that you analyze complex orchestras from output back to input because, normally, the audio output consists of one, easy-to-locate variable (or two in stereo, four in quadraphonic, etc.). Whereas the number of inputs usually is much larger. In this case, there are 21 continuous controllers, plus inputs for the note-number and the velocity of each note. Distinguishing at a glance the variables derived directly from physical inputs in contrast to the intermediate variables is not an easy task. The audio output is like the root of a tree, while input signals are like as branches or leaves of the tree.

Orchestra consists of two instruments:

- instr 100, containing MIDI-control-related opcodes (slider8 e slider16), main output and reverb line;
- instr 1, containing granular-synthesis-related code.

Instrument 100 is easy to read. Starting from the bottom toward the top (i.e. from the root toward the branches), notice that the global audio variables contained in the left and right channels (*gaout1* and *gaout2* variables) and the reverb signal (*arev* variable), are routed to the stereo output. These variables are then zeroed (together with *garev1* reverb line) with the *clear* opcode. The *arev* signal is generated by the *reverb2* opcode. *garev1* (global reverb line) is connected to the reverb after being filtered by a low pass filter (*tonex*). The filtering makes the reverb sound more pleasant when hearing it. The cutoff frequency in this filter is adjustable with slider 10 (*gk_10* global variable). Notice that *tonex* opcode consists of a bank of first-order filters, serially connected. This filtering produces a steeper cutoff curve which generates a warmer sound.

The arguments of *slider8* and *slider16* opcodes are split into several text lines which makes it more legible. (Remember that '\' character indicates a division of a single CSound statement into multiple lines that is recognized as single statement). Our orchestra has a total of 20 signals (adjusted by MIDI controllers). We used two opcodes. The first contains 16 sliders. The second has 8 sliders. So, four sliders remain unused, and can add additional variable parameters in the future by modifying the orchestra.

The following is a list of the global variables corresponding to parameters adjustable by MIDI sliders:

gk_1 select the table containing audio samples (this orchestra can use different samples at the same time);
gk_2 pitch offset, that can be selected by changing the index of a table containing a series of frequential ratios;
gk_3 grain repeat speed, i.e. number of grains per second;
gk_4 phase scanning speed of current sample. This parameter allows to change the duration of current sample without changing its pitch and vice-versa;
gk_5 end frequency of glissando of each grain (see *fof2* and *fof3* manual);
gk_6 total duration of each grain, scaled according to grain repeat speed;
gk_7 attack time of grains, scaled according to their total duration;
gk_8 decay time of grains, scaled according to their total duration;
gk_9 reverb send level;
gk_10 cutoff frequency of low-pass filter used by the reverb output;
gk_11 random amount of grain frequency;
gk_12 random amount of grain duration;
gk_13 left/right channel phase difference;
gk_14 random amount of starting grain phase;
gk_15 octaviation factor (see *fof2* and *fof3* manual);
gk_16 main volume control;
gk_17 harmonic tuning table number;
gk_18 amount of random changes in harmonic tuning table;
gk_19 left/right deviation of grain repetition speed;
gk_20 stating phase offset of grains. If the phase scanning speed of current sample is set to zero (*gk_4* slider), this parameter allow to 'scrub' sampled sound manually.
gk_21 random amount of grain starting time;
gk_22 not assigned;
gk_23 not assigned;
gk_24 not assigned;

Now, let's read instr 1, starting from the bottom.

The three lines of code containing the *vincr* opcode assign left/right channels and the reverb line to the corresponding global variables (*gaout1,gaout2,grev1*) which will be used as arguments in the main audio output located in instr 100.

Notice that reverb line (*garev1*) is obtained by mixing the left and right channels, and by multiplying the result by the current value of slider 9 (*gk_9*) or adjusting wet/dry ratio. Slider 9 also affects the level of direct signals (*a1* and *a2*) placed in the global variables *gaout1* and *gaout2*.

a1 and *a2* variables are generated by *fof3* opcodes. These are the heart of the granular synthesis engine. There are two calls to *fof3* which process a stereo file using the granular synthesis technique.

Even a mono sample can be granulated using two *fof3* modules with slightly different parameters. This produces a stereo effect.

fof3 opcode is derived by *fof2* which is derived by *fof*.

Initially, *fof* was not designed for granular synthesis, but for vocal synthesis using formants derived from IRCAM's *Chant* program (Xavier Rodet et al.).

Thanks to the internal structure, *fof, fof2* and *fof3* can be used in granular synthesis, as well. Compared with *fof* and *fof2*, *fof3* can handle 16-bit integer samples stored into a CSound table (whereas *fof* and *fof2* only handle 32-bit floating-point samples). For this reason, *fof3* is more efficient and wastes less memory. It stores double the amount of samples with the same amount of RAM. Furthermore, *fof3* uses linear interpolation to read samples, while *fof* and *fof2* don't. So, the audio quality is much better.

Let's analyze the input arguments of the first line of code for the *fof3* opcode (arguments on the second line are practically the same):

```
a1      fof3kampenv, kfund, kform, gk_15, 0, kris, kdur, kdec, iolaps, ifna, 101, 3600, kphs, kgliss
```

kampenv Amplitude envelope. In this case, signal is generated by the previous line of the *linenr* opcode. In this instrument the amplitude varies according to the note-on velocity received by DirectCsound from the MIDI port (see the line containing *ampmidi* opcode).

kfund When using *fof3* in granular synthesis (instead of vocal synthesis), this parameter indicates the grain repeating speed. During processing, *kfund* is variable and enables control over the temporal distance between grains. If *kfund* doesn't vary, or varies slowly and smoothly, we refer to the process as synchronous granular synthesis. If *kfund* varies chaotically, we refer to it as asynchronous granular synthesis. In this orchestra, the base speed of grain repetitions is adjusted by slider 3 (*gk_3* variable). The random variations in this base speed are adjusted with slider 21 (*gk_21* variable).

kform When *fof3* is used for granular synthesis instead of vocal synthesis, this parameter contains the pitch-transposition of the current grain. The value of *kform* is sampled at the start of grain and remains constant for the duration of the entire grain - even if *kform* varies in the meantime. The concept is the same for the initialization parameters which are 'sampled' at the start of a note and remain constant for entire note duration. The only difference is that,

in this case, *kform* remains constant only inside a single grain. So, if it varies during a note, the next grain will get a new frequency value, but the current grain continues to use the old value. *kform* is expressed in cps which indicates the number of times per second the entire table containing the audio samples is read. It should be clear that assigning a frequency value expressed in cps to this parameter is correct only when a single cycle of the sound waveform is stored into the table (for example, a sinusoid). When the table contains a complex sample, it is better to refer to the period of each cycle. (Period is the inverse of frequency.) In our example, the period corresponds to the duration of sampled sound contained in the table. Suppose to have a sample with a length of one second that contains a tone of 440 cps. If we want to play this sampling at 880 cps, we have to read the table twice fast by assigning 2 for a value of *kform*. If we want to play it at 220 cps, we have to assign 0.5 etc. If our sample has a duration of 1.5 seconds and we want to produce a tone of 440 cps, (the sampling frequency of the original) we have to set the period = 1.5 seconds. But since this value must be expressed in cps, (a frequency unit, not a duration unit) we have to assign the inverse of that period (1/1.5 = 0.6666). If we want to transpose up an octave, *kform* must be set to 1/(1.5/2) = 2/1.5 = 1.3333 (i.e. the inverse of half period, that is the double of frequency) and so on.
So it is important to take into account the total duration of the sample contained in the table, as well as, its original frequency (pitch) and original sampling frequency. We pay particular attention to sounds recorded at sampling frequencies that are different from the orchestra's sampling frequency. In our orchestra, the pitch transposition of grains can be adjusted by slider 2 (*gk_2* variable) and by a MIDI note number (*cpsmidi* opcode) while the random amounts of pitch variation of grains can be adjusted by slider 11 and 18 (*gk_11* and *gk_18* variables). Slider 18 allows a table with micro-tuning ratios to control the frequency of grains randomly. Each grain will assume a frequency value that corresponds to a ratio contained in the current micro-tuning scale.

gk_15 in vocal synthesis, this argument contains *octaviation index* which attenuates the level of odd-numbered grains. In vocal synthesis, this index produces an octave-lowering effect. In synchronous granular synthesis, it produces a rhythmic effect when this index is greater than zero. In our orchestra this parameter can be controlled by slider 15.

0 This argument is not used in the granular synthesis of this orchestra. In vocal synthesis, it expresses the bandwidth of the formant in Hertz.

kris Attack time of the trapezoidal envelope of grains. It can be varied in different grains. In our orchestra attack time can be adjusted by slider 7 (*gk_7* variable).

kdur Total duration of each grain. It can be varied in different grains. In our orchestra attack time can be adjusted by slider 6 (*gk_6* variable). Also, it is possible to adjust random variation of grain duration with slider 12 (*gk_12* variable).

kdec Decay time of the trapezoidal envelope of grains. It can be varied in different grains. In our orchestra decay time can be adjusted by slider 8 (*gk_8* variable).

iolaps Number of overlapping grains. If the time duration of the grains exceeds the time interval between grains, the grains will overlap. This parameter defines the maximum number of overlaps. If the number of overlaps surpass this number, CSound crashes. In this orchestra maximum number of overlaps is set to 10. It is recommended that number to this parameter is not too high. High numbers waste of processing time and degrade real-time performance.

ifna In granular synthesis this parameter must be filled with the number of the table containing the sampled sound.
In *fof* and *fof2*, this table is, usually, filled using *GEN01*. In *fof3* (as in the previous example), it is filled using *GEN22*. (It is identical to *GEN01* except that it fills table with 16-bit samples). In our orchestra it is possible to select a different table for each note by varying slider 1 value (*gk_1* variable).

101 Number of the table containing the shape of the attack and decay segment. It is usually a straight-line segment or a sigmoid. The sigmoid can be obtained by using a cycle of a positive sinusoid shifted 90 degrees out of phase with the first and last quarter of cycle are cut off (by using *GEN19*).

3600 Maximum note duration (not grain duration). In this orchestra is set to 3600 seconds.

kphs This parameter tracks the phase of the table storing the sampled sound. It start with zero and ends with 1. These numbers refer to the start and the end of table. To accomplish this task, normally the *phasor* opcode is used, which generates the phase for a table in which period (i.e. the inverse of frequency) coincides with the duration of table scanning.
By varying the frequency of *phasor*, we obtain different reading speeds. So, it is possible to *stretching* time without affecting the pitch of a sampled sound. If the frequency of *phasor* is set to zero, that is if the *kphs* parameter remains constant, the sampled sound will 'freeze'. In our orchestra, the *phasor* frequency (i.e. table scanning speed) can be adjusted with slider 3 (*gk_3* variable). It is also possible to set an offset defining the initial point of

table scanning. By varying such parameter and setting *phasor* frequency to zero, it is possible to 'scrub' manually by changing the corresponding slider value. In our orchestra this value can be adjusted by slider 20 (*gk_20* variable).

kgliss - In *fof2* and *fof3*, a glissando can take place in each grain. This parameter indicates terminal frequency of the transposition. It is expressed as a scale factor. Consequently, assigning 1 to such parameter leaving the frequency of grain unchanged; assigning 2 doubles the frequency at the end of the glissando (the transposition moves up an octave); assigning 0.5 halves the last frequency (i.e. it transposes down an octave down). If the grain's duration is very short, the glissando will sound like a timbral effect, or a sort of detuning. In our orchestra, this parameter can be adjusted with slider 5 (*gk_5* variable).

ampenv signal, contains the amplitude envelope which is generated by *linenr*. The absolute amplitude can be adjusted with slider 16 (*gk_16*), the main volume control. *iolaps* is set to 10. *kris* and *kdec* (grain attack and decay) are calculated as fractions of *kdur* these fractions can be adjusted by slider 7 and 8 (*gk_7* and *gk_8*).

Grain duration *kdur* is controlled by slider 6 (*gk_6*) and its the random variation can be adjusted by slider 12 (*gk_12*).

The frequency of *kgliss* (grain glissando) can be adjusted with slider 5 (*gk_5*).

The table that contains the sampled sound is scanned separately for the left and right channels (*kphs* and *kphs2*) with the two lines of code that call the *phasor* opcode.

The *phasor* input argument controls the speed of sampled sound scan. This argument (*kphsrate*) can be adjusted with slider 4 (*gk_4*). When *kphsrate* defaults to the value 0, sampled sound scanning is stops on a single point, and all grains are read from only one point of sampled sound table. It is possible to modify the scanning point manually, in this example, with means of slider 20 (*gk_20*). This offsets the current point in the scanning. It is, also, possible to modify the phase-difference between the left and right channel by adjusting slider 13 (*gk_13*). Offsets in the grain reading points of sampled sound table can be implemented using random jumps. The random offset (*krndphs*) is generated by *linrand* opcode and the random influence on sampled sound reads can be adjusted with slider 14 (*gk_14*). Actually, *phasor* generates a signal moving from zero to one like the numbers that represent the phase at the start and end of the table containing the sampled sound. Remember the table length must be a power of two, but the number of table entries needed to store a sampled sound is rarely a power of two. So, the number of sound samples and the total number of elements of the table are usually different. (The table length will be greater or equal to the number of sound samples). For this reason, the *nsamp( )*

function is used. This function returns the number of samples actually read from sample file.

The last part of table remains unused, and is filled with zeroes. If the entire table is scanned, we would hear sound only in the first part of table. For the remaining portion we wouldn't hear anything. To prevent this, the phase of table must not rise all the way to 1, but only to the last which holds a sound sample. (i.e. a number between 0.5 is half the table.) The scale factor *ilnDmem* represents the ratio between the sampled sound's length and the table's length.

In our example *phasor* operates at *k-rate*, but the *kphs* and *kphs2* variables must contain values at the initialization stage so that *fof3* can legally call those variables. For this reason, the two variables are initialized with zero values. The phasor frequency (*kphsrate*) is obtained by the multiplication of the output of *slider* 4 with *isrDdur* which is a scaling factor.

The frequency of granule repetitions (*kfund*) is controlled with slider 3 (*gk_3*) in combinations with a random offset (generated by *trirand* opcode). The value of this offset can be adjusted with slider 21. When the value is not zero, rhythm of the grains will vary.

The frequency of each grain is obtained by two variables *kform1* (left channel) and *kform2* (right channel).

Frequency values are influenced by several factors: MIDI note number, slider 2 (*gk_2*, that initiates a transposition), random generators which vary the frequency of each grain which is adjustable with slider 11 (*gk_11*), and random generators that choose an interval ratio stored in a table storing a scale which is adjustable with slider 18 (*gk_18*).

imemlen, ilen, ilnDmem, ifsr, isrDmem and *isrDdur* are re-scaling factors which affect various parameters. We avoid to go into mathematical details in order to don't annoy the reader, who can study their purpose for himself in any case.

ifna and *ifna2* are numbers of the tables containing the sampled sound (left and right channel). These numbers can be changed with slider 1 (*gk_1*).

iamp used to adjust the amplitude of notes, depending by MIDI note velocity.

ifmidi affects the grain frequency (as well as other factors). It is dependent by MIDI note number.

At the beginning of score several tables (1 to 20) are filled with sampled sounds using GEN22.

Table 100 contains a segment of exponential curve and is accessed with the *slider16* opcode. It is used to create a more natural response when adjusting some sliders.

Table 101 contains a sigmoid curve. Its purpose is to shape the attack and decay segment of each grain. The sigmoid curve is created by shifting a positive sinusoid 180 degrees out of phase 180 and then removing the first and the last quarter of period.

Tables 102, 103, 104 and 105 contain frequency ratios for micro-tuning scales.

Table 151 contains transposition factors.

At last, instrument 100 is activated for 3600 seconds, in order to allow an hour of Csound real-time performance.

At this point we end the lecture section regarding DirectCsound real-time examples.

How do we control all MIDI parameters in real-time? We could connect a MIDI fader box (several such mixers are available commercially) to the MIDI input port of the computer to provide the user with a number of physical sliders (potentiometers) which transmit MIDI control-change messages as they are moved (and are then recognized by the orchestra). Normally, MIDI fader boxes or MIDI mixers have only 16 sliders while the adjustable parameters of orchestras are more numerous. Our orchestra, for example, has 21 parameters.

An alternative to hardware devices is VMCI is a program designed to be used in conjunction with DirectCsound under Windows. This is more convenient in many aspects, as we will see in next session.

4. VMCI (VIRTUAL MIDI CONTROL INTERFACE)

VMCI GUI interface can send most kinds of MIDI messages (all VOICE messages: *note-on, note-off, poly after-touch* and *channel after-touch, control-change, program-change* and *pitch-bend*) to any MIDI port installed on the computer. VMCI is totally configurable and gives the user total control over MIDI message definitions. VMCI can be used in place of a MIDI keyboard or any external MIDI control device. It is possible to control DirectCsound via MIDI even without having any MIDI interface card installed on the computer. This program was specifically designed to control DirectCsound, but it can be used to control any MIDI instrument, hardware and software, as well.

4.1 VMCI modes.

There are two versions of VMCI:

1. *VMCI*
2. *VMCI Plus (commercial version with the unique hyper-vectorial synthesis and other enhanced features).*

In this lecture we only deal with the first version that has two modes:

- *Lite mode*
- *Pro mode*

LITE mode is *freeware.*
PRO mode is *shareware.* This mode can be only activated with a 'magic' code given to persons who pay for the software.

In order to control DirectCsound with VMCI, it is necessary to install «*Hubi's LoopBack device*», a virtual MIDI program which provides MIDI ports without any hardware MIDI interface. The «*Hubi's LoopBack*» package is freeware. It is possible to connect several devices to the same MIDI port. Thus, it is possible to control DirectCsound both with VMCI and a hardware master-keyboard at the same time.

VMCI Pro provides the following tools:

- four *7-bit slider panels*, up a total of 256 configurable sliders that can send any MIDI control-change message;
- two *14-bit sliders panels*, up a total of 64 configurable sliders that can send messages of with a double resolution;

- two *virtual joystick panels*, up a total of 16 configurable joystick areas, each one of these controlling two parameters at a time;
- a *virtual keyboard* panel capable to handle a total 960 different MIDI messages of any kind, according to user configuration. Any one of these message can be associated to a key of the alphanumeric keyboard;
- CSound editing and starting buttons, which makes Csound related operations easier;
- *copy board*, that allow to copy and paste parameter values from VMCI to a CSound orchestra o score.

4.2 The ACTIVATION BAR

When starting VMCI, the activation bar appears:

FIG.1 Activation bar

The *activation bar* is the main window and has the following purposes:

- Open and save setup files (with ***.stp*** extension). Setup files contain most settings made during the working sessions. The main settings are slider and joysticks positions (see below), text labels for every parameters and virtual keyboard configuration.
- Show and hide panels (containing sliders, joysticks, and virtual keyboard), by clicking the corresponding check-boxes.
- Open the «MIDI Setup» dialog-box, that allows to select MIDI out port (in «Plus» version it is possible to activate the MIDI in port too).
- Show and hide panel toolbars in order to gain more space and to enlarge vertical slider length.
- Enable automatic sending of note-on and note-off messages each time a slider is moved, in order to initialize a «global instrument» (i.e. a Csound instrument which handles global variables used by other instruments).

- Enable/disable visualization of numeric values of parameters when they change. Since updating visualization subtracts a lot of CPU processing time, this option is useful to enhance Csound realtime performance by freeing processing resources.
- Visualize and clearing «Copy Board» that contains all current slider positions.
- Csound related buttons («*Csound settings*», «*Run Csound*», «*Edit orc*» and «*Edit sco*» that allow to run up to two instances of Csound at the same time, and to edit corresponding orc/sco pairs. «*Csound Settings*» button allows to setup all parameter corresponding to Csound calling inside VMCI).

4.3 Slider-panels

Slider-panels contain a group of scroll-bars (the number of available sliders is different in LITE and in PRO mode). By moving these scroll-bars MIDI control-change messages are sent to the MIDI out port. Each panel emulates the functionality of a MIDI fader box or a MIDI mixer. Two different resolutions are possible in sending parameters: 7-bit messages covering a range of 0 to 127, and 14-bit messages (consisting of a pair of 7-bit messages) covering a range of 0 to 16383.

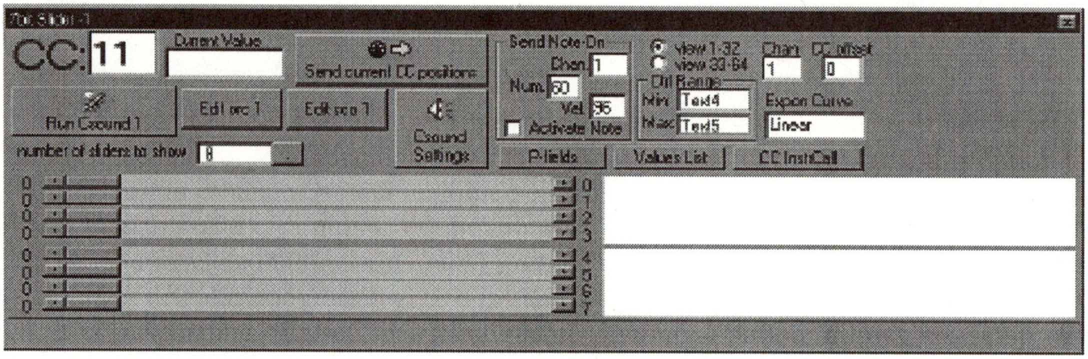

FIG.2 7-bit Slider Panel (horizontal)

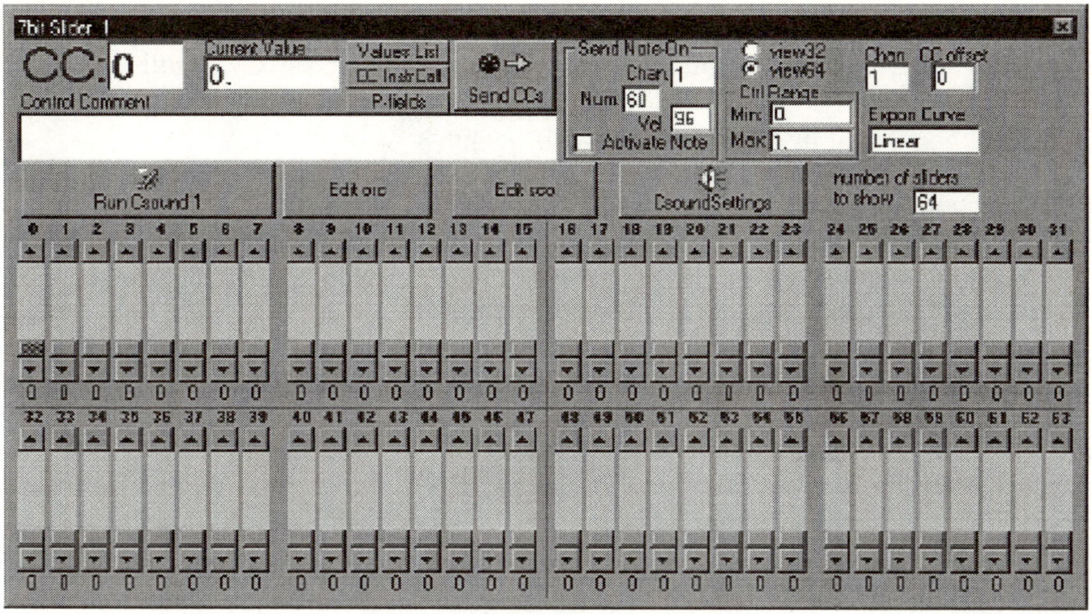

FIG.3 7-bit Slider Panel (vertical)

VMCI Pro mode allows to use up to six slider panels at the same time: two horizontal 7-bit slider panels (fig.2), two vertical 7-bit slider panels (fig.3) and two 14-bit slider panels (fig.4).

Each 7-bit panel contains a total of 64 sliders. The horizontal sliders can only display up to 32 slider at a time whereas the vertical sliders can display all 64 sliders. On the other hand, the horizontal ones display all the slider comments at the same time.

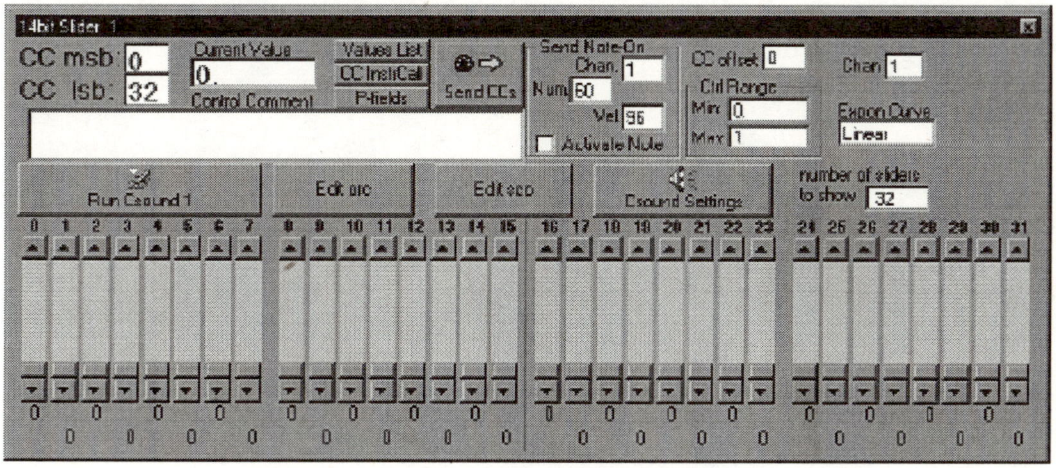

FIG.4 14-bit Slider Panel

When dragging a slider with the mouse, a stream of MIDI control-change messages are sent, and the following information is displayed in accordance with the slider position:

- control-change message number, corresponding to its actual configuration (that can be modified by the user);
- control-change message data value sent to the MIDI out port;
- re-scaled data, as it is interpreted by CSound (default re-scaling range is 0 to 1, and can be reconfigured by the user). Such value is useful to monitor what actually happens in the corresponding CSound instrument;
- slider comment (in horizontal slider panel the comments of all sliders are visualized at the same time), that can be defined by user for each slider.

VMCI allows to save all current slider positions of all panels in the setup file, and to send all MIDI messages corresponding to the present state of a panel by pressing «*Send current CC positions*» button. This restores the identical sonic configuration in a different CSound session, containing many parameters. This feature is normally not present in hardware MIDI fader boxes.

4.4 Virtual joystick panels

VMCI includes two panels, each one contains eight squares which emulate an analog joystick. By dragging a mouse over these areas, two different MIDI control-change messages are sent simultaneously. The first corresponds to the horizontal position of the mouse. The second corresponds to the vertical position. So, it is possible to control two parameters with a single mouse movement. An action which is impossible with sliders (fig.5).

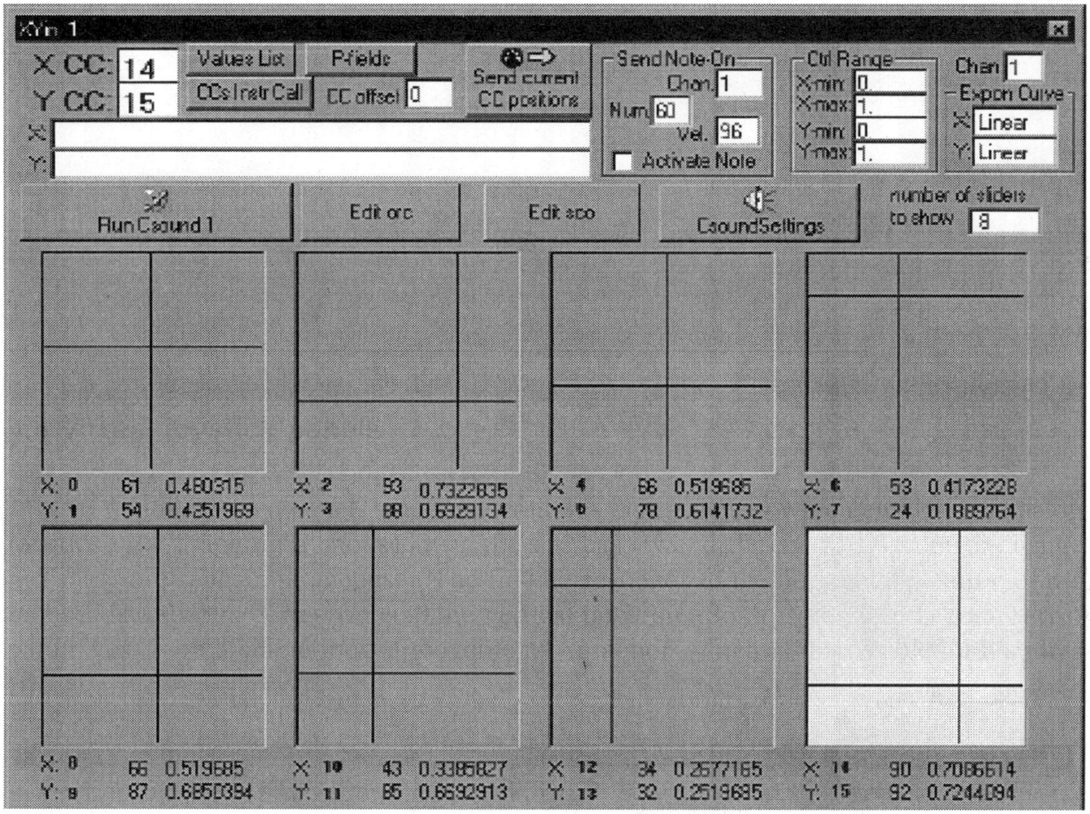

FIG.5 Virtual Joystick Panel

4.5 Virtual keyboard panel

Virtual keyboard panel (fig.6) sends any kind of MIDI VOICE messages, not only note-on and note-off messages.

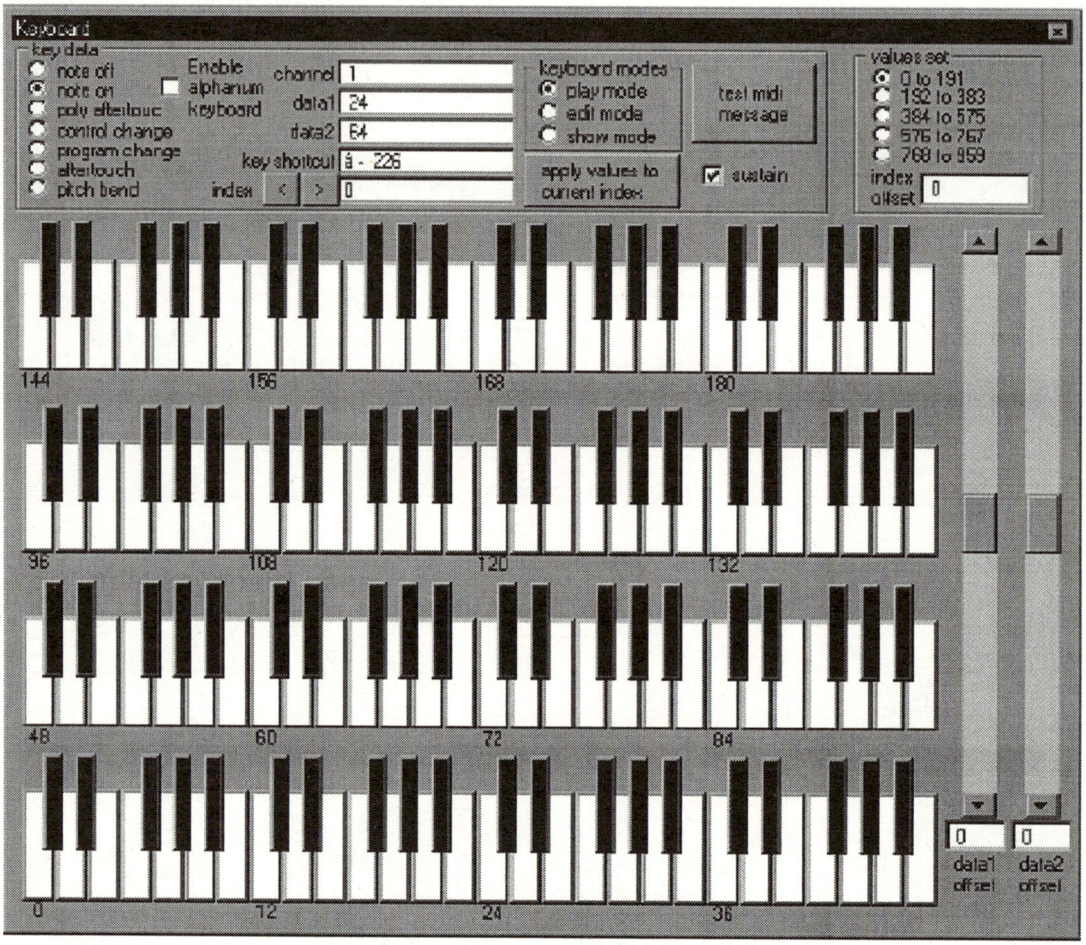

FIG.6 pannello della tastiera

Each button appears as a piano-key and can generate a note-on/off message, as well as program-change, pitch-bend, control-change or after-touch. Each key is totally configurable by the user and can send any VOICE message the user assigns to it. Furthermore, it is possible to assign each key of the alphanumeric keyboard to one of the piano-like buttons of the panel, making it possible to play the computer keyboard as it was a piano. Up to 959 MIDI messages can be assigned to the piano-like keys and current user configuration can be saved in the *.stp* file. Also, it is possible to add (or subtract) an offset to all data bytes in the current configuration by means of the two sliders located at the right of the piano-like buttons.

(Translated from the Italian by the author)

REFERENCES

Backus, J. *The Acoustical Foundation of Music*. New York, New York: Norton

Balena F., De Poli, G. 1987. 'Un modello semplificato del clarinetto mediante oscillatore non lineare', in *Musica e tecnologia: industria e cultura per lo sviluppo del Mezzogiorno*, Quaderni di Musica/Realtà Milano: UNICOPLI

Berry, R.W. 1988. 'Experiments in Computer Controlled Acoustical Modelling (A Step Backwards?)', in *Proceedings of the 14th Computer Music Conference*. Köln: Feedback Papers

Bianchini, R. 1987. 'Composizione automatica di strutture musicali', in *I profili del suono*. Salerno: Musica Verticale-Galzerano

Bianchini, R. 1996. 'WCShell e i suoi software tools per la generazione e la modifica di partiture in formato Csound', in *La terra fertile, Atti del Convegno*. L'Aquila

Cott, J. 1973. *Stockhausen. Conversations with the Composer.* New York, New York

De Poli, G. 1981. 'Tecniche numeriche di sintesi della musica', in *Bollettino LIMB n.1.* Venezia: La Biennale di Venezia

Dodge, C., and Jerse, T. A. 1985. *Computer Music*. New York, New York: Schirmer Books

Forin, A. 1981. 'Spettri dinamici prodotti mediante distorsione con polinomi equivalenti in un punto', in *Bollettino LIMB n.2*, Venezia: La Biennale di Venezia

Gabor, D. 1947. "Acoustical Quanta and the Theory of Hearing", in *Nature*, 159(4044)

IMUG. 1983. *MIDI Specifications*, Los Altos, California: MIDI International User's Group

Moles, A. 1969. "The Sonic Object", in *Information Theory And Esthetic Perception*. Urbana, Illinois: University of Illinois Press

Morresi, N. 1967. *Dispense di acustica applicata*, unpublished

Pousseur, H. (ed.), 1976. *La musica elettronica*. Milano: Feltrinelli

Prieberg, Fred K. 1963. *Musica ex machina*. Torino: Einaudi

Risset, J.C. 1981. 'Tecniche digitali del suono: influenza attuale e prospettive future in campo musicale', in *Bollettino LIMB n.2*. Venezia: La Biennale di Venezia

Risset, J.C., and Wessel, D. 1981. 'Indagine sul timbro mediante analisi e sintesi', in *Bollettino LIMB n.2*, Venezia: La Biennale di Venezia

Roads, C. 1978 'Automated granular synthesis of sound' *Computer Music Journal* 2(2): 61-62

Roads, C. 1985 'Granular synthesis of sound' in C.Roads and J.Strawn, eds.1985. *Foundations of Computer Music*. Cambridge, Massachusetts: The MIT Press

Roads, C., and Strawn, J. (ed.). 1985. Foundations of Computer Music. Cambridge, Massachusetts: The MIT Press

Roads, C. 1995. *The Computer Music Tutorial*. Cambridge, Massachusetts: The MIT Press

Seto, W.W. 1978. *Teoria ed applicazioni di Acustica*, Milano: ETAS Libri

Spiegel, M. R. 1974. *Manuale di matematica*, Milano: ETAS Libri

Smith, J. O. III. 1996. "Discrete-Time Modeling of Acoustic Systems with Applications to Sound Synthesis of Musical Instruments", in *Proceedings of the Nordic Acoustical Meeting*, Helsinki

Strawn, J. (ed.). 1985. *Digital Audio Signal Processing*, Los Altos, California: William Kaufmann Inc.

Tisato, G. 1987. 'Sintesi dei suoni vocali e del canto in modulazione di frequenza', in *Musica e tecnologia: industria e cultura per lo sviluppo del Mezzogiorno*, Milano: Quaderni di Musica/Realtà - UNICOPLI

Truax, B. 1988. 'Real-Time Granular Synthesis with a Digital Signal Processor', in *Computer Music Journal*, 12(2): 14-26. Cambridge, Massachusets: Summer M.I.T Press

Vercoe, B. 1986-1992. *Csound Manual*. Cambridge, Massachusetts: Media Lab - MIT

Wiener, N. 1964. "Spatio-Temporal Continuity, Quantum Theory, and Music". printed in *The Concepts Of Space And Time*, Boston Studies XXII, M.Capek (Ed.). 1975. Boston, Mass: D.Riedel

Xenakis, I. 1971. *Formalized Music*, Bloomington, Indiana: Indiana U.Press

CSOUND WEB SITES

1. MAIN SITES

Csound home page at MIT, Csound birthplace, run by Richard Boulanger:
http://mitpress.mit.edu/e-books/csound/frontpage.html

Other Csound home pages:
http://coos.dartmouth.edu/~dupras/Csound
http://www.leeds.ac.uk/music/Man/c_front.html

(the latter is not updated since 1/7/1997)

Csound FAQ (Frequently Asked Questions):
http://mitpress.mit.edu/e-books/csound/frontpage.html
ftp://ftp.hmc.edu/pub/csound/misc
http://coos.dartmouth.edu/~dupras/Csound/csoundpage.html

Semi-official site at Bath University (UK), run by John Fitch:
ftp://ftp.maths.bath.ac.uk/pub/dream

Mills College, contains Csound for PowerPC:
ftp://mills.edu/ccm/csound.ppc

Csound manual, version 3.56, in HTML, by Rasmus Ekman:
http://hem.passagen.se/rasmuse/Csound.htm

Version 3.56 of the Acrobat and zipped HTML manuals, by David Boothe:
http://www.geocities.com/~csoundmanual

EDISON STUDIO (Rome), contains WCShell for Windows by Riccardo Bianchini, a Csound front-end and more:
http://www.edisonstudio.it/

ConTempo, publisher of "Virtual Sound":
http://www.contemponet.com/

Hans Mikelson's Csound Magazine:
http://www.werewolf.net/~hljmm/Ezine/

DirectCsound for Windows by Gabriel Maldonado, with realtime in/out and MIDI support, and VMCI, a program to control Csound and other Midi instruments in realtime and to program configuration patches:
http://web.tiscalinet.it/G-Maldonado/download.htm

To Join the Csound Mailing List:
Send an e-mail to csound-request@maths.ex.ac.uk
In the first line of the message, submit this: subscribe your@email
After this e-mail has been processed (about 5 minutes), you will receive an e-mail from csoundrequest@maths.ex.ac.uk with further instructions. Follow these last few instructions, and your e-mail will be added to the Csound Mailing list.

To send message to the list, address the messages to
csound@maths.ex.ac.uk
Messages sent to the list are broadcast to all members of the list.

Other Csound (but not only) newsgroups:
comp.music
comp.dsp
alt.music.makers

2. SOFTWARE

mirror site of Bath University:
http://www.musique.umontreal.ca/electro/mirror/full - -r.html
http://www.parnasse.com/dx72csnd.shtml

orchestras emulating Yamaha DX7
http://www.bright.net/~dlphilp/dp_csound.html

Csound Tutorial by Dave Phillips
http://mars.let.uva.nl/gather/accci/index.html

Amsterdam Catalogue of Csound Computer Instruments (ACCCI)
http://ringo.sfc.keio.ac.jp/~eric

Eric Lyon's Csound instruments
http://home.earthlink.net/~radiobaton/

Richard Boulanger's home page
http://www.kgw.tu-berlin.de/~abart/CMaskMan/CMask-Download.htm

Cmask, a Csound score generator for Mac, SGI IRIX and Windows
ftp://ftp.musique.umontreal.ca/pub/cecilia/

Cecilia for Mac, Irix and Linux
http://www.snafu.de/~rubo/songlab/midi2cs

Midi2CS for DOS/Linux/SunOS, a MIDI-to-Csound converter
http://www.friends.panservice.it/pa2278/

MCC, a Csound score generator for DOS.
http://www.cis.ohio-state.edu/hypertext/faq/usenet/audio-fmts/top.html

audio file formats FAQ (Frequently Asked Questions)
file://ftp.cs.ruu.nl/pub/MIDI/DOC/bibliography.html

Piet van Oostrum's Computer Music bibliography
http://www.internexus.net/pub/sound/csound/Samples/

a tutorial with FOF examples for Mac
http://shoko.calarts.edu/~tre/SndHckDoc/

SoundHack, a Mac sound editor and converter
http://www.ccmrc.ucsb.edu/~doug/htmls/MiXViews.html

MiXViews, a sound editor for NeXT, Sun, Linux, and SGI
http://capella.dur.ac.uk/doug/res_site.html
a lot of computer music links

3. UNIVERSITIES, RESEARCH CENTERS AND ASSOCIATIONS

http://ccrma-www.stanford.edu/
Center for Computer Research in Music and Acoustics (CCRMA), Stanford.

http://www.ircam.fr/
IRCAM: Institut de Recherche et Coordination Acoustique/Musique, Paris

http://www.music.princeton.edu
Princeton University Faculty of Music

http://space.tin.it/musica/ilipc
Conservatorio 'S.Cecilia' (Rome) home page

http://www.aes.org/index.html
Audio Engineering Society home page

http://www-mitpress.mit.edu/Computer-Music-Journal/CMJ.html
Computer Music Journal home page

http://coos.dartmouth.edu/~rsn/icma/icma.html
International Computer Music Association home page

http://datura.cerl.uiuc.edu/schools/courses.html
computer music courses

Riccardo Bianchini
Milan, 1946

e-mail: rb@fabaris.it
www.fabaris.it/bianchini

Bianchini studied Piano, Composition, Electroacoustic Music, and Engineering at the Politecnico University. Since 1974 he has been Professor of Electroacoustic Music in the Conservatories of Pescara, Milan, and since 1987 in Conservatorio "S.Cecilia" in Rome.

He translated in Italian many important books on music, such as C.Rosen's "The Classical Style" and "Sonata Forms", His articles have been published in music reviews (Rivista IBM, Musica, Perspectives of New Music, etc.).

Since 1995 he is visiting professor in Universities of Uruguay and Argentina.

As a software writer, he is the author of many music related programs.

Since 1983 to 1991 he collaborated with RAI (Italian State Radio).

His compositions (orchestral, vocal, instrumental, electroacoustic, incidental), published and recorded by Edipan and BMG-Ariola, have been performed and/or broadcast in Europe, USA, Cuba, Argentina, Uruguay and Australia.

BIBLIOGRAPHY

Bianchini,R. 1973. "La nuova musica in Italia", in *Storia della musica Oxford-Feltrinelli, Vol.X.* Milan: Feltrinelli
Bianchini, R. 1976. "La musica elettronica", in *Rivista IBM*, 12. Milano
Bianchini, R. 1976. "Musica e letteratura (II)", in *Enciclopedia Feltrinelli Fischer.* Milano: Feltrinelli
Bianchini, R. 1976. "La musica contemporanea", in *Musica 1,2,3,4,5*. Milano
Bianchini, R. 1976. "La musica informatica", in *Musica Domani, 22*. Milano
Bianchini, R. 1985. *Computer Music: manuale di informatica musicale*. Unpublished
Bianchini, R. 1987. "Composizione automatica di strutture musicali", in *I profili del suono*. Salerno: Galzerano

Bianchini, R. 1996. "WCShell e i suoi software tools per la generazione e la modifica di partiture in formato Csound", in *La terra fertile, Proceedings*. L'Aquila
Bianchini, R, ed. 1996. Cristiano, C. *I territori di Montopoli e Bocchignano*. Montopoli di Sabina.
Bianchini, R. 1999. "La musica elettronica in Italia", in *Azzurra, 4*. Córdoba: Istituto Italiano di Cultura

TRANSLATIONS

1973. *Storia della musica Oxford-Feltrinelli, Vol.X*. Milan: Feltrinelli (translation of The Oxford History of Music)
Pousseur H., ed. 1975. *La musica elettronica*. Milan: Feltrinelli (translation)
Rosen, C. 1979. *Lo stile classico*. Milan: Feltrinelli (translation of The Classical Style)
Dick, R. 1979. *L'altro flauto*. Milan: Ricordi (translation of The Other Flute)
Rosen, C. 1984. *Le forme sonata*. Milan: Feltrinelli (translation of Sonata Forms)

DISCOGRAPHY

10 storie Zen, for flute, clarinet, vibraphone, piano, viola and cello.
WNC Ensemble. PAN PRC S2062
Roèn, for flute, clarinet, bassoon, horn, violin, viola, cello and piano.
L'Artisanat Furieux Ensemble, dir. T. Battista. PAN CDC 3010
Klimt, for flute, oboe, clarinet, violin, viola, cello, piano and tape.
Romensemble, dir. F.E.Scogna RCA CCD 3001
Machu Picchu, for flute, oboe, clarinet, bassoon, 2 trumpets, french horn, trombone, live electronics and tape.
Farfensemble, dir. R.Bianchini. ED0009

COMPOSITIONS

haiku, (1976, 10:00), piano and tape
Mirror, (1976, 05:00), flute and piano. C.A.S.
Collettivo II, (1976, 05:00), flute, oboe, clarinet, bassoon, violin, cello and piano. EDIPAN
Due racconti, (1979, 05:00), 2 clarinets, basoon, viola, piano. EDIPAN
La nave bianca (Preludio), (1980, 05:00), chamber orchestra. EDIPAN
La nave bianca (incidental music), (1980, 25:00), chamber orchestra and male choir
Roèn, (1982, 05:00), flute, clarinet, bassoon, french horn, violin, viola, cello and piano. EDIPAN

Riyàr, (1982, 05:00), piccolo, flute in C, flute in G, bass flute (1 flutist). EDIPAN
Sedrùna, (1982, 5:00), four hands piano. EDIPAN
Tre quadri immaginari, (1983, 10:00), harp. EDIPAN
Quattro canti: 1. "Di più cupi sentieri" (D.Villatico), 2. "La tierra que era mía" (J.G,.Durán), 3. "I have done" (J.London), 4. "Im wunderschönen Monat Mai" (R.M.Rilke), (1980-1988, 12:00), soprano and piano. EDIPAN
6 Preludi, (1980-1984, 11:00), piano. EDIPAN
Due fogli d'album, (1985, 02:00), flute and piano
Foglio d'album, (1985, 1:30), violin and piano
La principessa senza tempo, (1985, 14:10), flute and tape. EDIPAN
Alias, (1985, 5:00), 2 oboes and basson
Chanson d'aube, (1986, 6:00), 4 trumpets, 4 horns, 4 trombones
Rosengarten, (1986, 05:00) violin and orchestra
Our Faust, (1986, 17:00), clarinet, trombone, double bass and live electronics. BMG-Ariola
Arsól, (1987, 10:00), real time computer and quad tape
Divertimento, (1988, 8:20), for 13 instruments. EDIPAN
Somanón, (1989, 8:00), 11 strings. EDIPAN
Preuss (1989, 16:20), violin, cello and tape. BMG-Ariola
Fànes (1989, 8:00), flute in C and flute in G (1 flutist)
Alberi (1990, 6:00), sax quartet. BMG-Ariola
Saluto a Pablo (1990, 2:00), soprano, fute and clarinet
Cuando sonó la trompeta (1990, 7:30), soprano and tape. BMG-Ariola
Klimt (1991,10:50), flute, oboe, clarinet, violin, viola, cello, piano and tape. BMG-Ariola
Chanson d'aube II (1991,5:00), 2 oboes, 2 clarinets, 2 horns and 2 bassoons
Tre ricercari (1993, 5:00), 2 trunpets, horn and trombone
Machu Picchu (1993, 14:00), flute, oboe, clarinet, bassoon, 2 trumpets, horn, trombone, live electronics and tape
Poche note... per Enzo Porta, (1994, 2:00), violin
6 Preludi (II quaderno), (1994, 11:00), piano
Il contrabbasso poteva non esserci, (1995, 2:30), 2 flutes, oboe, piano and string quartet
Naste, (1995, 2:00), flute and cello
Howl, (1995, 6:30), male or female voice and tape
I dannati della terra, (1996, 28:00), actor, soprano, flute, percussion, tape and image projection
Ghe Xe, (1997, 5:00), flute in G and piano
Aria di Albertine (da "Doppio sogno"), (1997, 4:30), soprano, flute, oboe, clarinet, basoon, piano and string quartet

Canciones para las estrellas, (1997, 6:30), tape
Canciones para las estrellas, (1997, 8:00), piano and tape
Los pájaros del sueño, (1998, 9:00), clarinet and tape
Montevideana, (1999, 5:00), tape
How Deep the Sea, (1999, 5:30), Big Band (4 saxophones, 3 trumpets, 2 trombones, piano, bass and drums)
Alle Menschen werden Brüder, (1999, 7:40), violin, speaker and quad tape

TRANSCRIPTIONS AND REVISIONS

A.Gabrieli, *Ricercar nel duodecimo tono*, (1977), fl,ob,cl,fg,tr,cor,trbn
G.Gabrieli, *Quattro canzoni per sonar a quattro*, (1977), fl,ob,cl,fg,tr,cor,trbn
A.Willaert, *Ricercar X*, (1977), flute, oboe, clarinet, bassoon, trumpet, horn and trombone
J. da Modena, *Ricercar III,* (1977), trumpet, horn, trombone
Anonimi Francesi, *Suite di danze,* (1977), flute, oboe, clarinet, bassoon, trumpet, horn and trombone
H.Pousseur, *Icare apprenti*, (1977), flute, oboe, clarinet, bassoon, trumpet, horn and trombone
F.Schubert, *4 Ländler,* (1993), wind quintet
F.Schubert, *4 Ländler*, (1994), flute, oboe, clarinet, bassoon, string quartet
F.Schubert, *Deutsche Tänze*, (1994), flute, oboe, clarinet, bassoon, 2 trumpets, horn and trombone
W.A.Mozart, *Musiche di palcoscenico da "Don Giovanni"*, (1994), flute, oboe, clarinet, bassoon, trumpet, horn and trombone
H.Purcell, *Suite*, (1995), flute, oboe, clarinet, bassoon, trumpet, horn and trombone
D.Auber, *"Fra Diavolo"*, pot pourri dall'opera, (1995), flute, oboe, clarinet, bassoon, trumpet, horn and trombone
J.Lennon, P.McCartney, *Eleanor Rigby,* (1995), flute, oboe, clarinet, bassoon, 2 trumpets, horn and trombone
J.Lennon, P.McCartney, *Penny Lane,* (1995), flute, oboe, clarinet, bassoon, 2 trumpets, horn and trombone
J.Lennon, P.McCartney, *Yesterday*, (1995), flute, oboe, clarinet, bassoon, 2 trumpets, horn and trombone
J.Lennon, P.McCartney, *Girl*, (1995), flute, oboe, clarinet, bassoon, 2 trumpets, horn and trombone
J.Lennon, P.McCartney, *Lady Madonna*, (1995), 2 trumpets, horn and trombone
Bela Bartók, *Danze Rumene*, (1993), wind quartet
Bela Bartók, *Danze Rumene*, (1994), flute, oboe, clarinet, bassoon and string quartet

photo by Chris Bitten

Alessandro Cipriani
Tivoli (Rome), 1959

e-mail a.cipriani@virtual-sound.com
www.edisonstudio.it

Cipriani completed his studies in music composition and electroacoustic music at the Conservatorio S.Cecilia in Rome. He studied for a time with Barry Truax. Since 1989 he has worked on intermedia pieces, often in collaboration with visual artist Alba D'Urbano. More recently he has composed electroacoustic pieces with traditional religious singers for a new CD.
His works have received honors and/or have been selected for performance by government arts commissions, professional organizations and festival organizers including Bourges, Government of Canada Award, International Computer Music Conference, International Symposium on Electronic Arts, Musica Nova, Newcomp, etc. He has taught electroacoustic music at the Ist. Mus. V. Bellini in Catania since 1995. He has lectured about his music and his theory of 'electroacoustic tradition' at several Universities in Italy, Canada and the U.S. He has published analytical and theoretical papers in several journals and publications of the proceedings of various conferences.
His CD "Il Pensiero Magmatico" in collaboration with StefanoTaglietti is available on the Edipan label. Other pieces can be found in the ICMC95 and ICMC99 CDs. His music has been broadcast by RAI, CBC and other national radio networks as well as performed at festivals in Europe, Canada, South-America and the U.S.A.
He is one of the co-founders of Edison Studio in Rome.

BIBLIOGRAPHY

Cipriani, A. 1993 "Visibili..." in Atti del X Colloquio di Informatica Musicale, LIM-DSI Univ. degli Studi di Milano, Milano, pp.404-6

Cipriani A. 1993 Due tesi complementari sulle due versioni di Kontakte di K.Stockhausen - Tesi di Diploma in Musica Elettronica - Conservatorio di Musica S.Cecilia - Roma

Cipriani A. 1995 "Towards an electroacoustic tradition?" in Proceedings of the International Computer Music Conference, ICMA, Banff, pp. 5-8

Cipriani A. 1995 "Problems of methodology: the analysis of Kontakte" in Atti del X Colloquio di Informatica Musicale, AIMI , Bologna, pp. 41-44

Cipriani A. 1996 "Verso una tradizione elettroacustica? Appunti per una ricerca" in Musica/Realtà N°49 Marzo LIM Lucca pp.18-24

Cipriani A. 1996 "Tradizione orale, tradizione scritta, tradizione elettroacustica" in Atti del II Convegno La Terra Fertile - Incontro Nazionale di Musica Elettronica - Conservatorio di Musica "A.Casella", L'Aquila

Cipriani A. 1998 "Kontakte (Elektronische Musik) di K.Stockhausen: genesi, metodi, forma" in Bollettino G.A.T.M. anno V, n.1 GATM Univ. Studi Bologna

Cipriani A. 1998 "Musica e Internet: arte come esperienza, arte come codice" in Aperture n.5, Roma

Bianchini R.- Cipriani A. 1998 Il Suono Virtuale, Contempo, Roma

DISCOGRAPHY

A.Cipriani
QUADRO
for string quartet and tape
International Computer Music Conference '95 – PRCD1600

A.Cipriani-S.Taglietti
IL PENSIERO MAGMATICO
for tape, piano, percussions and mixed choir
EDIPAN – PAN CD 3059

A.Cipriani
AL NUR (La Luce)
for islamic chant, zarb, daf and tape
International Computer Music Conference '99 – PRCD2000

COMPOSITIONS

#1, #2, #3
Kreis
three works for video and electroacoustic music
Video by Alba D'Urbano
Music by Alessandro Cipriani
(1987-1991)
finalist at Locarno Video Festival (Switzerland)

#4
Kreis: la piazza
sound-video installation
(in collaboration with Alba D'Urbano)
presented at EASA - Berlin Kulturstadt Europas - Esplanade Berlin (Germany) Ago 1988

#5
Circolo Vizioso
sound-video installation
(in collaboration with Alba D'Urbano)
presented for the first time at
Internationaal Audio Visueel Experimenteel Festival 1989

#6
Circoscritto
sound-video installation
(in collaboration with Alba D'Urbano)
presented at
Centro di Video Arte (Palazzo dei Diamanti) - Ferrara within the exhibition "POLISET"
Dic.1991

#7
Luce di due soli
for piano, vibraphone and tape(dur. 25'25")
(1991)
(in collaboration with Giovanni Bietti)
Finalist at 1991 Newcomp Computer Music Competition
(USA) - First Performance
29th Festival of "Nuova Consonanza" - Roma

#8
Visibili
for two violins and tape (dur.8'30")
(1992)
MENTION AT "21e CONCOURS INTERNATIONAL DE MUSIQUE ELECTROACOUSTIQUE" - BOURGES (FRANCE) 1993
First Performance XV Festival Musica Verticale - Roma

#9
Quadro
for string quartet and tape (dur.10'30")
(1993)
INCLUDED IN THE INTERNATIONAL COMPUTER MUSIC CONFERENCE '95 CD
First Performance 18° Cantiere Internazionale d'Arte di Montepulciano

#10
Terra Fluida
for video and electroacoustic music
Video by Alba D'Urbano Music by A.Cipriani
(1991-1994)
MAIN PRIZE AT MUSICA NOVA ELECTROACOUSTIC MUSIC COMPETITION CZECH REPUBLIC RADIO-TV
World Premiere Musica Nova Praha Dec 1996

#11
Recordare
for bass and double-bass recorders and tape (dur.12'24")
(1994-rev.1997)
FINALIST AT 25e CONCOURS INTERNATIONAL DE MUSIQUE
ELECTROACOUSTIQUE" - BOURGES (France) 1997
First Performance 3 Nov '94 - Musica Verticale/Progetto Musica '94
Goethe Institut - Roma

#12
L'Acqua, il Musico, Lo Specchio
intermedia work for 5 musicians, two actors, video projections and tape (dur. 1h. 15 ca.')
in collaboration with Giovanni Bietti
(1993-94)
First Performance Dec 3rd '94 - Progetto Musica '94 (Spazi Aperti) Acquario - Roma

#13
In Memory of a Recorder
for tape(15' 45")
(1993-94)
First Performance Festival Animato 1995 Sala Uno - Roma 19 maggio '95

#14
Il Pensiero Magmatico
for magnetic tape, piano, percussions and mixed choir (dur. 53:00)
(1995-96)
in collaboration with Stefano Taglietti, texts by Bizhan Bassiri
World Premiere Oct. 18th, 1996 Musée FRC Le Creux de l'Enfer Centre d'Art Contemporain Thiers Francia

#15
Still Blue
Homage to Derek Jarman
(1996)
for magnetic tape, piano, cello,sax soprano, mime and projected video
First Performance Freon Ensemble - Progetto Dyonisos
Nov. 29th '96 - Acquario Romano - Progetto Musica '96

Religious Chant Trilogy (#16 - #19 - #21)

#16
Angelus Domini
(1996)
for gregorian chant and magnetic tape
First Performance Musica Verticale/Progetto Musica '96
Dec. 9th '96

#19
Al Nur (La Luce)
(1997)
for islamic chant, persian percussions, magnetic tape and projected video
First Performance Nov. 12th, 1997
Musica e Scienza /Progetto Musica '97 Goethe Institut – Roma
INCLUDED IN THE INTERNATIONAL COMPUTER MUSIC CONFERENCE'99 CD

#21
Mimahamakim
(1999)
for jewish chant and tape

#17
Pensiero Magmatico
(1997)
for video and magnetic tape
Video by Bizhan Bassiri
Music by Alessandro Cipriani
First performance Galleria Miscetti
March 1997 Roma

#18
Quem quaeritis non est hic
(1997)
Sound installation for quadraphonic magnetic tape
First Performance - Installation by Alba D'Urbano "Quem quaeritis..."
Kassel (Germany)
Martinskirche Jun-Sep 1997

#20
Still Blue
(Homage to Derek Jarman)
The Video
(1998)
Video by A.Cipriani, G.Latini and S. Di Domenico
Music by Alessandro Cipriani
First Performance Nuova Consonanza - Rome
SELECTED AT "CORTO CIRCUITO '98" EUROPEAN FESTIVAL OF AUDIO-VISUAL COMMUNICATION - NAPLES

#.22
Reflection of the Moon over two springs
(2000)
for tape

INDEX

B

C

D

E

F

H

I

K

L

M

N

O

P

S

T

U

V

W

OPCODE LIST

VALUE CONVERTERS

int(x)	(init- or control-rate args only)	
	frac(x)	" "
	dbamp(x)	" "
	i(x)	(control-rate arg; only)
	abs(x)	(no rate restriction)
	exp(x)	" "
	log(x)	" "
	log10(x)	" "
	sqrt(x)	" "
	sin(x)	" "
	cos(x)	" "
	ampdb(x)	" "
sininv(x)		" "
	sinh(x)	" "
	cosinv(x)	" "
	cosh(x)	" "
	taninv(x)	" "
	tanh(x)	" "
	taninv2(x, y)	" "

xr pow iarg, kpow

PITCH CONVERTERS

octpch(pch)		(init- or control-rate args only)
	pchoct(oct)	" "
	cpspch(pch)	" "
	octcps(cps)	" "
	cpsoct(oct)	(no rate restriction)

Tuning opcodes:

icps	cps2pch	ipch, iequal
icps	cpsxpch	ipch, iequal, irepeat, ibase

SIGNAL DISPLAY AND FILE OUTPUT

dispfft **xsig, iprd, iwsiz [,iwtyp] [,idbouti] [,wtflg]**
display **xsig, iprd [,iwtflg]**
print **iarg [,iarg,...]**

printk **itime, kval [, ispace]**
printk2 **kval [,ispace]**
printks **"txtstring", itime, kval1, kval2, kval3, kval4**

dumpk **ksig, ifilname, iformat, iprd**
dumpk2 **ksig1, ksig2, ifilname, iformat, iprd**
dumpk3 **ksig1, ksig2, ksig3, ifilname, iformat, iprd**
dumpk4 **ksig1, ksig2, ksig3, ksig4, ifilname, iformat, iprd**

SENSING & CONTROL

ktemp tempest **kin, iprd, imindur, imemdur, ihp,ithresh, ihtim, ixfdbak, istartempo, ifn [,idisprd, itweek]**
kx, ky xyin **iprd, ixmin, ixmax, iymin, iymax [,ixinit, iyinit]**
tempo ktempo, istartempo

TIME READING

kr **timek**
kr **times**
ir **itimek**
ir **itimes**
kr **instimek**
kr **instimes**

PROGRAM CONTROL

Jumps: **igoto label**

tigoto **label**
kgoto label
goto label

if ia R ib igoto label

```
if ka R kb    kgoto  label
if ia  R ib   goto   label

timout   istrt, idur, label
```

Reinitialisation:

```
reinit  label
        rigoto label
        rireturn
```

MIDI SUPPORT

MIDI converters

```
ival    notnum
ival    veloc
icps    cpsmidi
icps    cpsmidib
kcps    cpsmidib [irange]
kval    cpstmid  ifn
ioct    octmidi
ioct    octmidib
koct    octmidib [irange]
ipch    pchmidi
ipch    pchmidib
kpch    pchmidib [irange]
iamp    ampmidi  iscal[, ifn]
kaft    aftouch  iscal

kchpr   chpress  iscal
kbend   pchbend  iscal
ival    midictrl inum [, initial]
kval    midictrl inum [, initial]
```

MIDI controller input:

```
initc7/14/21   ichan, ictlno, ivalue
```

idest imidic7/14/21 ictlno, imin, imax [, ifn]
kdest midic7/14/21 ictlno, kmin, kmax [, ifn]

idest ictrl7/14/21 ichan, ictlno, imin, imax [,ifn]
kdest ctrl7/14/21 ichan, ictlno, kmin, kmax [,ifn]

nval chanctrl ichan, ictlno [,ilow,ihigh]
kbend pchbend [ilow, ihigh]

Misc MIDI input messages:

**kstatus, kchan, kdata1, kdata2 **

midiin

MIDI note output:

ion ichn, inum, ivel
ioff ichn, inum, ivel
iondur ichn, inum, ivel, idur
iondur2 ichn, inum, ivel, idur

moscil kchn, knum, kvel, kdur, kpause
midion kchn, knum, kvel
midion2 kchn, knum, kvel, ktrig

Output MIDI channel messages:

ioutc(14) ichn, inum, ivalue, imin, imax
koutc(14) kchn, knum, kvalue, kmin, kmax

ioutpb ichn, ivalue, imin, imax
koutpb kchn, kvalue, kmin, kmax
ioutat ichn, ivalue, imin, imax
koutat kchn, kvalue, kmin, kmax
ioutpc ichn, iprog, imin, imax
koutpc kchn, kprog, kmin, kmax

ioutpat ichn, inotenum, ivalue, imin, imax

koutpat kchn, knotenum, kvalue, kmin, kmax

Output MIDI system realtime messages:

mclock ifreq
mrtmsg imsgtype

Misc MIDI output messages:

nrpn kchan, kparmnum, kparmvalu
midiout kstatus, kchan, kdata1, kdata2

Extend MIDI events:

xtratim iextradur
kflag release

INSTRUMENT CONTROL

turnon insno[,itime]
ihold
turnoff

schedule inst, iwhen, idur, ...
schedwhen ktrigger, kinst, kwhen, kdur, ...

FUNCTION TABLE CONTROL

Table manipulation overview

Get information about function tables:

iafno ftgen ifno,itime,isize, igen, iarga[,...iargz]
ftlen(x) (init-rate args only)
ftlptim(x) (init-rate args only)
ftsr(x) (init-rate args only)
nsamp(x) (init-rate args only)

kr tablekt kndx, kfn [, ixmode] [,ixoff] [,iwrap]

```
ar        tableikt  andx, kfn [, ixmode] [,ixoff] [,iwrap]
ir        itableng  ifn
kr        tableng   kfn
```

Read/write function tables:

```
itablew   isig, indx, ifn [,ixmode] [,ixoff] [,iwgmode]
          tablew    ksig, kndx, ifn [,ixmode] [,ixoff] [,iwgmode]
          tablew    asig, andx, ifn [,ixmode] [,ixoff] [,iwgmode]
          tablewk   ksig, kndx, kfn [,ixmode] [,ixoff] [,iwgmode]
          tablewkt  asig, andx, kfn [,ixmode] [,ixoff] [,iwgmode]

ar        tablera   kfn, kstart, koff
kstart    tablewa   kfn, asig, koff

          itablegpwifn
          tablegpw  kfn

          tablecopy     kdft, ksft
          itablecopy    idft, isft
          tablemix      kdft, kdoff, klen, ks1ft, ks1off, ks1g, ks2ft, ks2off, ks2g
          itablemix     idft, idoff, ilen, is1ft, is1off, is1g, is2ft, is2off, is2g
```

SIGNAL GENERATORS

Linear signal generators:

```
nr line       ia, idur1, ib
nr expon      ia, idur1, ib
nr linseg     ia, idur1, ib [,idur2, ic[Ö]]
nr expsegia, idur1, ib [,idur2, ic[Ö]]
nr linsegr    ia, idur1, ib [,idur2, ic[Ö]], irel, iz
nr expsegr    Ia, Idur1, Ib [,Idur2, Ic[...]], Irel, iz

nr adsr       iatt, idec, islev, irel[, idelay]
nr madsr      iatt, idec, islev, irel[, idelay]
```

Phase generator:

nr phasor **kcps [,iphs]**

Table access:

xr table **indx, ifn [,ixmode] [,ixoff] [,iwrap]**
xr tablei **indx, ifn [,ixmode] [,ixoff] [,iwrap]**
kr oscil1 **idel, kamp, idur, ifn**
kr oscil1i **idel, kamp, idur, ifn**
kr osciln **kamp, idur, ifrq, ifn, itimes**

nr oscil **kamp, kcps, ifn [,iphs]**
nr oscili **kamp, kcps, ifn [,iphs]**
ar foscil **xamp, kcps, kcar, kmod, kndx, ifn [,iphs]**
ar foscili **xamp, kcps, kcar, kmod, kndx, ifn [,iphs]**

kr lfo **kamp, kcps[, itype]**

ar1[,ar2] **loscil xamp, kcps, ifn [,ibas] [,imod1, ibeg1, iend1] [,imod2, ibeg2, iend2]**

Buzzers:

ar buzz **xamp, xcps, knh, ifn [,iphs]**
ar gbuzz **xamp, xcps, knh, kih, kr, ifn [,iphs]**

Granular synthesis:

ar fof xamp, xfund, xform, koct, kband, kris, kdur, kdec, iolaps, ifna, ifnb, itotdur [,iphs] [,ifmode]
ar fof2 xamp, xfund, xform, koct, kband, kris, kdur, kdec, iolaps, ifna, ifnb, itotdur, kphs, kgliss
ar fog xamp, xdens, xtrans, xspd, koct, kband, kris, kdur, kdec, iolaps, ifna, ifnb, itotdur[, iphs][, itmode]
ar grain xamp, xpitch, xdens, kampoff, kpitchoff, kgdur, igfn, iwfn, imgdur
ar granule xamp, ivoice, iratio, imode, ithd, ifn, ipshift, igskip, igskip_os, ilength, kgap, igap_os, kgsize, igsize_os, iatt, idec [,iseed] [,ipitch1] [,ipitch2] [,ipitch3] [,ipitch4] [,ifnenv]

Time-streching:

ar [,acmp] sndwarp xamp, xtimewarp, xresample, ifn1, ibeg, iwsize, irandw, ioverlap, ifn2, [itimemode]

**ar1, ar2 [, acmp1, acmp2] **

sndwarpst xamp, xtimewarp, xresample, ifn1, ibeg, iwsize, irandw, ioverlap, ifn2, itimemode

Waveguide physical modeling:

ar wguide1 asig, kfreq, kcutoff, kfeedback;
ar wguide2 asig, kfreq1, kfreq2, kcutoff1, kcutoff2, kfeedback1, kfeedback2

ar pluck kamp, kcps, icps, ifn, imeth [,iparm1, iparm2]
ar wgpluck
ar wgpluck2 iplk, xamp, icps, kpick, krefl
ar repluck iplk, xamp, icps, kpick, krefl, axcite

ar wgbow kamp, kfreq, kpres, kratio, kvibf, kvamp, ifn[, iminfreq]
ar wgbrass kamp, kfreq, kliptens, idetk, kvibf, kvamp, ifn[, iminfreq]
ar wgclar kamp, kfreq, kstiff, iatt, idetk, kngain, kvibf, kvamp, ifn[, iminfreq]
ar wgflute kamp, kfreq, kjet, iatt, idetk, kngain, kvibf, kvamp, ifn[, iminfreq]

More physical models:

ar agogobel kamp, kfreq, ihrd, ipos, imp, kvibf, kvamp, ivibfn
ar marimba kamp, kfreq, ihrd, ipos, imp, kvibf, kvamp, ivibfn, idec
ar vibes kamp, kfreq, ihrd, ipos, imp, kvibf, kvamp, ivibfn, idec
ar shaker kamp, kfreq, kbeans, kdamp, knum, ktimes[, idecay]

4-operator FM instruments:

ar fmtbell kamp, kfreq, kc1, kc2, kvdepth, kvrate, ifn1, ifn2, ifn3, ifn4, ivfn
ar fmrhode kamp, kfreq, kc1, kc2, kvdepth, kvrate, ifn1, ifn2, ifn3, ifn4, ivfn
ar fmwurlie kamp, kfreq, kc1, kc2, kvdepth, kvrate, ifn1, ifn2, ifn3, ifn4, ivfn
ar fmmetal kamp, kfreq, kc1, kc2, kvdepth, kvrate, ifn1, ifn2, ifn3, ifn4, ivfn
ar fmb3 kamp, kfreq, kc1, kc2, kvdepth, kvrate, ifn1, ifn2, ifn3, ifn4, ivfn
ar fmpercfl kamp, kfreq, kc1, kc2, kvdepth, kvrate, ifn1, ifn2, ifn3, ifn4, ivfn

ar fmvoice kamp, kfreq, kvowel, ktilt, kvibamt, kvibrate, ifn1, ifn2, ifn3, ifn4, ivibfn

Emulation instruments:

ar moog kamp, kfreq, kfiltq, kfiltrate, kvibf, kvamp, iafn, iwfn, ivfn
ar mandol kamp, kfreq, kpluck, kdetune, kgain, ksize, ifn[, iminfreq]

ar voice kamp, kfreq, kphoneme, kform, kvibf, kvamp, ifn, ivfn

Random generators (uniform distribution):

nr rand xamp [,iseed, iuse31]
nr randh kamp, kcps [,iseed, iuse31]
nr randi kamp, kcps [,iseed, iuse31]

rnd(x)
birnd(x)

Random generators (various distributions):

xr linrand krange
xr trirand krange
xr exprand krange
xr bexprnd krange
xr cauchy kalpha
xr pcauchy kalpha
xr poisson klambda
xr gauss krange
xr weibull ksigma, ktau
xr betarand krange, kalpha, kbeta
xr unirand krange

SIGNAL MODIFIERS

Gain units:

kr rms asig [,ihp, istor]
ar gain asig, krms [,ihp, istor]
ar balance asig, acomp [,ihp, istor]

ar dam ain, kthresh, icomp1, icomp2, irtme, iftme

Signal limiters:

ir ilimit isig, ilow, ihigh
nr limit nsig, klow, khigh

xr wrap xsig, xlow, xhigh
xr mirror xsig, xlow, xhigh

Notification:

kout trigger ksig, kthreshold, kmode

Envelope lines:

nr linen kamp, irise, idur, idec
nr linenr kamp, irise, idec, iatdec
nr envlpxkamp, irise, idur, idec, ifn, iatss, iatdec [,ixmod]

kr follow asig, idt

nr adsr iatt, idec, islev, irel[, idelay]
nr madsriatt, idec, islev, irel[, idelay]

Interpolator:

ar ntrpol asig1, asig2, kpoint [, imin, imax]

Standard filters:

kr port ksig, ihtim [,isig]
ar tone asig, khp [,istor]
ar atone asig, khp [,istor]
ar reson asig, kcf, kbw [,iscl, istor]
ar areson asig, kcf, kbw [,iscl, istor]

ar tonex asig, khp[, inumlayer, istor]
ar atonex asig, khp[, inumalayer, istor]
ar resonx asig, kcf, kbw[, iscl, inumlayer, istor]

ar butterhp asig, kfreq
ar butterlp asig, kfreq
ar butterbp asig, kfreq, kband
ar butterbr asig, kfreq, kband

ar filter2 asig, iM,iN,ib0,ib1,..., ibM,ia1,ia2,...,iaN
kr kfilter2 ksig, iM,iN,ib0,ib1,...,ibM,ia1,ia2,...,iaN
ar zfilter2 asig, kdamp,kfreq,iM,iN,ib0,ib1,...,ibM,ia1,ia2,...,iaN

Specialised filters:

ar nlfilt ain, ka, kb, kd, kL, kC

ar dcblock asig [, igain]

ar lowres asig, kcutoff, kresonance [,istor]
ar lowresx asig, kcutoff, kresonance [, inumlayer, istor]
ar vlowres asig, kcutoff, kresonance, iord, ksep;

ar biquad asig, kb0, kb1, kb2, ka0, ka1, ka2
ar moogvcf asig, kfco, kres
ar rezzy asig, kfco, kres

Sample level operators:

kr downsamp asig [,iwlen]
ar upsamp ksig
ar interp ksig [,istor]
kr integ ksig [,istor]
ar integ asig [,istor]
kr diff ksig [,istor]
ar diff asig [,istor]
kr samphold xsig, kgate [,ival, ivstor]
ar samphold asig, xgate [,ival, ivstor]

Delays:

ar delayr idlt [,istor]
ar delayw asig
ar delay asig, idlt [,istor]
ar delay1 asig [,istor]
ar deltap kdlt
ar deltapi xdlt

ar vdelay asig, adel, imaxdel
ar multitap asig, itime1, igain1, itime2, igain2 . . .

Reverbs:

ar comb asig, krvt, ilpt [,istor]
ar alpass asig, krvt, ilpt [,istor]
ar reverb asig, krvt [,istor]
ar nreverb asig, ktime, khdif
ar reverb2 asig, ktime, khdif

Special effects:

ar harmon asig,kestfrq,kmaxvar, kgenfrq1, kgenfrq2, imode, iminfrq, iprd
ar flanger asig, adel, kfeedback, imaxd

FFT-based morphing synthesis:

asig cross2 ain1, ain2, ilen, iovl, iwin, kbias

OPERATIONS USING SOUNDFILE ANALYSIS DATA

Based on Heterodyne analysis:

HETRO.EXE - Fourier analysis for adsyn generator

ar adsyn kamod, kfmod, ksmod, ifilcod

Based on Phase vocoder analysis:

PVANAL.EXE - Fourier analysis for phase vocoder generators

ar pvoc ktimpnt, kfmod, ifilcod [,ispecwp]
ar pvadd ktimpnt, kfmod, ifile, ifn, ibins [, ibinoffset, ibinincr]
kfrq,kamp pvread ktimpnt, ifile, ibin
pvbufread ktimpnt, ifile
ar pvinterp ktimpnt, kfmod, ifile, kfreqscale1, kfreqscale2, kampscale1, kampscale2, kfreqinterp, kampinterp
ar pvcross ktimpnt, kfmod, ifile, kamp1, kamp2, [ispecwp]

tableseg ifn1, idur1, ifn2[, idur2, ifn3[...]]
tablexseg ifn1, idur1, ifn2[, idur2, ifn3[...]]
ar vpvoc ktimpnt, kfmod, ifile, [ispecwp]

Based on Linear predictive coding (LPC):

LPANAL.EXE - Linear predictive analysis for lpread/lpreson generators

**krmsr, krmso, kerr, kcps **

lpreadktimpnt, ifilcod[, inpoles][,ifrmrate]
ar lpreson asig
ar lpfreson asig, kfrqratio

lpslot islot
lpinterpolislot1,islot2,kmix

Using single Fourier analysis frame:

CVANAL.EXE - Impulse response fourier analysis for convolve operator

ar1[,...[,ar4]]] convolveain, ifilcod, ichan

OPERATIONS USING SPECTRAL DATA TYPES

Overview

wsig spectrum xsig, iprd, iocts, ifrqs, iq[,ihann, idbout, idsprd, idsinrs]
wsig specaddm wsig1, wsig2[, imul2]
wsig specdiff wsigin
wsig specscal wsigin, ifscale, ifthresh
wsig spechist wsigin
wsig specfilt wsigin, ifhtim

koct specptrk wsig, inptls, irolloff, iodd[, interp, ifprd, iwtflg]
ksum specsum wsig[, interp]
specdisp wsig, iprd[, iwtflg]

SOUND INPUT & OUTPUT

Sound input:

a1 in
a1, a2 ins
a1,...,a4 inq
a1 soundin ifilcod [,iskptim] [,iformat]
a1, a2 soundin ifilcod [,iskptim] [,iformat]
a1,...,a4 soundin ifilcod [,iskptim] [,iformat]
a1[,a2[,a3,a4]] diskin ifilcod, kpitch [,iskiptim][, iwraparound] [,iformat]

Sound output:

outasig
outs asig1, asig2
outs1 asig
outs2 asig
outq asig1, asig2, asig3, asig4
outq1 asig
outq2 asig
outq3 asig
outq4 asig

Panning and 3-D sound:

a1,...,a4 pan asig, kx, ky, ifn [,imode] [,offset]
aL, aR hrtfer asig, kAz, kElev, "HRTFcompact"
a1,..., a4 space asig, ifn, ktime, kreverbsend [,kx, ky]
a1,..., a4 spsend
kr spdist ifn, ktime, [,kx, ky]
a1,... , a4 locsig asig, kdegree, kdistance, kreverbsend
a1,..., a4 locsend